PERSPECTIVE

DO THE TRIUMPHS AND DISASTERS OF THE PAST HAVE A REAL MEANING FOR OUR CIVILIZATION TODAY?

This is the searching question which Herbert J. Muller discusses in this finely written and stimulating inquiry into the cultures that have preceded our own. The glories of Greece and Rome, the challenge of the Industrial Revolution, the adventure that was to be a New Russia, the mysticism of India and the humanism of China—these are examined in the light of their essential meaning for the twentieth century. What did they amount to—and why, despite their promise, did they fail? Was there a fatal flaw within these civilizations that is inherent in our own critical and turbulent society?

Outspoken and informed, lively and judicious, this unusual book presents a thoughtful and optimistic view of the chances of our civilization to survive. "We have to keep on making history instead of leaning on it," writes Professor Muller, and he recommends a firmer, bolder grasp on our ideals of freedom and individualism so that we shall be entitled to the collective hope of leaving an everlasting mark on history.

Here is bright assurance that catastrophe does not stalk us and that disaster in our day is not inevitable—a fascinating and rewarding book for all who strive to make the wisest use of mankind's common heritage.

"An exceedingly well-written and exciting inquiry into the way history works . . ."
—*The New York Herald Tribune*

Other MENTOR Books of Interest

THE LOOM OF HISTORY *by Herbert J. Muller*
A richly panoramic history of the fabled cities of Asia
Minor and its role at the crossroad between East and
West through the centuries.   (#MQ341—95¢)

THE ANVIL OF CIVILIZATION *by Leonard Cottrell*
This fascinating history of the ancient Mediterranean
civilizations reveals the long-buried secrets of the early
Egyptians, Hittites, Sumerians, Assyrians, Babylonians,
Greeks and Jews, brought to light by archeological
discoveries.   (#MP413—60¢)

PATTERNS OF CULTURE *by Ruth Benedict*
A famous anthropologist analyzes our social structure
in relation to primitive cultures.   (#MD89—50¢)

FOLKWAYS *by William Graham Sumner*
A classic study of how customs originate in basic human drives, this is an incredibly comprehensive analysis
of the cultures of primitive and civilized peoples.
        (#MT297—75¢)

TO OUR READERS: If your dealer does not have the SIGNET
and MENTOR books you want, you may order them by
mail, enclosing the list price plus 5¢ a copy to cover mail-
ing. If you would like our free catalog, please request it
by postcard. The New American Library of World Literature, Inc., P. O. Box 2310, Grand Central Station, New
York 17, New York.

The Uses of the Past

Profiles of Former Societies

By Herbert J. Muller

A MENTOR BOOK

Published by THE NEW AMERICAN LIBRARY

To Richard and Johnnie

Published as a MENTOR BOOK
by arrangement with Oxford University Press, Inc.,
who have authorized this softcover edition.
A hardcover edition is available from Oxford University Press.

FIRST PRINTING, JULY, 1954
SEVENTH PRINTING, OCTOBER, 1963

The Uses of the Past is published in
England by Oxford University Press.

MENTOR TRADEMARK REG. U.S. PAT. OFF. AND FOREIGN COUNTRIES
REGISTERED TRADEMARK—MARCA REGISTRADA
HECHO EN CHICAGO, U.S.A.

MENTOR BOOKS are published *in the United States* by
The New American Library of World Literature, Inc.,
501 Madison Avenue, New York 22, New York,
in Canada by The New American Library of Canada Limited,
156 Front Street West, Toronto 1, Ontario

PRINTED IN THE UNITED STATES OF AMERICA

Contents

v

Preface

THIS book is a series of studies of former societies, remote in time or space, and is designed to give perspective on the crisis of our own society. Since I am not a professional historian, it calls for some emphatic disclaimers. It is not a comprehensive survey of the history of civilization, of our own society, or of the particular societies treated in the separate chapters; it does not embody a complete theory of history, or a brand-new interpretation of it; it does not culminate in prophecy, or a guaranteed program for salvation. As a matter of principle, it is not an effort to say the last word about human history. Rather, it is an effort to counteract the popular simplicities that have been inspired by the complexities of our age, and to discount the last words that are being uttered so freely these days. In general, it is an approach to history in the spirit of the great tragic poets, a spirit of reverence and of irony, and is based on the assumption that the tragic sense of life is not only the profoundest but the most pertinent for an understanding of both past and present. In particular, it is an effort to apply a method of irony, the piety of deliberate impiety, stressing the inevitable ambiguities, incongruities, and paradoxes of human history, which among other things suggest why, 'in the final analysis,' there can be no final analysis.

The most obvious justification for this 'tragic' view is that the drama of history has been high tragedy, in the Aristotelian sense. All the mighty civilizations of the past have fallen because of tragic flaws; as we are enthralled by any Golden Age we must always add that it did not last, it did not do. All the civilizations have also had real grandeur, a glory that survives their fall; as we contemplate their ruins we need not feel merely that all is vanity. It is a great drama, somber and magnificent, which evokes the appropriate tragic emotions of pity and awe.

In this view it does not follow, however, that our civilization will necessarily share the fate of all previous ones. If an unhappy ending is all too conceivable, the Spenglerian thesis of inevitable decline—with the strangly attractive sense of being damned and doomed—is another simplification that calls for ironical discount. Civilization is a very recent adventure of the human race, a brief hour in its long history; it amounts to a dozen or so experiments, all under different conditions; and the rough analogies in the outcome of these experiments do not permit us to generalize and predict with anything like scientific certainty. This is why a layman may not be simply presumptuous in criticizing professional historians, and especially the greater historians. As they consider history an art, they naturally look for a plot, a grand design; as they consider it a science, they naturally look for laws, a comprehensive theory. Yet the only clear conclusion to be drawn from their radically different findings is that we do not know for sure the final meaning of the drama.

Meanwhile the layman has to consider the popular conclusions, the meanings that men are finding in our own history, and that influence the history we are making. An immediate inspiration of this book is Arnold Toynbee's *A Study of History*. It is a remarkably bold, rich, stimulating work—I should say the most impressive historical work of our time. Its popularity, however, seems due to its remarkably simple conclusion. Our one hope of salvation, Toynbee asserts, is a return to the 'One True God,' from whom we have fallen away: 'we may and must pray' that God will grant our society a reprieve if we ask for it 'in a contrite spirit and with a broken heart.' In effect, he seems to be saying that only a miracle can save us. I think he may be right. But I think we had better not live on this assumption. Toynbee's own study offers no evidence that prayer will save a society, any more than it saved the Roman world after its conversion to Christianity. If we want to save our world, not merely our private souls, we might better try to keep and use our heads.

Whether or not men turn to prayer, this book is based on the belief that even our godless civilization may deserve to be regarded with reverence as well as irony. As Whitehead said, the present is holy ground. It is all there is: the whole past is summed up in it, the future is implicit in it; and at worst it contains the values and ideals that inspire men to condemn it. In the incessant din of the mediocre, vulgar, mean, and fraudulent activities of a commercial, mass society, we are apt to forget the genuine idealism of democracy, the dignity of the long, painful struggle for liberty and equality. We may be too scornful even of our notorious material progress. Plumbing is not necessarily fatal to the good life, nor poverty or misery essential to spiritual elevation. If we are pleased to feel superior to the material well-being that we appear to enjoy, we should at least remember the generally wretched lot of the great masses of men in all previous societies, and the general acceptance of wretchedness as the law of nature or the will of God.

More simply, I am assuming that the modern world is in fact as revolutionary as everybody says it is. Its profound contradictions are not due to mere perversity or simple folly. They are due to the extraordinary developments in science and technology, which have led to far more rapid and radical change than any previous society has known, and than our sociey has been prepared to deal with. And because the paradoxes of our age are so violent, men have been violently oversimplifying its issues. On the one hand, many political and business leaders are still celebrating the triumphs of technology, science, and free enterprise as if there were nothing fundamentally wrong with our civilization, and the world depressions and world wars were unfortunate accidents. On the other hand, many intellectuals are ignoring the obvious triumphs, seeing only a monstrous folly and evil. I have assumed that it might be helpful to try viewing our world with both pride and alarm, both tempered by historical sense.

H. J. M.

Istanbul
January 1952

Acknowledgments

THE first chapter of this work is an expansion of an article, 'St. Sophia, and the Uses of the Past,' published in the *Virginia Quarterly Review*. Elsewhere a few short passages have been drawn from other published articles: 'Notes on World Culture' in the *Arizona Quarterly,* 'The Revival of the Absolute' in the *Antioch Review,* and 'The Relative and the Absolute' in the *Sewanee Review*.

I am grateful to various friends for their assistance, in particular to my colleagues Herbert L. Creek and Paul Fatout for criticism of the entire manuscript; to Robert Van Nice for the privilege of becoming acquainted with Hagia Sophia, during the course of his thorough study of this magnificent building; and to Ercüment Atabay for companionship and services as guide on expeditions to Nicaea, Pergamon, Sardis, Ephesus, Priene, and other ancient cities.

Above all, I am indebted to the many historians upon whose work I have drawn, directly and indirectly, to an extent that could not be acknowledged by quotations and footnotes. They are not responsible for my conclusions, of course, and may not welcome my intrusion; so I wish to declare that this intrusion has at least taught me a profound admiration for their collective undertaking, as well as their individual achievements, in at once reviving the wonder of the past and relieving its tyranny.

H. J. M.

I

Introduction: Haġia Sophia, or the 'Holy Wisdom'

1. ON WISDOM HOLY AND UNHOLY

When Henry Adams studied the glorious medieval cathedrals he was inspired to work out his 'dynamic theory of history,' and in particular his contrast between the Virgin and the Dynamo, as the symbols of medieval unity and modern anarchy. He came to feel that the love of the Virgin Mary, which had raised the cathedral of Chartres, was 'the greatest force the Western world ever felt,' or even 'the highest energy ever known to man.' As a philosopher of history, he resolved to concentrate on the Virgin's 'mental and physical energy of creation,' and not to yield to the charm of the 'adorable mistress'; but he was obviously smitten. He ended by drawing his wistful, charming picture of the Middle Ages, which has become still more charming as men have grown appalled by the folly and evil of our own age. Quite a few writers are now saying that the thirteenth century was the greatest of all centuries, the apex of Western civilization; and a chorus swells with the obvious religious moral.

I thought of Henry Adams when I was working, a few years ago, in the cathedral of Hagia Sophia, in Istanbul. Here was the great monument of Eastern Christendom, in which the Virgin had also been the favorite object of worship. From its famous dome one might get a still longer and larger view of history, for it was completed by the Roman Emperor Justinian in the year 537—six centuries before Chartres—and it looks down on both Europe and Asia. And so I too began to ponder the meanings of the past. Only, my reflections failed

13

to produce a neat theory of history, or any simple, wholesome moral. Hagia Sophia, or the 'Holy Wisdom,' gave me instead a fuller sense of the complexities, ambiguities, and paradoxes of human history. Nevertheless I propose to dwell on these messy meanings. They may be, after all, the most wholesome meanings for us today; or so I finally concluded.

At least I begin in simple piety. Although St. Sophia (as it is conventionally miscalled in the West) lacks the soaring grandeur of the Gothic cathedrals and today is rather shabby in its ornateness—like an overdressed dowager in decay—it remains a magnificent monument. It is not a degenerate form of classic architecture but a daring creation in a new style; among other things, its architects were the first to solve, on a large scale, the problem of setting a spherical dome on a square chamber. Despite its ornateness there is a majestic simplicity in its basic design, with the nave lined by towering columns of porphyry and verd antique and crowned by the great dome. One can still get a vivid idea of its original splendor, when the sunlight streaming in through the high windows of the dome made a glory of the acres of gold-leaf mosaic on its vaulted ceilings—some four acres of gold —and of the black, red, green, purple, and yellow marble of its paneled walls. And St. Sophia would be impressive enough simply because it has stood up for fourteen centuries, in constant use, withstanding hundreds of earthquakes, surviving the rise and fall of empires—living out a longer history than any other great building in Christendom.

Hence it is rich with the associations of all that has made Constantinople so memorable in history. For nine hundred years St. Sophia was the main stage for the high pageantry of the Byzantine Empire. Here presided the Patriarch of the Orthodox Church, the Bishops of Constantinople who struggled with the Bishops of Rome and finally established their supremacy in the East. Here the emperors were crowned and consecrated to the service of the true faith, and here they gave thanks for their victories over the enemies of Byzantium and God. In a real sense they owed their power to St. Sophia, for the Orthodox Church was the chief unifying force of a heterogeneous empire. It was the Church that inspired the heroic resistance to the all-conquering Arabs, which preserved Christendom in the East. Or it might be called the power of the Virgin; for more than once, in popular belief, it was only a miracle of the Virgin that saved Constantinople from conquest by the heathens.

Yet simple piety is hardly the key to the history of this worldly city, or even of St. Sophia. The Virgin no doubt had sufficient reason for allowing her cathedral to fall to the

Turks; in its subsequent history, at any rate, there is an insistent irony of the crude Thomas Hardy type; and thereby hangs my incongruous tale. Under the Ottoman Empire, Hagia Sophia served as a mosque, resounding with praise of the very masculine Mohammed. A few years ago this desecration was at last ended by Kemal Ataturk, the godless dictator who was himself attempting the miracle of creating a new Turkey on the Western model; he made the cathedral into a museum, in keeping with his policy of discouraging religion. An American architect was granted permission to make the first thorough study of the world-famous building. I relieved the architect of some routine work by making rubbings or copies of masons' marks—initials cut into the stones by the ancient builders. This simple task gave me the opportunity of crawling all over the stately monument, feeling my way back through the centuries, and working up a curious fond acquaintance with the anonymous masons. From these simple workmen I learned something more about the complexities of human history.

2. THE HISTORY OF ST. SOPHIA

According to Henry Adams, it was the 'attraction of power in a future life' that raised St. Sophia and the Gothic cathedrals. This might seem as selfish or vain a motive as it did to St. Bernard, who was horrified by the ostentation of church towers; but the more popular idea of Gothic art is that expressed by Ralph Adams Cram. He drew an ideal picture of the medieval artists and artisans, working freely together in a common love of beauty and of God. He contrasted their exalted piety with the crass materialism that raises the modern skyscraper, built by gangs of hired laborers to the greater glory of big business. And certainly we should be chastened by the Gothic cathedrals, the more when we consider the relatively poor little towns that erected them. The humble artisans who built St. Sophia—which Cram called 'the everlasting wonder of all Christendom'—gave me, however, chastening ideas of a different kind.

From all appearances, these artisans did not work in a holy, dedicated spirit. On some of the finer marble panels they left proud signatures, fancy monograms cut with loving care; but on most of the stones they chiseled out very crude initials. Apparently they made these marks in order to claim payment for their work; sometimes they signed a stone twice to make sure, with one signature upside down. I gathered that their primary motive was to get a job done and a living made, just as it is with workmen today. They differed from contemporary builders most obviously in that they did not work to exact specifications, but improvised as they went along. Their stones are generally rough-hewn, irregular in size or shape, and sometimes strangely imperfect. Instead of discarding, for example, a floor slab that had a broken corner or a crooked side, the masons cut the next one crooked so as to fit them together.

Upon close inspection, indeed, St. Sophia is an everlasting wonder in its anomalies. Its basic construction is honest, forthright, superbly solid; the more the architect learned about the secrets of its structure, the more he marveled at the resourcefulness and skill with which its builders had carried through an undertaking as bold and magnificent as the world had known, or yet knows. At the same time, there is hardly a straight line or a true curve in the majestic structure, even apart from the wear and tear of centuries. Everywhere one sees an exquisite care in the refinements of decoration, and an amateurish crudeness in the rudiments. The splendid columns of porphyry and verd antique are typical. Their capitals, and the arches resting on them, are elaborately carved; their bases are so roughly finished as to shame an apprentice. And in inconspicuous places even their ornamented capitals are likely to be unfinished. Everything stands; but everything is wavering, bulging, or askew.

The obvious excuse for such slovenliness in detail is the haste with which St. Sophia was erected; by a mighty effort, the Emperor Justinian succeeded in completing it in less than six years. This haste, however, suggests an unseemly impatience in his hopes of power in a future life. Justinian's piety is unquestionable—it is further proved by his savage persecution of heretics and his wars to extend the true faith. But it appears that he was also inspired by the hope of worldly fame that has led ordinary kings and capitalists to erect great monuments. At the dedication of his cathedral he raised his hands to heaven and cried, 'Glory to God, who has judged me worthy of accomplishing such a work as this! O Solomon, I have outdone you!' In other words, glory to God, and to the Emperor Justinian. Carved all over St. Sophia is the monogram of Justinian and Theodora, the brilliant courtesan who became his empress. Outside the cathedral he set up a colossal equestrian statue of himself, as a modern Achilles. In his palace near by he required all officials to swear loyalty to 'our divine and pious despots,' Justinian and Theodora; all who entered the royal presence had to prostrate themselves and call themselves slaves. He maintained a personal sovereignty more absolute than any emperor before him.

It seems clear that the central inspiration of Justinian's career was not God but imperial Rome. To revive the glory of the Roman Empire, he sacrificed both his subjects and himself over a long reign of almost forty years, working tirelessly, ascetically, ruthlessly. He surpassed all his predecessors in the persecution of heretics because he held himself responsible for the right theological opinions of all his subjects, to assure God's favor to the Empire. (As the contemporary historian Procopius wrote, 'He did not think that the slaying of men was murder unless they happened to share his own religious opinions.') For similar reasons he ordered his jurists to formulate the celebrated Justinian Code: he must be the supreme legislator and lay down the one Roman law for all. With the aid of his brilliant, devoted general, Belisarius (of whom he became jealous and suspicious), he recovered much of the ancient dominion of Rome in Italy and Africa. 'Never except under our reign has God granted the Romans to achieve such triumphs,' he rejoiced. 'That of which Antiquity did not seem worthy, in God's judgment, has been realized in our time.' God, however, appeared to be ungrateful. Justinian's empire was visited by the Great Pestilence, one of the most devastating plagues in all history. But even his triumphs came to seem meaningless, or even fatal. For his victories in the West he paid a high price to the Persians in the East; their triumphs included the utter destruction of the great Christian city of Antioch. In destroying the Gothic power in Italy, he destroyed all possibility of harmony between the Romans and the Christianized Goths, left Italy a prey to the heathen Lombards, and left Rome itself a city of ruins. And to meet the worldly costs of his zeal in enlarging and adorning his holy empire, he had to impose such heavy taxes that he was more hated by his Christian subjects than by his heathen enemies. Altogether, his reign was the most brilliant and glorious in Byzantine history, and the most disastrous. The builder of St. Sophia left an exhausted empire that began disintegrating after his death, and took a century and a half to recover.

The succeeding generations of worshipers in St. Sophia left humbler tokens of their own aspirations to immortality. Scratched on the columns and balustrades in the galleries, where the women sat, are many ancient initials and doodlings, including satirical drawings of bishops in their ceremonial robes. On the main floor the piety was purer, though of a superstitious kind. Hollows worn in the pavement beside the columns indicate where countless worshipers stood to kiss the holy icons; a hole in the 'perspiring column' of St. Gregory betokens the faith of countless more, who rubbed their fingers here to cure or prevent eye trouble. But less edifying are the memorials of royal worshipers. Among the superb mosaics, for instance, is a portrait of the Empress Zoe, who ascended the throne as a middle-aged virgin and devoted herself chiefly to making amends for her prolonged chastity. Beside her is her husband Constantine Monomachos, who looks somewhat strange because his head is set on shoulders belonging to somebody else; he had been preceded by two husbands who turned out badly.

On the whole, the history enacted in the cathedral of the Holy Wisdom seems little holier or wiser than the goings on in most worldly capitals. Justinian the Great had strengthened the claim of the emperor to appoint and control the Patriarch of the Church; his successors received a divine right from the ceremonial of consecration in St. Sophia—they all wear halos in their official portraits; and whether or not they were 'divine and pious,' they usually dominated the Orthodox Church. Occasionally a high-minded Patriarch defied an unprincipled emperor, or a bigoted Patriarch defied a wise emperor. More often the spiritual father accepted the policy of his worldly master, whose support he was pleased to enlist in struggles against rival bishops and the Roman Popes.

The only notable triumph of the Church was in its long struggle with the Iconoclasts, the emperors who tried to restore the purity of early Christianity by suppressing the worship of images. One result of this triumph is the beautiful mosaic of the Virgin that adorns the entrance to St. Sophia. Another was the canonization of the Empress Irene—the imperious beauty who, as regent, brought up her son in utter dissipation in order to unfit him for the exercise of his royal prerogatives, and, when he nevertheless asserted himself, had him dethroned and blinded. She later became St. Irene, because the Church remembered only her devotion to images: she had assembled the Council of Nicaea that pronounced 'anathema on all who communicate with them who do not worship images,' and that thereby reversed the Council of Constantinople of thirty-odd years earlier, in which 348 bishops had unanimously decreed that images were inventions of the devil. Although two more Councils later assembled, to reverse each other, the images were finally restored once and for all, in the year 843, by a solemn ceremony which thereafter was annually commemorated in the cathedral of the Holy Wisdom.

Altogether, the Byzantine Empire is likely to look strange

and unattractive to a Western eye. It was a nation without nationality—an artificial empire that called itself Roman, that we call Greek, and that in fact was made up chiefly of assorted Asiatics, of some twenty different nationalities. Culturally, it had little of the glory that was Greece. It maintained a brilliant capital, preserved the ancient learning, produced a notable architecture and ornamental art, and civilized the Slavic East; but it contributed nothing of importance to literature, philosophy, science, or the life of reason generally. Politically, it was an Oriental despotism that had something of the grandeur of Rome but more of its rottenness. Its haloed emperors were above all law, subject only to the wiles of eunuchs or other court favorites and to the plots of ambitious generals. Although many of them were able statesmen and brave warriors, hardly one was distinguished for Christian virtue; most were unscrupulous and cruel—ruthless adventurers or dissolute weaklings who alike earned the assassination that they often got. Their brilliant capital was usually turbulent and licentious. Its history in this aspect is a story of incessant intrigue and brawl, centered about St. Sophia, the Sacred Palace, and the Hippodrome. On almost every page somebody is having his nose cut off or his eyes put out.

In this whole drama Arnold Toynbee finds a wholesome moral. He declares that the Byzantine Empire broke down about the year 1000 (though it took four more centuries in dying), and that the cause of its crumbling, just when Western Christendom was starting a vigorous growth, was the imperial domination of the Orthodox Church. The imperial ideal, a relic of old Rome, not only smothered the vitality of the Church but led to a fierce war with the Bulgarians, fellow Christians who refused to be dominated; although the empire finally won this war, it was softened up for the oncoming Seljuk Turks. Toynbee's moral is 'the universal nemesis of idolatry,' the 'perverse and sinful' idolatry of an ephemeral institution, in which worship is transferred 'from the Creator to the creature.'

Unhappily, Toynbee proves too little—or too much. The Byzantine Empire was always fighting wars, for one reason or another, and almost any war might have served to destroy it. The victorious one against the Bulgarians appears no more inevitable, or inevitably fatal, than countless others waged in the name of either the Creator or his creatures. If anything, Toynbee seems to prove the universal failure of religion. The sinful idolatry of worldly institutions has been common to all civilizations, and to their religions; established religions have typically been allied with imperial or aristocratic interests. The fact remains that the Orthodox Church approved of the Bulgarian war. It seldom exerted its authority in behalf of purer worship of the Creator.

In the closing scenes of Byzantine history, at any rate, one may also remark the nemesis of the orthodox kind of idolatry. On the night before the final Turkish onslaught on Constantinople, in 1453, the Emperor Constantine Palaeologus, the last of the Constantines, received communion in St. Sophia. Then, accompanied by the Patriarch and a large crowd, he proceeded to the church of St. Theodosia, to pray to this martyr who had been manufactured in the struggle against the Iconoclasts and whose relics were famous for exceptionally miraculous powers. At dawn of the next day, which was St. Theodosia's day, he returned with a small band to the city walls, to fight and die gallantly. Most of his subjects spent the day in the churches, praying to their saints for another miracle instead of aiding their emperor. When the Turks fought their way into Constantinople they found ten thousand persons in St. Sophia, still praying. One legend has it that Sultan Mehmet illustrated the lesson of nemesis with the head of the last Constantine, which he exposed outside at the foot of Justinian's statue.

3. EAST AND WEST

'O, city, city, head of all cities!' lamented the historian Ducas, an eye-witness of the fall of Constantinople. 'O, city, city, center of the four quarters of the world! O, city, city, pride of the Christians and ruin of the barbarians! . . . Where is thy beauty, O paradise? Where is the blessed strength of spirit and body of thy Lord? . . . Where are the relics of the saints, where are the relics of the martyrs?' The fall of the 'New Rome' also made a terrible impression on Western Christendom, which had failed to come to the aid of its Eastern brethren. 'I am ashamed to be alive,' Aeneas Sylvius wrote to the Pope, 'and wish that we had all had the luck to die before this happened'; and he spoke at some length about his 'speechless grief.' Horror was intensified by fear of the advancing Turkish power, and by dismay at the loss of commercial privileges that Italians had enjoyed in Constantinople. For some ten years after the disaster prelates kept calling for another Crusade, to preserve Europe from the Turks.

The excitement soon subsided, however. Western Christendom was too absorbed in its own wars and commercial rivalries to keep worrying about the Turks, especially when the infidels permitted European merchants to trade in Constantinople again. From the beginning, moreover, many Westerners had regarded the disaster as a long overdue judgment of God upon the Greeks. The Greeks were notoriously a 'vicious people, steeped in sin,' as one traveler reported; they were greedy, treacherous, corrupt, and—above all—heretical. 'The Turks are enemies,' Petrarch had written, 'but the Greeks are schismatics and worse than enemies.' For the efforts to reconcile the Roman Catholic and the Orthodox Church had failed. Although the last Byzantine emperors, in their desperation, made sweeping concessions to the Papacy in hope of aid, the Orthodox masses stubbornly resisted the Roman heresy. The last of the Constantines got a Roman cardinal instead of the military aid he wanted; and when the cardinal solemnly celebrated the union of East and West in St. Sophia, just five months before the city fell to the Turks, he only provoked a fiercer dissension. 'It is better to see in the city the power of the Turkish turban than that of the Latin tiara!' exclaimed one dignitary. And so Constantinople, for all its thousand years of stirring history as the citadel of Christendom, soon faded from Western memory, or lived only as a ghostly, enigmatic symbol of a distant past. The future now belonged to Western Christendom, while St. Sophia became a mosque.

Meanwhile the Turks suggested another unwholesome moral. As pious Moslems, they plastered over the mosaics in St. Sophia, since all representations of the human form were sacrilegious, and they obliterated the crosses of the infidel Christians. They even effaced the crude little crosses in the signatures of some of the old masons. But they were almost as careless of detail as the original builders: they overlooked quite a few crosses and did not bother with the inconspicuous ones. Likewise they did not destroy the sacrilegious mosaics but merely covered them with plaster; hence it has been possible to restore them in recent years. More important, the Turks preserved St. Sophia for posterity by a thorough, skilful job of repair. For they respected the splendid capital of Eastern Christendom. They respected even the Patriarchate, granting it religious freedom, exemption from taxes, and civil authority over Orthodox Christians throughout the Ottoman Empire; by their conquests they gave it a wider jurisdiction than it had had in its heyday. The unwholesome moral is that in spite of their initial cruelties, the terrible Turks were more civilized and humane than the Christians of the Fourth Crusade, who had captured Constantinople before them.

Setting out to fight infidels, with the blessing of the great Pope Innocent III, these Crusaders were more inspired by the attraction of wealth and power in this world. They began by destroying the Christian city of Zara, to satisfy the Doge of Venice who was providing their transportation, and they ended by fighting the Byzantine Empire. When they took Constantinople they fired large sections of the city, massacred thousands of their fellow Christians, and for some days wantonly pillaged and destroyed. 'Since the world was created,' boasted one of their leaders, 'never had so much booty been won in any city!' They looted St. Sophia as they did other monuments, carrying off some of its treasures, melting down others to make coins.[1] The priceless accumulations of nine centuries were part of the price of the Fourth Crusade. And this happened in the year 1204, the beginning of the thirteenth century, when the Virgin was reputedly at the height of her power.

So in fairness to St. Sophia, whose history we have been looking at from a prejudiced Western point of view, we might now look at the happenings in and around the cathedrals of the West. The thirteenth century also saw the founding of the Inquisition, the increasingly systematic persecution of Jews and dissenters, the atrocious extermination of the Albigenses. Such violent intolerance was no doubt logical, given the Devil. The Devil was also very real at this time; he was known to command a formidable army of witches, goblins, werewolves, and assorted demons, all in human shape. Nevertheless the violence raises some question about an age supposedly united in a loving faith. As for the great multitude, the social records of the period make clear that their faith was woefully impure, shot through with pagan superstitions—and at that was not sufficient solace for their hard lot on earth. Churchmen constantly lamented that drunkenness and crime were most prevalent on Sundays and holy days. As for the churchmen themselves, there was notorious venality among the lower orders, and at the top a fierce struggle for worldly power. Hence Dante—now regarded as the symbol of this greatest of ages—believed that it was morally and spiritually bankrupt and consoled himself by torturing its leaders in the ghastliest of hells.

The thirteenth century was in fact extraordinary in its twin cults of the Virgin and the Devil, its blend of chivalry and brutality, love and lust, faith and fear; but it was a tragic

---

[1] Thus some famous bronze statues of antiquity, which Constantine the Great had collected to adorn the first capital of the Christian world, were made into pennies to pay off the common soldiers. Of the 'holy relics' that were carried away, most disappeared during the French Revolution.

century for Western Christendom. In Toynbee's sympathetic account of it, its main outcome was the failure of the ideal proclaimed by the Hildebrandine Popes—the lofty ideal of a universal Christian society, united under their spiritual dominion; and the failure was due to the arrogance of the Church. From the beginning, this holy end had been corrupted by the use of violent means, and it steadily degenerated into a lust for power. By the thirteenth century the Papacy was engaged in a remorseless, vindictive struggle with the emperors. It was fatally injured even by its victories, having undermined its spiritual cause and armed the worldly powers that were to overthrow it. The aftermath—the Great Schism, the Reformation, and the bloody religious wars—only emphasized the spiritual disaster that had already occurred.

According to Toynbee, then, the Eastern Christian Society failed because the throne dominated the Church, and the Western Christian Society failed because the Church tried to dominate the throne. Or one might say that the power of the Virgin—'the highest energy ever known to man'—was not high enough to create a really Christian society. Neither Chartres nor St. Sophia inspired any notable holiness or wisdom in political and economic life. In both, the masses of men were taught to seek their well-being in the life to come, and to endure without complaint the hard lot that enabled the ruling classes to enjoy well-being in this life. The Eastern and Western Churches clashed because both were politically ambitious, and because both—unlike the religions of the Far East—taught that salvation was possible only to their own followers, thereby automatically condemning the overwhelming majority of mankind to eternal torment. As for the conspicuous differences between the two societies, the pious Westerner may remark that Byzantium produced no Aquinas, no Dante, no Innocent III. The impious may remark that the West became the dominant civilization in the world after it had shaken off the domination of the Church, and set about cultivating natural sources of power; while Byzantium, trusting its Virgin and its saints to the end, went down ignominiously.

4. THE MYSTERIES OF BYZANTIUM

'In the revolution of ten centuries,' Gibbon summed up his history of the Eastern Roman-Byzantine Empire, 'not a single discovery was made to exalt the dignity or promote the happiness of mankind. Not a single idea has been added to the speculative systems of antiquity. Not a single composition of history, philosophy, or literature has been saved from oblivion by the intrinsic beauties of style or sentiment, of original fancy, or even of successful imitation.' Until the last century, most Western writers echoed this verdict on Eastern Christendom. Yet St. Sophia still stands, an everlasting wonder. After noting all the crudities in the detail of its construction, one still gets a total impression of magnificence, unsurpassed in its blend of the monumental and the ethereal. And after noting all the anomalies in the history played out in it, one must face a final question about the society that built it —a society that for all its apparently rotten foundations had an astonishing vitality. Offhand, the Byzantine Empire had every reason to go down as Rome did; yet it survived the fall of the 'Eternal City' by a thousand years, maintaining a high civilization despite constant pressure from barbarians and infidels. It outlasted all contemporary empires, such as the Gothic, the Persian, the Arabian, and the Frankish. Why? What kept it going? Its vitality seems still more mysterious if we accept Gibbon's verdict. It suggests that youthful Westerners might try to take a more sympathetic look at the venerable religious, political, and cultural institutions of the Byzantine Empire.[2]

With its icons, its cult of relics, its hosts of dubious saints and miracles, Orthodox Christianity is apt to strike a Westerner as a mass of superstition. Cardinal Newman described it as 'doctrine without principle.' Clearly it did emphasize cultus more than principle, ritual more than reason; its heart was the mystery of the Mass—a holy mystery to be felt, not explained or understood. Still, this would not make it simply

[2] Toynbee disposes of the mystery by killing off the Eastern Roman Empire, which he declares was dead for all practical purposes by A.D. 602; in 717 he starts a new Byzantine Empire, which made the mistake of reviving the 'ghost' of its predecessor, and so broke down only three centuries later. Almost all other historians, however, stress the essential continuity of the Eastern Roman-Byzantine Empire through all its ups and downs, beginning when Constantine the Great solemnly inaugurated his new capital in the year 330. For Toynbee's supposedly dying Roman Empire built St. Sophia, the greatest masterpiece of Byzantine art. During the seventh century, when according to him the empire had ceased to exist, the Patriarch continued to preside at St. Sophia; an unbroken succession of emperors, including the famous Heraclius, maintained their capital at Constantinople and kept issuing gold coins that were accepted as standard everywhere in the East; and Toynbee himself notes that the corpse performed the 'magnificent feat' of repelling a simultaneous attack by Persians from Asia and Avars from Europe. His scheme accordingly seems to be a high-handed way of teaching a religious moral.

alien or heretical. Christians in the West believe in angels, demons, heaven, hell, the resurrection of the flesh, and other doctrines that on rational grounds also look like superstitions, and can be demonstrated only on the grounds of a supernatural revelation. In this view, the East completely accepted and frankly glorified the mysterious, supernatural basis of all Christian belief. Orthodox Christendom was in fact more orthodox. Its Thomas Aquinas was John of Damascus, who as early as the eighth century summed up and virtually sealed its theology. John was a compiler who made no pretense of fresh interpretation or synthesis; at the outset of his compendium he announced, 'I will say nothing of my own.' Western thinkers continued to elaborate and complicate their theology, often saying profound things of their own, but moving farther away from early Christianity. The apparently silly controversy over the *filioque*, the chief doctrinal reason for the official break between East and West in the eleventh century, actually represented a fundamental difference. The Roman Church, following St. Augustine, maintained that the Holy Ghost proceeded from both the Father and Son; it thereby completed the logic of the Trinity and glorified a rational principle. The Eastern Church maintained, rightly enough, that there was no Scriptural basis for this doctrine; it adhered to the ancient Creed that stated that the Holy Ghost proceeded only from the Father. Today it still stands where it stood in the eleventh century.

Spengler and Christopher Dawson, among other historians, have pointed out that Eastern Christianity can be best understood as a phase of the revival of ancient Oriental cultures in the centuries after Christ, and their triumphant reaction upon classical culture. The East seized on the mystical elements of Christianity, elaborating the mystery cult that had first made it popular; the Roman West developed the ethical and legal elements. One of the national heroes of Byzantium was always the stylite or ascetic monk, who symbolized the Oriental other-worldly spirit; the Roman West put him to work. Likewise the East stressed the Holy Spirit more than the Father or the crucified Son. Its churches were not soaring cathedrals, symbols of tense aspiration—they were 'cupola caverns' (in Spengler's phrase), magical with gold gleaming on wall and ceiling, mysterious with the presence of the Spirit in their shadows. In general, Orthodox Christianity was given to neither the crusading zeal nor the *Sturm und Drang* of the wilful West. (Nicolas Berdyaev reports that its mystics know nothing about the 'dark night of the soul' through which their Western brethren usually have to pass.) But its holy mystery remained the most vital force in an Asiatic Empire, surviving the inglorious end of the state.

The Byzantine political system is much harder to admire, unless one agrees with George of Pisidia: 'How fair a Rule is monarchy, when God-sustained.' God had to sustain all the emperors elected by the army or the aristocratic senate, and all the successful assassins of these emperors; with their coronation, legitimate successors and usurpers alike automatically became sacred; and about the only real limit to their power was the danger of assassination. The most that can be said for this system of 'Caesaro-papism' is that it produced some illustrious emperors—statesmen and warriors genuinely devoted to the empire. Although the idea that they were 'Equals of the Apostles' could not save them from being murdered, it helped to keep alive something of the old Roman tradition that their position was an obligation, not merely a personal privilege. They needed Roman fortitude, since their empire was always under pressure from nomads and powerful neighbors, and their capital itself often besieged. Norman Baynes suggests that the notorious deceit, brutality, and cruelty of Byzantine history might be forgiven because of the constant tension of its life.

Another source of strength was the civil-service tradition inherited from Rome. Wasteful, cumbersome, often corrupt, the bureaucracy nevertheless had a basically sound organization that enabled it to maintain a degree of law and order in periods of anarchy and to resist tyranny as well as reform. Especially notable were its financial and military departments. For some eight hundred years, Baynes points out, the government issued coinage that was universally respected, and it never stopped payments or declared bankruptcy—a record of stability unparalleled in either the ancient or the modern world. The Byzantine military also made an excellent record by efficiently organizing its relatively small forces, and making a science of the business of war. What most obviously sustained the monarchy was not God but its money and its army.

As for Byzantine culture, it has been traditionally overpraised for its preservation of the Greek heritage, and traditionally underrated for the same reason: it was confused with late classical culture, and then disparaged as a degenerate phase of it. By now Byzantine art and architecture are generally recognized as a great independent style, no less original because it is a fusion of classical, Christian, and Oriental elements. For a Westerner, its most distinctive elements are Oriental. From the Near East it got not only such specific forms as the dome but its passion for color and ornament, and for symbolism and abstract design. Its Christian subjects were highly formalized even after the image-worshipers triumphed over the Iconoclasts (who represented something like the Mohammedan spirit). And though a Westerner is apt to prefer the humanism of Greek art, or the relative naturalism of medieval art, only the hidebound realist can deny the splendor that Byzantium gave to the Christian story. The first great age of Byzantine art that produced St. Sophia also created a style that endured for many centuries, spread over Italy, Greece, and the Slavic world, contributed to medieval and Renaissance art, lived on in Russia, and is still an important influence in the Near East.

The common objection to this style, as to Byzantine culture generally, is its rigid conventionalism, the stiffness and sameness of its forms through the centuries. Again, however, we must first acknowledge its remarkable vitality. In the last centuries of Byzantium an intellectual and artistic renaissance gave a splendid glow to the dying empire. It built some of its most exquisite churches; it produced famous mosaics (notably those in the church of the Chora in Istanbul) worthy of comparison with Renaissance art in Italy; it produced scholars and teachers who were revered in the West. Its temporary capital at Nicaea became so noted for its brilliant culture that it was hailed as a second Athens. It even caught something of a humanistic spirit, which might have led to a profound renaissance had the empire survived. As it was, the death agonies of Byzantium were prolonged by its ancient reputation as a mighty empire, which gave it enough diplomatic power to keep struggling for the remnants of its domain and to expose it to further humiliation by Italians and Turks; but at least it maintained its dignity as a high culture. It earned the obituary pronounced by Charles Diehl: 'the champion of Christendom against Islam, the defender of civilization against barbarism, and the educator of the Slavic East.'

This is a decent enough achievement for a civilization. It deserves a much fuller account, and perhaps a more enthusiastic one, than I have sketched here. Yet even enthusiasts seldom rank Byzantium with such civilizations as Greece, Rome, India, and China. Although it conserved much, it created little. Aside from art, it in fact contributed nothing 'to exalt the dignity or promote the happiness of mankind.' There remain the profound ambiguities in the history of St. Sophia, the unholy wisdom and the holy folly associated with this 'everlasting wonder of all Christendom,' which make one wonder why the Byzantine Empire endured for a thousand years.

Granted that one man's holy mystery is another man's primitive superstition, and that an outsider cannot do full justice to the distinctive piety of Eastern Christendom, it is nevertheless possible to make certain objective observations. The Orthodox Church was ultra-conservative, and conserved primarily a mystery cult. Her greatest writers and thinkers—such as Athanasius, John Chrysostom, and the Gregories of Nazianzus and Nyssa—came in the fourth century; her theological development ended with the ceremony in St. Sophia that commemorated the final defeat of the Iconoclasts, and in effect confirmed the popular belief in the miraculous powers of images. 'To the faith of the Fathers she has remained splendidly loyal,' comments Norman Baynes, 'but that very loyalty of the heart has made it difficult for her to worship her God with all her mind.' This is to say the Church was indifferent or hostile to the pursuit of truth, and helps to explain why Byzantine civilization contributed so little to the life of reason. Similarly the Church failed to inspire new ideals or encourage new aspirations. It made nothing of the revolutionary implications in the teaching of Jesus. The Virgin herself, it appears, symbolized chiefly the hope of mercy in the life to come; she did not insist that men be gentle, merciful, and kind in this life. One motive for the common piracy in the Byzantine Empire was the need of financing pilgrimages for Our Lady.

Nevertheless this mystical Church was in other respects quite worldly. Although historians conventionally describe Byzantine culture as essentially religious, dominated by the supernatural, religion itself was plainly dominated by the throne and had a much less apparent influence on secular behavior. Justinian's bishop stated the law laid down by Justinian: 'Nothing should happen in the Church against the command or will of the Emperor.' The Emperor was often pious, in a royal fashion, and sometimes fancied himself a theologian, as Justinian did; but his main interests were imperial. Most of his subjects were as earthy. If one type of national hero was the fanatical monk, another was the winner of the chariot races in the Hippodrome adjoining St. Sophia; the *spina* of the Hippodrome has been called the axis of the Byzantine Empire. The considerable power that religion did exert, moreover, was not always conducive to either the material or the spiritual welfare of the empire. If the Church was the main source of its unity, it was also a major source of weakness and dissension. The very numerous monasteries, exempt from taxation, immobilized much of the wealth of the empire and were a constant drain on its limited manpower.[3] The influential monks were now fighting among themselves, now fighting the emperor, now supporting him in the persecution of schismatics. Religious persecution alienated so many citizens in Syria, Palestine, and Egypt that these provinces offered little resistance to the Moslems, even welcoming their relatively tolerant rule. And in the last centuries of Byzantium the Church disastrously weakened the state by its jealousy of Rome. It forced a complete break with Rome, and later thwarted all efforts at reconciliation by imperial statesmen. In finally asserting itself against its imperial masters, it destroyed whatever chances of survival the empire had.

As for the imperial system itself, it remained a naked despotism, habitually unprincipled in its policies and brutal in its methods. It recognized the traditional demand of the populace of Constantinople for bread and circuses, but it recognized no political rights whatever. It commanded loyalty only through the fiction that the Emperor was the elect of God; otherwise it was a purely artificial creation, whose heterogeneous subjects could be loyal only to individuals or through blind habit. It introduced occasional administrative reforms but created no new political institutions and inspired no new political ideas. In its last crisis it was still clinging to its timeworn fictions. A Spanish visitor to Constantinople in 1437 commented on how 'sad and poor' its inhabitants were, but added, 'The Emperor's state is as splendid as ever, for nothing is omitted from the ancient ceremonies.' Its one enduring legacy was its brilliant pageantry, which was inherited by the Vatican.

Pageantry—the purely decorative—is also a conspicuous quality of Byzantine art. The whole culture of the church-state was hidebound by tradition, and the basic tradition was a formalism that always tended to artificiality. It suffered from its greatest achievements, whose forms became fixed, sacrosanct, and arrested further development. Large provinces of culture were so blighted by the tyranny of conventional-

---

[3] There was an enormous increase in monasteries during the reign of Justinian, when the rest of his subjects were groaning under taxation. Here again Justinian's motives in encouraging the monks were not wholly disinterested. 'If they, with their hands pure and their souls bare, offer to God prayers for the State,' he wrote, 'it is evident that it will be well with the army, and the cities will prosper and our land will bear fruits and the sea will yield us its products, for their prayers will propitiate God's favor towards the whole State.' Such bargains recall the old hymn:

> Whatever, Lord, we lend to Thee
> Repaid a thousandfold will be;
> Then gladly will we give to Thee
> Who givest all.

ism that there was no healthy development at all. Byzantine poetry, for example, is a maze of fantastically elaborate, obscure rhetoric. (Baynes reports that the best work of its one good religious poet—Romanos, in the sixth century—is so simple and clear that it was dropped from the service books, and then forgotten.) During the last renaissance of Byzantine culture, its poets and philologists revived the 'pure' Attic dialect, and began revising the ancient texts in this wholly artificial literary language.

Herein is the crowning paradox of the most celebrated contribution of Byzantium—its preservation of Greek culture. According to Toynbee, 'Orthodox Christian piety' preserved this heritage. Actually this piety was inimical to Greek humanism, and at times openly hostile. Justinian passed a law forbidding anyone 'infected with the madness of the unholy Hellenes' to teach any subject; it was he who closed the schools of Athens, ending their history of eight hundred years. Classical learning never disappeared from Constantinople, to be sure. In time Greek became the official language of the empire (though to the end it called itself the 'Empire of the Romans'). Yet Byzantium never caught the essential Greek spirit—free, curious, critical. Piously it preserved its invaluable heritage, without ever really understanding it or benefiting from it; its classical tradition was not so much an inspiration as another incubus. Hence it could not propagate this tradition among the peoples it civilized.[4] To the Slavic East Byzantium passed on only its art, religion, and Caesaro-papism.

Altogether, it was an essentially static culture, whose apparent energy was rooted in little apparent moral, intellectual, or spiritual initiative. Once Proclus sounded its keynote in the advice he gave to the Emperor Anastasius: 'I have never learned to accustom myself to innovations, and I fear them above everything else, for I know full well that in making innovations safety can in no way be preserved.' This spirit hardly makes for a glorious history, or even a sensible one. It does not actually make history safe. 'The Byzantine culture faithfully preserved its original tradition,' concludes Christopher Dawson, 'but it was powerless to create new social forms and new cultural ideals'; so when the church-state crumbled there was no other source of energy, no basis for a new communal effort. It had not learned to accustom itself to the innovations that history was forcing on it.

Still, it had managed to carry on for a thousand years

---

[4] Historians have now discredited the old textbook theory that the flight of Greek scholars to Europe, upon the impending fall of Constantinople, was a prime cause of the Renaissance. Although the West learned something from Byzantine scholars, it learned more from the Arabs.

after Rome fell. The original question remains: What kept this static civilization going? Why was it preserved by a tradition that failed to preserve Rome? I can see no very good reasons, or at least none that illustrate a satisfying philosophy of history. Offhand, the advantages of the Byzantine Empire seem accidental or incidental. It had a strong walled capital, with an excellent location for purposes of trade and defense; as at once the economic and the political capital, Constantinople was less parasitic than Rome. It had the secret of 'Greek fire,' the diabolic weapon that scattered or destroyed enemy fleets besieging Constantinople; probably this military secret did more to preserve the empire than did its whole Greek heritage. Above all, it had good luck in its emperors during its worst crises, being periodically saved by the emergence of a strong, able ruler. This looks like mere luck, because the rise of such a savior was not provided for by any peculiar wisdom in its political institutions; it was facilitated by the customary intrigue, turbulence, and corruption that also enabled worthless adventurers to seize power. One is tempted to believe that it was indeed the Virgin who kept saving the empire, for some unfathomable feminine reason.

At least none of the popular theories of history clearly accounts for the history of Byzantium. With its ups and downs, and its gradual transition from a Roman to a distinctively Byzantine civilization, it does not fit into the neat cyclical patterns of Spengler, Toynbee, Sorokin, and others; on a graph only its final decline makes a decent curve. Its seemingly fortuitous climaxes illustrate no dynamic law. The brilliance of Justinian's reign, for example, is an understandable human achievement but not a predictable one; and then his work might have stood up better except for the disastrous plague that not only depopulated but demoralized his empire—another natural but not inevitable event. Perhaps least applicable are the 'iron laws' of Marxist theory, even apart from its inability to explain the glory of St. Sophia itself. The peculiar culture of Byzantium reflected no peculiar economic structure, or change in its material conditions; its history was marked by no class struggle between the haves and have-nots but only by intrigue and strife within the small ruling class. From the orthodox Marxist point of view it had no real development or history. Yet Byzantium had much to do (as we shall see later) with the shaping of the Soviet Russia that has been established in the name of Marx.

Perhaps the most we can say is that the kind of despotism established by Diocletian and Constantine, and cemented by Justinian, was naturally congenial to the East. Rome tried to become what its Asiatic provinces were by nature, but it lacked the essential spirit, the force of ancient tradition. In all the historic empires of the East there has been little spirit of liberty or faith in the power of reason. The peasant masses had no voice, and little will but to work and to worship. To a democratic Western eye, accordingly, there is always an instructive moral in the eventual collapse of these empires; but the trouble remains that they often flourished for centuries. So Egypt endured for more than two thousand years after its despots, in their monstrous obsession with power in a future life, took to building pyramids out of the blood of their people; and their pyramids are likely to outlast Western civilization, or possibly the human race itself.

5. THE METHOD OF TRAGEDY

What, then, does St. Sophia have to tell us? I should not restrict its meaning to the few implications I have chosen to stress from the drama of fourteen hundred years. I should insist only that there is no one simple meaning, and that we must realize the profound incongruities of the drama if we hope to rise on stepping stones of our dead selves to higher things. St. Sophia remains an inspiring monument, glorious and vainglorious. It is a symbol of humility and pride, of holiness and worldliness, of the power of faith and the limitations of faith. It is an everlasting triumph, of a society that failed. It may epitomize all the great societies and golden ages of the past, which also failed and still inspire. It calls for reverence, and for irony.

For most contemporaries the plainest need is more reverence, or simply a decent interest in the past. An American lady who paid ten cents to visit St. Sophia was so disappointed that she wanted her money back. 'They call it a museum,' she said in disgust, 'and there's nothing in it.' So there is nothing in the past for too many Americans, except some blurry notions of their own brief history as a chosen people; and so they cannot really know who they are or where they are. Others are likely to desecrate St. Sophia by regarding it as merely a museum, finding it picturesque; for nothing is more undignified than a past become quaint. But it is we, of course, who really suffer from such impiety. The naïve, uncritical faith in material progress that has made Americans feel so superior to the past is still a menace to a hope of any kind of progress. It is also liable to as naïve a despair. Once infatuated with our unprecedented achievements, men are now appalled by the realization that history is big enough to swallow them up too.

For this reason, however, more sensitive spirits have been tending to the opposite extreme, the ancient habit of overrating the past. Literary men are always apt to get sentimental about the past for much the same reason that simple men get sentimental about their happy, carefree childhood days, which in fact were full of childish cares. Looking back, they see the great monuments, the enduring records of the highest aspirations. They do not see all the trivial, paltry, vulgar, foolish ends of the unheroic dead—the mean stuff of daily existence that by its nature is perishable, and perishes with little trace. They forget the constant complaint of great men about the mediocrity of their age; or they remember only the nobly expressed complaint, not the mediocrity. We must indeed be grateful for the enchantment of the past, its magical power to lift us above the sordid, petty, nagging concerns of everyday life, and at worst to leave us brooding over the tragic dignity of man's life instead of the indignities of the cost of living. Yet we cannot afford to spare the past its troubles. Such enchantment makes the present seem only more unintelligible, and more intolerable, unless we appreciate as well the value of disenchantment—of an awareness that all the generations whom death has made stately in stillness once strutted and fretted even as we. Too many writers have the habit of representing the loftiest ideal of some former age as its essence, and then contrasting it with the meanest actualities of the present. So the thirteenth century is celebrated as if it were summed up by St. Thomas Aquinas, Dante, and the Virgin of Chartres, while the twentieth century is reduced to Hitler, Hearst, and the sex queens of Hollywood.[5]

As it is now easy to be ironical about our vaunted progress, so it is easy to fail in decent respect for the living. A steadfast reverence—a reverence for the human spirit, not merely a few selected dead—itself calls for a more robust, catholic irony. And here St. Sophia may symbolize a wisdom holier than its builders knew, in the sense in which holiness is akin to wholeness, haleness, and healing. Its paradoxical history comes down to an age-old story, as familiar as fantastic. It is the story of a 'rational animal' who thereby lacks the sureness of instinct, is a prey to irrational desires,

[5] A distinguished classical scholar, Sir Richard Livingstone, offers another example in his *Greek Ideals and Modern Life*. To Livingstone Greece is chiefly Plato, and he assumes that he has characterized modern life when he contrasts Plato's political thought with the campaign speeches of our politicians. It apparently does not occur to him that he might as fairly contrast William James or Woodrow Wilson with the innumerable demagogues who led Greece to ruin.

and of all animals leads the least sensible life; who alone is free to choose and aspire, and so is forever torn by doubt and discontent, from which spring at once his loftiest values and his ugliest hates and fears; who alone can know truth and virtue, and by the same token is prone to error and evil, capable of a folly and brutality unknown to dumb brutes. In a time of troubles, it is the story of how the best is apt to become the worst, as high, fixed principles lead to the use of unprincipled means, and an uncompromising sincerity ends as the terrible falsity that inspired the old proverb, May God deliver us from the lies of honest men. At all times it is the story of the inescapable hazards that man brought upon himself when he took to playing with fire and then, without forethought, set out on the extraordinarily bold adventure of making over his world; while ever since he began to reflect he has been seeking a repose that he can find only in the death he fears.

Our theme, in short, is high Tragedy. We start with the absurd incongruities that are the main theme of Comedy too: 'O Lord, what fools these mortals be!' But Tragedy heightens the incongruities by invoking the emotions of pity and awe, adding that man is the most wretched and sublime of fools. In its supreme manifestations, such as the tragedies of Sophocles and Shakespeare, it is an all-inclusive experience, embracing the extremes of good and evil. It takes on the most awful possibilities of human life, to display the most splendid possibilities of the human spirit. It goes through the worst, and by going all the way through it earns an honorable peace, which is more secure because it is peace without victory. It may therefore afford a deeper pleasure than the happy endings of Comedy, or even a more exhilarating pleasure than 'calm of mind, all passion spent.' And the principle of its paradoxical success—its resolute complication of its issues, in a spirit at once ironic, compassionate, and reverential—may be broadened into a principle of historical analysis: a way of viewing history that might not be precise, rigorous, or decisive enough to be dignified as a logical or scientific method, but that can be comprehensive, consistent, disciplined, roughly systematic, generally incisive, and always pertinent.

In historical terms, the incongruities inherent in the nature of man are as naturally heightened by social order and social change. An order requires institutions, officials, routines, conventions, habits; and this indispensable bureaucracy, in thought as in administrative affairs, is always a threat to social health. An order is necessarily a selection from diverse possibilities, and as such it requires the suppression of other possibilities, has the defects of its virtues, and tends to overemphases—

as William James said, without too much we cannot have enough, of anything. Social change as necessarily brings further conflict and contradiction, through cultural lag. All creative achievements are disruptive, and create new problems. All victorious creeds and policies have unintended by-products, which may defeat their purposes. All social movements that have the force to go far enough are apt to go too far and so to call out counter-movements, the pendulum swings of history.

The 'tragic view,' accordingly, may not only comprehend but anticipate the technical analyses of sociologists and historians. Without prejudice to science, it may help us to realize the value that Lionel Trilling attributes to literature, as 'the human activity that takes the fullest and most precise account of variousness, possibility, complexity, and difficulty.' By systematically complicating all issues, stressing the defects and the excesses of all values, insisting on tension, imbalance, uncertainty, and contradiction as the essential conditions of civilization, and the source of both its glory and its tragedy —by ironically qualifying the great triumphs, and reverently qualifying the great failures, we may get both a richer appreciation of the poetry and drama of history and a clearer understanding of the fact, the 'reality' that concerns social science. We may hope to be at once more humane and more realistic, more generous in our sympathies and more sober in our judgments.

For this reason I have been discounting the obviously wholesome morals, in particular Toynbee's moral that the root evil in human history is pride. *Hubris,* or the insolence of pride, was indeed the main theme of the Greek poets who originated Tragedy. Historically it was the nemesis of Athens itself, as of the Great Kings of Persia, the Pharaohs of Egypt, the Caliphs of Bagdad, the Autokrators of Byzantium, the Popes of medieval Rome. Yet the tragic poets have not seen a clear justice in man's fate, nor a shining hope in the gods; and history hardly bears out such hopes. Toynbee's own study shows that when religious belief was strongest it bred the worldly pride from which it is supposed to deliver us, and was most deeply involved in the moral failures of both Eastern and Western Christendom. The 'universal nemesis of idolatry' is so universal that, like 'nature,' it explains nothing. Pride in man's own creations is common to all societies, including the longest-lived, and perhaps most common in their vigorous youth and prime. It may be considered the mainspring of civilization.

Here again St. Sophia gives the clue to a basic ambiguity.

Pride goeth before a fall—but first it lifts men to real heights. Without pride the tragic hero would not be a hero; without it there would be no tragedy in history because no civilization at all. And without it there would be no higher religions. It was pride that built St. Sophia. It was still pride that led thousands to pray in St. Sophia in the miserable last days of Byzantium; for in their abjectness they were still assuming that the Almighty took such a keen personal interest in the inhabitants of one small region of this planet that he would perform a miracle to lay low the inhabitants of other regions. Even the loftiest manifestations of the religious spirit may be described as overweening pride. Nothing is prouder than the humility of the ascetic or other-worldly spirit that proclaims itself superior to the whole natural world, or than the mysticism that renounces the self only to commune with God himself.

In short, we are all proud of one thing or another, if we have any self-respect or any faith in anything at all. Since we can all recognize the dangers of pride in others, our apparent task is to define and ground our faith, in an awareness of the limitations and the excesses of all faiths. And for this purpose, finally, I draw a specific, positive lesson from the history of St. Sophia. The root evil of Byzantine civilization was not simply its worldly pride—it was a blind faith, a basic unreason. It was exemplified in the tyranny of convention but most concretely in the tyranny of the church-state. Both Church and State claimed absolute authority, without enlisting the free consent of their subjects or permitting free criticism of the principles of their authority. Both were hostile to the life of reason.

Another object of this book will be to define and ground the pride or faith implicit in this judgment. It is a liberal, rationalistic, humanistic faith, rooted in the Greek heritage that Byzantium unthinkingly preserved and betrayed. One of its basic tenets is the dictum of Pascal: 'Thought makes the whole dignity of man; therefore endeavor to think well—that is the only morality.' I assume that thought is most dignified and moral when it recognizes its own limitations, and the hazards it inevitably introduces into the life of man. In confronting history, it must at least begin with the tragic view. It must acknowledge that no civilized society ever has had or can have the stability and security of the far more ancient ant and bee societies, which are regulated by the more efficient, economical mechanism of instinct. Today it must acknowledge that the rationalistic faith that has built the modern Western world is implicated in the frightful state of this world. Nevertheless I continue to believe, in pride, that our only possible hope lies not in prayer but in more thought, and in more earnest, responsible endeavor. The plainest lesson I get from the history of St. Sophia is that men cannot count on miracles.

II

The Nature of History

1. THE PHILOSOPHY OF HISTORY

'Happy is the people that is without a history,' wrote Christopher Dawson, 'and thrice happy is the people without a sociology, for as long as we possess a living culture we are unconscious of it, and it is only when we are in danger of losing it or when it is already dead that we begin to realize its existence and to study it scientifically.' There are still such happy people among us, on farms, in business offices, and in congressional chambers. But those who are cursed by consciousness cannot become unconscious by an effort of will, and many have grown unhappier because they know too little history and sociology. A little consciousness is the most dangerous thing. And so we had better strive to become clearly and fully conscious, of who we are, where we are, and how we got this way.

From the outset, we are faced with the striking contradictions of the modern world. Our age is notorious for its want of piety or sense of the past; up-to-date men have been too busy making gadgets, automobiles, depressions, and wars to care much about anything older than the minutes of the last meeting. Our age is nevertheless more historically minded than any previous age, and has a much longer, wider, clearer view of the past. Its contributions to historical knowledge, over the last hundred years, are among its most honorable achievements. In studying the past scientifically, unearthing its monuments, recovering its vanished life, historians have performed a work of unprecedented piety. For despite their deep sense of the past, the ancients had little understanding of it. Thucydides, the most objective of ancient historians, began his history of the Peloponnesian War by stating that nothing of great importance had happened before his time; and in his ignorance of all that lay behind his age he could not realize the unique glory of Athens, which for us makes the Peloponnesian War even more momentous and more tragic than he felt it to be. Modern historians are far better acquainted with the early history of the Greeks, as of the Egyptians, the Hebrews, and the Romans, than were these pious peoples themselves.

The triumphs of this historical research involve further ironies. They have been triumphs of the scientific spirit and method. Hence they fostered the illusion that often inspired them—the illusion that history is or should be an exact science, free from all taint of art or philosophy. 'Do not applaud me,' Fustel de Coulanges told his rapt students. 'It is not I who address you, but history that speaks through my mouth.' This claim of utter impersonality encouraged the monumental unimaginativeness of German scholarship, which still awes American universities and dehumanizes the humanities. It implied that the significance of human history was to be discovered by a systematic avoidance of significant generalization or judgment. It was based, Carl Becker remarked, on the strange philosophical assumption that by not taking thought a historian could add a cubit to his stature. 'Hoping to find something without looking for it, expecting to obtain final answers to life's riddles by resolutely refusing to ask questions—it was surely the most romantic species of realism yet invented, the oddest attempt ever made to get something for nothing!'

Now this naïve faith was understandable, and up to a point quite laudable. Historians of the last century were striving to make their subject intellectually respectable in an age of science. (As late as 1880 there were only eleven professors of history in American colleges.) They had to combat the common tendencies to entertain and edify, to exploit the dramatic and spectacular, to teach political and religious lessons, or to leap to grandiose philosophies of history. These tendencies are still so popular that we can scarcely afford to ridicule any aspiration to objectivity and exactitude. Nevertheless the 'scientific' historians had a shallow conception of science, art, and philosophy. They thought of the true scientist as one who deals in plain, unvarnished facts, never making assumptions and never being harried by doubt and dispute over fundamentals. They thought of art as the antithesis of science, as if imagination deals only with the imaginary and can be indulged only when knowledge fails. They thought of philosophy as metaphysical speculation, another inferior substitute for knowledge or threat to it. They failed to see that science itself is an imaginative interpretation of reality, based on philosophical assumptions.

Their very ideal of objectivity and exactitude, in other words, calls for a more exact idea of the nature of historical knowledge, and the limits to its objectivity. The aim of history, said Ranke, is simply to state 'what has actually happened; but this is far from being a simple business, even apart from the fact that we can never hope to know all that has actually happened. If we did know all, we should have to forget almost everything before we could understand anything—just as our memory is an aid only because we remember no more than a minute fraction of our past experience. As it is, the main problem is not so much to fill in the many gaps in our factual knowledge as to make sense out of the vast deal that we do know. For a historical fact never speaks for itself. We begin by singling out the 'important' happenings; we then try to determine their causes and effects, or their connections with other happenings that we decide are relevant and important; we finally try to determine their significance, their connection with our own purposes. And in this whole process of selecting, interpreting, and evaluating the facts, attempting to answer the unavoidable questions, how, why, and what of it, we are unavoidably committed to questionable assumptions about the nature of man and the world, and about his possible or his proper destiny. We cannot help having some philosophy of history, however vague or unconscious. So we might try to have a clear, conscious, coherent one.[1]

This book is based on the ancient conception of history as 'philosophy teaching by experience.' It is also based on the 'new history,' the contribution of this century, which ultimately

[1] As an example of the kind of innocence to which historians are prone, I cite C. N. Cochrane's *Christianity and Classical Culture*. 'It is none of my business as an historian to pronounce upon the validity of Christian claims as opposed to those of Classicism,' Cochrane states in his Preface. 'My task is simply to record those claims as an essential part of the historical movement which I have attempted to describe.' In his text he proceeds to demonstrate why the failure of the Roman political ideal was 'inevitable,' because of the 'insoluble riddles' it involved, and then to demonstrate the validity of the Christian claims as represented by St. Augustine, explaining away all the riddles that other historians have found in Augustine's thought. 'There can be little doubt,' he pronounces, 'that his work resulted in a fuller and more adequate knowledge of man and of his universe than anything of which Classicism had proved capable.' Actually, of course, there is considerable doubt. Otherwise there would be no real problem for historians and philosophers, except perhaps the mystery of why Augustine's ideal also failed when the medieval papacy attempted to realize it—a failure that Cochrane neglects to mention.

involves new philosophies of history. More specifically, it is based on the following assumptions:

1. That the ideal of history, in the words of Morris Cohen, is 'an imaginative reconstruction of the past which is scientific in its determinations and artistic in its formulation';

2. That history is more genuinely scientific in spirit as it takes into account the reasons why it cannot be utterly objective or strictly scientific in method;

3. That among these reasons is the necessity of dealing with a complex of factors—physical, biological, psychological, cultural—that cannot be measured, isolated in controlled experiments, or reduced to a single cause;

4. That among these factors is the force of human will—of mind and character, ideas and ideals;

5. That this force makes it necessary to pass ethical judgments on history, and that such judgments are in fact implicit in the works of the most resolutely amoral historians;

6. That our scientific, esthetic, and moral interests alike call for a world view, a kind of anthropological study of civilizations, as a perspective on our own civilization;

7. That in this perspective we can make out universals or underlying uniformities but cannot claim possession of the absolute truth about man and the universe, cannot hope for complete certainty about beginnings and ends; and

8. That this is not simply a depressing conclusion.

Though most of these propositions may seem elementary or harmless, all are controversial. All are contested by eminent thinkers, in practice when not in theory, and have still more controversial implications. I therefore propose to amplify them somewhat before beginning my survey of the drama itself.

2. THE PREMISES OF INQUIRY

1. Although the practical value of a knowledge of history is commonly exaggerated, since men do not appear to learn readily from the mistakes of their ancestors, and historians themselves are not always conspicuous for their wisdom, I suppose that few would deny the practical necessity of this knowledge. When Henry Ford, in the good old boom days, said that 'history is bunk,' he merely illustrated the ignorance of the hard-headed industrial leaders who were leading the country straight to a crash. History has also been described as a series of messes, but only by a historical analysis can we determine how we got into the latest mess,

and how we might get out of it. The very idea that we are in a mess involves assumptions about the 'natural' course of affairs, as do all policies for dealing with it. Practical men who distrust 'mere theory' are especially fond of pointing out that 'history shows' something or other—usually showing that they are fearful of all change and incapable of learning from the failures of their conservative forebears. In any event, we are forever drawing upon the past. It not only constitutes all the 'experience' by which we have learned: it is the source of our major interests, our claims, our rights, and our duties. It is the source of our very identity. In an eternal present, which is a specious present, the past is all we know. And as the present is forever slipping back, it reminds us that we too shall in time belong wholly to the past.

For such reasons our interest in history is more poetic than practical or scientific. It begins as a childlike interest in the obvious pageantry and exciting event; it grows as a mature interest in the variety and complexity of the drama, the splendid achievements and the terrible failures; it ends as a deep sense of the mystery of man's life—of all the dead, great and obscure, who once walked the earth, and of the wonderful and awful possibilities of being a human being. 'History is neither written nor made without love or hate,' Mommsen wrote. The historian is inevitably an artist of a kind as he composes his narrative, selecting, shaping, coloring. The greater historians, from Herodotus to Toynbee, have generally been distinguished for their imaginative reach and grasp, not necessarily the soundness of their conclusions. Gibbon remains one of the greatest, despite his apparent prejudice and his untrustworthiness in detail, because of his artistic mastery of an epic theme.

Nevertheless history must always aim at literal truth. As Trevelyan said, its very poetry consists in its truth. 'It is the fact about the past that is poetic'—the fact that this was the actual drama of actual men, and that these men are no more. A lover of history loves it straight, without chasers of fancy; he is especially irritated by merely picturesque history, or by such bastard offspring as the fictionized biography. This concern for literal truth helps to explain why historians, the lovers of the past, have been more disposed to condemn their predecessors than poets have been. Over two thousand years ago Polybius noted how each successive historian 'makes such a parade of minute accuracy, and inveighs so bitterly when refuting others, that people come to imagine that all other historians have been mere dreamers.' So the scientific historians of the last century inveighed against the dreamers before them, and have in turn been ridiculed in this century.

In this view, one might wonder just where the truth comes out, and why one should put any trust in the latest version of it. It is always easy to be cynical about history, as 'a pack of tricks we play on the dead.' Yet it is impossible to deny the impressive advance that has been made in the last hundred years. Historians have built up an immense body of factual knowledge, knowledge that is no less genuine because it is subject to different theoretical interpretations. They have systematically widened, deepened, and clarified the sources of knowledge by philological, paleographical, archaeological, and ethnological research. They have come to realize the importance of commonplace, everyday events, in particular the economic activities that have been neglected in favor of the political and military. They have learned a great deal about the influence of both the physical and the cultural environment, what lies below factual history and above it. They have become aware of evolution, of origins and growths, of the history of history itself. Their very ignorance is suffused with knowledge, which at least keeps them from being ignorant of their ignorance.

The progress in historical knowledge, accordingly, has not been a steady advance toward absolute truth, a steady reduction in the number of universal laws to be discovered. It has been a progressive clarification, a fuller consciousness of what has happened, and how and why. When historians offer some fifty different reasons for the fall of the Roman Empire, we may at first be simply confused; yet we have a better understanding of the fall than if we assumed there was only one reason, or no reason except Fate. In spite of all their disagreement, moreover, historians are now generally agreed in discounting the most obvious explanation, that Rome succumbed to barbarian invasions; they have a deeper insight than the great Gibbon had, and perceive the dry rot that had set in during the Golden Age he celebrated. For they now have the advantage of a vast, international, cooperative enterprise, conducted in a scientific spirit. Although every historian remains fallible and subject to bias, his work remains subject to correction and criticism by his fellows, in professional journals and congresses. The relative objectivity of contemporary social science, as Karl Popper points out, is due not to the impartiality of all the social scientists, but to the publicity and community of the scientific method.

2. A particular gain is summed up in my second proposition—the very awareness that historians can never attain the impersonal exactitude to which they must always aspire. There can be no 'pure history'—history-in-itself, recorded from nobody's point of view, for nobody's sake. The most

objective history conceivable is still a selection and an interpretation, necessarily governed by some special interests and based on some particular beliefs. It can be more nearly objective if these interests and beliefs are explicit, out in the open, where they can be freely examined and criticized. Historians can more nearly approach the detachment of the physicist when they realize that the historical 'reality' is symbolic, not physical, and that they are giving as well as finding meanings. The important meanings of history are not simply there, lined up, waiting to be discovered.

Up to a point, all this implies something like Croce's principle, that true history is always contemporary history—history 'for the occasion,' of what is alive for us. The past has no meaningful existence except as it exists for us, as it is given meaning by us. In piety and justice we try to see it as it was, or as it seemed to the men who lived it, but even this poetic interest is not disinterested; in our contemplation of the drama we see what is most pertinent for our own hopes and fears. Hence the past keeps changing with the present. Every age has to rewrite its history, re-create the past; in every age a different Christ dies on the Cross, and is resurrected to a different end. Today the Peloponnesian War and the decline of the Roman Empire have a special significance for us that they could not have had for the Middle Ages or the Renaissance; by the same token, they will have a different significance for a Hindu or Chinese than for a Western historian. Our task is to create a 'usable past,' for our own living purposes.

Yet this admission of relativity does not permit us to create whatever we have a mind to, make over the past to suit ourselves. Old Testament and early Christian historians could freely tamper with the facts because they knew the divine plan of history; the only important use of facts was to illustrate the all-important religious truth. We cannot simply stick to the facts but we cannot disregard them either, and must derive our meanings from them in the knowledge that they are both stubborn and ambiguous. Our distinctive interests and beliefs make it possible for history to be relatively disinterested and impartial. Through Marx, Freud, Sumner, Pareto, Boas, Spengler, and many others, we have become more aware of the inveterate habit of rationalization and the sources of bias —the class interests, the *mores,* the conditioned reflexes of culture, the unconscious assumptions, the 'climate of opinion.' Although we can never entirely escape or control our climate, never attain a God's-eye view, we can more freely discount and supplement—at least when we read the other fellow's history. The very crisis of our civilization is in this aspect an aid to understanding. In a stabler society we might expect to have a simpler, stabler past, whose primary meaning was the wisdom of the ancestors. We are not naturally wiser than our ancestors; but the revolutionary conditions of our thought and life have forced a realization of relativity and complexity, the uncertainties of all history, and the ambiguities of the good old days that somehow led to these very bad days.

3. Meanwhile the most apparent reason why we cannot generalize about history with scientific certainty and precision is that we cannot isolate, measure, or graph the multiple forces that determine it. Race, the natural environment, the pressure of surrounding cultures, technological inventions and discoveries, genius or great leadership, institutions economic, political, and religious—the complex, continuous interaction of these and other factors defies equation or controlled experiment. Considered separately, even a seemingly incidental factor may look decisive. Thus Simkhovitch argued plausibly that hay has been a major influence. The introduction of grass seed and clovers, by which soil can be restored in a few years, was 'the greatest of revolutions, the revolution against the supreme law, the law of the land, the law of diminishing returns and of soil exhaustion'; the Roman failure to make hay was a basic reason for the decline of their empire. Hans Zinsser argued as plausibly for the importance of rats, lice, and fleas, the carriers of diseases that have decided more decisive battles and campaigns than has brilliant generalship; the Roman Empire was also fatally weakened by terrible plagues. But we cannot measure the relative importance of such factors, much less explain history by them. With hay, and without plagues, history in this century looks more complex than ever.

A further complication is that the 'natural' causes we can point to often have unpredictable, disproportionate, seemingly unnatural results. Cortez and a handful of adventurers confronted the mighty Aztec empire, a civilization in some respects superior to their own; but they toppled the empire and destroyed the civilization because they had gunpowder. This historic event is quite understandable—and it is supremely irrational, philosophically absurd. History is full of still more trifling, fortuitous events that had momentous consequences. In 1920, for example, the pacific King Alexander of Greece died of blood-poisoning, due to the bite of a pet monkey; a general election led to the recall of King Constantine, who thereupon started a disastrous war on the Turks. Winston Churchill observed, 'A quarter of a million persons died of that monkey's bite.'

Needless to add, causes go much deeper than the immediate event that sets off a historic train of events. The deeper we go, however, the more ramifications we find; and I stress the incalculables and imponderables because analysts are always prone to reduce the interaction of many forces to the action of a single force, such as race, environment, or economic activity, and then to 'explain' history by it. Tocqueville remarked that an exaggerated system of general causes is a consolation to second-rate historians as well as statesmen: 'it can always furnish a few mighty reasons to extricate them from the most difficult part of their work, and it indulges the indolence or incapacity of their minds, while it confers upon them the honors of deep thinking.' If the desire for great laws of history is quite natural, rooted in the ancient notion that 'nature loves simplicity,' the laws so far proclaimed prove only that man loves simplicity, and that he has not really found it. They are always arbitrary, man-made laws that men can break, as they cannot break the law of gravitation. Just as conservative businessmen appeal to inviolable laws of supply and demand, which they are the first to violate whenever they get a monopoly, so Communists appeal to iron laws of history and inevitable outcomes to justify their efforts to make history come out to suit themselves, and to excuse their merciless liquidation of Marxist-lawbreakers.

4. This is to repeat my fourth assumption: that we cannot ignore the human agency in history, cannot escape the implication that within limits it is a free agency.[2] Historians have been stressing the deep, impersonal, unconscious processes that govern social change, as in the growth of a vast industrial civilization that nobody had planned and few understood. They have accordingly tended to minimize the power of ideas and ideals, or even to deny this power. The complexities that make it difficult to find the great law of history also strengthen the impression that man has no real freedom to make his history. Yet the problems we face are clearly of man's own making. However unplanned, the industrial revolution was a vast human effort, a conscious exploitation of new power got

[2] I feel free to waive the metaphysical problem of free will. Although it may be hard to see just how man can go his own way in a presumably lawful universe (not to mention the theological assumption of an omnipotent God who wills all), his freedom is less mysterious if it is not conceived as a purely spiritual state, an ability to be utterly unaffected by the world about him. Most plainly, it is the ability to do things in and to the world. And this is not only compatible with lawful necessities but increased by a knowledge of such necessities. Knowing the law of gravitation, I cannot be carefree and jump off a cliff; but I am free to save my neck—or if I choose, to kill myself in this manner. Science, which has fathered the doctrine of determinism, is the most striking example of man's determination and ability to bend nature to his own purposes.

by scientific ideas and ideals. 'Invention is the mother of necessity.'

The fundamental fact is that man is the only culture-building animal. Culture means a man-made environment, which is primarily a mythical or 'spiritual' environment. In this enterprise he is aided by the seeming biological handicap of prolonged infancy and immaturity, during which he learns what his ancestors have made. The kind of culture he builds is conditioned by the natural environment but not determined by it; his creativity or freedom of action is indicated by the variety of Indian cultures developed on the American plains, or the long series of different societies in the same environment of Asia Minor. And the most powerful influence on him is the unseen environment of his own creation. We may deny, for example, the validity of belief in the supernatural, but we cannot deny its tremendous power. It has often proved stronger than the elemental impulses of self-interest and self-preservation, inducing men to give up their worldly goods, to deny the claims of their senses, to mortify their flesh, to welcome martyrdom—to defy the oldest laws of nature and society, in order to devote themselves to biologically preposterous behavior. Civilization, or culture grown more varied and complex, represents a more conscious, determined, resourceful effort to master the natural environment and set up a world of man's own. Amid its complexities one may see only that the individual is a product of his society, which in turn is a product of impersonal forces. Nevertheless the whole enterprise of civilization is a rare human creation, a triumph of mind and will; and the impersonal forces work only through the ideas and beliefs of men.

Similarly with the influence of great men. In the revulsion against the 'hero' theory of history, proposed by such thinkers as Fichte, Hegel, and Carlyle, historians have tended to picture the great men as mere agents of impersonal forces, and thereby to reduce the issue to a false antithesis—whether they make history or are made by it. The actual problem is to determine both their effect on their environment and its effect on them. Many seem dispensable despite their greatness; if Columbus had not discovered America or Watt invented the steam engine, it seems fairly certain that somebody else would have before long. Other men of greater genius, who achieved what nobody else could have, had little apparent influence on the course of history; despite my conviction that Shakespeare was the greatest writer who ever lived, I cannot believe that his work made any appreciable difference to the subsequent history of Western civilization, or even of literature. Still others—in particular many famous generals and monarchs—owe their fame more to their accidental position than to qualities of greatness; like the little Dutch boy who saved the dykes, Sidney Hook has remarked, they needed only a finger and the chance of happening by at the right moment. All the heroes of history required the great moment or the right moment, the forces to work with. Had Alexander the Great been born in Macedon three centuries earlier or three centuries later than he was, he could never have embarked on his conquest.

Yet the great man may indeed be epoch-making, by the decisions he makes, the direction he gives to the forces at his disposal. Although it is clear—in retrospect—that the time was ripe for such adventurers as Alexander, Mohammed, Jenghiz Khan, and Lenin, their *success* was not clearly inevitable. Their will—even their whim—made a profound difference in history. Moreover, the mere ideal of greatness is a force. All peoples have clung to it, and responded to it; all have their national heroes. If the immediate achievements of the hero may be discounted, the hero as symbol, or even the mythical hero, continues to make history.

Although the admission of such imponderables is likely to be displeasing to scientists and philosophers who want strict law and order, it does not destroy all possibility of lawfulness and predictability. The 'spiritual' forces are still recognizable universal forces. At any rate, here are the given terms of our problem. The scientific determinist himself must reckon with the power of beliefs, sacred traditions, new ideas, great leaders, simply because they are among the most recognizable, determinable causes in history. Otherwise he is forced back on a kind of mystical, inhuman fatalism that would be fatal to the historical sense. If everything that has happened is the only thing that could possibly have happened, we might as well close the book. The reason we don't is that even the determinists and fatalists are always implying that there were real alternatives, and that men made the wrong choice. Whatever we believe in theory, we continue in practice to think and act as if we were not puppets.

5. It is this inescapable sense of human responsibility that fills the past with poignant 'might-have-beens,' and the future with portentous 'ifs.' And so the idea that history is made, and suffered, by men is not pure idealization. As we recognize the real power of knowledge, reason, and conscious aspiration, we are forced to recognize the greater power of inertia, ignorance, stupidity, and irrationality. The very respect for conscious human purposes calls for stress on the human obstacles to their fulfilment. It calls, finally, for conscious ethical judgment. My fifth proposition is that such judgments are im-

plicit in whatever significance we find in history, and had better be explicit.

Conflict and change are the essence of the drama. As we study the great historic conflicts we naturally take sides; as we study the great changes we as naturally judge that they were for better or worse. When we talk of the progress or decadence of a society we are implying some standards of value. When we lament any of the tragedies of history, such as the decline and fall of Rome, we are committing ourselves to the values of civilization; we are refusing to rejoice with the Huns, who no doubt were proud and happy enough during the worst days of Rome. The most impartial, objective historians are constantly passing judgment on leaders and policies. Their factual narratives are full of such adjectives as wise, cruel, just, unscrupulous, benevolent, brutal, corrupt, vicious—adjectives that seem factually accurate only because of the general agreement on the ethical standards implicit in these judgments. And none are prone to judge more freely, or more harshly, than those—like the Puritans and Marxists—who ostensibly believe in predestination or determinism.

Here again the very advances in our knowledge and understanding have tended to obscure the ethical issues, the judgments finally required by the faith in reason that has produced this knowledge. In our awareness of evolution and cultural relativity we can understand any stupidity or atrocity by simply dating it. We can excuse Aristotle and St. Paul for taking slavery for granted; we can appreciate the exalted fervor that led the noblest Crusaders to rejoice in the massacre of heathens; we can see that it was piety and ignorance, not mere sadism, that burned old women at the stake as witches. We can do a fine justice, indeed, to the past. Still, we do condemn—we must condemn—the cruelties of slavery, fanaticism, and witch-burning. In being charitable to the doer of the deed, we cannot afford to condone the deed itself. And least of all can we afford to explain away our own shortcomings as historic necessities. Although the irresponsibility of America after the First World War was quite understandable and predictable, it was not strictly inevitable. It was a moral and intellectual failure, for which Americans were responsible. They have learned something from it, and must continue to learn; for in all history no nation has faced such staggering responsibilities as face America today.

6. It is therefore a commonplace that we must establish some kind of world order, and cannot hope to do so without breadth of understanding and sympathy. Our scientific, esthetic, moral, and urgently practical interest alike call out my sixth proposition, of the need for an anthropological view of

our history, an effort to see in perspective not only our nation but our civilization. Although this may seem to be a harmless exercise, in practice it will meet violent opposition. It involves what practical men call globaloney or un-Americanism, and what pious men call indifference to principles or betrayal of the true faiths. It involves still another contradiction of our age: that we now have a far wider view of history than our ancestors, a view in which we can appreciate the astonishing variety of human aspiration and achievement, and that we have also developed stronger prejudices than any other civilization, raised new barriers to understanding and community.

The ugliest example is racial prejudice. Even though few reputable historians continue to find the key to civilization in the innate superiority of the white, the Nordic, or the Anglo-Saxon race, this vulgar theory still colors the thought and feeling of a great many men who do not openly commit themselves to it. In the Anglo-Saxon world, indeed, feeling about color is so strong and deep that men assume it is instinctive, and even the tolerant are likely to be repelled by the thought of racial intermarriage; whereas such feeling has actually been rare in history. All peoples have been pleased to regard themselves as superior, but few have identified their superiority with the color of their skin. And since the great majority of the world's population are what Americans call colored, and consider naturally inferior, it becomes necessary to repeat that this attitude is strictly a prejudice, inconsistent with the principles of democracy and Christianity, and with no scientific basis whatever. Biologically, races are not pure or sharply defined, racial differences are only a small fraction of man's common inheritance, and the clearest differences— as between white skin and yellow, long heads and broad, straight hair and kinky—have no clear importance for survival. Historically, mixed races have usually produced the golden ages, all races have proved capable of civilization, and no race has led the way throughout history. The 100 per cent American today is a parvenu who owes 99 per cent of his civilization to a mongrel antiquity.

More common in history is the prejudice of nationalism, based on the universal 'in-group' feeling. It is not simply an ugly sentiment, or a refuge for scoundrels. It has inspired high ideals of duty, devotion to the common welfare, sacrifice for a greater good. It has fertilized Western culture with a rich variety of national traditions. Yet the historic claim to national sovereignty, with the sentiment of devotion to one's country right or wrong and the natural conclusion that it is practically always right, is now an apparent anachronism. And if such ancient sentiments will scarcely be eradicated by a study of world history, at least they should not be fortified by historians. Until recently, most histories were national histories, written from a nationalistic point of view; today most school texts are still of this provincial kind. They give a false idea of the self-sufficiency and the manifest destiny of the nation. They slight the common foundations, the unity and continuity of Western civilization, and the great indebtedness to other civilizations. They foster the common misconceptions of the past that are much more dangerous than simple ignorance of the past.

Less conspicuous but still pervasive is religious prejudice, the exclusiveness that has distinguished Western civilization from all others except Islam. Despite the growth of tolerance, most Christians still assume that theirs is the only true religion, and that their Christian duty is to convert the rest of the world. The rest of the world, which happens to include the great majority of mankind, still resents this assumption; and in the light of religious history it does look like an arrogant assumption. One may reasonably argue that Christ is the most nearly perfect symbol of the one God that all the higher religions have sought to comprehend. One cannot reasonably take for granted the certain truth of an exclusive divine revelation: a revelation that was granted to an obscure group at a particular moment in history, that was recorded by fallible men in narratives marked by manifest inconsistencies, that cannot be proved by independent reason, and that Christians themselves have never been able to agree upon, much less to embody in a Christian society. Yet Western writers, including historians, cling to the parochial attitude symbolized in our calendar. The appearance of Christ is regarded as the turning point of all history, and the confused records of his appearance as conclusive proof of a higher truth known only to Westerners.

This religious self-righteousness is both cause and symptom of a general cultural chauvinism. All peoples, to repeat, have tended to assume the superiority of their culture. (Thus the Eskimos of Greenland believed that the white men came there to learn good manners and morals from them.) With its technological triumphs, however, Western culture has been able to achieve an unprecedented domination of all other cultures, and to express an almost unprecedented contempt for them. The early stages of this domination involved such savagery as the extermination of Indians and enslavement of Negroes, who were thereupon called savages. The later stages involved an economic exploitation that was less atrocious but more offensive because of the increasingly sanctimonious talk about the white man's burden, and the constant insistence on his moral and religious superiority. And though contemporaries are both more curious and more sympathetic, even borrowing freely from the 'backward' peoples, there is still too little regard for their rights or respect for their customs, and too little appreciation of the significance and the value of cultural diversity. One result is that almost all Western nations are plagued by the problem of cultural minorities, intensified by racial, religious, and even linguistic prejudice.

The point here is not merely the moral need of a better understanding of other peoples. It is the intellectual need of a better understanding of ourselves, and of our possible destiny. Toynbee suggests an apt analogy in his account of the horizon of the great emperor Babur, who founded a mighty empire in India about 1500. As a Turk, Babur was the agent of manifest destiny, ruling at the heart of civilization; for centuries Turkish people had been riding out to conquer, spreading from Mongolia to Algeria and the Ukraine, and they now dominated most of the civilized world except China. As a cultivated man, Babur knew that some Frankish barbarians had threatened civilization by invading the holy lands of Islam centuries before, though of course they had finally been thrown out; and no doubt he knew that these rude infidels still existed on a corner of the peninsula of Asia known as Europe, though he never bothered to mention them in his brilliant autobiography. He also failed to note that some Frankish ships had reached India a few years before he did. For he could never have dreamed that descendants of these infidels were going to dominate the whole world, including incidentally his own empire. Three hundred years later, Toynbee notes, the great Egyptian historian Al-Gabarti still looked at the world from Babur's point of view. In recording the events of an extraordinary year, Al-Gabarti remarked somberly that 'the most portentous was the cessation of the Pilgrimage' from Egypt to Mecca, an unprecedented event that showed again how Allah alone ruled history; for this was the year when Napoleon descended on Egypt.

No more can we predict the fantastic course that history will have taken some centuries hence, or be sure what are the most portentous events taking place today. But we can at least imagine the possibilities. We might be somewhat wiser, and less self-righteous, if we did not take for granted that the future belongs to America, or even to the West. We might learn, as Toynbee remarks, from our great historic achievement. 'By making history we have transcended our own history'—laying the foundations of a world order, making possible the union of mankind. Easterners have been forced to learn from this achievement of the West; many have profited from the study of both their history and ours, gaining a perspective on civilizations in clash and in crisis. Westerners remain more provincial than Babur, without his excuse for short-sightedness.

7. Indeed, we might well go further than Toynbee, and question his own seemingly provincial assumption that it is the Christian God who rules history. If we try to think in really universal terms, we cannot talk easily of universal truths. The eternal verities we hear so much about usually look like selected beliefs of our own society, and in a long view they turn out to be mutable. History itself is the deadliest enemy of the Eternal and Absolute. The whole history of thought is a refutation of the finality to which thinkers have endlessly aspired. I conclude, accordingly, that in first and last matters we cannot conclude with absolute certainty.

But I should at once add that the admission of *ultimate* uncertainty does not mean *complete* uncertainty. The absolutist tradition of Christendom leads men to assume that if we don't have absolute standards we can't have any standards, and that if we are not standing on the Rock of Ages we are standing on nothing.[3] Actually, we can and do know plenty of objective truths without knowing the whole or final Truth. Beneath the manifold diversity of human history, more specifically, we can discern the basic uniformities and continuities that make it an intelligible history, not a chaos. They are implicit in the common structure of man, and the common requirements of social existence in the natural world. Thus all societies have to deal with the problems of birth, growth, education, sex, toil, and death. All display an esthetic sense, an interest in creating beauty; all have and enforce a code of morality, which generally comes down to something like the Golden Rule; all recognize the existence of unseen forces greater than man, which remain high and unseen whether they are called demons, God, or energy; all have standards of excellence, values that defy mortality. The very diversity in their ways of life points to such fundamental truths as the remarkable adaptability of man, and the universal power of custom or habit in fixing any one way of life.

In general, the uniformities and continuities of human experience are what make significant thought possible; the manifold possibilities of experience are what make critical thought necessary. Hence a refusal on principle to say the last

[3] As one of innumerable examples, I cite Cleanth Brooks: 'Once we are committed to critical relativism, there can be no stopping short of a *complete* relativism in which critical judgments will disappear altogether.'

word about human history is not a refusal to say any word, or to pass any firm judgment. Rather, it defines the conditions of judgment. Say that our most cherished beliefs are matters of opinion and it is then our business to get sound opinions, based on honest thought and the best available knowledge; only a fool will say that any opinion is as good as any other opinion—and even a fool is apt to seek expert opinion when he gets sick. Say that our final preferences are matters of taste and it is then our business to cultivate good taste; cultivated men may dispute the relative merits of Donne and Shelley, but they can and do agree that both are better poets than Eddie Guest. Because of the flagrant disagreement among the wise men, we are apt to forget the very general agreement on who were the great men—and to overlook the implication of this agreement, the tacit admission that there are diverse forms of goodness and greatness. As for history, we are confronted by societies embodying radically different ways of life, but it remains our business to judge the historical consequences of those ways. We can hope to make more intelligent judgments if we are aware of the many ways, and do not take for granted that our own is necessary or necessarily superior to all others.

Here, it seems to me, is the basic problem of thoughtful men today. We do not know the final truth about God and the world; the most certain knowledge we do have about the history of man belies all pretense to absolute certainty. We must nevertheless have principles, standards, faiths; many men have been demoralized by a shallow relativism that denies us the right to judge anyone or anything, while we perforce keep judging. The problem, then, is to maintain principle and morale in the face of ultimate uncertainty, on grounds that permit both the faith and the tolerance required by the pursuit of truth and goodness; just as the problem for statesmen is to compromise and reconcile without a cynical indifference to principle, in order to accommodate fundamentally different ways of life in a world order. The immediate objection to all partisans of absolute truth is that they evade the given terms of this problem.

8. I am therefore led to my final assumption, that the admission of a principle of relativity and uncertainty should not be simply depressing. It does not destroy all possibility of knowledge and judgment. Rather, it is the outcome of comprehensive knowledge, and the means to further knowledge of man's history. It enables a higher objectivity, a fuller understanding of present and past. It enables wiser choices among the possibilities open to us—among goods that are no less real because they are relative, and that are more

relevant than artitrary absolutes. Above all, this principle encourages a positive faith in positive values: of liberality, breadth of spirit, hospitality to new ideas, willingness to adventure, humility in admitting one's own fallibility and the limitations of the human mind—of the tolerance that is indispensable for the pursuit of truth, for social harmony, and for simple humanity. If these are not the highest values, none are more essential to the hopes of world order and peace.

They also entail obvious dangers, of confusion, halfheartedness, demoralization, despair. One cannot be confident that mankind is yet ready or able to surrender the ancient illusion of certainty in its idealisms. Nevertheless this illusion intensifies the confusion and dismay of our times. It obscures the actual uncertainty in which men have always lived and which they take for granted in daily life. It obscures the goods that actually sustain men—such goods as creative work, appreciation of beauty, friendship and love, or simple comradeliness —and that do not require metaphysical or supernatural sanctions. It obscures the living faith of Western democracy. Thus seven Princeton professors asserted in a manifesto, 'The Spiritual Basis of Democracy,' that democracy cannot endure without a belief in an 'objective moral and spiritual order' established by a 'cosmic spiritual power'; whereas this belief is not logically required by a faith in democracy, which is rather an agreement on the right to disagree peaceably about religious or any other belief. And those who do believe in such a divine order are as likely to support an authoritarian regime—and historically they usually have.

All in all, we doubtless suffer from too much doubt. But we are likely to suffer much more because too many men are too sure of themselves.

III

The Adventure of Civilization

1. THE COSTS OF CIVILIZATION

We have been dealing with history as a branch of knowledge. As we turn to the past itself, the subject of that knowledge, we might well begin with a pious tribute to our nameless prehistoric ancestors, who by inconceivably arduous and ingenious effort succeeded in establishing a human race. They made the crucial discoveries and inventions, such as the tool, the seed, and the domesticated animal; their development of agriculture, the 'neolithic revolution' that introduced a settled economy, was perhaps the greatest stride forward that man has ever taken. They created the marvelous instrument of language, which enabled man to discover his humanity, and eventually to disguise it. They laid the foundations of civilization: its economic, political, and social life, and its artistic, ethical, and religious traditions. Indeed, our 'savage' ancestors are still very near to us, and not merely in our capacity for savagery. Although the primitive survives most obviously in the superstitions and fetishes of simple men, it survives as well in quite respectable customs, such as the tabooed word, the initiation ceremony, and the national totem. Our everyday language is alive with its animism: skies still 'threaten,' seas and fires 'rage,' forests 'murmur,' and 'Mother Earth' beckons us to rest. Our literature, religion, philosophy, and science all retain elements of the myth and magic out of which they grew.

For such reasons men have looked to primitive societies to discover human nature in its 'pure' state. In fact, however, we cannot find such a universal state of nature. We find instead a fantastic diversity in designs for living, and often an outrageous disregard of the reputed laws of human nature.

And this commonplace of modern anthropology is pertinent because first of all we have to deal with primitivism—the familiar idea that civilization is a disease, and that the only possible cure for it is a return to nature and the simple life. Although this idea is commonly identified with Jean Jacques Rosseau, it is an ancient and universal one. The myth of the noble savage is at least as old as Homer, who mentions 'the noble mare-milkers and the mild-drinking Abieo, the most righteous of men' (an apparent reference to the Scythians); while later Greek and Roman literature is full of homilies on the happier, more virtuous life of rude peoples. Everywhere we find civilized man troubled by misgivings about his most remarkable achievement, pining for a lost Eden. Such misgivings are natural, given the inevitable complications of civilized life, and may be salutary. Simple peoples can often teach us simple lessons in good will and good sense. (So the dictators might take a lesson in wit from the Ashanti in Africa, who have an annual ceremony during which the people are not only permitted but required to ridicule and upbraid their rulers.) But with all respect for primitive cultures, primitivism is a shallow, sentimental attitude.

Usually it is based on a misunderstanding of primitive life, whose apparent simplicity is complicated by rigid taboos and black magic. At best, however, the primitivists cherish an impossible desire. They wish to appreciate the simple life with all the self-consciousness and sensitivity that only civilization makes possible; they wish to be children of nature and also poets and philosophers celebrating nature. Above all, they fail to make clear why civilization is 'unnatural'—why a stone axe, say, is according to nature, but a power-driven saw is not. They evade the basic issue of just what is the natural life for man—the issue that is the final concern of all philosophy and religion, and that is constantly confused by the ambiguities of the term *nature*. If the term is taken to mean the entire universe, with all its phenomena, then everything that goes on is bound to be natural, and it is meaningless to tell man to follow nature. If the term is taken to mean the entire universe apart from man, then it is inhuman to tell man to follow the ways of other animals, and to discourage his efforts to understand and control nature. Or if the term is taken to mean native or essential character, as in 'human nature,' then the distinctively human lies in consciousness, and the civilized effort to widen, clarify, and enrich consciousness would seem quite natural.

We cannot absolutely prove that it is better to be a civilized man than a caveman, or even that it is worth being a human being. We can say that if conscious life has no value, nothing has value and all thought is meaningless. No man in his senses really wishes to change places with a contented imbecile or a pig in his sty. But then we have to pay for our knowledge of good and evil. The price of conscious life is discontent, fear, and pain unknown to other animals. The conditions of civilized life are richer values and higher costs. By its more elaborate, complex organization of life a civilization provides more goods, both material and spiritual, than a primitive society can; and it thereby creates more tension, friction, instability, insecurity.

Adventure, as Whitehead maintained, is quite literally the key to civilization. This highest achievement of man is a 'program for discontent.' Likewise Toynbee suggests that the terms of the adventure may be summed up in Faust's wager with the Devil:

> If ever time should flow so calmly on
> Soothing my spirits in such oblivion
> That in the pleasant trance I would arrest
> And hail the happy moment in its course,
> Bidding it linger with me...
> Then willingly do I consent to perish.

By the grace of Goethe, Faust was saved, as civilizations have not been; but unlike them he stuck to the terms of the bargain. They have typically succumbed to complacency or conservatism, losing their creative energy or readiness for adventure; and only in stagnation and death can they approach the stable equilibrium they seek. The stablest element in human history is precisely the most primitive and formless—the peasant masses that have no real history. The great creative ages, on the other hand, have been conspicuously unstable. When bookmen celebrate the golden ages, now changeless, composed, and serene in splendor, they are apt to falsify the spirit of these ages; for no man who craves security and peace of mind would have been happy in Periclean Athens, Renaissance Italy, or Elizabethan England. When Henry Adams concluded his *Education* with the faint hope that the future might see 'a world that sensitive and timid natures could regard without a shudder,' he was even fainter than he thought. Such natures are doomed to shudder in any civilized world.

Today, at any rate, there is no mistaking the necessity of adventure. The pace of revolution is strictly unprecedented; centuries in Egypt, China, and India, or even in Greece and Rome, brought less radical change than a lifetime today. We are all too aware of the risks, the costs we pay for the goods of our kind of civilization. For this reason, however, we are apt to magnify the costs, or to regard any costs as unprecedented. We forget that men have always had to live dangerously, above all when they were living near the height of their powers. So we might do well to review the distinctive means and ends of civilization, the main articles of its program for discontent.

The adventure begins with some improvement in technology that enables a surplus of material goods, and a release of energy for other purposes than a mere livelihood; thus men illustrated the value of adversity by developing the irrigation systems of the Nile and the Euphrates, creating their own Garden of Eden in a desert. Then rises the city, which is the first clear sign of civilization. In the city the economic surplus is collected and managed, or squandered, and energy is further stimulated by close association, division of labor, and the pursuit of more wealth or the competition for a larger share of the existing wealth. One result of this stimulus is the invention of writing. Apparently developed for the practical purpose of keeping accounts, writing turns out to have immense, unforeseen consequences, in the growth of learning, literature, holy scriptures, and all forms of culture. And from all this activity emerges the self-conscious individual, the creator who is nevertheless the product of civilization; for in primitive societies a potential Shakespeare, Michelangelo, or Newton would have no chance of discovering his genius, much less of cultivating it.

These distinctive achievements of civilization are real gains, real goods. Only in a civilized society can man contemplate his inability to live on bread alone, and dream of better ways of living. The material surplus provides the leisure for cultivating spiritual interests; the city is the main center of creative activity, the spiritual as well as the commercial and political capital; writing is indispensable to the transmission of a high culture; the self-conscious individual at his best is the glory of civilization, or even the only justification of the whole enterprise. At the same time, these creative achievements automatically create new problems or new evils. The surplus wealth breeds inequality and injustice; the city becomes Babylon, the central source of babble, disorder, corruption, and decay; literate learning sanctifies and perpetuates the superstitions, prejudices, and injustices of the past; the self-conscious individual is always a threat to the security of the group, or a victim of it. The freedom that has been gained not only permits the familiar abuses of freedom but heightens the awareness of the limits to human freedom, and raises the ultimate problem—freedom for what? Having learned his strength, man rediscovers his weakness.

The conclusion of all this is not a fatalistic acceptance of inevitable evil. Evil will always be with us, to be sure; but the specific forms of evil are not static, absolute, and irremediable. In creating them, civilization likewise creates the standards by which we judge them, and stimulates the effort to eradicate them. In deploring the limited success of this effort, we may forget that we have set higher standards and goals, that we seek to do away with conditions (such as slavery) once accepted as inevitable or even proper—that in this way too we make evils by making good. My immediate conclusion, again, is that the adventure of civilization is necessarily inconclusive; or at least that its issues call for further complication before we jump to conclusions.

2. THE MATERIAL BASIS OF CIVILIZATION

It would seem obvious that material wealth and power are the essential basis of civilization, and that they are essentially only the basis, the means to other ends. No high civilization, no golden age, has been poor and weak. The creation and transmission of the spiritual achievements of a society depend upon its material achievements, its monuments testify to both its artistic and its technological power, its ideals and its wealth. Yet the values of the mind or spirit remain the 'higher' values, the ends of civilized life. Although the great writers and thinkers do not agree on precisely what they are, almost all describe the good life by such terms as wisdom, virtue, love, beauty, peace, and holiness; their disagreements come down to different versions of the abiding trinity—the Good, the True, and the Beautiful. Although simple men think in terms of happiness and are likely to identify it with material success, they too know at heart that wealth is no guarantee of happiness; and almost all pay at least lip service to 'the finer things of life.'

I begin with these platitudes because it seems very hard for men to see their material progress steadily and whole, in its necessity and its insufficiency, its values and its evils. The ruling classes of former societies evidently enjoyed their wealth but were generally contemptuous of the artisans and merchants who provided it for them; the high cultural tradition found an honorable place for war and aristocratic sport but not for practical, useful activities. In the last century, however, business and technology have been honored above all other activities; most Americans pay only lip service to the 'higher' values as they boast shamelessly of their high standard of living. This gross materialism has in turn driven many intellectuals into a corner, where they cry out a shallow, futile scorn of material progress. Even the hardy Thoreau took civilization with him when he turned his back on it and went to the woods; he still needed its tools and materials, to live and to record his protest against it. Critics of modern industrialism make far more liberal use of its products and services, with as little acknowledgment. We cannot in any event do away with business, or call a halt to technology. If we hope to humanize them we need to recognize their human value, as indispensable means to civilized life and as creative activities in their own right. It might be good strategy to begin with a reverent view of the material achievements of man, and an ironic view of his spiritual achievements.

To judge by all the available evidence, the rise of civilization was not a gift of the gods or a tribute to them. It was a technological affair, an economic enterprise inspired by practical motives. Through inventions and discoveries, men were able to take care of their physical wants more efficiently; in the leisure, comfort, and relative security thus achieved, they were able to develop social graces, fine arts, literate learning, and higher religions. In all civilizations before our own, agriculture remained the chief source of wealth; because most aristocracies were landed aristocracies, agriculture had more prestige than commerce—as it still does among literary devotees of the ancient cultural tradition. Nevertheless civilization flourished with the growth of industry and trade, which were far more extensive in antiquity than is commonly realized. The great adventure of Greek civilization in particular began as an adventure in trade, or specifically with the exploitation of the humble grape and olive; the production of wine and olive oil enabled the enterprising Greeks to enter the world market and compete with the Phoenicians (one of the few known peoples whose brilliant culture was frankly identified with commerce, and organized to promote commerce). The first notable achievements in Greek poetry, philosophy, and science were contributed by Ionia, the colonial cities in Asia Minor that were the first to develop a thriving commerce. The glory of Greece reached its zenith in Athens, at the zenith of the Athenian adventure in economic imperialism.

Whitehead declared that commerce is the beginning of civilization and freedom in that it is intercourse by persuasion instead of force. For all the loose talk about free private enterprise, it does in fact promote enterprise, initiative, personal independence—the adventurous spirit on which a flourishing civilization depends; arrested commerce is one of the surest signs of a civilization in decay. For all the sordid motives involved in commerce, it inspires daring adventures such as no merely practical man would embark upon. Thus the commercial Phoenicians led the way for the Greeks, exploring the whole Mediterranean, exploring even the whole coast of Africa (a feat that no Greek or Roman dared to attempt); thus Marco Polo ventured across a vast unknown continent, Columbus discovered a new continent, Magellan circled the world. Commerce also acts as a major stimulus to civilization by promoting commerce in ideas, an exchange of spiritual as well as material goods. Thus the acquisitive Greeks in Ionia acquired knowledge of older civilizations, and speculation in business led to speculation in thought, which is another gamble.

Commerce in turn is but one example of the division and diversification of labor resulting from the advance of technology and the accumulation of an economic surplus. Men are apt to underrate the very great gains this has made possible. Resenting their confinement to a particular task or regretting their dependence, they are fond of cultivating the illusion of being as self-sufficient as their pioneering ancestors by hunting their own game, building their own shacks. Yet specialization—by the individual and by the community—is the clearest index of human development. The self-sufficient man has little to contribute to the community, the self-sufficient community has little to contribute to other communities. Both may still be found—in the most primitive parts of the world. (One may even find 'natural' economies so close to a bare subsistence that they cannot afford such specialists as the priest or witch-doctor.) Specialization alone has enabled the extraordinary man to discover and develop his genius, and the ordinary man to discover and develop his individuality.

As plainly, however, it may narrow, warp, and impoverish individuality. In our own world specialization has produced the machine-tender and the bookkeeper, the technician and the academician—the hordes of cultural illiterates and expert ignoramuses. It denies millions the opportunity of really creative work, the elemental satisfaction of saying, 'I made this.' Even the wealth of opportunities it affords is a wealth of square holes for round pegs; in a civilization there are many more possibilities of going wrong, or—as bad—of restless doubts that one has made the best choice. We have innumerable educational agencies for guiding choices of occupation, or for intensifying the confusion by multiplying the possible choices; but we are only beginning to educate for the all-important problem, of co-ordinating and humanizing our specialized knowledge, bringing our experts together, teaching our technicians to speak a common civilized language. In short, division of labor naturally leads to excessive division, or sharp separation; and it brings us back to the familiar complex of good-and-evil. So too with commerce. All the energy, initiative, and daring that go into it help to promote the indolence and conservatism of privileged classes. Still plainer, commerce breeds fraud, greed, strife, war.

And so with the major problem, the everlasting problem, raised by the surplus wealth that made civilization possible. It posed the question who was to own the surplus, and for what purposes was it to be used. The historic answer has invariably been the creation of a hierarchy of classes, more or less rigid. In every civilization the wealth and the power that goes with it have been concentrated in the hands of a few. Among the early specialists were experts in consumption—a class whose chief functions included what Veblen called conspicuous consumption,—or vicarious consumption for the edification of the producing classes.[1] We may assume that the rise of privileged classes was largely unconscious, not a deliberate plot by greedy men. We may also assume that the problem of sharing the wealth, or approaching equity, will plague even the 'classless society,' since power has to be exercised by a few and is always liable to abuse. But the basic paradox remains that for great masses of men civilization has always meant less material well-being than primitive men usually enjoy. It has meant a man-made misery, which was aggravated by increasing inequality as in time the privileged came to exploit the masses more deliberately and systematically. And with the Industrial Revolution came still more glaring contradictions, of more wretched poverty and impotence amidst vastly increased wealth and power. An astounding triumph of technological efficiency created unemployment and want, bringing on periodic depressions and panics by producing more goods than could be sold, while millions needed those goods. For the first time in history, society has been plagued by abundance rather than scarcity.

To this whole problem we shall keep recurring. Meanwhile we may note another fundamental difference between modern civilization and its predecessors. The historic result

---

[1] That this can still be a humane function is apparent from the crowds that gather at the entrance of the Metropolitan Opera House when the season opens. Few of the hangers-on seem bitter or resentful as they watch the wealthy ladies enter in their furs and jewels. Most appear to be happy, even grateful to these ladies who so arduously perform the duty of consuming for them.

of the material surplus has not been the constant class struggle pictured by Marxists, between the few who have and the many who have not. Although such class wars have broken out occasionally, as in ancient Greece and Rome, the significant struggles have usually been within the upper classes, involving kings, priests, warrior nobles, and in time wealthy merchants. Throughout most of history the peasant masses accepted their lowly status. Their infrequent rebellions, in times of extreme want or oppression, were blind uprisings, not planned revolutions in the name of democratic rights, and had no profound, lasting results. With the rise of democracy, however, the masses have become a real factor in the problem of sharing the wealth. Despite the marked inequalities, the advanced democracies have unquestionably raised the standard of living of the great majority of their citizens. The ordinary man now has opportunities for a richer life than he dreamed of in the past. What he does with these opportunities, how he conceives the rich life, is another problem, to which we shall also recur. But it would seem dishonest as well as futile for well-fed, well-clothed, well-housed intellectuals merely to deplore the common desire for material well-being.

3. The City as Center and Symbol

Among the literary tendencies of recent years has been the revolt against the City. The emancipated young writers of the 'twenties who scorned Main Street and the Bible Belt, flocking to Chicago or New York in search of freedom, art, and Life, are now fleeing the city and celebrating the free, wholesome life of the village. This is an old story. The city has always bred a contempt for the peasant—the 'villein,' the hayseed, the yokel—and then bred weariness and disenchantment, a wistful idealization of the pastoral life. The modern industrial city has indeed blasted the landscape as has no other, achieving a unique drabness and ugliness; but for congestion, filth, noise, and mongrel disorder it is hardly worse than ancient Rome, medieval Paris, or Elizabethan London. And always we read the same complaints, of the vulgarity, the artificiality, the immorality and irreligion, the physical and spiritual squalor, the soullessness—the age-old follies and vices of Babylon, which in every age seem new. So the story is true, as far as it goes. The city is always vain and wicked enough to provoke the prophet of doom. 'Wail, O inhabitants of the Mortar!'

Yet the old story is also superficial and vain—if we value civilization itself. *Civilization* means literally the making of cities and city life, and it is literally impossible without them. The village world has been relatively stable (at least until the Industrial Revolution) because of its inertia; what energy was left over from the labor of supporting life was spent in maintaining the ancient rites and customs, or resisting the newfangled ones coming from without. The rise of the city has been the historic sign of a society on the march; it stimulated further adventure by bringing people together, pooling their efforts, promoting change by exchange, enlarging the world through contact with other peoples and cities. The great city became the center of unrest and disorder because it remained the center of creative activity. In time the poet or the philosopher might flee to the village (or more often the villa), but his very understanding and appreciation of nature were a product of the city; his work was inspired by it, addressed to it, circulated and preserved by it. Without London and Boston Thoreau could have had no Walden, or no spiritual interests to take there. Although civilization has always rested on the labor of the village world, its history is the history of Babylon, Jerusalem, Athens, Rome, Constantinople, Paris, London.

Even religion owes its highest achievements to the city. Simply because the village is conservative, orthodox, and pious, while the city is given to heresy and unrest, the higher religions have grown up in cities. Thus Jesus, the Galilean, went to Jerusalem to enact the climactic scenes of his failure and his triumph. His Apostles spread the gospel in the cities of the Roman Empire. The first great churches were established in the great cities of Ephesus, Antioch, Alexandria, and Rome, which among other things were famous for their mobs, their luxury, and their vice. The bulk of the early converts to Christianity came from the despised city rabble. The last to be converted were the peasants or 'pagani'—who in the backward sections of Christendom still worship pagan deities, under the guise of patron saints. The village remains the stronghold of the old-time religion, which may not be good enough for the future.

Hence we might discount somewhat the notorious evils of city life—the life that has always attracted the more ardent, enterprising spirits from the countryside. Its popularity is not due simply to the inducements of the big money. It is doubtful whether the ordinary city-dweller is more grasping than the French peasant, say, or even the sturdy New Englander. Nor are his morals necessarily lower than the countryman's (apart from the latter's rude mode of education in the facts of life). As Morris Cohen observed, the stabler *mores* of the village do not permit the freedom that may be abused in the city: yet stability is not the *summum bonum,* and freedom is essential if morality is to be rational and responsible. Traditionalists are like to deplore city life because they have something of the attitude of the small-town moralist.

The basic truth, however, is that the city is a symbol of both the best and the worst in civilization, and all the risks of its bold presumptions. It is open to a much wider world than the village and walled off from the natural world; by its variety, bustle, and commotion it stirs new interests and aspirations, and weakens old faiths and natural pieties. As the political capital, the seat of rule and misrule, it launches the national adventures in statesmanship and conquest, and loses the victories or squanders the spoils. As the social capital, it is the school of grace, urbanity, intrigue, and frivolity, the arts of living and of living on others. As the cultural capital, the marketplace of ideas, it is the birthplace of new movements in art thought, which may mean regeneration or degeneration.

In the modern world the terms of this problem have been at once magnified and altered. All past societies were predominantly agricultural and rural. Even in the Greco-Roman world, which was conspicuously a city world, the bulk of the population were still peasants. Modern civilization is predominantly industrial and urban. The great majority of Americans live in or about the city; the big, sprawling, fast-growing city—Chicago, Cleveland, Detroit—is the most distinctive product of the Industrial Revolution. At the same time, industrialism has been radically transforming the ancient village world. Main Street has undergone a remarkable change within a generation, and is no longer isolated from the city, physically or spiritually; the hayseed or yokel survives only in the backwoods or on the vaudeville stage. And city life itself is being altered by the growth of the suburb. New means of transportation, in particular the automobile, have enabled increasing numbers to combine the advantages of the city with some of the advantages of the village. With this have come efforts at city-planning and decentralization, which are still in their infancy but are potentially revolutionary.

In any event, it seems plain that the city is here to stay, at least as long as our civilization, even though it may have to go underground in the atomic age. The Southern agrarians of yesteryear, with their glorification of the gentleman-farmer and the dignity of the life of the soil, were playing a variation on an ancient theme, in the usual minor key and to the usual negligible effect. We may hope to beautify the city, to eliminate its slums, to quarantine its worst diseases, to bring the country into it, to facilitate escape from it. Nevertheless, it remains indispensable, to both the cultural and the commercial life of civilization.

4. THE AMBIGUITIES OF THE SPIRITUAL ACHIEVEMENT

I have said that as we share the venerable faith in the Good, the True, and the Beautiful, as the ends of civilization, we should do well to begin with an ironic view of the spiritual achievements of man. For this faith is strictly a faith: one that is always vulnerable to the taunts of practical men, who may seem to get along well enough with their material wealth and coarse pleasures, and as vulnerable to the analysis of skeptics and cynics, who may ask what good has come of all this spiritual achievement, and how we know that it is good. The faith is always threatened as well by the falsities and absurdities of its disciples: the pursuit of virtue, truth, and beauty has inspired egregious evil, error, and ugliness. We should not be surprised to find that the highest manifestations of civilization have involved the deepest contradictions.

The historic source of these contradictions, Ralph Turner points out, was the invention of writing. Literate learning, the major means to intellectual growth and creative achievement, has also been a major aid to the conservative forces that resist growth and adventure. From the outset it encouraged a purely verbal kind of learning that was confused with natural knowledge, and a liturgical kind that discouraged free inquiry. It helped to standardize and sanctify the codes, classics, and scriptures that embalmed the ignorance and prejudice as well as the wisdom of the ancestors. As the possession of a privileged few—especially the priestly class—it consolidated the power of the upper classes, raising them still higher above the illiterate masses, who were condemned to blind obedience and blind worship.

One result of this aristocratic monopoly on learning has been an inevitable distortion of history. The records of the past, which reflect chiefly the interests of the upper classes, give only an incidental or indirect view of the life of the masses, the everyday business of hewing and hauling. Thus Gibbon wrote his celebrated description of the Roman Empire under Trajan, Hadrian, and the Antonines, as the period in the history of the world during which 'the condition of the human race was most happy and prosperous'; but he was not actually talking about the 'human race.' He was describing the condition of the prosperous upper classes. There is some evidence that the great majority of the population—the peasants, the city proletarians, and the slaves—were not especially happy or prosperous at this time. The main point, however, is simply that we do not know and cannot know much about their lot. And so with all the other great empires. When the anonymous masses enter history it is chiefly to be slaughtered in battle, to die of famine or privation—to illustrate the failures of their betters; apart from these calamities we can only conjecture how contented they were under their priests and kings, and whether they enjoyed the golden ages. We have the mighty pyramids, but no first-hand account of the feelings of the wretches who built them. We have the sublime *Meditations* of Marcus Aurelius, but no diaries of his countless subjects who had greater need of his stoicism. Or when we can make out the best and the worst in past societies, we still cannot be sure of the balance, the average, the quality of the commonplace, the level of everyday life—the proportions of pomp and misery, fine art and dirty work, high endeavor and petty concern. We have the exalted tragedies of Aeschylus, but we do not know to what extent they exalted the citizens of Athens, or could compete with such attractions as the Olympic games.

A related effect of the aristocratic monopoly was the cultivation of knowledge for decorative, honorific, esoteric, or sacred purposes, rather than practical or productive ones. Invented to facilitate business transactions, writing soon became the medium for transactions with the gods or the god-kings, and those who carried on this elevated business naturally looked down on the lowly business of the world, the vulgar doing and making of artisans, merchants, and slaves. Applied knowledge was not merely degraded but divorced from the higher learning; the 'useful' was opposed to the philosophical and the spiritual. Hence the advance of science in the Western world was not a clear gain but a constant 'problem': it jeopardized traditional beliefs that had been cut off from natural knowledge. Since the last century, to be sure, the tables have been turned. Now useful knowledge has become almost sacred, as the means to our wealth and power; our 'institutions of higher learning' have been specializing in a practical training that is neither high nor learned. But the ancient aristocratic bias still persists. The immense visions of modern physics and astronomy are considered less imaginative than the most tortured imaginings of modern poets, less spiritual than the mildewed metaphors of conventional churchmen. In general, the limitations of modern culture are due not only to the narrowness of scientists and technicians, and the grossness of businessmen, but to the fastidious exclusiveness of literary and learned men, jealous of their traditional prerogatives as custodians of a higher or holier kind of truth.

Apart from the classiness of the classical, however, the glorious accomplishments of the mind and spirit have always had inglorious consequences. Today the conspicuous example is science. Its enormous extension of knowledge has meant not only a narrowing of consciousness for many specialists but an impoverishment of consciousness for the many others who have regarded its severely limited descriptions as complete explanations, the whole truth about the world. Its triumphant advance in the understanding and control of nature has weakened man's belief in his own importance in the cosmic scheme, or even in the reality of his spiritual values; many thinkers concluded that man is a mere mechanism whose behavior is blindly determined. More recently, the triumphs have culminated in discoveries about the subatomic world that appear to undermine the basic assumptions of uniformity and causality on which science has rested, and that give man a power which conceivably may destroy science and all its work. Altogether, the most successful instrument of human reason has shaken the faith in reason that has been the mainspring of Western civilization.

But the humanities have also been inhuman, or all too human, in their conceit. Religion everywhere has exhibited the paradoxes of St. Sophia. The higher religions have commonly grown out of the failures of civilization, bringing promises of eternal life to dying societies. Although they survive these societies they bear the marks of their defeatist origins; the most characteristic sign of their loftiness is the abasement of man and this earth, an other-worldly or life-denying spirit. They are therefore always liable to conflict with the creative forces of a flourishing society, and thence to profound inconsistencies or ignoble concessions. Above all, they are invariably corrupted by their worldly success. As they become popular their revolutionary spiritual ideals are translated into popular hopes, fears, and desires; the loftier they are, the wider is the gap between the idealism of their founders and the practice and belief of most of their followers. As they become institutionalized they suffer the fate of all other worldly institutions. A priesthood ceases to propagate new values and devotes itself primarily to conserving the old ones, piously reducing them to routine rituals and dead dogmas. An established church also tends to ally itself with other vested interests, and thus to become infected with the worldly pride it was born to combat. And the periodic reactions that follow— the efforts to reinterpret the original revelation or recapture the original purity—revitalize the faith at the cost of splintering it into more sects and further confusing the nature of the original revelation.

All such perversions of high tradition are intensified by traditionalism, the occupational disease of guardians of culture. The guardians tend to forget that tradition has always been the great enemy of the founders of great traditions: that Socrates was a radical who did corrupt the youth of Athens by impiously urging them to question the time-honored ways; or that the teachings of Christ were an outrage to precisely the most cultivated, respectable, God-fearing people of his time; or that the American Revolution was strictly a revolution, illegal, violent, and bloody. In particular, the traditionalists abuse our Western heritage by singling out some one school of thought as the 'essential' or 'true' tradition; whereas diversity and non-conformity are the very soul of this heritage. It is the richest tradition that man has ever known simply because it includes so many disparate elements from diverse sources, and has never been at rest.[2]

Yet the last word must be spoken in piety. We have said enough about the abuses of the higher values to enable us, in realism and in honor, to declare their supreme value. While man is immensely indebted to the past for practical knowledge and skills, he cherishes the past for its contributions to the life of the mind or spirit. Ultimately he has never really honored the material wealth and power he has always sought. Reverently he recalls the great failures, ironically the mere conquests or triumphs of power. Assyria was a mighty empire, Sparta succeeded in dominating all Greece, the Mongols under the extraordinary Jenghiz Khan swept out of nowhere to conquer most of the known world. But who mourns the fall of Nineveh and Sparta, or the disappearance of the Mongols into the obscurity whence they came? Athens, Jerusalem, and Rome exemplified the limitations and excesses of great cultural achievement, all the paradoxes of glory and grandeur. But who rejoices at their fall?

Since the higher values are usually given a high metaphysical or religious sanction, it is worth observing that they require no such sanction. Like the simple goods of physical well-being, they are intrinsic goods, good for their own sake. And since, as capitalized abstractions, the Good, the True, and the Beautiful are apt to seem highfalutin' in an age of busi-

---

[2] T. S. Eliot, perhaps the most famous of contemporary traditionalists, is one of the most exclusive, rejecting a great deal of the political, philosophical, and religious heritage of the Western world. For all his subtlety and sincerity, Eliot argues much like the politicians and businessmen who maintain their power and prestige by laying claim to the true American tradition, of Jefferson or of Lincoln, and denouncing their opponents as enemies of the American Way.

ness and technology, it is well to stress their homely origins. The Good is rooted in the fact that man is a social animal, naturally gregarious, whose 'soul' may come from God but in any event can come simply from his relations with his fellows, and his natural desire for their esteem; his very self is a social product, or itself a society, which becomes self-conscious only as it becomes aware of other selves. The True is rooted in natural curiosity, the desire of all men to know something about whatever they are interested in, whether the workings of an engine or of a universe; the most abstruse concepts of science and philosophy grow out of a simple fondness for observing the out-of-doors. The Beautiful is rooted in the esthetic sense and creative impulse common to all men, and apparent even in the hard-headed man who thinks Art is effeminate; when he admires his new tool or gadget he says, 'It's a beauty.' The 'higher' values may be considered simply a fuller development of these natural human impulses, a fuller realization of the distinctive but natural possibilities of being a human being.

5. THE CONSCIOUS INDIVIDUAL

The social-contract theories that once were popular usually implied that society sprang from a deliberate, conscious agreement by individuals who originally had lived in a free, lawless 'state of nature.' Finally having the wit to realize that their freedom gave them no security, these individuals agreed to surrender certain of their natural rights to a central authority, in return for protection of their lives and their property. It is not generally recognized that the community came first, and that the individual with his rights is the product of a developed society. As far back as we can see we find men living in groups, comparable to the flocks, herds, swarms, and schools of the animal world; and only when we come to civilization do we find a high degree of individuality. Although primitive societies are not so static and homogeneous as commonly thought, they prescribe rigid modes of behavior and provide little room for individual differences; primitive man typically submits without question to the totems and taboos of his group, does not think of its demands as infringements of his natural rights or lawful liberties, and has little independent belief. Civilized man also accepts without question the great bulk of the customs and beliefs of his community; despite the reigning gospel of individualism we can still say with Oscar Wilde that most people are other people,

or with Bertrand Russell that most people would sooner die
than think—and in fact do so. Nevertheless civilized man is
far more self-conscious, and conscious of himself as an individual apart from the group.

The emergence of the individual with a mind of his own
may be considered, once more, the chief justification of civilization. He also sums up its paradoxes. The individual has always been a threat to the social order that produced him. Now
an inspired prophet introduces new ideas that disrupt settled
ways of thinking and feeling; now an ambitious leader leads
his society to conquest of other societies, or to disaster; now
an impassioned rebel starts a revolution. The self-conscious
individual is always prone, moreover, to be conscious chiefly
of his selfish interests, and to exploit others for his own good.
Hence many other individuals have suffered in civilization as
prehistoric men did not. They have been conscious chiefly of
injustice, oppression, tyranny, cruelty—of outrages on their
new sense of rights.

Civilization has accordingly created the problem of adjusting rights and duties, harmonizing the interests of the individual and of the group. The most conspicuous and most difficult
aspect of this problem is the political. Here we encounter the
ancient, universal story of privilege and oppression, the long
struggle for social justice and personal liberty, and the new
complications introduced by the ideal of individualism. But
the problem affects all spheres of culture. Religion usually demands conformity to a uniform faith, which may produce a
serene piety, or may violate individual conscience and kill the
religious spirit; the prophet crying in the wilderness may then
unsettle the ancient faith, perhaps preparing the way for a
nobler ideal, perhaps stirring up hysteria or fanaticism. Poetry
and art usually impose conventional forms or modes, which
may facilitate the expression of talent or may cramp the
original genius; the individualist who rebels may be a great
innovator or a mere eccentric. Even science now faces this
problem. It has represented the closest approach to the pre-
sumable ideal in these matters: an international co-operative
enterprise based on complete freedom of thought, in which
the individual scientist freely subjects himself to a rigorous
discipline that is never arbitrary or despotic, and makes his
findings freely available to society. Hence scientists could
zealously pursue the truth, innocently unconcerned about the
consequences of their discoveries, almost unaware that they
were shattering the traditional foundations of thought and revolutionizing their society. With their unlocking of atomic
power, however, they have suddenly awakened to an urgent
sense of social responsibility; while at the same time the state

has limited their freedom of inquiry, and in Russia has prescribed the truths they must find.

At any given moment, this whole problem is a matter of
stress. In a democratic society with a tradition of rugged individualism, and a perhaps excessive fear of all forms and
constraints, one might stress that there is no such thing as an
absolute individual with absolute rights. The individual is inseparable from his society, which has created his rights, furnished the materials for his prized individuality, furnished
even the principles for his rebellion against it. Similarly one
might remark that most of the great poets and artists of the
past did not make a cult of self-expression, strain for originality, or proclaim the sovereign rights of genius; they managed
to express themselves freely and fully enough while accepting conventional forms and modes, subordinating their art
to the interests of religion or the state, or even remaining
anonymous. Usually, however, this is not what most needs to
be said. There has seldom been too much freedom for too
many individuals, nor is such freedom the great menace today. Given the long historic record of oppression, the painfully slow, erratic growth of the ideal of personal liberty, the
natural conservatism or inertia of mankind, the immense
force of custom and convention, the vast reserves of ignorance
and prejudice—given all the political and cultural pressures
for conformity even in the advanced democracies, the final
stress should be on the claims of the individual, the ideal of
freedom to think and act for oneself.

6. THE MEANING OF HISTORY

Time will tell, we say; but we may not be aware of the difference that is made by our very conception of time. To
the Greeks and Romans time was characteristically a slow
but inexorable enemy of man, telling the destruction of all
his works. To the Hindu sage it was static or illusory, resem-
bling a deep pool rather than a flow or a river; so the splash
of history made ripples that vanished as they spread, distract-
ing only the foolish. To the modern Westerner, on the contrary, time is all-important. He tells it, keeps it, lives by it
punctually. In America he has a passion for making it and
saving it (though what he saves it for may not be clear). It
has been his great hope, in its promise of ever bigger and
better things to come. And if he is now much less hopeful
he has a more vivid sense of the horrors that time may bring.

For him, in any event, things always keep moving. Time Marches On!

In short, our feeling about time—however vague or unconscious—ultimately involves a philosophy of history. It leads to a momentous question. Given all the drama of human history, what is the plot, the grand design, the final meaning of the whole show? Positivists will tell us that this is a meaningless question. Manifestly we cannot give it a precise, positive answer: we cannot state it in terms that permit either empirical verification or rigorous logical analysis. But neither can we escape it. Although we naturally come to it as we hope to make sense of history, we are forced to consider it if only because men persist in answering it. Thus Westerners have declared that history is a progress, and in this faith have made extraordinary history. Today Communists are still so positive the drama will have a happy ending, in a classless society, that they threaten to precipitate a war which might make any society impossible, put a literal end to history. Others have therefore been led to reject the whole faith in progress—and their negations may also have positive consequences. Time will tell in any case; but what it will tell depends on what men say and do right now.

This is to reject the Indian view that history is mere appearance or illusion. In certain moods, to be sure, we all know the feeling that the 'real' reality is changeless and timeless—the feeling of eternity as a quality of the present, which is perhaps the most valid intimation of immortality. Even so worldly a philosopher as Bertrand Russell has said that 'there is some sense, easier to feel than to state, in which Time is an unimportant and superficial characteristic of reality'; and almost all the wise men have agreed that wisdom begins with a realization of its unimportance.[3] Still, Westerners have good reason for sticking to their senses as they do. The very insistence of the Hindu sages on the necessity of renouncing or transcending the temporal world, and their arduous disciplines for shaking off the illusions of sense, indicate that this world is real enough. And as students of history, at any rate, we are bound to take time seriously. The pertinent theories of history concern dramas that are played out in time, by flesh and blood actors, on a real stage. The most common theories involve three main kinds of movement in time—progress, decline, and cycle. Because the idea of progress is

[3] A further difficulty with the Western man's common-sense notion of time is that if he begins to think seriously about it, he soon runs into the unthinkable. He cannot really conceive an eternal universe: it must have a beginning, if not an end; yet neither can he conceive of the state before the beginning, or after the end. Time cannot march on forever, but neither can it stop.

so familiar, we may forget that it is a very novel Western idea, only a few centuries old; so we might first consider the alternative theories, which have the prestige of endorsement by the most illustrious thinkers of the past.

As I have already indicated, the theory of decline is the hoariest theory of history. Men used to locate Utopia in the remote past instead of the future—as in the Garden of Eden of Babylonian-Hebrew mythology, or the Golden Age of Hesiod. Even the sophisticated literature of the Greco-Roman world is shot through with the notion that civilization is a disease or degeneration. (Lovejoy and Boas offer a comprehensive account of the early career of this theory in their *Primitivism and Related Ideas in Antiquity*.) Although it was generally assumed that the utopian simple life had actually been lived somewhere, the conceptions of it varied widely. Hedonists pictured it as a carefree life in which men were good and happy; Stoics pictured it as a hard, rugged life that bred the manly virtues wanting in their effete society. Usually primitivism was an earnest criticism and exhortation, implying that man could mend his civilized ways; but the explicit conclusion was usually a gloomy belief that he lacked the sense to do so, implying that civilization is an incurable disease. A similar diversity appears in modern versions. Dostoyevsky and Tolstoy found their ideal in primitive Christianity, and their hope in the Russian peasant; whereas D. H. Lawrence glorified the intuitive, instinctive life or 'phallic consciousness,' but could never find a satisfactory historical model.

As all this implies, theories of decline cannot be taken seriously as literal outlines of history. There is no evidence whatever of the historical existence of a Garden of Eden or Golden Age, or of an ideal primitive stage in evolution. Such fictions may be useful as metaphors, symbolizing the actual corruptions of civilization and the natural corruptibility of man, but it is essential to remember that they are fictions, pure and rather too simple. Usually they reflect a shallow view of history, or a sheer ignorance of it.[4]

Hence the deepest thought of antiquity led rather to the conclusion that history is an endless cycle. Aristotle saw a continuous 'coming to be and falling away'; he speculated that

---

[4] A modern version typical of such fictions was a recent speech by the president of an alumni association. He edified the old grads with an account of the golden age of our society, which he dated about 1910—with no hint that this businessman's Eden was breeding its own serpents, and that its fruit was war and depression. Although his speech was no doubt inspired by the beery sentimentality appropriate to alumni reunions, it expressed the sober attitude of many business leaders, congressmen, and newspaper publishers.

there had already been countless civilizations, which had passed through a uniform destiny. Stoics and Epicureans alike dwelt on the inevitable recurrences. The rational soul, wrote Marcus Aurelius, 'considers the periodic destructions and rebirths of the universe, and reflects that our posterity will see nothing new, and that our ancestors saw nothing greater than we have seen.' Or in the words of Ecclesiastes, 'The thing that hath been, it is that which shall be; and that which is done is that which shall be done; and there is no new thing under the sun.' This theory of cycles has been maintained by such Western thinkers as Bodin, Vico, and Nietzsche, and in our time has been given its most systematic, comprehensive formulation in Spengler's *Decline of the West*. Spengler argued that all civilizations necessarily pass through parallel stages and necessarily die a natural death—unless (like the Aztec) they are prematurely destroyed by accident.

Whether one is comforted or depressed by this fatalistic view of history is presumably a matter of temperament. Most thinkers have chosen to dwell on its pessimistic implications. The cycles appear to be rhymes without reason, even when God is made their author. The eternal inanity of the cosmic process is most conspicuous in the Hindu and Buddhist versions, as summarized by Sir Charles Eliot: 'An infinite number of times the Universe has collapsed in flaming or watery ruin, aeons of quiescence follow the collapse, and then the Diety (he has done it an infinite number of times) emits again from himself worlds and souls of the same old kind.' Babylonian and Aztec myths likewise stressed the melancholy idea that the cycles are punctuated by universal catastrophes. Men are most disposed to take such a view of history, moreover, when they believe that their society is on the downswing, headed for catastrophe. Like the primitivists, the 'cyclists' usually believed that the best days were behind them, and they had even less hope of the future. So we have the curious spectacle of civilized man forever marching with his face turned backward—as no doubt the cave-man looked back to the good old days when men were free to roam instead of being stuck in a damn hole in the ground. And so the theory of cycles has again become seductive, as men again fear the worst. Spengler, Sorokin, and Toynbee have presented different versions of it, but all agree that the West is on the decline.

The most obvious argument for this theory is its correspondence with the processes of birth, growth, decay, and death in the natural world. Given the fate of all other higher organisms, it seems reasonable to assume that a civilization cannot maintain itself indefinitely, but in time must age and die. Offhand, the theory also corresponds with the actual history of civilizations to date: all but our own have died, or have been dying. (Thus we have unearthed several of Aristotle's 'lost' civilizations, such as the ancient Indic and the Minoan, and in the huge statues on Easter Island see evidence that there might once have been a high civilization in the South Pacific area.) Everywhere we find a monotonous recurrence of the basic themes of selfishness and greed, fear and hate. But most pertinent is the evidence of cyclical movements within civilizations, the familiar patterns of rise and fall. In *Configurations of Cultural Growth*, A. L. Kroeber surveys the major cultural achievements of all the great societies; and the most striking fact that emerges from his anthropological study is the fact of configuration and cycle.

About 1400, for example, the notable Dutch-Flemish school of painters arose suddenly, out of nowhere, with the Van Eycks; about 1700 the whole movement ended as suddenly, for Rembrandt, Hals, Teniers, Ruysdael, and the rest had died within a few years of one another; and ever since there has been practically no Dutch-Flemish painting of consequence. So it has been with all the major growths in art, literature, philosophy, and science. This phenomenon of the golden age is so familiar that we may forget how strange it is. All our knowledge of genetics indicates that the appearance of genius in any given society should be more or less constant—yet it never has been. Except for a very few isolated great men, such as John Scotus Erigena, genius has appeared only when there was a movement afoot; most potential greatness evidently goes to waste. And the movements appear to have specific limits as well as potentialities: they move to fulfilment, and then to exhaustion. All this implies a kind of predestination that Kroeber regrets. Nevertheless 'the empirical data, over and over again, and with really remarkably few exceptions, compel the conclusion that there are whole arrays of events in the history of culture which are objectively describable only in terms of the metaphors of "growth," "realization," "exhaustion," and "death," as our vocabulary stands today.'

This much seems clear. The picture as a whole, however, is not at all clear. Although we can make out configurations everywhere, they are irregular in their growth, diverse in their content, and inconstant in their associations. After medieval philosophy reached the end of its development, about 1350, there was no important philosophy in all Europe until the rise of the moderns with Descartes, after 1600; yet this long slump coincided with the Renaissance, a period of abounding intellectual activity. Kroeber's survey indicates that such apparent anomalies are the rule. Ancient Greece has fixed the common notion of a golden age as a rich growth in all fields of art and thought, a whole culture on the surge; but this glory has so profoundly impressed men because it was indeed unique. Thus the splendid Elizabethan Age produced no painting or sculpture to speak of, whereas the splendor of the Italian Renaissance was largely confined to the representative arts. Similarly there are conspicuous gaps in great civilizations. Egypt, Mesopotamia, and Japan produced no significant philosophy, Rome no science, Islam no painting, sculpture, or drama.[5] Furthermore, the golden ages of culture appear to have no necessary connection with national expansion. Greek culture flowered before and after the little city-states had their brief hour of military glory; the Italians made their greatest contributions when their cities were torn by civil war and largely dominated by other countries; the Germans led all Europe under Beethoven, Goethe, and Kant while they were being overrun by Napoleon's armies, and their great creative period was over by 1870, when their great national expansion began.

Altogether, Kroeber can make out no 'true law' in cultural history: 'Nothing cyclical, regularly repetitive, or necessary.' And in the history of whole civilizations, regular cycles are still harder to find. Civilizations are much less discrete and homogeneous than the cyclical theory presupposes, and their geographical, political, and cultural components do have a uniform destiny. (We have already seen that when 'Rome' fell, its Eastern Empire lived on.) Historians cannot even agree on their location in time and space—Toynbee makes out at least twice as many civilizations as Spengler did. Neither can they agree on criteria for marking the peak of a society, or on the symptoms of growth and decay. And most dubious are the neat parallels, the efforts to make all societies swing through exactly the same cycle. On the face of it, civilizations start at different points, building on different pasts in different environments, exploiting different possibilities. Spengler, the most systematic exponent of this theory, kept his cycles orderly only by a Teutonic forcing and drilling of the facts, with a ruthless suppression of all unruly facts.

Above all, the *necessity* of the cycles is unproved, and unprovable on the basis of present knowledge. The only cause

[5] With Islam, an obvious explanation is the Mohammedan law prohibiting the representation of the human form; but since native sculpture had been dead in this region long before this taboo, its absence might be considered the reason for the taboo. Kroeber warns against the conventional 'explanations' in our texts. Although Elizabethan drama, for example, is usually explained by the defeat of the Spanish Armada, it might be as reasonable to explain the defeat by the rise of Elizabethan poetry. The truth probably is that both were manifestations of some deeper cause that has yet to be defined.

suggested by Spengler is a biological analogy that cannot bear scientific analysis. 'The Biology of the future,' he declared, 'will undoubtedly find the point of departure for an entirely new formulation of its problems in the concept of the preordained life-span of the genus and species'—a span, he added, which is 'a numerical value of almost mystical significance.' Mystical is strictly the word for it. Biology gives no signs of accommodating him; and even if it attempted this new departure (or aspired to the exaltation of a capital B) it would not prove his point, since a society is neither a genus nor a species.

What biology still does teach is the theory of evolution; and this brings us back to the modern theory of progress. Although past societies were often complacent enough about their superiority over barbarians, there are only a few scattered hints of any hope for a continuous advance. The nearest thing to it was the Hebrew vision of the Messiah, which bred the Christian visions of the Millennium and the Second Coming, but these all depended upon a direct intervention by God; they stirred no hope that man, by his own efforts, could achieve a steady improvement of his earthly condition. Only with the rise of science did men begin to entertain seriously the possibility of progress. At length the possibility was transformed into a gospel, a certainty. History became a success story, of a race that was bound to make good. 'Progress is not an accident but a necessity,' proclaimed Herbert Spencer. 'What we call evil and immorality must disappear. It is certain that man must become perfect... Always toward perfection is the mighty movement.'

Now in the long evolutionary view, reaching back to the cave-man and ape-man, there unquestionably has been progress—always granted the assumption that it is worth being a human being. Man has achieved greater mastery of his natural environment, greater freedom of action, and thereupon has discovered the finer possibilities of life implicit in his distinctive power of consciousness. In historic times there have been clear gains in intellectual and spiritual as well as material wealth and power. Christian thinkers who now ridicule the faith in progress forget the assumption of progress in their own concept of 'higher' religions, and of the progressive revelations of God through Abraham, Moses, and Christ; and hardly any thinker will deny that the religion of Jesus is loftier than that of Moloch. If all specific gains are disputable, there remains the general advance that man has made, from blind obedience to the totems and taboos of the tribe to conscious, reasoned loyalty to ideals of humanity. All the savagery that persists seems more frightful because it no longer seems inevitable or proper. In general, the tragic failures of civilization have left substantial residues of knowledge, skills, arts, ideas, ideals—of enduring goods that men do not willingly give up, once they are known, but that we are apt to forget because we take them for granted.

Simply as we cherish the possibilities of progress, however, we must severely qualify the popular notions about them. The progress has not been steady or in a straight line: history is not a succession of civilizations rising to ever greater heights, coming ever closer to the distinction of having produced us. The progress has not been progress pure and simple: all the gains in freedom and power have enabled men to do more evil as well as good, to destroy as well as create. Above all, the progress has not been automatic and inevitable: it has resulted from arduous human effort, an 'expense of greatness' that has often been squandered by later generations. Hence continued progress is not guaranteed by any known law of nature. Nothing in history assures the success of our civilization; history tells us only that the incalculable possibilities open to us are more likely to be for worse than for better. Nothing in biology assures the indefinite progress or even the indefinite survival of the human race; devolution or extinction has been the common fate of the more complex forms of life, while the simple amoeba is a good bet to last to the end. At that, the exciting story of the evolution of life is a local affair, an interlude confined to a speck in interstellar space. Those who make 'emergent evolution' the key to the cosmic plan have little more scientific authority than the Book of Revelation; for our most certain knowledge indicates that all life on this planet is ultimately doomed to extinction, and that its disappearance will make no apparent difference to the universe. The only enduring result of man's works, Santayana has said, is that the earth may cast a slightly different shadow on the moon.

7. THE OPEN SOCIETY

What, then, is the meaning of history? The answer presumably should come at the end of this work, where conclusions belong. My conclusions were in fact modified during the course of my studies, and will be restated at the end. Yet it would be idle to pretend that we are now about to embark on a voyage of exploration, with no idea of our destination. My answer has been implicit in all that I have written so far, and will determine the content of the chapters that follow. It amounts to a basic assumption, a premise that should be laid face up on the table. Briefly, my answer is at once a negation and an affirmation. History has no meaning, in the sense of a clear pattern or determinate plot; but it is not simply meaningless or pointless. It has no certain meaning because man is free to give it various possible meanings.

His freedom is sharply limited, of course. Man has to choose within the conditions imposed by his biological structure, his natural environment, and his cultural heritage. He cannot do whatever he has a mind to, and at that his mind has been largely made up by his ancestors. For such reasons he is always prone to believe that history somehow makes itself, in spite of his efforts, by the automatic operation of natural laws or God's will. Still, at any moment he has a wide range of choices and is willy-nilly making more history, discovering the meanings of his past and determining the meanings of his future. The most significant 'facts' he has to face are of man's own making. Marxism, for all its theoretical determinism, is the clearest illustration of how history is made by men's beliefs about what has happened, what is happening, and what should happen.

This insistence on human freedom is not simply cheering. It means that we have to keep making history, instead of leaning on it, and that we can never count on a final solution. It means the constant possibility of foolish or even fatal choices. Yet the dignity of man lies precisely in this power to choose his destiny. We may therefore welcome the conclusion that we cannot foretell the future, even apart from the possibility that it may not bear knowing. Uncertainty is not only the plainest condition of human life but the necessary condition of freedom, of aspiration, of conscience—of all human idealism.

It is the business of the future to be dangerous, Whitehead remarked; and we can always trust it to keep on the job. I again stress the uncertainties, however, because the dangers are always intensified by the pretensions to absolute certainty or finality. These are the ultimate source of corruption, the reason why the best becomes the worst and crusaders for heaven make a hell on earth. And none is more insidious than the principle of historical predestination. Knowing in advance how history is going to turn out, men climb on the bandwagon, ride the wave of the future.[6] They can then indulge any policy, from supine resignation to ruthless violence.

---

[6] James Burnham is especially agile in the performance of this feat. In the name of hard-boiled realism, he has so far ridden at least three waves—the Marxist revolution, the managerial revolution, and the imperial destiny of America. Presumably he has a weather eye open for the next wave; but meanwhile he still tends to deride visionary idealists who are more interested in making history than in predicting it.

So the Communists can justify the most barbarous behavior: like hangmen, they are merely executing 'the verdict of history.' They corrupt morality at its very base by implying that it is man's duty to fight for the inevitable, or that historic might makes right. Even in self-sacrifice they are profoundly irresponsible. Our business as rational beings is not to argue for what is going to be but to strive for what ought to be, in the consciousness that it will never be all we would like it to be.

Among the possible 'meanings' of history—to restate my premises in these terms—the most significant is the growth of this power of self-determination, or freedom to make history. I assume that for interpreting the past and choosing a future we must begin with a full acknowledgment of the claims of reason: a humble reason that makes no claim to finality or metaphysical certitude, because such claims cannot be rationally substantiated, and that recognizes its finiteness and fallibility; a proud reason that nevertheless maintains its authority as the final judge of all claims to truth, insisting that its tested knowledge is no less real and reliable because it is not a knowledge of ultimate reality, and that only by a further exercise of reason can its limitations and its fallacies be clearly discerned. We are not forced to choose between reason and faith in the conventional sense—we may choose between more or less reasonable faiths. The ideal of rationality in turn requires the ideal of freedom, the right to be an individual. A rational person is not merely one who has good habits or right principles, but one who knows what he believes and assumes the intellectual and moral responsibilities of his beliefs; and first he must be free to think for himself, make up his own mind. Although non-rational behavior may exhibit admirable qualities, such as the loyalty, fortitude, and daring found in barbarians, or even in the animal world, these qualities are not wholly admirable, or trustworthy, unless they are conscious, responsible choices. The only possible virtue in being a civilized man instead of a barbarian, an ignoramus, or a moron is in being a free, responsible individual with a mind of one's own.

The best society, accordingly, is that which is most conducive to the growth of such persons. It is what Karl Popper has called the 'open society.'[7] It is an adventurous society that has broken with the universal, prehistoric custom of regarding ancient customs as magical or sacred, that views its institutions as man-made for human purposes and examines

---

[7] *The Open Society and Its Enemies*, London, 1945. Popper is somewhat unfair to its enemies, of whom he makes Plato No. 1. Otherwise his book is a cogent argument for the views I am expressing here.

their suitability for these purposes, that welcomes variety and change instead of enforcing rigid conformity, and that accordingly provides its members with personal opportunities and responsibilities beyond mere obedience. It is Athens as opposed to Sparta.

Today it is us; and thereby hangs our tale. Because we have made the farthest advance toward the open society we are likely to feel more impotent than men have ever felt before. The novel idea of progress, or simply of 'opportunity,' has been so deeply engrained in our everyday thought and feeling that we are incapable of passive acceptance and endurance; in a crisis we take for granted the possibility and the need of 'doing something about it.' Having accumulated a vast deal of sociological and historical knowledge, we are also more aware of the difficulty of doing anything about it, and are more critical of the simple faiths that once made it easier for men to do or die for God, king, and country. We bear the cross of consciousness. In a fuller consciousness the burden may be eased—and this is the reason for the chapters that follow. Our adventure in freedom is so recent that what appear to be our death rattles may be growing pains. But in any event the pains are unavoidable. For a society as for an individual, the hardest problems begin with freedom. Today the future of the open society is wide open, to triumphs or to disasters of a magnitude hitherto undreamed of.

IV

The Legacy of Israel

1. JESUS AND JUDAISM

If the spirit that erected Hagia Sophia was impure, mixed with worldly ambitions, its Christian inspiration involved a profounder irony. Few pagans would have been less impressed by the magnificence of the cathedral, the mystery of its Masses, or the authority of its Patriarchs than would the historic Jesus. For in all the mystery that shrouds the person and the mission of Jesus, nothing seems more certain than that neither he nor his first followers had any intention of founding a new religion, much less so ceremonial a one. It appears that the author of Christianity never dreamed of it. The synoptic Gospels, written a generation or so after his death, still stress his Jewish ancestry, both physical and spiritual. He was a descendant of King David; he constantly quoted the Scriptures of Israel; he came not to destroy the Law but to fulfil it; he came to fulfil the prophecies of the great prophets. Addressing his fellow Jews, he preached a simple ethical and apocalyptic gospel in the prophetic tradition. In time he might have been included among the true prophets of Israel had not St. Paul, in spreading his gospel among the Gentiles, taken liberties with the Law. As it was, Jesus was crucified as the King of the Jews; on the Cross he appealed to the God of the Jews. He died, as he had lived, a devout Jew.

At least this aspect of his human life needs to be stressed in simple justice to Judaism. When the Christians broke away, taking the Old Testament with them, they assumed that no virtue was left in Judaism. They were now the chosen people; the Jews were something worse than pagans, because they had rejected Christ. Within a century or so Christians knew nothing about the living religion of Israel. To this day orthodox churchmen have ignored its independent claims to truth, treating it as a poor, wayward relation rather than an elder brother. Liberal churchmen, on the other hand, have usually dwelt on the unfortunate influence of the Old Testament on early Protestantism, which made a gospel of its harshest texts. Few have done justice to a remarkable religion that has held its own for some three thousand years.[1]

The story of this religion is enthralling in itself, but it also has immense historic significance for all Christendom. Besides Jesus himself, Judaism gave Christianity Yahweh—the One God, and a living God. It contributed a Sacred Book—its own Testament and the idea for a New Testament. It contributed a historic tradition that made all life purposeful and all history meaningful. Christianity went on to offer private salvation by sacramental means, the popular attractions of the mystery cults that were flourishing all over the Roman Empire; but given the heritage of Judaism, its eucharist was not merely the 'drug of immortality' that intoxicated St. Ignatius. Had the early heretic Marcion succeeded in his effort to divorce Christianity from Judaism, it might well have become simply another mystery cult, and like the others succumbed to gross superstition. Certainly Marcion would have made the appearance of Jesus in Palestine wholly arbitrary. It is mysterious enough that the Saviour of mankind should confine his mission to one of the lesser provinces of the Roman Empire, and not make himself known to the great contemporary civilizations of China and India. The only intelligible excuse for this partiality is the lofty tradition of Israel.

The opponents of Jesus, moreover, were not simply betraying this tradition. It is again typical of Christian bias that the Pharisees are remembered only as legalists, and that 'Pharisaic' is given in our dictionaries as a synonym for self-righteous and hypocritical. Actually, Jesus quarreled with them over matters of relative stress rather than basic principle; for his main teachings about God and man came from them. Despite their concern with external forms, they were not indifferent to the spirit of religion; their famous Rabbi Hillel also taught that true religion was summed up in the two great commandments, to love God and love thy neighbor. Likewise the Pharisees were not reactionaries. They were liberals, seeking to adapt the traditional faith to new conditions, tol-

[1] *Judaism and Christianity*, an admirable book by James Parkes, is in this respect depressing. An Anglican minister, Parkes feels obliged to write like a missionary as he expounds the living truth in Judaism; and it is surprising to read that he was surprised as he discovered this truth for himself. Apparently nothing in his theological training had prepared him for such a discovery.

erating wide differences in opinion, and welcoming such new ideas as the resurrection in a hereafter, which Jesus also took over. As for the serious faults that he denounced, these were not peculiar to them but common to all established religions; Christianity itself would soon stress forms and ceremonies as much as they did. Altogether, if the Pharisees failed to appreciate the spirit of Jesus, they at least succeeded in doing away with the kind of idolatry that flourished in St. Sophia, and in giving Judaism the essential form that enabled it to hold together a people hounded as no other has been in history.

Yet the historic outcome of this quarrel was profoundly ambiguous. By driving the Christians out into the Greek world, Israel enabled them to profit from pagan culture and develop a universal religion. Then Israel turned in on itself and its Law, renouncing all dalliance with Hellenism. It succeeded in holding its own, but at considerable cost in narrowness and exclusiveness. As Christianity triumphed, on the other hand, it accentuated some of the most dubious potentialities of its heritage from Judaism. A personal God, a Sacred Book, a divine purpose in history, a chosen people to fulfil this purpose—these ideas may be splendid incentives to high aspiration, but they are not clearly suitable to a religion that claims universality. They are the source of the major difficulties that have beset Christianity in recent centuries. They make it advisable to go back to the first principles of religion itself.

2. RELIGION AS DOGMA AND AS MYTH

Although religion is one of the universals of human culture, its universal essence is not easy to define. In a historical view, we are confronted not by Religion but by a multiplicity of religions, which are alike in certain 'primitive' elements, such as the basic acts of ritual and prayer, but which still differ in fundamentals. The high gods may be local or universal, personal or impersonal, immanent or transcendent; they may or may not be creators of the universe, or issue moral commandments, or promise heavenly rewards. As diverse are men's ways of dealing with them. Worship may be individual or communal, secret or public, improvised or formalized, ecstatic or grave. Yet implicit in all this diversity are two general ideas—that there are higher, unseen powers, and that men must deal with them. Religion might therefore be defined, broadly, as an effort to make sense of a mysterious world, and to get into satisfactory relations with the mysterious powers that control it.

If this definition does not seem exalted enough, it at least assumes that religion serves a rational purpose, responding to cognitive as well as emotional needs, and that these needs are as vital for civilized as for primitive men. In trying to make sense of the world, religion may range from animistic myth to metaphysics; but in any case it deals with questions that science does not answer, or even raise at all. Science explains *how* things happen; it does not explain *why* things are, or why they are as bad as they often seem. It explains the immediate causes of suffering and death but not the pathos of mortality, the reasons why man must suffer and die. Likewise knowledge alone does not bring peace and wisdom. Men still have to come to terms with what they know, and don't know. They have to accept their universe, whether it be the universe of Einstein or of Augustine.

The multiplicity of religions also implies, however, that whatever divine reality there may be is not clearly known, 'The idea that religion contains a literal, not a symbolical representation of truth and life is simply an impossible idea,' Santayana declared. Rationally considered, it is indeed impossible. The whole history of religious thought makes plain that no truths about God can be conclusively demonstrated; otherwise the saints and sages would long since have agreed. If some one creed is literally true, then all others are to a considerable degree literally false. The only possible way to do justice to the innumerable lofty expressions of the religious spirit is to regard them all as symbolic representations, naturally conditioned by their time and place as well as by the limitations of the human mind, which could not be expected fully to comprehend the divine mind.

An ardent believer may properly object that no rational, historical approach can reveal the deepest secrets of his religion. But it is not the business of a historian to communicate such secrets. Because he has to deal with many varieties of ardent belief, he must begin by stressing that the possession of a secret is no guarantee of its truth. Absolute conviction may provide an extraordinary stimulus to man's creative powers, or it may produce a 'convict,' a man chained by his beliefs; in either event it does not constitute proof. Even the overwhelming experience of mystics, who claim the most immediate knowledge of God, proves only the power of their belief, not its validity. If we must always respect what men feel in their most exalted moments, we still cannot accept all such experiences at their face value. Many African tribes also enjoy their supreme religious experience when the god 'comes to the head' of the worshiper, who may then be completely transformed. Melville Herskovits reports that for them this experience is not at all abnormal, exceptional, or incomprehensible; the possession of the god is so natural an outcome of the beliefs and practices they have learned that the unfortunates who 'have nothing in the head' are apt to be the maladjusted ones. Still, just what they have in the head is an open question.

At the same time, to view religion as symbolism is by no means to reduce it to mere fancy. Since man developed language he has always lived in a symbolic universe. 'Instead of dealing with the things themselves,' writes Ernst Cassirer, 'man is in a sense constantly conversing with himself. He has so enveloped himself in linguistic forms, in artistic images, in mythical symbols or religious rites, that he cannot see or know anything except by the interposition of this artificial medium.' Even in his most practical activities he is not face to face with the things in themselves or facts in the raw; his whole 'reality' is experienced through a language of symbols. All human reality is in some sense a spiritual reality, since it perforce includes things that are not seen. Religion is only the clearest example of a controlling symbolism. Call it mythology and it is still not a primitive way of misinterpreting or escaping the facts of life, but a comprehensive way of organizing and accepting the facts. The greater mythologies, such as the Greek and the Hebrew, symbolize ideas and ideals whose realism, range, and depth may be appreciated more fully if they are not taken for gospel truth.

Now, many civilized peoples have been content to accept their religion as a symbolic representation, tacitly if not openly. The Greeks and Romans took for granted that every people should have its own gods, and felt free to adopt foreign ones; the practical Chinese entertained hosts of deities, in a spirit of skepticism as well as hospitality; the deeply religious Hindus always assumed that Brahma had many different manifestations. All could respect the sacredness of other religions. The Western world, however, has had a radically different tradition. The Israelites introduced a very literal belief in a jealous God, who would tolerate no rivals. When Christianity took over the God of Israel, it intensified his concern with right belief; he punished not only the worship of other gods but erroneous opinion about his own unknowable nature. Mohammedanism, regarding itself as a purer form of these religions, was even more literal in its dogma.

In the past this dogmatism led to violent religious conflict, on a scale unknown to other civilizations. For centuries Christians persecuted Israel, warred on Islam, and fought most fanatically with one another; they were never able to agree on what was the literal truth. In the last century or so the traditional dogmatism has created a new problem for Christians. Orthodox Christianity has staked its whole authority on the historical truth of its sacred narratives, and this truth has been steadily eroded by scientific, historical inquiry. Scientific standards of truth are not the only possible standards, of course, but they are the necessary standards for claims to literal, factual, historical truth. They do not apply to the question whether Christ was the Son of God; they do apply to the question of just what he said and did on earth. Hence the claims of the orthodox churches not only appear contrary to fact but defy the principles on which reliable knowledge rests. Dogma, which has an evident value when it is innocent and unquestioned, may now produce an intellectual dishonesty fatal to the religious spirit.

Historic Christianity has also prepared means of escaping from this impasse. It has always insisted that the divine mind is literally incomprehensible, and warned against the presumption of declaring an intimate acquaintance with it. 'Thou thoughtest wickedly,' God said through the Psalmist, 'that I am even such an one as thyself.' St. Augustine added that if one knows the object of his belief, then what he knows is not God. Elsewhere Augustine said that the Incarnation was the only Christian doctrine he did not find in Platonism—and he could have found even this doctrine, in embryo, in the mystery-cults of the ancient world. Since Christian rites and beliefs were anticipated by pagan religions, their value need not depend on an exclusive divine revelation. Worshipers of a God of love should be pleased to think, with the Hindu, that he is above favoritism and has always revealed himself to all men who sought him—though none, of course, could expect to know him wholly. In any case, the fact is that from the outset Christianity developed a rich symbolism and mythology, which linked it with much older religious feeling.

A beautiful illustration of this development is the myth of the Virgin Mother, the symbol of love and mercy. In the Gospels Mary is mentioned very briefly, if only because of the natural embarrassment about the human family of Jesus; she does not appear as the merciful mother or play any part in his career. The legend of the virgin birth was apparently a later growth, since St. Paul never mentions it, and Luke and Matthew, the only Gospel authors who do mention it, are eager to stress that Jesus was a lineal descendant of David, through Joseph. Her rapid rise to popularity was not remarkable, however, for the ancient world had long known the Great Mother, and in Isis particularly had worshiped the loving and sorrowing mother. So she triumphed over the opposition of early theologians, who regarded the idea of a mother of God as a reversion to paganism. She became the chief patron of Eastern Christendom and later of medieval Europe, presiding over Chartres as over St. Sophia. A century ago she rose to new heights with the papal proclamation of the Immaculate Conception—a popular idea long opposed by eminent theologians (such as St. Thomas Aquinas) because it has no textual basis whatever in the Bible. Now her career has been crowned by the recent proclamation of the dogma that she went bodily to heaven, though the authors of Scripture knew nothing of this either.

As a historical figure, then, the Virgin Mother is legendary. Certainly her popularity has not been based on knowledge of the life of Mary; nor has her power over men been strengthened by the effort (of a Bishop of London, for example) to give the virgin birth some scientific standing, on the grounds of parthenogenesis in insects. As a symbol of man's hopes and ideals, however, she remains as lovely as ever. She is still the most vital religious symbol for millions of simple worshipers, for whom the Trinity is much too remote and abstract, and God himself too awful. That millions more have ceased to love her is no proof of the depth of their religious feeling and understanding, or of the wisdom of the churches. It is a melancholy comment on the state of religion in America today that Notre Dame, or Our Lady, is best known for her football team.

Hence she symbolizes the dilemma of modern Christianity. The Virgin was enthroned by the Roman Catholic Church, which has accumulated a remarkable wealth of symbolic representations as it cultivated the poetry of Christianity; yet it remains the most obstinate in maintaining the historical truth of its mythology, while making other concessions to temporal interests which vulgarize its magnificent poetry. Protestantism has renounced much of this poetry, tending to frown on the Virgin Mother as a Catholic superstition; yet its own literal versions of the Christian story seem as arbitrary, and are often harsher. Modernists are generally uneasy about both the myth and the dogma. While taking considerable liberties with traditional doctrines, they wish to preserve the traditional authority of whatever doctrines are dear to them, and are seldom willing to say unequivocally that these are symbolical. Others who are disposed to believe are of two minds and half a heart because they are unable to say plainly that Christianity is 'true'—true, that is, in the absolute sense it has claimed.

An example of how traditional attitudes confuse even 'advanced' thought is John Crowe Ransom's *God Without Thunder*. As a poet, Ransom is not merely content to accept religion as mythology—he glories in the myth. Its very virtue, he insists, is that it does not aspire to historical or scientific truth; it can therefore transcend the qualitatively meager abstractions of science and symbolize the fullness of history, in particular its most remarkable aspects. He condemns Westerners for their failure to see that myths are 'frankly' fables, which 'do not propose to compete with natural history.' Nevertheless Ransom wishes to retain the God of historic, institutional, orthodox Christianity, which has never regarded its myths as fables, and has always proposed to compete with natural history—for reasons that Ransom approves. Myths do not work in human civilization, he says, 'except when they are dogmas, tolerably hard, and exceedingly jealous of their rivals.' He defines the really religious person as the Fundamentalist, one who 'originally' chose his myth in the full consciousness that it was a myth, but then gave it his whole belief.[2] *'In effect,"* he writes, (the italics are his), *'the Fundamentalist does not any longer distinguish myth and fact';* and he adds, 'Why should he, if the myth is worth believing in?' In other words, myths are not facts but should be taken as facts; when they compete with facts one may simply say that they do not really compete; and so the poet still has the cake he ate.

Ransom also points to the final difficulty. Just as we respect myths, and recognize their necessity, we have to assert preferences among them. Ransom's preference is the Yahweh of ancient Israel. His *God Without Thunder* is an argument for a God *with* thunder: a God whom he frankly describes as stern, arbitrary, inscrutable, unaccountable, even frightful; a God who is not moral or rational by human standards, who is 'beyond good and evil,' and who visits his terrible wrath on the righteous and the wicked alike. One may agree that this God symbolizes the fact of human history more realistically than does the lawful, benevolent deity of liberal Christianity. One may wonder, however, why he should be worshiped, if worship is to be more than an act of fear or an ultimately vain effort at propitiation. An honest man may prefer the attitude of John Stuart Mill: 'Whatever power such a being may have over me, there is one thing which he shall not do; he shall not compel me to worship him. I will call no being good who is not what I mean when I apply that epithet to my fellow creatures; and if such a being can sentence me to hell for not so calling him, to hell I will go.'

This, of course, is the voice of mere reason. Still, it must

---

[2] This Fundamentalist, it might be noted, is a myth invented by Ransom, which also competes with natural history. The God of orthodox Christianity has rarely, if ever, been chosen in this spirit.

question faith, just as faith must question reason; for the greatest religious myths lead to profoundly different ways of life, and are the most liable to terrible abuse. (Hitler's creed, for instance, included versions of the basic Hebraic-Christian myths of a revelation, a golden age and a fall, a chosen people, a divinely inspired prophet, and a divinely constituted authority.) The rational approach to religion as a symbolical representation of the ideal, rather than a literal representation of the actual, might even promote a deeper piety. It might help to restore the feeling of richness that the modern world so often lacks in its religion, as in its philosophy, literature, and art. It might preserve the actual richness of Christianity—the wealth of ideal symbol, which in the form of dogma is apt to look as irrational or absurd as Mohammedan dogma looks to most Christians.[3] At any rate, our historical knowledge remains among the given terms of our religious problem. In these terms I am reviewing the legacy of Judaism: a splendid legacy that may stir a deeper, purer reverence than St. Sophia can, but that also calls for irony.

3. YAHWEH, A LIVING GOD

No drama in history is more fascinating than the rise of Yahweh. Starting out as an obscure deity of a despised people, apparently incapable of protecting them from their enemies, he nevertheless triumphed over his far more powerful rivals and eventually conquered a mighty civilization. Offhand, it is the very model of the success story—the story of a local god who made good, against terrific odds. And it is a story of character, not luck.

Toynbee brings out its moral by comparing Yahweh with Zeus. Both began their careers as barbaric warlords, tribal deities who had proved themselves in tribal warfare. Zeus was the first to be civilized, in the image of Greece. As a super-Greek he was concerned chiefly with his Olympian affairs, and had no particular purpose in mind for his human subjects. Hence he looked uneasy when poets and philosophers later tried to make him serve as the One God, the guarantor of a universal moral order. It was not merely that he had

[3] They may smile when Mohammed, a very literal prophet, describes heaven as 'The Garden,' a paradise with streams of milk and honey, silk garments, fair maidens, and other frankly sensual attractions; yet these heavenly furnishings are no more inappropriate than the golden streets and pearly gates of the Book of Revelation, and are less incongruous than the gunpowder that Milton's revolting angels dig up in *Paradise Lost*.

a disreputable past—he simply wasn't interested in the job. Eventually the Greeks paid him off with a heavenly sinecure, which enabled the peaceful old age suitable to his easygoing ways; but they sought their religion elsewhere. Yahweh, on the contrary, could grow with his people because he was always intensely purposeful, and had no other interests except his people. Once he had been endowed with benevolent purposes, and taught to concern himself with all mankind, he could become, as he did, the God of Judaism, Christianity, and Mohammedanism. As the Almighty, he still had a great disadvantage over the powerful rivals who had succeeded Zeus, the dying-gods of the popular mystery cults; for he alone was the creator and ruler of the universe. He gave meaning and purpose to the whole history of man.

The most inspiring theme of this story is the education of Yahweh himself. 'The Lord is a man of war!' Moses had exulted. In victory he was merciless, commanding his people to slaughter their enemies, man, woman, and child. The Lord was also an Oriental despot, fiercely jealous of his prerogatives; he was apt to slaughter his own people for disrespect, and announced that he would punish even their children unto the third and fourth generation. In his inordinate hunger for flattery he at first had little interest in the moral principles of his subjects. What is apparently the earliest recorded version of the Decalogue (in Exodus 34) makes righteousness purely a matter of ritual. 'Thou shalt not seethe a kid in his mother's milk,' Yahweh concludes, sanctifying a primitive taboo that reflects as little concern for the maternal sentiments of goats as for the ideal aspirations of man. In general, the ancient religion of Israel was about as depressing as other primitive religions. 'It is pathetic,' writes Santayana, 'to observe how lowly are the motives that religion, even the highest, attributes to the deity, and from what a hard-pressed and bitter existence they have been drawn. To be given the best morsel, to be remembered, to be praised, to be obeyed blindly and punctiliously—these have been thought points of honor with the gods, for which they would dispense favors and punishments on the most exorbitant scale.'

With the rise of the prophets, however, Yahweh was committed to moral principles. Amos declared that he cared nothing for ceremonial worship but only for justice and righteousness. Hosea stressed not merely his righteousness but his love, and made him lovable. Micah summed up this new ideal with a sublime simplicity that no other religion has surpassed: 'He hath showed thee, O man, what is good; and what doth the Lord require of thee, but to do justly, and to love mercy, and to walk humbly with thy God?' Then

Isaiah made Yahweh the One God of all mankind. The Israelites remained his chosen people but they had been chosen to make him known to the rest of mankind, and so to make possible universal salvation. Although Yahweh was still an anthropomorphic God, the prophets remade him in an ideal image of man—of man as he aspires to be in his loftiest moments.

Or at least they approached this ideal. Unfortunately there was still much of the old Yahweh in the God of Israel, much that survives to this day; and here is the root of our religious problem. He had announced himself to Moses as a 'jealous God,' commanding first of all that no other gods should be tolerated, and he remained jealous when his sway was extended to the whole race of man. Under Christianity and Mohammedanism he was able to become militant—in Israel he was less aggressive if only because his nation was weak. And in this 'relentless intolerance' of Yahweh Toynbee sees the primary reason for his astonishing triumph. The gods of the pagan world were easy-going, willing to live and let live; so all went down before this implacable adversary who was content with nothing short of 'total victory.'

Such contempt for 'false' gods may appear as a supreme piety, a reverence befitting the One True God. In Israel it looks offhand like a supremely selfless faith, since God blessed his chosen people by chastening them, requiring them to endure an earthly lot considerably worse than that of his other children. Yet their scorn of religions sacred to other peoples also looks like provinciality, bigotry, and conceit. It was essentially an irrational sentiment, based on sheer ignorance of most other religions, and fortified by a refusal even to consider their claims. It had terrible consequences, in the long, bloody history of persecution. It explains why Christianity, with its message of peace and good will, has been a major cause of war and ill will. Toynbee concludes that only through a 'spirit of uncompromising exclusiveness' can man firmly grasp 'the profound and elusive truth of the unity of God.' If so, it appears that the cost of God's unity will remain the profound disunity of mankind, and even of his own worshipers; for the elusive truth continues to elude most of mankind.

Yahweh himself, it seems, was sometimes disposed to tolerance. Thus Isaiah expected him to 'do a new thing,' delivering the righteous of all nations in a universal peace. But these different moods of Yahweh raise another problem. The simplest way of symbolizing the manifold diversity of the universe, and of its ideal possibilities, is to create many gods, like the Greeks, or to recognize different incarnations of the

One God, like the Hindus. Under a pure monotheism it is difficult to harmonize this diversity. The actual result in the Western world has been widely different representations of the divine personality, which have inspired as different kinds of behavior. For the moment we may distinguish two main traditions. In the Old Testament Yahweh is occasionally represented as a kind Father, whose children should accordingly love him and love one another. More often he is represented as a Lord, a King, whose servants should fear him.

Christianity has emphasized the Father, whose loving kindness is symbolized chiefy by the Son and the Mother. From the Fatherhood comes the ideal of the brotherhood of man, with the most distinctive Christian virtue of charity. The sublime example is the life of St. Francis of Assisi, but perhaps the greatest glory of Christianity is the least conspicuous—the forgotten blessing of all the simple pastors who have worked in this spirit, and all the humble lives that have been sweetened by it. At the same time, such gentle ideals are apt to soften into sentimentality. Liberal Christianity of the last two centuries may fairly be charged with tender-mindedness and shallowness, in particular a blindness to the tragic realities of evil. There are also logical difficulties when the symbol of the loving Father is taken as the literal, essential truth about God. Love is so far from being the ruling principle of the creation, with its endless pain, strife, and misery, that Christianity itself has described the world as a vale of tears. The chief proof of God's love then turns out to be the hope he offers that some of his children may escape the evils of his handiwork.

For such reasons Christianity has also retained the fierce Yahweh, the symbol of the King who inspires fear. 'How are you going to love,' asked Tertullian, 'unless you are afraid not to love?' There was good reason for being afraid. Under Christianity Yahweh had grown ever fiercer, creating a hell in which he could torture his enemies through all eternity.[4] As an Oriental king, at any rate, he tended to be arbitrary. Although he might be gracious and kind, men had no claims on his kindness, no rights to justice. Thus he never really answered Job's anguished questions about the unmerited suffering of the righteous: he simply boasted of his power and skill in the art of world-making, rejecting any responsibility for making his scheme intelligible to man. (The Hollywood happy

---

[4] Judaism, it should be added, did not officially accept this hell. In so far as it speculated on punishment in an after-life, it generally conceived something like the Moslem hell—a purgatory in which punishment is terrible and prolonged but not eternal. Yahweh was too powerful to permit a Satan to lord it eternally over a realm of his own.

ending, in which Job is given twice as much wealth as he had had, together with a second set of children, only emphasizes the capriciousness of Yahweh.) Many Christian thinkers have been more explicit in denying the moral claims of man. St. Paul asserted that God bestowed his saving grace without regard to merit, and St. Augustine, Luther, and Calvin systematized this arbitrary scheme of salvation. To the natural complaints about its apparent injustice, all answered that man has no right to set up his own standards or to assert his own merits; God's infinite goodness is sufficiently displayed by his willingness to save any men at all. Both Judaism and Christianity have maintained that God must be given the credit for all the goodness in human history, and that man must take the blame for all the evil. Nor is this kind of theology outmoded. Karl Barth, one of the most influential of modern Protestant theologians, is the most vigorous champion of the stern, unaccountable Yahweh. Nicolas Berdyaev deplores the assertion of human standards of justice and goodness as 'an unwillingness to accept the will of God.' John Crowe Ransom condemns it as 'fastidious,' and his realism maintains stoutly, even proudly, that Yahweh can be simply awful.

Such views of God no doubt make some sense in their very denial that there must be sense by human standards. There would be no religion, indeed, were there not this vast, awful unknown. Yet one may face the mystery humbly without groveling before it, or exalting its most awful, unintelligible aspects. It is one thing to recognize that the ways of deity are beyond human reason; it is another thing to despise reason, and to condemn loyalty to the highest ideals that man can conceive. Without such loyalty religion is reduced to a worship of mere power, and men might as well worship Satan or the law of gravitation. Archbishop Whateley summarized the issue:

If one attaches no meaning to the words 'good' and 'just' and 'right' except that such is the divine command, then to say that God is good and his commands just is only saying in a circuitous way that he is what he is, and that he wills what he wills, which might equally be said of any being in the universe.

Hence the revival of the old Yahweh in recent times does not suggest a genuine reverence. It looks like what Toynbee himself calls archaism—'a withdrawal according to plan rather than a pilgrimage inspired by faith.' Its most apparent value is not in inspiring men to do their best but in preparing them to endure the worst.

Even the reformed Yahweh, however, finally raises another problem—the problem of any God conceived as a person. Through all his mutations Yahweh remained very personal. He was indeed He—a Somebody, not an It. Christianity came to endow him with an elaborate set of intellectual and spiritual attributes, purely verbal qualities derived from the assumption that his nature could not be expressed in words; yet it clung to his person. It brought him even closer to men by granting them a personal immortality comparable to his. (In their awe of the Lord, the authors of the Old Testament had assumed that he alone was immortal.) Today so subtle a theologian as Étienne Gilson still discovers a supreme importance in the fact that Yahweh means 'He who is'; whereas the God of Plato and Spinoza is merely a 'that which is,' unreal and inhuman.

The advantage that Christianity had in this legacy is evident enough. A personal God enables other persons to come into vital relation with him. If simple people in particular need a human God, even the most thoughtful may appreciate him when they consider, say, the purely logical God of Aristotle. As the Unmoved Mover, it has no interest in what it has moved; as Pure Thought, it has nothing to think about except itself. It is utterly self-sufficient, and nothing less than itself can be worthy of its concern. It is everything that an absolutely perfect God ought logically to be. Everything, that is, except God. For our living purposes it amounts to a Nonentity, mindless, impotent, and inane. It may inspire contemplation of its own self-hypnotic kind, but it cannot inspire creative thought or bless any effort. Worship is pointless, since it is rapt in a ceaseless, sufficient contemplation of itself. Only by giving this pure abstraction the name of God can man create the illusion that it is adorable.

Still, an Absolute is clearly more rational than Yahweh; and here is the dilemma. The authors of the Old Testament had no philosophy. They had a simple, absolute faith that the Lord *was,* that the whole universe testified to him, and that all this was self-evident. They did not have to find him by introspection or mystical experience; they did not have to formulate a creed or rationalize their faith. If, like Job, they were troubled by Yahweh's behavior, they never dreamed of questioning his existence or his majesty. The logic of their faith was simply that Yahweh had declared himself, to Abraham, to Jacob, and most completely to Moses. So too with Christianity. Though it took to philosophy when it entered the Greek world, it always based its authority on the apostolic tradition, the teaching of those to whom Jesus had declared himself. It is on a divine revelation that the claims of both Judaism and Christianity finally rest. And when one surveys the history of civilization, these claims may look arbitrary and provincial.

Thus Gilson concludes a subtle metaphysical proof of the necessity of a personal God by making a sudden leap. 'He who is,' he says flatly, is 'the God of Abraham, of Isaac, and of Jacob.' If so, the vast majority of mankind might wonder why he did not reveal himself to them too. They might object even to claims of more liberal theologians, such as James Parkes. Parkes grants that the historical reality of a divine revelation cannot be proved, but believes that there was such a revelation at both Sinai and Calvary; only so can we understand the enormous influence of these two obscure happenings. It seems clear that something very important did happen at Sinai and Calvary. But something important also happened at Mecca, in ancient Persia, and in ancient India. Parkes does not mention Mohammed, Zoroaster, or Buddha, who exerted as enormous an influence on the basis of quite different revelations. To Buddha it was revealed that God was not. So it seems necessary to make the commonplace observation that had Gilson, Parkes, or any of the rest of us been born in India or China, we should not be talking about 'He who is,' and might never have heard about Yahweh.

The chief difficulty, however, is even more obvious. The whole assumption that man is the special concern of a personal Creator, or even the reason for the creation, may have been plausible when this earth was believed to be the center of a cozy universe, but it seems wildly improbable in the light of our present knowledge. Contemporaries have to reconcile their idea of God with the idea of millions of island universes, and millions of centuries before man appeared on this obscure planet. With all respect for the conscious life of man, they may be unable to believe that its recent emergence is the main point of so stupendous a spectacle.

Many religious philosophers have accordingly tended to conceive of an impersonal or a limited deity. To William James God was the ideal tendency in things; to others God is the mind or soul of the universe. This deity is apt to be given such unattractive names as Infinite and Eternal Energy, or Principle of Concretion. It leaves open the question of where all the unideal tendencies come from. It is emotionally less satisfying than Yahweh. Nevertheless the deepest religious thought of other societies, such as Greece, India, and China, has not required this kind of emotional satisfaction. The felt need of a personal God—not to mention a personal immortality—is a product of our tradition, not a requirement of human nature or the religious spirit itself. Simply to preserve the value of this tradition we need to see it in perspective and feel free to readapt it. Gilson maintains that 'any religious God whose true name is not "He who is" is nothing but a myth'; but it is the God of Abraham, Isaac, and Jacob who seems mythical today. With all his anachronisms, Yahweh has become a source of perplexity and embarrassment. A literal insistence that he is the personal ruler of the stellar universe may force the religious spirit to seek elsewhere for illumination.

4. THE SACRED BOOK

When the early Christians took the Old Testament with them as they set out to convert the Gentiles, they had an inestimable advantage over all their rivals. No other religion in the empire possessed a Book. The mystery cults no doubt had some advantage in the secrecy of their initiation rites, but for the long run there was a far more powerful appeal in the possession of a Book—an open book, available to all men. Christians entrenched themselves behind it as they fought off pagan critics. They were not the upstarts they appeared to be, but the inheritors of a sacred tradition much older than Rome itself. They had God's own word, eloquent and explicit, for his grand plan, his commandments, his covenants. Above all, they had a book magnificent in its own right—the greatest single work, I should say, that man has produced. In spite of its unmystical and unmetaphysical spirit the Old Testament reaches exalted conceptions of the unity of God, and of men before God; because of this spirit it remains a rich source of inspiration for all men, instead of a book of secrets for priests and theologians. It surpasses all other scriptures in the range and variety of its religious poetry and drama. Its prophets in particular stand out from other religious leaders of mankind in the eloquence of their protests against social injustice.

In short, men had reason to believe that so noble a work was the work of God himself. But this belief again raises the bogey of literalness. A Sacred Book is always likely to obstruct both moral and intellectual enlightenment, by sanctifying the prejudices as well as the inspired visions of its time and place. It is always a source of confusion and controversy, often leading to bigotry and hatred; for the word of God never proves to be clear and consistent.

These difficulties vanish when the Old Testament is taken for what it unmistakably is in the light of scholarly research —not a uniformly inspired expression of a uniform creed, but a record of the moral and religious evolution of an extraordinary people. In this view we can easily explain all the prehistoric taboos, naïve superstitions, and barbarous customs embedded in it, and as easily discount all the Oriental bombast inspired by a ferocious tribal deity. We may even sympathize with the old Yahweh because he was so obviously fallible, 'repenting' what he had said or done, and sometimes wrathfully suspecting that his whole idea of creating man had been a mistake in the first place; like De Lawd of *Green Pastures,* he is often unhappy at the way things keep going on his earth. More important, we may realize the full grandeur of the prophets, who rose from the idol to the ideal, transforming an ordinary tribal religion into a unique ethical monotheism. We may admire the most remarkable quality of the 'peculiar people,' which was not their fidelity to their ancient Yahweh but their earnest quest of God. For it is as a quest that the whole religious history of mankind can be best understood and appreciated.

Whatever he may think, no educated Christian actually accepts the whole Bible as literally true. The most orthodox resorts to historical or metaphorical explanations as he deals with manifest inconsistencies, or explains away the plain meaning of such texts as 'Thou shalt not suffer a witch to live.' Indeed, the ministry could hardly survive without figurative interpretations; every Sunday thousands of sermons resound with meanings that the authors of the Bible could never have dreamed of. Nevertheless most churchmen still maintain that the Sacred Book is in effect the word of God, on a different basis from the Scriptures of all other religions. They reject the basic findings of the 'higher criticism'; they insist on the literal truth of all texts involving their dogma; they constantly quote Scripture to clinch their contradictory arguments. They are at once so highly fanciful and so profoundly unimaginative in their use of the greatest of books that we are again forced to begin at the beginning.

The beginning was sufficiently ironical. The early scribes felt quite free to edit the narratives that were to form the basis of the Pentateuch, even though their editing was careless and uncritical by modern standards. Then the prophets introduced their revolutionary new conceptions of Yahweh; they were considerably more radical than the Christian modernists of our day. As revolutionary was the Book of Deuteronomy, discovered in the late seventh century B.C. Among other things, this 'second' statement of the Mosaic law forbade the traditional worship at the 'high places' of Israel and decreed that henceforth sacrifices could be offered to Yahweh only in Jerusalem, a city unknown to Moses. This new revelation, however, was the turning point. Even while the prophets were transforming the Yahweh of the old writings, the priests began canonizing these writings. By the end of the fifth century they had become fixed. One reason for this halt to the religious growth of Israel was simply the magic of the written word, which has always awed simple minds; but the immediate reason was the priestly interest in a strict observance of the Law. Before fixing the sacred writings, accordingly, the priests again revised them—inserting the deadly genealogies, elaborating the Law in minute detail, editing the historical narratives to prove that the fortunes of Israel had always depended on the observance of the Law. At worst, their devotion to forms and ceremonies reduced an extraordinary religious history to a dead letter; they give the impression, as Frazer remarked, that the creation itself was merely a prelude to the institution of the sabbath. At best, they kept the letter alive by inculcating habits that made for piety, weaving the Law into daily life. At any rate, Israel became the 'people of the Book.'

The New Testament had a similar history. Jesus himself had taken liberties with the Scriptures of Israel that he revered. 'It hath been said, An eye for an eye, and a tooth for a tooth: But I say unto you—' and with this refrain he rejected a series of the traditional teachings. When his followers broke away from Judaism they had to take further liberties, since they were no longer obeying much of the ceremonial Law that was plainly enjoined in the Scriptures. Meanwhile they also had to formulate their new tradition. Thus we have four different Gospels because the early Christians had no one authoritative narrative. St. Luke declared that he wrote his because he 'had perfect understanding of all things from the very first' and wanted his excellent friend Theophilus to 'know the certainty of those things'; but if so, the other authors had an imperfect, uncertain understanding. The Gospel according to St. John introduces so different an interpretation of the life and thought of Jesus, in the light of Greek thought, that it amounts to a 'higher criticism' of the other gospels. It even suggests something like an evolutionary view of religion in its promise of further revelation: 'I have yet many things to say unto you, but ye cannot bear them now. Howbeit when he, the Spirit of truth, is come, he will guide you into all truth.'

The canonization of these writings was again due to priestly needs. The scattered Christian churches, which St. Paul's Epistles make clear had been established before the gospels were written, naturally felt the need of a uniform, authoritative belief. The Epistles also indicate the fierce controversies

among the early Christians, and illustrate the seemingly haphazard processes of divine inspiration. Paul wrote his letters
in bad Greek, sometimes hurriedly, often vehemently; in his
haste he was apt to be casual or imprecise, in his passion, to
be immoderate or obscure; and he never had a thought that
he was writing a New Testament.[5] Then later Christians, involved in different controversies, decided that these letters
were verbally inspired Scriptures that expressed nothing more
nor less than the truth.

Now, the authors of both the Old and the New Testament
narratives, like most Orientals, had little regard for truth by
modern standards. They were by no means dishonest—they
were simply devoted to a 'higher' truth, to which all facts
and legends had to conform. They were writing something
much more important than history. Still, they were not trustworthy historians. The evident inaccuracies, inconsistencies,
and fabulous aspects of their narratives were bound to raise
difficulties for more learned philosophical readers; and in the
Greek world Christianity had to face these difficulties. St.
Augustine stated the problem baldly: 'I should not believe in
the Gospel if I had not the authority of the Church for so
doing.' A more rigorous logician might observe that since the
Church derived its authority from the Gospel, his belief was
quite arbitrary.

The Greeks also suggested a solution to this problem, in
the method of allegorical interpretation they had cultivated
when they discovered that their immortal Homer had told
lies about the gods. Philo, a Hellenistic Jew, made elaborate
use of this method, and the Church Fathers were generally
fond of it. Origen, the great master of it, was at times as
forthright and bold as a modern critic; he not only denied the
literal truth of much of Genesis but treated some stories in
the New Testament as fables. And though Origen was later
condemned by the Church, the search for allegorical meanings was still permitted. St. Augustine was pleased to see in
the drunkenness of Noah a symbol of the death and passion
of Christ. The Church itself was pleased to accept allegorical
interpretations of some unholy texts. 'Thy two breasts are
like two young roes that are twins, which feed among the
lilies,' sings the sensual lover of the Song of Solomon. Here,
according to the translators of our Bible, Christ setteth forth
the graces of the Church.

These phantasies, however, indicate why the method of al-

---

[5] To the Galatians he wrote, 'Now a mediator is not a mediator of
one, but God is one.' A theologian reports that his fellow-scholars have
given some 430 different explanations of this text, and wonders what the
unfortunate Galatians could have made of it.

legory as practiced hardly made the revelation more intelligible or consistent. Fancy was allowed to run wild in embroidering the Sacred Book, but the exercise of critical judgment was not allowed. Origen expected, the allegorical interpreters were neither scholarly nor genuinely imaginative. They knew little or nothing about the origins of the sacred writings, had no idea of religious evolution. They were not distinguishing fact from fable; they were simply looking for cryptic truths beneath the literal truths. They could not do otherwise, within the Church. The Church condemned Origen because his principle of individual judgment threatened both its authority and the authenticity of the Biblical narratives. Hence the Sacred Book was made a closed book, effectively sealed against objective analysis and judgment. Later the Church would discourage ordinary Christians from even reading it.

The historical consequences of this whole development are incalculable. Merely as religious poetry and drama the Bible is inspiring enough to many men; but unquestionably it has inspired many more, and more deeply, because of the belief that it is the very word of God. We cannot begin to estimate all that this belief has contributed to the life of Western man, in solace and joy, and in incentive to simple goodness. Unhappily, however, we can estimate some of its deplorable consequences. The victims of the sacred text include many thousands of old women who were burned at the stake because a witch shall not be suffered to live. We can roughly count the casualties of the frightful epidemics of credulity and cruelty—not to mention the holy wars—during the sixteenth and seventeenth centuries, the age in which the Bible was read more diligently than ever before or since. But the chief victims were the Jews themselves, the people of the Book. Even the Old Testament contributed to their prolonged martyrdom: they suffered the more because of the unsparing honesty of their prophets, who were quoted against them. The New Testament provided more explicit texts. Christians might well have overlooked the increasing animosity reflected in the Gospels, from Mark to John, remembering the words of Jesus: 'Father, forgive them; for they know not what they do.' Instead, they chose to take literally the appalling text in St. Matthew, when the people demand that Pontius Pilate crucify Jesus: 'His blood be on us, and on our children.' With the triumph of Christianity, the children of Israel had to repay his suffering a millionfold.

In this century Jewry has been persecuted on political and racial rather than religious grounds. Prejudice and intolerance have taken new forms; the most violent hatreds can no longer be attributed to bibliolatry or religion. Nevertheless religious prejudice still smolders all over the Christian and Moslem worlds, and still has the sanction of their Books. It flares up often enough among the orthodox. We dare not take for granted that it is a mere anachronism, certain to disappear; there remains a vast store of ignorance and misunderstanding, which are the more inflammable because of the deep anxieties of the modern world. At least those who believe in tolerance need to consider the sacred sources of intolerance. Even today the churches have too seldom taken the lead in the struggle against anti-Semitism, if only because the ultimate source of anti-Semitism is the New Testament itself. But the spirit of Jesus appears to have been different. This spirit is the final argument for the moral obligation to regard the Scriptures as human interpretations of a possibly divine revelation, not stenographic transcripts of the word of God.

5. The Divine Purpose in History

Prophetic Judaism is especially pertinent for us today because it was born of pain and evil, matured during desperate crisis, and triumphed in catastrophe. From the disasters of the nation, the prophets drew a high, unique moral. They declared that these disasters were a divine judgment on the chosen people, who had departed from the paths of righteousness and holiness, and that the people could be saved only by a return to these paths, not by politics or military victory. This was a heretical afterthought: the old Yahweh had plainly fallen down on his appointed job as warlord and protector of the tribe. As the priests went on to reinterpret the whole history of Israel in these terms, they freely suppressed, distorted, and invented. (Thus Omri, who founded so great a dynasty that the mighty Assyrians mentioned it in an inscription, was dismissed in a single verse, because he had tolerated the ancient worship of golden calves.) But in falsifying the actual history they helped to create a more significant history. The prophets had evolved a more rational, responsible theory of history than any other people had yet conceived. Instead of foisting history on Fate, they explained it by human character and conduct. Even in their utopian visions of the Messiah and the restoration of Israel they retained their moral realism. The idea of progress implicit in these visions was no automatic progress; man would first have to learn, through suffering, to be righteous and just. Meanwhile the prophets saw history as tragedy, and they did not soften it by easy promises of heaven for their followers or hell for their enemies.

The moral value of this conception of history is plain. It puts the issue squarely up to man, declaring his responsibility for good and evil. It demands that the rulers of this earth serve a higher law than the state. It warns the Church itself against the besetting sin of self-righteousness, emphasizing that God judges his own community most severely. And if the prophets let Yahweh off too easily, in absolving him of all responsibility for his creation, they put him too on his best behavior. It was not metaphysical speculation but the idea of history as a moral order that led them to the idea of a universal God. They came to realize that as the author of such an order Yahweh could have no real rivals, and that he could not be a merely national god either. No less important was their simple conviction that life is real and earnest. While most of the higher religions have denied man's history on earth any intrinsic value, seeking chiefly to escape it, the prophets of Israel insisted that it was intensely meaningful. When they asked men to renounce worldly wealth and power they invoked higher worldly goods. Life had to fulfil itself on this earth, or nowhere.

For such reasons the gospel of the prophets was always a social gospel, not a means to private salvation. They were not saints bent on saving their own immortal souls; they did not dwell on the ecstasies of their personal relations with God; they did not preach 'the value of religious experience' as a means of feeling uplifted. They themselves represented the highest ideal of Judaism: prophets exhorting their fellowmen to follow God through righteousness and social justice. For the divine purpose in history as they conceived it could be fulfilled only by a community. The individual was not an end in himself; he could be truly good and truly happy only by living and working in harmony with other servants of God. Judaism was unique in its idea of a dedicated community, a whole people that had a covenant or social contract with God, and that in time came to realize that this covenant was not merely a special favor but an awful responsibility.

Like all noble ideals, this gospel was patently liable to abuse. The later priests dwelt lovingly on the legal terms of the contract; they never wearied of expounding 'Israel's title-deeds.' The very idea of a covenant is apt to encourage self-righteousness. For all its exalted possibilities, it comes down to an extravagant version of the tribal conceit that all peoples have. Even in disaster, as Morris Cohen observed, the people might be too complacent, and indulge in the futile satisfaction of telling their enemies 'Our Father is a Policeman.' The prophets themselves repeatedly fell back upon naïve versions of the messianic dream, in which Israel triumphed at the expense of the rest of mankind.

At best, however, their interpretation of history calls for considerable discount. To begin with, we cannot take it literally. The prophets all believed that the Day of Judgment was close at hand, and generally agreed that the new age would come through a direct intervention by God; in the continued absence of any clear signs from God we must regard their prophecies as symbolic of a hope, an ideal. We need to discount as well their basic idea of history as the scene of God's judgment upon human evil. Although they will always appear to be right, since men are always sinful enough to justify almost any catastrophe that befalls them, their belief was based on considerable ignorance. They had little notion of natural causes, physical or social. The failure of crops, defeat in war, fire, famine, flood, plague—all were due to God's will, or man's sin; the prophets had no criterion for distinguishing between curable and incurable evils. And the conclusion of the drama was essentially arbitrary. The future they looked forward to was not a natural, logical consequence of the past: like the *deus ex machina* of Euripides, God would simply step in and arrange a happy ending.

Even as a symbolic interpretation of history, accordingly, the prophetic vision calls for further reservations. It represents the tradition of 'Hebraism' that Matthew Arnold contrasted with Hellenism.[6] This is a lofty tradition, and always pertinent; no doubt men cannot be reminded too often, or too earnestly, of their moral responsibilities. It is also a narrow tradition, and apt to become harsh. The prophets were indifferent to the arts and sciences, to other forms of excellence besides righteousness, or to the ideal of excellence for its own sake. They could not do justice to the wondrous pageant of history, including the many glorious works that man has created in spite of his sinfulness. They ignored the uses of reason and knowledge even in their own cause of social justice and moral responsibility. In general, they had little understanding or appreciation of civilization itself. Essentially they were primitivists, calling for a return to the

---

[6] Israel itself, of course, was not so single-minded or austere as its prophets. The Old Testament also contains the richly varied sentiments of the Psalms, the idyllic charm of the story of Ruth, the humor of the Book of Jonah, the Epicurean broodings of Ecclesiastes, the love songs of Solomon, and the tormented doubts of Job.

simple virtues of the ancestors. They could see the natural evils of civilization but not the positive contributions that had made possible their own noble visions. They were unable to realize that the Patriarchs were not prophets like themselves, and in their primitive society could not have been.

Altogether, the prophetic vision of history reflects an unconcern about history as we understand it; and it forces a vital issue if we still wish to make history. The prophets were not merely indifferent to worldly wealth, power, and wisdom—they were content to see their society destroyed, in their sublime confidence that God's purposes would thereby be fulfilled. It was enough for them that a 'remnant' would survive the destruction, to usher in the new age. Today, judgment of their policy will finally depend on the opinion whether or not our civilization is worth saving. One who regards it as essentially vile will naturally tend to be indifferent, like the prophets, to worldly strategies for preserving it. His only faith can be in the will of God; his problem, as stated by G. Ernest Wright, is 'How does one become a member of the remnant?' One who believes, on the contrary, that our civilization is not simply evil may still welcome most of the teaching of the prophets, in particular their impassioned denunciation of injustice; but he must also seek more worldly wisdom and invest more faith in human effort. His problems, needless to add, are manifold.

6. Epilogue: The History of Israel

Henceforth, said Johanan ben Zakkai when Jerusalem was destroyed in A.D. 70, the Jews would have only the Almighty and his Law; but this would suffice. That it did indeed suffice, and through far worse trials than he could have foreseen, is the unique glory of Judaism. The covenanted community was scattered over the face of the earth, despised, oppressed, persecuted, exposed to a martyrdom more cruel and prolonged than any other people has had to endure; yet it preserved its identity and its faith. It outlived all its more powerful and prosperous neighbors. It survived while Assyria, Babylon, Persia, Greece, Rome, Byzantium, and Arabia went into the shades.

For the Western world, the plainest meaning of the history of Israel is the ugliest. It is Christendom that has made this history so heroic, and so appalling. The martyrdom that Christians suffered in their early history was negligible compared with the martyrdom they later inflicted on the Jews.

The victims of the Roman Empire were a few thousand in number, and their fortitude was made easier by the promise of an immediate reunion with Christ in heaven. Israel cannot number or name its millions of martyrs, and has given them no halo, no guarantee of a heavenly reward; although the idea of an after-life became popular as the national hopes were disappointed, it did not become a flaming conviction or essential article of faith. Nor have the anonymous millions been granted the ordinary consolations and exaltations of dying for a cause. In the Roman Empire they could fight and die heroically; in Christendom they were simply massacred, in sudden, meaningless pogroms. This is an old story, and a monotonous one. It is so familiar that it is too easily forgotten—as already American leaders seem to have forgotten the millions slaughtered by Germany in the last war.

The recent shift from religious to racial prejudice only accentuates the barbarous irrationality beneath the surface of Western civilization. The medieval Church at least did not scorn Jews as a race; it constantly sought to convert them (and by its failure proved their integrity, since by conversion they could have escaped all persecution). In fact, the Jews are as mixed a race as most other peoples, including the Nordic. In various parts of Asia they are apparently indistinguishable from the natives, looking and acting like Chinese, like Arabs, like highlanders of the Caucasus. Their 'racial' characteristics in the West have largely been created by the West. They were segregated in ghettos, and then accused of clannishness; they were forced to wear a yellow badge of infamy, and then accused of furtiveness; they were encouraged to be moneylenders—a profession that jeopardized a Christian's chances of salvation—and then accused of avarice. In America today they are condemned for being shrewd, mercenary, and acquisitive, or in other words for beating other Americans at the national game; but they are also feared because they dominate certain trades and professions, into which they are forced because they are discriminated against in other trades and professions.

What chiefly distinguishes the Jews, indeed, is not merely their stubborn faith but their adaptability. 'We are not a commercial people,' Josephus explained to the Romans, '... and have no inclination to trade.' Under the later empire, however, they were among the chief traders. Similarly with their habitat. A predominantly agricultural people, they settled in cities after the diaspora; when they were excluded from Western Europe and made Eastern Europe their center, they returned to the countryside; when they emigrated to America, they became an urban people again. Likewise, the fierce enemies of Hellenism have developed a reputation as a peculiarly intellectual people, with a passion for learning. Under the relatively tolerant rule of Islam they made important contributions to philosophy and science; Maimonides created an impressive theology that is as remote from Biblical Judaism as the theology of Aquinas is from the Gospels. With the coming of the Enlightenment in Europe, they produced so many brilliant composers, mathematicians, and scientists that they have been credited with a racial genius for such pursuits. Actually, the only apparent genius is an indomitable energy and resourcefulness that are concentrated on whatever opportunities are open to them.[7] But in any event they can count on being attacked by their frustrated neighbors: because they have become assimilated, or because they have not become assimilated; because they are nationalistic, or internationalistic.

This resourcefulness, however, brings up the ambiguous implications of the history of Israel. In retrospect, the national tragedy of the dispersion was also a blessing. The fall of Jerusalem destroyed the power of the priestly aristocracy. It strengthened the inwardness of the prophets, the stress upon spirit instead of forms. It purified Judaism by forcing the substitution of the synagogue for the temple, of prayer and conduct for sacrifice and ceremony. It rescued Judaism from the worst excesses of its tendencies to legalism and to militancy. After the dispersion there could hardly be a papacy to impose dogma, or an Inquisition to punish heretics. When the autonomous communities looked to some great teacher or commentator, they were influenced by his prestige, not by his official position. Over the centuries during which Christendom has been inflamed by the popular lies of an international conspiracy of Jewry, there has never been a central authority or conclave. (Although an attempt was made in the sixteenth century to center religious authority in Palestine, it was denounced by the head of the College in Jerusalem and came to nothing.) And like early Christianity, Israel was strengthened by persecution. It was not merely faith that held the covenanted community together—it was Christian violence. Christian practice gave them little reason for regarding their

---

[7] A. L. Kroeber notes that the line of Jewish world champions in chess, unbroken over some years, might have suggested a peculiar Jewish genius for chess; but then the line was broken, by Cuban, Russian, and Dutch champions. One reason for such spectacular local successes, Kroeber adds, is that their coherence as a minority group enables the Jews to mobilize more quickly and win temporary dominance in a new field—as in recent times, for example, they have dominated psychoanalysis and Broadway entertainment.

own religion as inferior, and it helped them to maintain a loftier, more consistent social morality.

Yet they were also warped by the national disaster. Before the first captivity in Babylon, Judaism had been a growing, creative religion. Now the loss of political freedom brought a loss in religious freedom. As Israel fell back on the Law, the Law was made rigid, tight, and binding. The prophet gave way to the high priest and then to the annotator; the religious genius that had created the Old Testament was confined to the commentaries of the Talmud; then the Talmud, too, was closed. Moreover, the Law fixed the national role as a peculiar people. Their jealous God made them intolerant, their religious food laws made them unsociable. Hence they antagonized the tolerant, civic-minded Greeks, who were at first inclined to respect them as a community of 'philosophers' because of their strange habit of discussing religion in their temples; their contempt of pagan beliefs and customs led to pogroms in Alexandria long before the ascending of Christian intolerance. And they fatally antagonized the Romans. Their suicidal uprisings in Palestine, which ended in the death or enslavement of more than a million Jews, took place during the *Pax Romana,* when the rest of the Mediterranean world was enjoying a peace that it had never known before.

Ultimately, both the glory and the tragedy of Israel sprang from the exalted, inhuman conviction that they, and they alone, were God's chosen people. Chosen peoples are not apt to make good neighbors. Their refusal to make peace with their Greek neighbors and their Roman rulers could be highminded and heroic, or it could be narrow-minded and perverse. Often it was plain fanaticism. The chosen people resented the tolerance and humanism of Hellenistic civilization as fiercely as they resented its immorality and paganism. When the ruthless, able, statesman-like Herod the Great restored the glory of Palestine, they could forgive his brutality but not his alien birth or his fondness for Greek culture. When they were exploited by their own rich, priestly aristocracy they were docile—until the aristocracy grew friendly with the Greeks. 'As has always been the case in the East,' writes Kirsopp Lake, 'the people submitted to extortion but rebelled against civilization.' And in their periodic uprisings their Zealots were as brutal as their rulers, massacring thousands of Gentiles, and murdering many of their fellow-Jews who opposed their violence. In general, the people were incapable of the humble, charitable attitude implicit in the teaching of their greatest prophets. The history of Israel, like the history of Christian Europe, suggests that no nation and no sect can afford to regard itself as the elect of God.

Today the spirit of Israel is rather different. After two thousand years the people have regained their national independence; as the prophets predicted, Jews from all lands are gathering in Palestine. In the struggle for independence there were again Zealots who resorted to terrorism, and no doubt there were rapt ancients who looked for the literal fulfilment of the Biblical prophecies. Many more appear to be fired by the hope of reviving the dead past, although it was never glorious politically; they are building up the nationalistic and racial sentiments from which they themselves have suffered so much. Orthodox zeal is also seeking to revive their dead language, Hebrew. For the most part, however, the leaders of Israeli are not strictly orthodox. The prophets had declared that the kingdom would be restored by the intervention of God, through a messiah, and would usher in an age of universal peace. As it is, the people restored the nation by their own efforts, without the direct assistance of God or of a son of David, and presumably they do not hope to convert the world. The nation has to maintain itself in a kind of world the prophets never dreamed of, and would hardly approve of. Although it can still find in them a rich source of inspiration, it is not basing its national and international policy on their vision of history. For better or worse, it is striving for a worldlier wisdom.

V

The Romantic Glory of Classical Greece

1. THE ROMANTIC TRADITION

When Shelley was writing his poem 'Hellas,' his ironic friend Trelawney took him aboard a Greek caique at Leghorn, so that he might meet some Greeks in the flesh. Trelawney reports how he found a dirty little ship infested by a gypsy crew, 'shrieking, gesticulating, smoking, eating, and gambling like savages,' and captained by a trader who was upset by the Greek war of independence, because it was bad for business. He was appalled to find not the faintest trace of the 'lofty and sublime' spirit of Hellas—he was reminded only of Hell. If Shelley could visit Athens today, when the Greeks have enjoyed independence for more than a hundred years, he would no doubt remain disenchanted. He would find a gay, gregarious people, charming in their friendliness and vivacity, but volatile, restless, noisy, disorderly, garish, and generally unplatonic. They are shrewd businessmen, with a special talent for trade. They have a quick, sharp, practical intelligence but seem little concerned with fundamentals or universals. They are passionately interested in politics but more as a game, or struggle for power, than as a conflict of principles and ideals. Their national life has usually been a Balkan melodrama, a tragic farce of intrigue and brawl, animated by a spirit of liberty that has precluded law and order but permitted rule by oligarchs and dictators.

Shelley concluded that not a drop of the old Hellenic blood was left. Some scholars have argued that this is literally true, because for some two thousand years Greece was repeatedly devastated or overrun, in particular by Slavic peoples. It is certain that very little of the old blood can be left, and as certain that except for the Greek language there has been no cultural continuity. While the Parthenon kept gleaming on the Acropolis, the Athens that huddled around it was for centuries a small town, often wretched, whose mongrel inhabitants made no effort to preserve its heritage, much less to revive its ancient glory. The old Greece faded away; modern Greece is a new adventure, by a new people.

Yet Shelley was wrong. He overlooked a deeper irony of history, which his own disenchantment illustrates. The point is that there was always considerable hell in Hellas. It is that in many ways the modern Athenians bear a striking resemblance to the ancient Athenians, from whom they are not descended.

We are dealing with a great romance. In all history, Spengler observed, no culture has so passionately adored another culture as the Western has adored the ancient Greek. This cult of the classic is a becoming tribute to a glorious people —the most remarkable people in history, I should say—to whom we owe the beginnings of most of the values of our civilization. Nevertheless the passion is romantic; and as usual in such affairs, the image of the beloved one is a creation of the lover. The Greek world that lives in the Western mind is the kind of world pictured by the aging Goethe: a world of beautiful form and order, perfect in harmony and proportion, controlled in emotion and balanced in thought, altogether 'classical' in its simplicity, restraint, poise, serenity. It is the chaste world of Matthew Arnold, suffused with 'sweetness and light.' Actually, the Greeks were one of the most restless, immoderate peoples in history. They were as impulsive, volatile, turbulent, and generally unplatonic as the modern Greeks. They were also shrewd and acquisitive— among the smartest traders of antiquity. (The Emperor Cyrus of Persia described a Greek market as 'a place set apart for people to go and cheat each other on oath.') The Athenians in particular were much too brilliant and high-spirited to be 'sweet.' In the words of Thucydides, 'they were born into the world to take no rest themselves and to give none to others.'

Thucydides is perhaps the best guide to both the reality and the romance of Greece. He is a splendid representative of the traditional classic ideal—the ideal that is in fact embodied in Greek sculpture and architecture, and repeatedly expressed in Greek poetry and philosophy. His history of the Peloponnesian War resembles Greek tragedy in its stress on the punishment of insolent pride, and in its esthetic distance —a detachment especially admirable because he was himself deeply involved in the war, suffering disgrace and exile. (Thus he simply states, in the third person, that the general Thucydides was exiled after the loss of the city of Amphipolis—making no effort to defend or excuse his conduct.) Yet his history indicates that the classical ideal of 'nothing in excess' was enjoined so insistently because the Greeks were so excessive a people. In admiring the dignified restraint with which he tells his story, we are apt to forget the story itself. It is a story of fantastic contradictions, of shrewdness and naïveté, courage and cowardice, loyalty and treachery, generosity and cruelty, idealism and cynicism, wisdom and folly. It is a ridiculous story, of brave soldiers who are easily panicked and given to wailing; of canny generals whose strategy is finally determined by eclipses or the entrails of birds; of life-and-death campaigns held up by oracles, festivals, and games; of piddling victories disputed in the haste to set up trophies; of bloody defeats honored by pious truces to bury the dead. It is an appalling story, of a silly war that marked the failure of the most brilliant civilization in history, and that gives the impression of high-spirited, precocious schoolboys playing a stupid, vicious game. It is a supremely classical account of wildly romantic excess.

To us, Greece means Athens; and that Athens lost this war should remind us of the very mixed glory of Greece. Sparta, the conqueror of Athens, was almost its exact antithesis: the most sober, disciplined of the city-states and the least Greek, which made its one contribution to the high culture of Hellas by suggesting the totalitarian features of Plato's *Republic*. There was also famous Corinth, wealthy, vulgar, and soft—famous chiefly for its commerce and its commercialized pleasures, in particular its prostitutes. There was Thebes, with its glamorous legendary past and its unglamorous historic record: a city of prosperous, smart businessmen given to collaboration with the Persians, with as little patriotism as the captain who shocked Shelley. And the national shrines, the symbols of the unity and continuity of Hellas, might also have depressed him. There was Olympia, dedicated to Zeus and to athletes, the heroes of Hellas: a splendid, luxurious establishment, not very chaste or austere, to glorify the games which were celebrated for over a thousand years, and to which the Greeks flocked even when the Persian host of Xerxes was invading their land. There was the national sanctuary of Delphi with its temple to Apollo, the god of light and civilization, the most characteristic and beloved of the Greek gods: a rich temple-bank that was highly commercialized, and whose oracles were exploited for sordid political purposes, when not purchased by bribes.

Athens itself was the home of the smart, acquisitive businessman, the prototype of the modern Greek. Whitehead once remarked that the type of modern man who would feel most at home in ancient Greece is the average professional heavyweight boxer; but even an American businessman, for all he would miss in Periclean Athens, would have got along better there than the ordinary classical scholar. Athens rose when it took to trade and industry, while Sparta remained agrarian; its brilliant cultural enterprise rested on its enterprising business life, notably its invention of the practice of banking. Its lovely pottery, which to us is a sign of the Greek instinct for beauty, was a sign as well of the energy, shrewdness, and resourcefulness of the Greek businessman. Athenian pottery helped to bring on the Peloponnesian War by driving all other pottery off the Italian market, thereby inflaming the enmity of Corinth and Megara. A more general cause of this disastrous war was the economic imperialism of Athens. Still, the fruits of this imperialism, together with the spoils of war, provided the wealth that made possible the adornment of the Acropolis, which was also a symbol of power.

Even the art of Greece is not so chaste as tradition has it. When Sorokin declares that until the third century B.C. Greek art contained 'nothing vulgar, coarse, or debasing,' nothing of the crudity of our own 'sensate' art, he has presumably forgotten Aristophanes, the satirists and polemists, the phallic images, the many-breasted Artemis of Ephesus, the celebrations of sexuality and homosexuality—all the Dionysian or Bacchic elements of Greek culture that led the barbarian Scythians (according to Herodotus) to deplore the Greek fondness for frenzy. But the Acropolis of Athens is the clearest illustration of the deceptive magic of time. Time has purified it, sweeping away the gaudy confusion, leaving only the stainless marble; the Parthenon stands alone in majestic simplicity, in the perfect proportions of its skeletal outlines. And so we forget that these temples were once painted in lively colors and decorated with gold leaf, in something like Oriental luxuriance. We forget the huge statues of the gods that were crowded into them, and about them, in utter disregard of harmony and proportion. We forget the astonishing clutter of slabs, statues, and monuments that filled the Acropolis—a hodge-podge that makes Radio City seem a model of architectural restraint.

In general, a people actually devoted to the 'classical' ideal would never have made the history that the Greeks did, though they might have lived a much longer and happier one. The golden age of Athens is especially dazzling because it was so brief. In the early years of the fifth century B.C. Athens saved all Greece by throwing back the Persians at Marathon and Salamis. This feat made possible its magnificent flowering, and then the suicidal Peloponnesian War that broke out only fifty years after Salamis. The interim, the Age of Pericles that to us is so brilliant, was to contemporaries a black period. In this century, Herodotus wrote, 'more woes befell Greece than in the twenty generations preceding Darius'—woes caused not only by the Persians but by constant strife within and among the Greek city-states.[1] By the end of the century Athens had gone down to defeat. The strife continued for two or three more generations, until all the Greek city-states went down before the Macedonians. Then there arose the great classical schools of moral philosophy, notably the Stoic and Epicurean, which taught different versions of the same wisdom—measure and sobriety.

I have exaggerated, of course, the unclassical incongruities in the life of Greece. We must finally value a society for its greatest, enduring achievements, and these include the ideals it consciously set for itself, even if it fell short of them. Many ordinary Greeks, as well as some famous ones, undoubtedly did exemplify the restraint, composure, and poise of the conventional classic ideal. But my motive in stressing these incongruities at the outset is not to tarnish the glory that was Greece. It is first of all to make possible a calmer, easier look at the dazzling achievement, so that we may not be simply overawed or blinded to our own achievement; many contemporaries also manage to be restrained, composed, and poised. It is finally to do ampler justice to a people who were still more original, imaginative, daring, versatile, and many-sided than the falsetto scholars would have them. If we remember that the Greeks were rather different from their sculptured gods, we can better understand their failures and better appreciate their triumphs.

2. THE UNIQUE ACHIEVEMENT OF GREECE

In his treatise *Against Apion,* addressed to Roman Gentiles, Josephus defended the importance of Jewish history by attacking the Greeks. 'I cannot but greatly wonder at those

---

[1] Elsewhere Herodotus gives a vivid glimpse of the emotional, immoderate Athenians. They were so affected by *The Capture of Miletus,* a drama by the poet Phrynichus, that 'the whole theatre burst into tears.' Thereupon they fined the poet, and passed a law that his drama should never be exhibited again.

who think that we must attend to none but Greeks as to the most ancient facts, and learn the truth from them only . . . For you will find that almost all which concerns the Greeks happened not long ago, nay, one may say, is of yesterday and the day before only . . . How can it then be other than an absurd thing for the Greeks to be so proud, as if they were the only people acquainted with antiquity . . . ?' The Greeks themselves told stories about their apparent absurdity. 'You Greeks are mere children, talkative and vain, and knowing nothing of the past,' an Egyptian priest told Solon. Again, when Hecataeus informed the priests at Thebes of his descent from a god, his sixteenth ancestor, the priests took him into an inner temple and showed him images representing 345 generations—which still didn't end in a god. Yet the important point is that the Greeks told these stories themselves, and that they got the real point, as probably the Egyptian priests did not. While standing in awe of the venerable Egyptians, they could still take a judicious pride in their own uniqueness. And elsewhere Josephus himself suggested a good reason for their pride. 'The Egyptians,' he observed, 'appear never in all their history to have enjoyed one day of freedom.' The talkative, vain, brash Greeks were the first free men in recorded history, the first to have minds of their own. Life as we feel it and know it began with them.

Since Americans are even brasher, they cannot be reminded too often of the phenomenal achievement of Greece. Within the space of fifty years Athens alone, a little city-state of only a few hundred thousand, produced such men as Pericles, Aeschylus, Sophocles, Euripides, Aristophanes, Socrates, Thucydides, Phidias, the architects of the Parthenon—men whose equals are hardly to be found in our whole history. I do not propose, however, to review this achievement in the detail it deserves. My concern is the Greek spirit—the spirit that led them to embark, without maps, charts, or guides, on the adventure of freedom and the life of reason. It involved the penalties and the paradoxes that are the immediate theme of this book, and are reflected in their own creation of Tragedy. Out of its failures sprang Hagia Sophia: designed by Greek architects, presided over by Greek Patriarchs, but built by a bigoted, despotic emperor who also closed the academies of Athens, to the glory of a faith that was unfree, incurious, and unadventurous. Still, the spirit of Athens proved more vital, inspiring new adventures in the West while Hagia Sophia fell to the Turks; and though it has got us into trouble too, this book is dedicated to its values. For better and worse, it is the primary source of the historical importance of Greece.

The first question, naturally, is how this spirit arose. We cannot explain it by any mystique of race, blood, or Kultur. The Greeks were a mongrel people who never prided themselves on racial purity, were evidently stimulated by their wandering and intermingling with older peoples, and borrowed freely from Crete, Egypt, Phoenicia, Babylonia, Lydia, and other ancient cultures. More helpful is Toynbee's principle of challenge-and-response, or the virtues of adversity. Greece was no comfortable cradle of civilization but a rocky, bony land, which could not support a growing people in its scattered valleys and plains; hence the Greeks had to take to the sea, develop trade and industry, and send out colonizers.[2] Later they rose magnificently to the challenge of invasion by the mighty Persian empire. Yet all this does not really explain the adventure of the Greeks. Countless other wandering, mongrel peoples who faced similar challenges, or had the advantage of adversities, remained barbarians. We do not know just how or why some peoples rise to splendid achievement. All we know for certain is that at least as early as Homer the Greeks were already a free people, standing on their own feet, living their own lives in an ordered world in which monsters, demons, and other irrational horrors had largely been tamed or exterminated.

Now, the Eastern civilizations before them must have had more freedom, variety, initiative, and stir than their rigid structures suggest. They had made remarkable discoveries, carried on extensive trade, created art forms, built imposing cities, organized powerful kingdoms. Nevertheless what we know of these societies indicates that as they became established, they all tended to settle into the same invariable pattern. They were ruled by gods and god-kings who were alike despots. They lived in a profoundly irrational world, haunted by fear, controlled by magic, framed by inviolable custom. Their basic principle was absolute obedience to customs and institutions that were not reasoned about because not regarded as man-made. They had codes of justice and knew some happiness, but they had no idea of personal liberty or a right to happiness. Apparently their subjects never conceived the possibility of a better kind of society, for we do not hear of great rebels or popular uprisings.

Against this historical background the saying of Anaxagor-

[2] Toynbee points out that one of the poorest regions of Greece was Attica, whose land was already denuded in Plato's time, whereas Boeotia had exceptionally fertile, deep-soiled plow-lands. Yet the Boeotians were known to the rest of Hellas as a sluggish, rude people—'Boeotian swine.'

as becomes more luminous: 'All things were in chaos when Mind arose and made order.' The Greeks were apparently the first to put their trust in Mind and by conscious thought to introduce order into the universe and man's life. When Thales of Miletus stated that 'all things are made of water,' his apparently naïve fancy was an astonishingly bold advance in thought. In the face of the multifarious, shifting appearances he was assuming that nature was intelligible, in natural rather than supernatural terms; and with this assumption philosophy got under way. 'The fact is that invoking the gods to explain diseases and other natural events is all nonsense,' declared Hippocrates (or one of the legendary men known as Hippocrates). '. . . In nature all things are alike in this, that they all can be traced to preceding causes.' Earlier societies had accumulated considerable medical knowledge and skill, but not until this denial of magical or supernatural causes could medicine become a science. 'Hecataeus of Miletus thus speaks: I write what I deem true; for the stories of the Greeks are manifold and seem to me ridiculous'—and with this skeptical utterance the study of history really began. From such beginnings the Greeks went on to make impressive contributions to philosophy, science, and history, but their all-important contribution was the beginnings—the critical, inquiring spirit. And as they discovered Nature, so they discovered Man. The motto inscribed in their national shrine at Delphi was not 'Fear God' but 'Know Thyself.' They created the ideal of culture—the conscious cultivation of human nature.

The best example of this new spirit is Herodotus, if only because in him it is still so youthful and fresh, and so striking against the background of the ancient world he traveled over. 'I traveled for the sake of learning, for the sake of inquiry,' he writes (and incidentally never mentions the hardships and perils involved in travel at that time). He sought to learn from peoples who remembered and recorded but rarely inquired. At first glance, his credulity seems as remarkable as his curiosity. Although he repeatedly states that he is a mere reporter, who feels obliged to tell all he heard but not to believe it all, he obviously believes some whoppers; his criterion for distinguishing fact from fancy is hopelessly unclear. Yet he is essentially a critical as well as eager inquirer, and his uniqueness is most evident when he visits Egypt, the land of whoppers. Thus he is 'particularly anxious' to learn about the marvelous river Nile, its sources and the reason for its annual inundations; and when the priests and natives can give him no information, he considers several

explanations that had been suggested by Greeks, finally offering a theory of his own. His theory is far from the truth. Still,
the point is that he was looking for a natural cause, a rational
explanation—and that the venerable, learned Egyptians could
tell him nothing whatever about the river their whole civilization had depended upon for thousands of years.

Still more to the point is the central theme of his history—
the Persian War as a struggle for liberty. 'A slave's life you
understand,' Herodotus has the Greeks tell a friendly Persian
satrap who advises submission to the Great King, "but never
having tasted liberty, you cannot tell whether it be sweet or
no. Had you known what freedom is, you would have bidden
us fight for it.' Although Persian rule was more liberal than
that of earlier empires, the noblest Persian was in fact a
slave of the Great King—a vassal at any moment liable to
be buried alive or cut in two by his royal master, whose whim
was law.[3] And although the motives of both sides were mixed,
as Herodotus characteristically makes clear, he singled out the
issue that made the Persian War perhaps the most momentous in all history. In its actual consequence it was a struggle
between despotism and the ideal of liberty, blind faith and
the ideal of reason. Only the valor and steadfastness of Athens saved the Greeks from enslavement; and with the victory
of Athens the Greek spirit found its fullest expression.

'We are the school of Hellas,' asserted Pericles in his Funeral Oration. That this was, as he said, 'no mere boast
thrown out for the occasion' was proved by the disastrous
aftermath of the occasion; for after its humiliating defeat by
Sparta Athens remained the cultural capital of Hellas, still
more deeply admired by Greeks everywhere. Pericles did
not boast of the masterpieces it had produced, though in
view of the size and the material resources of Athens the
civic effort that adorned the Acropolis was extraordinary. Primarily he boasted of the type of man that Athens produced—
a man not only public-spirited and loyal but self-reliant,
resourceful, enterprising, and versatile, who cultivated 'refinement without extravagance and knowledge without effemi-
nacy.' The Athenian best exemplified the Greek ideal of
wholeness, an 'excellence' of body-and-soul—in Matthew Arnold's terms, a general, harmonious expansion of all the
powers that make the beauty and worth of human nature.

[3] The basic irrationality of the often gracious, tolerant Persians is
epitomized by the behavior of King Xerxes when a great storm destroyed his bridge across the Hellespont. He 'straightway gave orders
that the Hellespont should receive three hundred lashes,' Herodotus
reports. His wrath still not satisfied by this punishment of the sea, he
then beheaded the overseers who had built the bridge.

And the primary condition of this achievement, Pericles emphasized, was freedom.

'At Athens,' he said, 'we live exactly as we please.' Whereas Spartans 'by a painful discipline seek after manliness,' Athens trusted to the native spirit of its citizens and encouraged individualism, a rich variety of interest and effort. Granted that Athenian democracy extended only to the minority who were citizens, for its citizenry it was as pure and complete a democracy as history has known. Some Americans, to be sure, would consider it a dangerously socialistic 'welfare state.' The Athenian government did not merely referee disputes, jail lawbreakers, protect businessmen, maintain an expensive navy—it built the Parthenon, financed the great festivals, and in general spent lavishly to provide a full as well as secure life. Nevertheless the citizens were masters of their government, and did not fear it as an external, alien power. They were also free from both the conformity and the competition imposed by sharp social distinctions. (Even slaves, an aristocratic observer complained, could hardly be distinguished in dress and manner from wealthy citizens.) They were freer in their private lives, by law and by custom, than Americans are today. They had no blue laws, no priesthood, no Committee for un-Greek Activities. Altogether, Athens dominated the lives of its citizens more than any other state except Sparta, but it dominated because it gave them both the opportunity and the incentive to develop and express their individuality. It was the first great experiment in the 'open society.'

Sketchy and inadequate as is this account of the unique achievement of Greece, it may seem a tedious rehearsal of the commonplace. A devotion to freedom is no longer unique. The breathtaking speculations of the early Greeks are now pedestrian exercises, or no exercise at all; their brilliant ingenuities are matters of common sense, a string of old quotations. Who can be thrilled by the counsel of harmony and wholeness? Such stale familiarity may be tribute enough to the Greeks, as evidence of how pervasive and profound their influence has been. Yet the familiarity may obscure the pertinence of their achievement, which remains unique. If we take seriously their ideal of harmony and wholeness, we may still get a fresh perspective on not only the mass life but the high culture of the modern world.

For the Athenians, Matthew Arnold's ideal of culture was not literary or 'cultural' but a wholly natural, almost unconscious living ideal, because it was deeply rooted in the life of the community. The talented man who fully developed his

individuality was not a bohemian or a highbrow but an active citizen—a public man like Socrates. Civic life was the
scene and occasion alike of their architecture, sculpture, painting, and poetry. Tragedy, the supreme expression of their culture, was enacted at the greatest of the civic festivals, for the
benefit of the whole citizenry; among other things, it expressed
their deepest religious thought and their loftiest national ideals.
For the Greeks did not separate their major interests. They
considered politics, religion, learning, art, and sport as alike
natural, and naturally related. Both the Olympic games and
the dramatic festivals were national festivals, presided over
by the Muses and dedicated to the gods; the games were
embellished by works of art, the tragic dramas were accompanied by rowdy comedies. If the Beautiful appears to dominate Greek culture, it is only because it was inseparable from
the True and the Good, and from their everyday life.

In modern America, on the other hand, the chief unifying force is business. While men still clamor that the government must be kept out of business, and in effect have
developed a special ethos for business, it has profoundly influenced government, religion, science, art, education, sport,
and all other interests. Otherwise we make a point of sep-
arating these interests. We make the separation of Church
and State an ideal, and try to keep both of them out of
education; we cultivate 'pure' science and 'pure' art, as ends
in themselves; we dignify our national festivals by pure
oratory, or make them an occasion for pure sport; we profes-
sionalize learning and sport alike, turning them over to specialists. The True is the domain of science, with separate,
more or less jealously guarded provinces for the 'higher'
truths of literature and religion. The Good is the domain of
religion, at least for one day a week, with different provinces for private, business, and political life, all more or less
carefully insulated against scientific knowledge. The Beautiful is the domain of the 'fine' arts, with museums to be
visited on special occasions by waifs and strays from the
separate domain of the popular arts.

Now, we cannot hope to achieve the vital unity of life in
little Athens, where most of the citizens could get together
on great occasions, take an active part in civic life, and center their common aspirations on a compact, visible Acropolis.
Our world is much too vast, complex, and heterogeneous. It
requires a great deal of highly specialized interest and activity; it must train a host of professionals, technicians, experts.
We have been forced to separate some major interests, moreover, simply for the sake of harmony. Given a religion that

claimed exclusive possession of absolute truth, but whose followers disagreed violently on the nature of this truth, we have learned that we cannot afford to allow the Church to control education or share the power of the State. Similarly we have learned the value of 'pure' research, independent of political or social interests. We have learned that the Athenian ideal of individualism requires the partial separation of the individual from the state, the constitutional establishment of a realm where he is free to pursue happiness in his own way. In our civilization, the degree of unity that Athens achieved freely and naturally could only be imposed arbitrarily, by the totalitarian or Spartan methods that Pericles condemned.[4] And our heterogeneity has its own values. It is the potential means to a more abundant, richly varied life than the Greeks knew.

Yet for this very purpose we need to cultivate the Greek ideal. The need is plainest for all our stunted, lopsided, 'practical' men, who leave culture to their womenfolk while they assiduously narrow their minds and stifle their sensibilities, devoting themselves so slavishly to the business of making a good living that they become incapable of enjoying or even conceiving a good life. The Greeks had a word for this type of man: it has become our word 'idiot.' In beating this dead horse, however, writers may overlook the strong tendencies to narrowness and lopsidedness among the elite. Such tendencies are most conspicuous in scientific or scholarly specialists, but they are more insidious in artists, critics, and intellectuals generally. Such specialists in culture, unhappily, are more or less isolated from the main sources of power and prestige in a mass civilization; usually they address so small an audience that they find it hard to regard their work as a vital force in the communal life, and may feel that they are merely talking to one another. Consequently they are disposed to make a virtue of their isolation, cultivating aloof, fastidious, exclusive attitudes that amount to a policy of cultural isolationism.

Long ago Matthew Arnold complained of the 'incredible

---

[4] The Communist doctrine, for example, that all art and literature should serve the interests of the state is in theory a thoroughly Greek doctrine; the Greeks never glorified self-expression or the romantic rights of genius. In practice, however, the Greek artist worked much more freely and spontaneously than the Soviet artist. To the Athenians art was never a mere tool of the state, an incidental means to higher ends; as a natural form of excellence it was inseparable from the excellence of the whole. Trusting the native spirit of their artists, and taking a broad view of the interests of the state, they did not feel obliged to set up cultural commissars.

vagaries' in our culture. 'Sanity—that is the great virtue of the ancient literature,' he declared; 'the want of that is the great defect of the modern, in spite of all its variety and power.' But to more popular critics sanity in literature means the affirmation of 'sound' moral or political ideas, when not a wholesale wholesomeness. Hence the 'new critics' seek to preserve the dignity of literature by a kind of esthetic puritanism. They not merely concentrate on form and technique, the neglected esthetic values—they frown on a concern with the social uses and bearings of literature, its 'ulterior' values. They are embarrassed by explicit moralizing or philosophizing, in which Greek writers freely indulged; they bridle at any suspicion of 'literary nationalism,' which was a primary inspiration of Homer, Pindar, and Aeschylus; they consider it a kind of prostitution when a poet (such as Archibald MacLeish) enters public life, where Greek poets felt at home. In effect, they preach a doctrine of art for art's sake that would have shocked the supremely artistic Greeks. And behind all such tendencies lies a habit of thought engrained by the Hebraic-Christian tradition and fortified by the drive to 'efficiency'—the assumption that responsible thinking must be militaristic or authoritarian. The common aim is a monopoly on truth, the common password 'Either-or.'

'To make the individual at one with the state, the real with the ideal, the inner with the outer, art with morals, finally to bring all phases of life under the empire of a single idea, which, with Goethe, we may call, as we will, the good, the beautiful, or the whole—this,' wrote G. Lowes Dickinson, 'was the aim, and to a great extent the achievement of their genius.' Almost all readers applaud such familiar tributes to the Greeks. But most remain committed to very different aims. They continue on principle to separate the individual from the state, the ideal from the real, the inner from the outer, art from morals; or when they seek a single unifying principle they find it in science *or* religion *or* the religion of the state—in some idea of the whole that suppresses most of the natural goods of human life. Then they complain that our world is in pieces.

3. THE LIMITATIONS OF GREECE

No war in history seems more appallingly stupid than the Peloponnesian War, which signaled the failure of the glorious Greeks. It is still more disheartening because democratic

Athens was a prime instigator of the war, not an innocent victim of it. This is the story that Toynbee emphasizes: Athens, the 'liberator of Hellas,' became the 'tyrant city.' Edith Hamilton stresses in particular its moral corruption. She tells how the men who fought against Persia had stood for ideals of justice and honor, fearing and hating most of all the insolence of wealth and power. Then, within a generation, the men of imperial Athens became self-seeking, unprincipled, cynical, losing all regard for the rights of others; and though they continued to applaud their great tragic poets, Miss Hamilton declares that the bright young men could no longer understand these poets. Hence the Athenians met the fate of proud Persia before them. And the whole story is still more pertinent because the unenlightened self-interest and unholy self-righteousness of the Greeks led to vicious class war within the city-states, as well as suicidal war between them. We know these ancient evils: they remain the major threat to our own civilization.

For this reason, however, I think we need to begin with the usual complexities and incongruities. We cannot afford to take so simple a view of the Athenians, as a noble people who suddenly went rotten. For their imperialism did not spring from sheer lust for power; like Britain, Athens was dependent upon imports for food and had to protect her sea routes or lifelines.[5] At that her empire was not seething with rebellion, except among the wealthy classes; she seems to have been generally popular with the common people of her allies, as a champion of democracy against oligarchy. In any event, the flowering of Athenian culture coincided with the rise of Athenian imperialism. By the time her citizens are reputed to have become thoroughly corrupted they were building the Parthenon, flocking to the plays of Sophocles, Euripides, and Aristophanes, listening respectfully to the Funeral Oration of Pericles, listening eagerly to Socrates and other philosophers. I suspect that the unprincipled young men of Athens really did have some understanding of these remarkable goings on. Meanwhile there were plenty of pious conservatives to uphold the ancient traditions of Athens. They were busy attacking Pericles, deploring the reckless extravagance that adorned the Acropolis. They banished Anaxagoras, reviled Euripides, and in time killed Socrates.

[5] Frank Burr Marsh pointed out that if Athens had not transformed a free confederacy of Greek city-states into a compulsory union of vassal states, the whole Aegean world probably would have fallen prey to the still mighty Persian empire. The confederacy was starting to break up before Athens refused to allow members to secede.

The evils were there, but they were indeed ancient—they were not a sudden blight. The fatal militarism of the Greeks was a product of their whole tradition, from Homer down. They had always regarded war and piracy as legitimate, as did all other peoples around them; nor were they accustomed to fighting for ideals of justice, or any cause holier than self-defense. Even in the Persian wars, their most heroic and honorable struggle, Herodotus reveals much the same blend of idealism and cynicism, loyalty and treachery, that marked the Peloponnesian War. The Greeks were mercenary, jealous, and suspicious of one another; many tried to sit on the fence, while many others fought on the Persian side; tyrants and oligarchs often betrayed their cities to the Great King, in order to maintain their own power; and some of the greatest heroes, including the Athenian Themistocles, later became traitors. At all times the curse of Hellas was disunity and strife, springing from envy and greed but also from its very ideals of freedom and individualism. And so it is a mistaken piety that glosses over the many embarrassing customs and convictions of the brilliant Greeks. Simply as we value their way of life we need to see clearly both their shortcomings and their inherent limitations, the defects of their virtue.

In the first place, these ancients were very young, only a few centuries removed from barbarism. Their youthfulness is most apparent in the prehistoric superstitions that were embedded in their high culture as well as their folkways, and which influenced their national life to an extent difficult for us to realize. If the Athenians had lost the battle of Marathon, they probably would have become subjects of the Persians, and never developed a Periclean Age; yet Herodotus reports that they did not begin this momentous battle until 'the victims showed themselves favorable,' and their chances were jeopardized by the absence of the Spartans, who could not march out of Sparta because the moon had not yet reached the full. (It appears that the course of history may also be determined by the entrails of animals and the phases of the moon.) Again, in the fatal campaign against Syracuse, the turning point of the Peloponnesian War, the Athenian expedition was on the point of sailing home to safety when an eclipse of the moon occurred, and their soothsayers prescribed a wait of thrice nine days; so the Athenians waited, to be utterly destroyed by the Syracusans.

Similarly the Greeks had little historical sense. The student of their history, Toynbee wrote, has the advantage of sitting through the whole play and listening to its beautifully articulate protagonists, who had 'the wisdom of greater experience and the poignancy of greater suffering than ours.' After such esthetic appreciation, however, the student had better discount and supplement this wisdom. The Greeks could only speculate about their early history because they had no records, no lists of kings, no dates, no chronology except for the Olympic games; when they grew critical of their traditional legends they had no ready means of substituting reliable knowledge, and surprisingly little interest in trying to get such knowledge. After a few pages of speculation, Thucydides simply says that nothing of great importance happened before his time. The Greeks accordingly had no idea of growth and development, no clear perspective on their heritage. Homer was their Bible; his half-amused, ironic portraits of the immoral gods became the models for respectable piety; and when the more thoughtful became distressed by his 'lies' about the gods, they could not understand him as the product of an earlier culture, a phase of cultural evolution.

It followed that the Greeks had a sharply limited understanding of the history that they themselves were making and recording. Herodotus finally referred everything to the will of the gods. 'Evil had to befall' so-and-so, runs his refrain; although remaining quite cheerful himself, he repeatedly drew the melancholy moral that the gods humble or destroy the mighty simply because they are mighty. The more scientific Thucydides did not go much deeper. While considering the Peloponnesian War the all-important event in history to his time, he slighted the greatness of Periclean Athens that alone made it important. (We know little about what was presumably the greatest period in Greek history—the period between the defeat of the Persians and the outbreak of the Peloponnesian War—because nothing of 'historic' importance happened in that period: there were no great wars.) Thucydides could not understand the underlying causes of the war because he had little idea of the profound influence of the past, or immediately of economic forces. Admirably fairminded though he was, he could not be fair to Athens because he did not understand its economic problems. 'Nowhere but in a few men of that generation,' remarks F. M. Cornford, 'shall we find so much independence of thought combined with such destitute poverty in the apparatus and machinery of thinking.'

The apparatus remained relatively poor, chiefly because the Greeks failed to develop scientific habits of thought. In their rational pursuit of natural causes they displayed an amazing prescience: Democritus offered an atomic theory,

Anaximander a theory of evolution, Aristarchus a Coperni-
can theory. But the Greeks themselves could not realize the
brilliance or importance of these theories. They were not in
the habit of going to school in the natural world, or of
subjecting their theories to empirical tests; they did not keep
asking the critical question—what are the facts? Even Aristotle, who founded the science of biology by making a close,
first-hand study of nature, and was the first great thinker
to recommend and pursue such study, continued to deduce
the final truths about nature from 'self-evident' premises.[6] His
logic and his speculative physics were much more influential
than his biology; his glory became the syllogism, a logic that
had no means of testing its major premises and could not
serve as a logic of discovery. Despite its freedom and variety,
Greek thought was therefore prone to a kind of unconscious
dogmatism, a habit of arbitrary assertion. Despite its essentially practical interests, it was prone to an intellectualism
that carried it away from material and social realities. Lacking the guiding idea that new empirical truths could be
discovered, it came to deify Pure Reason, and to stress pure
contemplation as the ideal of Reason. In our own world, we
could do with more contemplation, less emphasis on the need
of incessant applying and doing. The Greeks might have
done better with a more pragmatic view of knowledge.

As it was, their greatest thinkers positively scorned the commerce, industry, and technology on which their civilization
was based. To them the practical uses of knowledge were
ignoble, and the 'base mechanic arts' unworthy of a citizen.
According to Aristotle, the trade of laborers, artisans, and

[6] Aristotle's *Politics* illustrates this basic confusion in his thought. He
derived his conclusions from an empirical analysis of the main types of
Greek government, carefully specifying the various kinds and degrees
within each type; in his pragmatism he recognized that no one form of
government is necessarily the best for all peoples, at all times, under
all circumstances. Yet his acute study was always limited, and sometimes vitiated, by uncritical assumptions about 'Nature'—a concept as
vague and ambiguous in his systematic thought as it was later to be in
idealistic thought of the eighteenth century. Thus he made Nature bear
the brunt of the human institution of slavery: Nature had designed
slaves for the benefit of superior men, just as she had designed animals
for the sake of men, and vegetables for animals. He regarded Nature
as a kind of deity, which 'makes nothing either imperfect or in vain'—
a strange statement for an observant biologist. Elsewhere, however, he
remarks that good men should breed true, 'and this is what Nature desires to do, but frequently cannot accomplish'; so it appears that Nature may be imperfect, because of the opposition of some unspecified
force. He also slips in another standard, declaring that a man who acts
in accordance with reason will often oppose Nature as well as custom. But in general Aristotle's Nature is an obliging deity who approves
whatever Greek customs he considers 'natural.'

merchants 'renders the body and soul or intellect of free persons unfit for the exercise and practice of virtue.'[7] Here again the Greek concern for the 'higher' values is pertinent for a society that glorifies the practical. We could do with much more of their stress on knowledge as Virtue or Wisdom, not as Power; we might admire the Athenians more because they never boasted of their plumbing, and preferred a rich civic life to a high standard of private living. Nevertheless there is no necessary virtue in poor sanitation, or an indifference to the practical uses of knowledge, or an ignorance of the national economy. The foundations of Greek society might have been stronger if its citizens had done more of the work that was left to slaves and foreigners, if its scientists had applied more of their knowledge and developed a superior technology, and if its intellectuals had had more understanding of its economic problems. The subsequent event was unkind. With the fall of the city-states, the higher values had no firm social foundation. The enterprising, many-sided Greeks inspired the genteel, one-sided humanism of the 'classical' education of the Western world, which gave as little understanding of the scientific and industrial revolutions that were transforming this world.

In short, the Greeks were cribbed and cabined by their ideal of excellence. To follow for a moment Spengler's analysis of the Classical spirit, they lived in a tidy Euclidean world, finite, static, complete. They had no feeling for horizons, prospects, or backgrounds, and no word for 'space'; they had such a horror of infinity that the idea was virtually taboo. They had no desire to explore the whole world, to convert it, or to master it by technology. In their colonizing adventures they did not venture into the hinterlands or seek to establish a 'new land'; their colonies clung to the Mediterranean, the mother-city, and the ancestral god. They had no Protestantism, no Romantic Movement, no stirring revolutions in art and thought; they had critics and reformers but no great rebels or missionaries consciously in advance of their time. They did not look to the future, or when they did they saw endless cycles, repetition rather than change. (They dropped Anaximander's theory of evolution.) They had so little interest even in keeping time that they were slow to make use of the clocks and calendars developed by Egypt and Babylonia. In general, their world was a world of forms, not of forces,

---

[7] It should be noted that Homer's aristocratic society did not regard manual labor as degrading. His heroes were not at all genteel or scornful of the mechanic arts, and their wives were not ashamed to assist slaves in the housework. Trade and industry became undignified only after they had made possible more wealth and leisure.

and their main effort was to keep it small, clear, orderly, statuesque.

Spengler goes on to show how this effort shaped all the major creations of the Greek genius. Their political ideal was the well-ordered little *polis,* the state as statue. Their Olympian gods were superlative shapes, not omnipotent wills or superlative forces, and their mode of worship was a pious observance of forms, not a soaring aspiration. Their science was based on the concepts of matter and form, not of mass and energy; always true to form, Nature 'abhorred a vacuum.' Their mathematics was plane and solid geometry; they had no dynamics, no differential or infinitesimal calculus, no irrational numbers, no zero as a number. Their great ethical systems, such as the Stoic and Epicurean, alike held up an ideal of 'statuesque steadiness'; their common aim was to limit rather than fulfil desire, to order rather than expand life. Their painting had no horizon or perspective, no sense of space or depth. Their architecture concentrated on the temple, the smallest of the great architectural forms, and to the end was based on the simple post and lintel. 'Everything that is Classical,' Spengler sums up, 'is comprehensible in *one* glance.' Greek culture has been so popular if only because it is the tidiest, most understandable of the great cultures.

As usual, Spengler ignores a great deal in order to keep this pattern neat. Like the classical scholars he derides, he falls into the error of identifying all Greece with its Apollonian ideal, slighting the strong Dionysian tendencies, the bold adventures in thought and political life, the restless, wilful spirit that led to endless war between classes and states. He becomes preposterous when he declares that 'the Greeks willed nothing and dared nothing.' Yet the Greek spirit was in fact considerably less daring and dynamic than the spirit of the Western world, which has sought to harness the forces of nature, searched out the subatomic world and the stellar universe, discovered new continents and 'lands of opportunity,' begot the idea of Progress, set off great revolutionary movements, sent out missionaries and crusaders—which has explored and exploited the whole world, and endeavored to make it over in its own image, whether of Christianity, democracy, capitalism, or communism. The Greeks accordingly avoided the excesses of this 'Faustian' spirit, the penalties of a reach that exceeds a grasp; but they had to pay a price for their kind of perfection. Their failure was not merely a failure to realize their ideal—it was due as well to the limitations of this ideal.

Simplicity, clarity, perfection of form—these excellent qualities are not necessarily the supreme excellence, or the ultimate criteria of truth and beauty. They may sacrifice too much of the variety, complexity, fluidity, and ambiguity of human experience, the manifold possibilities of value; the deepest thought or the loftiest imagining is usually not the clearest.[8] But the great danger that besets the classical ideal is classicism—its tendency to a static, sterile perfection. Although the Greek temple became a marvel of harmony and proportion, it had no future; its basic form of post and lintel was suitable only for small buildings; yet Greek architects clung to this simple form to the end. Hence the very perfections of the Greeks were bound to paralyze art and thought unless their admirers could recapture the spontaneous, adventurous spirit that had created the masterpieces. As it was, the classical spirit led to an excessive generality, a lifeless formalism, an artificial dignity, a rigid repose, a restraint that restrained no emotion to speak of. It led to the kind of classicism that we find in later Rome, and in Europe after the Renaissance, but also in the decline of Greece itself. For centuries Athens continued to admire itself as the 'school of Hellas' while it rehearsed the old lessons, and failed to learn its own lesson.

In civic life, this classical spirit was tempered by the individualism and enterprise of the Greeks. It helped to make possible the ideal balance of impulse and control, freedom and order, that Athens approved. Nevertheless it contributed to the disunity and strife that destroyed Greek freedom. Their individualism was apt to become strident because it was rooted in the aristocratic tradition of their revered Homer, the passion for personal fame and glory, but was not clearly provided for in classical theory, political, philosophical, or religious. In their concern for form and order, the philosophers evaded such confusing, disrupting issues as the claims of the individual soul, the rights of man as man. The Greeks could be generous and humane, or they could be callous and cruel (as beauty lovers so often have been); but

---

[8] Although Greek tragedy, for example, majestically represented the universal story of Man against Destiny, it could not sound the depths of a Hamlet or the brothers Karamazov. Edith Hamilton notes that Lady Macbeth is at first very much like the Clytemnestra of Aeschylus in her single-minded passion, but that she then grows complicated. While waiting for Macbeth to kill the king, she says to herself, 'Had he not resembled my father as he slept, I had done't.' This sentence, Miss Hamilton observes, blurs the clear outline; Aeschylus would never allow his Clytemnestra to lapse into such femininity because he was interested in her type, not in her inmost personal life. It cannot be said that Shakespeare's realism is perforce artistically truer, nor is it necessary to make invidious comparisons. Yet one who has come to know Shakespeare will find it hard to deplore his interest in the inner life of individuals, or to regard the Greek mode of tragedy as necessarily superior.

in either event they did not recognize such ideas as the interests of mankind. Nor were Plato and Aristotle effectually concerned with such interests. The good as they conceive it was not open to all men; it could be known only by a privileged leisure class in a Greek city-state—a local, temporal political arrangement. It required the majority of mankind to confine themselves to the hard, dirty work.[9] Women as well as slaves were merely servants of men, means to the good life. The best woman, said Pericles, is she 'of whom there is least talk among men whether in praise or in blame.'

Hence there was no higher law to restrain the wars within and between the states. Here the vision of the Greeks was limited by their greatest political achievement—the free, self-governing city-state. The separate cities all aspired to self-sufficiency and claimed absolute sovereignty. They developed no common law, no system of linking highways, no effective system of international co-operation; their abortive alliances and confederacies aimed chiefly at domination or balance of power. Like the classical temple, the city-state was incapable of growth. It could not grow into a United Greek States because it had no institutional means of assimilating the free citizenry of other states, transforming confederacies into a genuine federation; a Greek citizen always had to be within hailing distance of the popular assembly. (If Athens ever did think of granting its scattered little allies the privileges of Athenian citizenship, it developed no system of popular representative government on a large scale.) And while the city-state was failing, Greek thinkers failed to work out new political possibilities. Plato and Aristotle still aspired to nothing beyond a well-ordered city-state. They did not conceive of a united Greek nation, much less an international order; they did not tackle the problem of national sovereignty, or order among the states. In effect their only foreign policy was war—even Plato's Utopia had a warrior class, educated only to be patriotic warriors. At best they had a healthy realism, seeking to study the world as they found it, but their realism ultimately came down to a fatal provincialism. Plato in particular wrote as if Herodotus had never written. When all of Hellas lost its independence to Macedon, the leading

---

[9] Although it might be argued that Plato and Aristotle were simply being realistic in recognizing the natural inferiority or incapacity of most men, both generally accepted the terms of life in a Greek city as necessities of human nature. They gave little thought to the claims of ordinary men because they assumed that mean, slavish behavior was congenital, not the result of social institutions that forced men to lead mean, slavish lives.

schools vied in justifying the ancient institution of monarchy, or else turned their backs on the political problem.

In this view, the enterprising, creative Greeks were not enterprising or creative enough. They were unequal to the challenge of their own achievements, or specifically to the new possibilities of tension, friction, and disorder created by their new ideal of freedom. If the immediate cause of their failure was the corruption of pride, a further cause was the circumspection of the classical spirit. Behind their ideals of form and order lay a deep-seated fear of change. Greek thinkers typically sought to dismiss change, as mere appearance or illusion, and in practical life to arrest change. Their typical way of adapting themselves to a world that kept changing in spite of them was the way of contemplation, of resignation, or of withdrawal. In this respect the Greeks were less proud and wilful than the Hebrews. The Hebrews had a passion for justice on this earth, demanding the final establishment of terrestrial peace and order; the promises held up by their prophets were the fighting faith of their zealots. The Greeks could fight bravely for their city-state, but they had no such passion for the cause of justice or any ideal state on earth.

In other words, the freedom-loving Greeks lacked a deep faith in the power of freedom. While they conceived man as essentially a rational animal and believed that he could order his private life, they did not believe that he could progressively improve the collective life. They had little sense of history as creation or actual adventure, little confidence in man's ability to make his own history. Their ultimate principle remained Moira—a Fate to which the gods themselves were subject. Their greater writers usually asserted that this universal order was a rational, moral order, which punished *hubris,* but they often wrote as if it were a blind or hostile order; and in any case man could do nothing about it. He realized his rationality by contemplating or submitting to a given metaphysical order, not by seeking to create a new social order. This fatalism, which from the outset lay behind Greek thought, at the end dominated thought and paralyzed will. Moira became Tyche, or Chance.

All this is by no means to discredit the Greek genius. They were pioneers in the life of freedom, with no precedents to guide them, no settled democratic traditions to steady them. It is no wonder that their thought was conditioned by their social arrangements and reflected their limited knowledge and experience. The wonder remains that these fledglings dared and achieved so much. Say the worst about their political philosophy, and then one must add with Zimmern that they made the all-important contribution to political philosophy—they invented it. Grant that their society was based on slavery, and that Aristotle defined a slave as an 'animated instrument' who was 'nothing of himself,' it is much more remarkable that Euripides and other Greeks began to denounce this universal institution, which was accepted by Jesus and St. Paul centuries later, and still defended by Americans in the last century. In all fields of thought the Greeks took the necessary first steps. We are more knowing than they because we have had the privilege of knowing them, and the wit to carry on their pioneering adventure. My point, again, is simply that in justice both of them and to ourselves we need to see the Greeks as they were, taking full advantage of the perspective afforded by our much wider experience and greater knowledge. We are unjust to Athens if we merely moralize about the sins of pride, forgetting the superstition, ignorance, immaturity, and provinciality that clouded its brilliance. We are unjust to ourselves if in any branch of art or thought we regard the Greek word as the last word, as pertinent today as ever.

Our analysis has carried us far from the Age of Pericles. The men of Athens were not wanting in enterprise or faith in man's powers; they were bold and exuberant, heedless of the traditional wisdom. Their living ideal was not so much an Apollonian suppression of excess as a balance of excesses, a harmonizing of Apollonian and Dionysian ideals. Even so, their adventure took place in a classical world, a world of frieze. Their ideal of excellence was a design for living in this small world, and included elements as unsuited to our life as the Greek cornices on our early skyscrapers, or the Greek columns stuck on the walls of our county courthouses. In particular their city-state was a very small affair, whose administrative problems were negligible by comparison with ours. 'It is difficult, if not impossible,' wrote Aristotle, 'to govern properly a very numerous body of men'; but we have attempted this difficult or impossible task. We have not only created great nations but sought to enable the entire population to participate in the whole life of the nation. Now we have set up the ideal of a United Nations, the extension of freedom to all the peoples of the world. We are dealing with problems the Greeks hardly thought of.

4. PLATO AND THE AMBIGUITIES OF IDEALISM

The real tragedy of the Peloponnesian War, writes Edith Hamilton, was not merely the fall of Athens but the defeat of the cause of humanity: 'Greece's contribution to the world was checked and soon ceased.' To a lover of Athens, however, the real tragedy was more paradoxical. The fact is that the Greeks made their deepest mark on the world in the centuries following this defeat. It was only after their independent history ended that they entered world history, conquering the East, educating the Romans, and in time Hellenizing Christianity. In like manner their philosophers now became concerned with universal issues, turning away from the city-state, inward to the soul of man. While piously celebrating the Age of Pericles, the Western world has drawn much more heavily on this later Greek thought. It has drawn especially on Plato, whose thought was the clearest response to the fall of Athens; Plato has had a greater influence on our intellectual tradition than any other Greek. Only it is an ambiguous influence. It forces the main question, how well the cause of humanity made out in this later phase of Greek thought.

As an extraordinarily fertile thinker, who remains the greatest symbol of the perennial idealism in the history of philosophy, Plato has inspired an exceptional degree of pious confusion. A distinguished example of such confusion is Sir Richard Livingstone's *Greek Ideals and Modern Life*. Livingstone's main theme is that Greece in the fifth and fourth centuries B.C. went through the same spiritual revolution that we are now suffering from, but saved itself and civilization for another seven hundred years—'thanks in the first instance to Plato'; hence we should 'study closely the medicine which he devised for his age.' Actually, Greece was not saved by Plato's medicine: the Hellenistic period that followed was an age of increasing spiritual confusion, which maintained its vigor by quite unplatonic means. Plato himself was not fully cured by his own medicine, judging by his later works: the almost desperate insistence of his *Laws* on absolute unity and order suggests a disunity in his soul. For his idealism was not the epitome of 'Greek ideals.' It was finally a repudiation of the spirit that had created Periclean Athens. It was born of disillusionment, in a period of shock and strain. And although the historic origins of Plato's thought by no means determine its final significance or value, they do throw considerable light on its historic influence, and on its special pertinence for our own age of shock and strain.

To begin with, Plato represents a mystical, other-worldly current in Greek culture that was older, deeper, and stronger than many lovers of Athens have recognized. The mystery religions, associated in particular with the names of Dionysus and Orpheus, had become popular cults long before his time. Based on the ancient idea of a savior-god, a dying-god who had been resurrected, the mysteries offered the Greeks a hope of immortal bliss denied them by the Olympian gods. (The gallantry of the Homeric heroes is the more admirable because they knew that after death they would all go to Hades, a shadowy underworld.) The development of these religions illustrates the Greek ideal of balance or all-inclusive harmony, instead of mere suppression of excess. At first the priests of Apollo opposed the worship of Dionysus, a non-Olympian who became popular as a god of intoxication and inspired chiefly frenzy or mad ecstasy; but when the barbarian continued to sweep the country, the Greeks managed to order and humanize his worship, in a national festival dignified by the works of their tragic poets. Still, the growing popularity of the mysteries makes clear that the Greeks were not simply clear-eyed, fearless naturalists. In the period of their greatest glory they apparently felt increasing need of supernatural aid and comfort.

Of these mysteries Aristotle observed, 'The initiated do not learn anything so much as feel certain emotions and are put in a certain frame of mind.' One may question how spiritual this frame of mind was. In the *Republic* Plato ridiculed the hocus-pocus of the mystery religions, their promise of purification and release from sin by 'agreeable child's play.' The initiated did feel some good emotions, however, in their communion with a savior-god who could really be loved. They might be purified by the perennial feeling of man, that to live he must first die to his old life; the resurrected god might inspire a genuine spiritual rebirth.[10] As salvation religions, at any rate, the mysteries contributed ideas that outlived the Olympians. Orphism was especially influential in its concern with the immortal soul. Although its disciples were apparently uncertain about the after-life, some believing in transmigration, others in heaven and hell, they were generally agreed that the soul was 'a son of the starry heaven,' that its enforced dwelling in a body was a form of original sin, that its earthly life was a source of corruption, and that its natural aim was to transcend this life. This dualism was at the heart of Plato's idealism.

Now, Plato discussed his famous theory of Ideas only once

[10] Orphism in particular became so lofty a faith that some scholars, such as Jane Harrison, question whether it has ever been surpassed. Orpheus might be considered the ideal symbol of religion, as at once a musician, a poet, a theologian, and a mystagogue, who not only promised immortality but taught men to seek beauty, truth, and goodness. Some early Christians were so impressed by him that they thought he must have been a disciple of Moses.

or twice, in the early dialogues; so scholars are still debating the nature of these Ideas and their relation to the sensory world. One reason why Plato has been so germinal a thinker is that his philosophy is not clear, systematic, or complete. His habitual use of the Socratic dialogue implies a measure of skepticism, an ironic reserve; but whether or not he was deliberately inconclusive, he was ambiguous enough to enable different thinkers to admire or attack different Platos. We need not worry here, however, over metaphysical or epistemological detail. The main Plato—the traditional Plato who has so deeply influenced the poetry, philosophy, and religion of the West—stands for a basic idea that is clear enough. He teaches that the 'real' reality is a spiritual one. It is not the physical world of transitory appearances perceived by the senses, but an unseen realm of essences or 'forms,' immutable, eternal, perfect, which can be apprehended by the mind, and of which the material world is only a shadow or imperfect copy. It is an ideal order whose highest form is the idea of the Good.

One can easily understand why Platonic idealism, in these general terms, has charmed, inspired, and sustained so many poets and thinkers. It elevates the mind above the passing show of things, the distractions and oppressions of the everyday world. It declares the spiritual independence of man, providing a cosmic bill of rights for all visions of the ideal. It encourages man to trust his highest aspirations, affirming that what he values most in his best moments is the very essence of truth, written in the constitution of the universe. It assures man that all that is really real is good, and can never die. If such idealism is a delusion it is a noble delusion, very flattering to the universe or its creator; for the children of nature generously refuse to admit the manifest imperfections of their parent, dismissing the evidence of their senses, and holding the creation up to the highest standards they are capable of.

To many men, therefore, idealism will always appear to be a pathetic wish-fulfilment. If the mind alone gives us knowledge of reality, it is still a tremendous leap to the conclusion that mind alone *is* the true reality. The leap seems more arbitrary because it is never clear why the mind should have been handicapped by the endowment of misleading senses, or why this world of mere appearance should ever have come to be. But the main issue for our present purposes is the attitude that the idealist takes toward the natural world—the world which most men persist in believing is very real, and in which history perforce is made.

As Santayana remarks, even naturalists may welcome a

great deal of Plato's thought as a guide to an ideal fulfilment of life in the natural world. His idealism is a transcendence but not simply for transcendence' sake; it is often a means of discriminating natural goods, achieving natural goals. Certainly Plato was less platonic than many of his later disciples, and to the end was deeply concerned with the business of this world. Like his master Socrates, moreover, he was habitually an inquirer, seeking the absolute but in a more catholic spirit than the absolutists of Western tradition. As a highly imaginative poet he thought habitually in terms of tale, myth, and symbol rather than dogma. In general, a student of literature and philosophy should dwell on the breadth, depth, and rich variety of his dialogues, in which men of all schools can find beauty and truth.

A student of history, however, must dwell as well on Plato's dualism. He sometimes tended to divorce the ideal from the natural, and to find goodness only in his imagined world. In the *Phaedo*, for example, he pictured the body as merely the prison of the soul, asserting through the genial, robust Socrates that the true philosopher is 'always occupied in the practice of dying'—dying to bodily pleasures and natural interests, and dying, one might add, to the Greek ideal of harmony. It was this unearthly spirituality that became the ideal of later Platonists in the ancient world. Early Christianity in particular seized on the extreme implications of his dualism. The Christian fear or contempt of ordinary human nature and the natural world came less from spiritual Israel than from Greece.

Such 'pure' idealism is not purely wholesome, or simply inspiring. While it declares that the human spirit is forever superior to the world, attuned to the Absolute Spirit, it also declares that man is forever an alien in his natural home. It debases the only world he can be sure of. (In the words of Robert Frost, 'The woman you have is an imperfect copy of some woman in heaven or in someone else's bed.') At least this was not the spirit of Homer or of Periclean Athens; it could not have created the unique glory of Greece. Nor was it the savior-gods of the mysteries who inspired the efforts that made Athens great; their growing popularity signified a lack of faith in natural means to the good life. And so this whole advance to a loftier spirituality was also the beginning of a retreat.

The retreat began as a withdrawal from civic life. Like the good soldier Socrates, Greek thinkers had typically been active citizens. Plato sought to continue this tradition, studying political problems, advising tyrants, devoting his declining years to the composition of his dull, thorough *Laws*. He was deeply troubled by the increasing separation of thinkers and men of action, the disappearance of the type of Pericles. Nevertheless he was repelled by the political life of Athens after its fall, and did not embark on the public career that as a young man he had been eager for. Unlike Socrates, who talked to all-comers in gymnasium and agora, he set up his Academy, a school designed to educate rulers but destined to become academic. He foreshadowed the tendency of philosophers to form closed schools, to teach a wisdom suited chiefly for private life, or even—like the Cynics—to rebel against civilized or civic life.

In this detachment Greek philosophers were able to make their invaluable contributions to ethical theory. They created more universal ideals, notably the Stoic ideal of citizenship in the 'Great Society' instead of the city-state. These ideals might be pallid, however, because they were not really communal ideals based on a vital faith. Philosophy, the rare love of wisdom, the fine flower of serenity, has commonly flourished in ages of disruption or decay—in the sickness of China, Rome, and Islam as of Greece; and it has commonly aggravated the sickness by inducing thoughtful men to turn their backs on the basic social problems of cause and cure. So the Greek philosophers now aspired chiefly to conduct an orderly retreat. The wisdom of the Stoics was resignation, not gladness or fullness of life; their austere devotion to Nature could be an inhuman acceptance of all natural 'necessities' as equally right and good. The wisdom of the Epicureans was a serene happiness that included more positive joys but required a cautious, retiring kind of life; as Will Durant comments, their design for living was excellent for a bachelor but hardly for a society. In general, Greek philosophy moved toward the passivity of the Orient.

Given such tendencies to withdrawl, Plato's realm of ideal essences naturally became a refuge from the actual world of change and uncertainty. Here the mind is free to contemplate, follow the gleam of the heart's desires. Or here, in other words, it is relieved of its natural responsibilities. The ultimate outcome was the bankruptcy of Greek philosophy, the collapse of the whole enterprise in critical inquiry. In the Neo-Platonism of Plotinus the world was still rational, even though it could not be known by reason, and it might still be enjoyable; if Plotinus was generally 'ashamed of being in the body,' as his pupil Porphyry said, he could sometimes write like an ancient Greek. ('Do not suppose that a man becomes good by despising the world and all the beauties that are in it.') His followers, however, dwelt chiefly on the ascetic, irrational elements of his thought. They became

contemptuous of science, natural philosophy, or reason itself.
They sacrificed their whole priceless heritage for the sake of
the mystical trance, 'the escape of the alone to the Alone'—
the ecstatic assurance that they were not really alone after all.
'In this ecstasy,' writes F. M. Cornford, 'Thought denies itself; and Philosophy, sinking to the close of her splendid
curving flight, folds her wings and drops into the darkness
whence she arose—the gloomy Erebus of theurgy and magic.'

Likewise the spirituality of Platonism and the mystery religions ended in primeval darkness. Toynbee has traced the
common career of the religion of the elite in a disintegrating
society—the course from curiosity through devoutness to superstition, of an alien, exotic kind.[11] At the beginning of the
Republic, Socrates remarks that out of curiosity he had paid
his respects to the Thracian goddess Bendis recently imported
to Athens, and Plato manifests a similarly detached interest
in the many myths—as of transmigration and the judgment of
the dead—that perhaps came from the Orient. Both were at
once critical and essentially devout. But Plato also foreshad-
ows the bizarre superstition in which such devoutness ended.
In his old age he apparently approved of the Babylonian cult
of the Seven Planets, which produced the Music of the
Spheres as they wheeled through the heavens; soon there was
a widespread literal belief in this heavenly Music. Although
the Epicureans generally held out against such beliefs, most
Stoics succumbed to them; Chaldean astrology was congenial to Stoic fatalism. Later thinkers became dissatisfied
with the celestial harmonies only because the Seven Planets
represented a realm of inevitable necessity, and they therefore sought magical means of escaping to some Eighth Region, where they could be alone with God. At the end, Greek
religion and religious philosophy were a riot of popular
superstitions, largely from Oriental sources, which were ven-
erated for their 'vast antiquity,' and which in fact were pre-
Hellenic or prehistoric.

This is a far cry from Plato's idealism, and is by no means
his responsibility. It is still pertinent, however, as an example
of the potential and the actual corruptions of Platonism, with
which both the philosopher and the historian must reckon.
His thought was peculiarly liable to abuse because his ultimate criterion of truth was intuitive and subjective, not empirical. Trusting his spiritual vision, he taught men to look
for the essential truths in their own minds rather than the

---

[11] Aldous Huxley, one might say, has illustrated the speed of modern
life by going through in a lifetime a course that took centuries in ancient Greece. His sincere devoutness has carried him through enough
fads and cults to earn him his reputation as the 'Hollywood yogi.'

world around them; and once they have got this congenial idea they can naturally find whatever they have a mind to. But the main point remains that Plato's thought was symptomatic of the sickness of Athens, the apparent failure of its humanistic ideal. It was colored by a defeatism that is especially pertinent today, when men are again proclaiming the failure of humanism.

The defeatism is most apparent in Plato's political thought. The ideal state described in the *Republic* is the social equivalent of the perfect order in the Realm of Ideas. Because Plato advances many proposals that still seem radical—such as the community of wives and property, and the scientific regulations of child-breeding—his pious readers often fail to recognize how literally reactionary his political ideal is by democratic standards. His main concern is not the rights or the happiness of individuals but the stability of the State. He explicitly repudiates the ideals of liberty and equality. Assuming that the great majority of men are incapable of self-government, fit only to work or fight for the State, he devises a sort of caste system of workers, warriors, and philosopher-kings. The workers are barely mentioned, since their vulgar activities call for no serious attention. The warriors are carefully educated but are not allowed to have minds or lives of their own; their reading and even their music are rigorously censored. Only the philosophers may become rational, responsible human beings; they are given a thorough training because they must do all the thinking for the society. Briefly, Plato's ideal republic incorporates the ideal of the bee-hive, in which there is no freedom, no individualism, no desire for self-realization, but only an unthinking devotion to the prescribed task. His chief concession to the potential humanity of the common people is the 'noble lie' that the philosophers will tell them about their origin, in order to keep them content with their menial status.

Given the elevation of Plato's thought as a whole, it is grossly unfair to dismiss him as a 'Fascist philosopher.' One of his primary objects in the *Republic* was to refute the Fascist principle that Justice is the will of the strong, the interest of the superior few. He would never have condoned the irrationality and brutal tyranny of the dictators. None the less it is important to recognize that Plato was in line with Fascism in rejecting the principles of liberty and equality, tacitly denying the dignity and worth of the individual, even anticipating the technique of deliberately lying to the common people. For his ideal totalitarian state was conceived in the same disillusionment with democracy that led to the rise of Mussolini and Hitler. Having seen Athens fail, Plato had lost his faith in ordinary human nature. He was no longer able to put up with the risks of the 'open society.' For the sake of order and security he was willing to sacrifice even the spirit of his beloved master Socrates. Socrates would have been the first victim of his *Laws,* in which he not only banished poets from his ideal state but prescribed jail or death for open criticism of the state religion.[12]

Today Plato's ideal is still seductive, as men are again being frightened by the riskiness of the democratic adventure; so we might again pause to take our historic bearings. Athens fell, for good reasons. From Thucydides to Toynbee, historians have dwelt on the follies and injustices of Athenian democracy. It illustrated all the excesses that democracy is liable to; its equality bred demagogues, its liberty became license. Yet it was not merely democracy that failed in Greece. The tyrannies and oligarchies provided no more stability and security, not to mention justice and independence. To preserve their privileges, they were typically the first to sell out to the enemies of Greece (just as monarchists and big businessmen in Europe were the leading collaborators with the German conquerors). When the Athenian aristocrats came into power at the end of the Peloponnesian War— after repeated efforts to betray their city to Sparta—they were guilty of much worse excesses than any democratic regime before them. And Sparta, the victor, which gave Plato a working model of discipline, order, and complete subordination of the individual to the State—Sparta failed more quickly and miserably than Athens. Its superbly disciplined and devoted citizens had no other object than to maintain their iron control of the masses of helots; in victory it had nothing to offer the rest of the Greek world, of which it was always suspicious; lacking imagination or idealism, any capacity for

---

[12] Some scholars still argue that the *Republic* is not primarily the work of the aging Plato but contains much of the thought of Socrates. Since I am in no position to settle the issue, I am content merely to point to the unmistakable difference between the Socrates of the *Apology* and the Socrates of the *Republic.* The former does not know all the answers but teaches men to keep asking the first and last questions, insisting that 'the unexamined life is not worth living'; he chose to die rather than to sacrifice his own conscience to the State. The latter not only is more dogmatic but prescribes an unexamined life for almost all of his citizens; he lays down principles that justify the execution of the historic Socrates.

Other scholars have defended the *Republic* as a 'tale' of the individual 'writ large,' designed to illustrate the need for rigorous self-discipline, and not to be taken literally as a political scheme. Ordinary readers, however, cannot help feeling that Plato was quite serious about the political principles he took the trouble to expound at such length. And the principles recur in his *Laws,* which was certainly not intended as a mere 'tale' or political *jeu d'esprit.*

the arts of peace, it became arrogant and corrupt, earning the hatred of all Hellas by selling to Persia the liberties that Athens had won, for Persian aid in its wars against other Greek states; and within a generation it was overthrown, by hitherto inglorious Thebes.

Sparta was not Plato's ideal. It was a "timocracy," whose rulers were not philosopher-kings but warriors. Plato ranked timocracy above democracy, however, arguing that it produced a better type of man. It is accordingly significant that Sparta in its prime contributed nothing to Greek culture, built nothing worth excavating. In the spirit of Plato's ideal legislators it rigorously censored the arts and banned public discussion of philosophical issues. On the other hand, it is no accident that the Greek genius flowered most brilliantly in Athens, the freest, most democratic of the city-states. Those who deplore Athenian democracy are hardly entitled to celebrate the extraordinary creativity of the Age of Pericles. The abundant life that Plato himself pictured in such dialogues as the *Symposium* makes plainer the poverty of his civic ideal.

To my knowledge, Plato has not had a significant influence on political theory and practice. Men have seldom had to be taught to distrust democratic ideals; when conservatives have drawn on Plato's arguments I imagine it was chiefly to justify principles that they had already come by, all by themselves. Yet the *Republic* remains significant as a classic statement of the recurrent longing for the 'closed society.' It illustrates the un-ideal tendencies to which idealism is prone when it becomes too good for this world, disdainful of ordinary human nature and natural goods. While it is unfair to dismiss Plato as a Fascist philosopher, it is also unfair to regard him as a serene spiritual doctor, devising medicine for a troubled society. We may make better use of the freedom he gives to the human spirit, and of the wealth of suggestion for the ideal use of this freedom, if we see him in his historic context, as neither a timeless spirit nor a supreme Greek, but a disillusioned Athenian whose world was in fact a dim reflection of the ideal, changeless order he dreamed of.

5. The Hellenistic Age

Although the Hellenistic period has commonly been viewed as a decline, an epilogue of fading glory, contemporary Greeks felt quite differently. Those who followed in the wake of Alexander the Great believed that they were living in a 'new era'—not the end but the beginning of an age, which was more prosperous, enlightened, 'modern.' And they had reason for their pride. The aftermath of the fall of Athens and Sparta was truly a vigorous, exuberant, creative period. The conquest and Hellenization of the Eastern world was perhaps the most remarkable adventure of the Greeks, the most striking proof of their vitality and versatility. Where they had once clung to the shores of the Mediterranean, in colonies that were transplanted bits of Greece, they now ventured into a continent, settling in new cities among strange peoples. In adjusting themselves to this larger, more varied world, they made some new contributions, which classicists have tended to neglect but which have had more influence on our civilization than such purely classical masterpieces as the Parthenon, the sculpture of Phidias, and the tragedies of Sophocles. Their achievement has an especial interest for us, finally, because of some suggestive parallels between the Hellenistic world and the New World of America. The last great adventure of the Greeks brought them closer to us.

Granted that this achievement was due initially to a single man, Alexander the Great, it was essentially a creation of the Greek genius, inspired by their unique heritage. Alexander himself was an ultra-romantic pupil of Hellas who claimed descent from Achilles, worshiped the *Iliad*, and believed that his conquest of the Persian Empire completed the mission his ancestors had begun in the Trojan War. As a self-conscious crusader he founded some seventy new cities, to be centers of Greek culture, and his successors founded at least two hundred more. Homer was now read more widely than ever before; Athens was revered everywhere as the educator of Hellas; the scattered Hellenes became still more conscious of their common identity.

Yet the chief stimulus to their new achievements was their cosmopolitan life in new lands. For mainland Greece, after a brief spell of prosperity, the Hellenistic age was indeed an age of decay, economically, politically, and culturally; by the time the Romans moved in, Greece was exporting little except antiquities. The continued reverence for Athens, or even its continuous cultural activity, has a pathetic aspect, suggesting the old professor who was once scintillating, exciting, inspiring, but is now unaware of his mental enfeeblement, mulling over his old notes, repeating his old lectures, talking abstractedly to respectful students whose minds are elsewhere. The stirring goings on were outside of Greece. Where an intrepid Herodotus had traveled to the lands of the 'barbarians' alone and agog, hundreds of students, teachers, artists, and assorted adventurers now wandered freely from city to city. In this restless, variegated world there grew up revolutionary ideas—such ideas as the 'civilized world,' or even 'humanity,' which were beyond the ken of Plato's little Republic. In time Polybius would write a 'universal' history, of Rome's conquest of the whole Mediterranean world; other thinkers nurtured the idea of 'cosmopolis,' a universal society instead of the *polis*. Still later, a heretical Jewish sect could spread over the Hellenistic world and become the universal religion of Christianity.

Meanwhile the most impressive achievements of the Hellenistic Greeks were material or utilitarian. They became builders on a large scale, of highways, aqueducts, and harbors, and of splendid cities, such as Alexandria, Antioch, and Pergamon. They developed the art of city-planning, laying out whole cities instead of merely adorning an acropolis; their engineers promoted hygiene and comfort by building well-paved, well-drained streets and introducing water into the home. With the growth of this practical spirit there arose the professional and the specialist, alike in government, business, sport, art, and learning. In Alexandria the Ptolemies founded the famous museum, or 'house of the muses'—the first known state establishment for the advancement of literature and science; then Pergamon built up a rival library. (Athens had no public library until the time of the Roman Emperor Hadrian, centuries later.) Such establishments bred a new type of intellectual—the grammarian, editor, critic, scholar: a dull type, by contrast with the creative geniuses over whose work they pored, but useful because they preserved this work for us. In particular the professional spirit led to a systematic promotion of natural knowledge, instead of bold but haphazard speculation by brilliant amateurs. The impressive roster of Hellenistic Greeks, and their successors under Roman dominion, includes such names as Euclid and Apollonius in mathematics, Posidonius and Strabo in geography, Aristarchus, Hipparchus, and Ptolemy in astronomy, Archimedes in mathematics and physics, and Galen in medicine. With Archimedes, for the first time in history, thought became a conscious inquiry into nature for the sake of controlling nature. He was the Newton of technology, inventing the science of mechanics and laying the theoretical foundations of engineering.

All this activity sprang from a vigorous expansion of trade and industry. The Hellenistic age was perhaps the greatest age of business before our own. It was an age of prosperous bourgeois, frankly devoted to material well-being. Yet they were also devoted to the ancient cultural values, especially the tradition of beauty. It might be profitable for both intellectuals and businessmen today to consider the very high level of gracious, civilized life that the Hellenistic world attained at its best. Pergamon, the 'second Athens' is the most brilliant example; but Priene is more striking, simply because it was never great or famous.

Priene was a small city of some four thousand inhabitants, overshadowed by neighboring Miletus, known chiefly for its perfect temple to Athena. To build this temple, its citizens had called in Pytheus, the architect of the Mausoleum of Halicarnassus—one of the Seven Wonders of the ancient world. They called in the best artists of the time to adorn all their public buildings, and had lovely statuettes in their homes as well. Their art treasures now adorn the museums of Europe, but the bare ruins that remain still testify to the high Greek traditions maintained by little Priene. It had its temples, standing proudly up on the mountainside overlooking the Gulf of Latmos.[13] It had a dignified *bouleterion,* where its town council met; it had a charming theater; it had its palestra, stadium, and marbled marketplace. It was a beautifully planned city, compact within its walls, but seemingly spacious because built in terraces on the slope of the mountain. Altogether, the citizens of Priene evidently enjoyed a combination of comfort and culture that would put to shame the ordinary American town. And it was not a wealthy suburb or resort but an autonomous city, once wholly independent. It was one of a hundred such cities in Asia Minor alone.

Then we must add that Priene, and its fellows, never produced such men as did Athens in its prime. Apparently it was not a highly creative city; it had to import most of its art and artists, it looked to the past for its culture. Even its time-washed ruins give some impression of bourgeois complacence that might settle into lethargy, degenerate into vulgarity. We may assume that like the Hellenistic world at large it suffered from both the corruptions and the limitations of its success.

Thus the increasing wealth of the Greeks brought the familiar vices of luxury; moral disorder was aggravated by the cosmopolitanism of an uprooted people. Their specialists included professional athletes, mercenary soldiers, and unproductive dealers and speculators, who typified the increasing venality and selfish individualism. Their art tended to be-

---

[13] This gulf has since become a plain, filled in by the Meander River. The once great port of Miletus, across the gulf from Priene, is now a poor Turkish village, miles inland. So one may moralize on the vanity of human history—or on its heroism, in the face of such whims of nature. Miletus put up a long struggle as it kept receding from the sea.

come more sentimental, ornate, or grandiose reflecting a bourgeois vulgarity that was to be inherited by Roman and Victorian architecture; their sculptured gods were less god-like, more like human giants. Their scholarly and critical work tended to become pedantic, foreshadowing the sterile Atticism of later Roman times. Because of this pedantry, ironically, little of their own literature was preserved—it was not written in a pure Attic style; but they wrote epigrams, idylls, and prose romances rather than epics or tragedies. And all these tendencies reveal the failure of the Hellenistic Greeks to solve their basic problems.

Of this failure Priene is also a symbol. Most obviously, it typified the chronic, fatal particularism of the Greeks. It often fought in the wars among the Greek cities; its primary aim was always self-sufficiency in its own little world. Alexander gave the Greeks a great world to live in, but upon his death they began re-enacting on a large scale the same dismal story of incessant strife. His empire at once broke up into kingdoms, which for two centuries fought one another as the little city-states had, until all fell into the lap of Rome.[14] The tragedy was intensified by a contradiction of the kind we suffer from today. The Greeks were developing humanitarian ideals, as well as a stronger feeling of solidarity, yet the warfare became increasingly barbarous, with Greeks enslaving fellow-Greeks, massacring non-combatants, sacking their most sacred temples. And from all this strife the chief sufferer was mainland Greece, the heart of Hellas. Here the warfare was most devastating and atrocious, the moral indignation most horrified and helpless.

Priene likewise typified the internal evils that undermined the prosperity and power of the Hellenistic kingdoms. As we admire it we must remember that its citizens were largely well-to-do landowners, whose comfort and culture rested on the labor of slaves and sullen natives in the surrounding country. Neither the peasantry nor the city proletariat shared in the prosperity of the Hellenistic age. In times of war they were always liable to enslavement; in times of rising prosperity they commonly became poorer, as prices

---

[14] Here again historical accidents raise portentous might-have-beens. If the brilliant Alexander had not died so prematurely at the age of thirty-two, he might have succeeded in consolidating his conquests and setting up the great Greek state of which he dreamed. But the fact remains that the Greeks were never able to achieve political unity or maintain peace by their own efforts. Their closest approach was the Achaean League in the Peloponnesus—a democratic federation of free states that maintained itself until the Romans moved in. This feat of the hitherto obscure Achaeans only accentuates, however, the repeated failure of Athens and the other great cities.

rose while slave labor kept wages low. Yet no great reformer or philosopher ever tried to solve this problem of extreme inequality, or to bridge the widening gulf between private morality and social practice. No thinker clearly realized the unsoundness of an economic system in which the impoverished masses limited the market for productive enterprise, and grew more hostile or more apathetic.

All such problems were aggravated by the essential artificiality of the Hellenistic kingdoms, which were unified only by the military force of the kings. Alexander apparently dreamed of establishing a genuine cosmopolis and made some effort to fuse the cultures of Greece and Persia. Even his announcement of his divinity, as the son of Zeus-Ammon, may not have been a delusion of grandeur but a deliberate concession to Oriental ways. This missionary spirit was foreign to the Greeks, however, and what survived Alexander was chiefly the idea of the sacred monarchy, later to be inherited by Rome and Christendom. Those who followed him did not come to Hellenize or to extend the blessings of liberty and law—they came to make a better living for themselves. Knowing and caring only about the freedom of the city, they were unprepared to establish anything like democracy on a large scale, even had the natives been ready for such government. The Greeks too were now disposed to accept the ancient institution of monarchy that the East had always accepted. Yet there was little reverence for most of the Hellenistic kings, among either the Greeks or the oppressed natives. Likewise the cultural fusion was incomplete. Although the Greeks mingled freely with the upper classes of the natives, adopting some customs and leaving their own mark on the native cultures, they lived mostly in their own cities—little Greek islands in an Oriental sea—and they made virtually no impress on the peasant masses. Hence the mongrel Hellenistic kingdoms were rent by profound divisions, between slave and free, proletariat and bourgeoisie, city and country, Greek and native, which made them an easy prey for the Romans.

We shall return to these issues when we come to the Romans. Their greater success in organizing the Hellenistic world and their ultimate failure to sustain it are more pertinent for contemporaries. Meanwhile there remains a suggestive analogy.

In *The Passing of the European Age*, Eric Fischer notes the resemblance between America and the Hellenistic world, as vigorous offshoots of a parent society in a new environment. The Greeks, it is true, moved into old, civilized areas and lived among the natives, whereas the Europeans moved to a new continent and drove away or exterminated the natives. (The Spaniards, who did encounter high civilizations, first enslaved the Indians and then converted them to Christianity; but by this policy they as effectually destroyed the native culture.) Nevertheless both peoples emigrated to new lands that became melting pots, both took a new lease on life; and recent history has paralleled Hellenistic history in the decline of the old country. With the world wars, the climax of its failure to achieve unity, Europe has lost its practical and economic leadership, as Greece did after its civil wars. Germany might have restored the supremacy of Europe, but it has failed catastrophically in two attempts to dominate the Continent; so now, as in the Hellenistic age, the offspring are greater powers and are laying down the law to their parents. Even the cultural leadership of the mother country is on the wane. Although the Americans still look to the Continent—especially to Paris—as the Hellenistic Greeks looked to Athens, they are developing independent cultures, based on the European tradition but containing original elements. Europe has often admired their contributions, in the manner of an indulgent parent proud of its bright offspring; but it is also resisting their influence, as immature, crude, or alien, just as Athens clung jealously to its traditions when the most vigorous creative work was being done outside of Greece. Hence European intellectuals are especially prone to gloomy views of the future, because to them the decline of Europe means the decline of Western civilization. They tend to ignore or resent the possibly healthy growths in the new centers outside Europe.[15]

Americans may welcome this whole analogy, as a confirmation of their manifest destiny. If so, they had better consider it closely. They have not yet produced men worthy to be

---

[15] Some of Spengler's 'symptoms' of Western decline, for example, are conspicuous only in Europe, or even only in the Germany of his day. Thus he proved that modern philosophy is sterile by describing it as purely academic, completely removed from the public life, as in Germany it might have been; but American philosophy has been characteristically pragmatic, and its most influential thinker—John Dewey—has been the most actively concerned with public life, exerting a profound influence on education. Similarly Toynbee is unable to do justice to such possibly rich growths as Mexican painting. To him, the new movements in the various arts stemming from non-European sources are examples of 'vulgarization and barbarism'; in cultural matters he is an ultra-conservative, with a fine taste for the classical tradition but a professorial distaste for the unorthodox or unrefined. (Had he lived in the Elizabethan age he would probably have been repelled by the vulgarity and barbarism of Shakespeare's plays.) And the sweeping generalizations about Western civilization indulged by Spengler and Toynbee alike do not clearly apply to such large areas as Canada, Brazil, and Australia.

ranked with Aquinas, Michelangelo, Shakespeare, Montaigne, Newton, Beethoven, and Goethe; today they cannot claim superiority over contemporary European culture, and in most branches are only beginning to approach European achievement; and as for the future, they might remember that except in science and technology the Hellenistic world never did equal the achievement of Athens. Still more important is the immense responsibility of their possible mission. The enterprising Hellenistic Greeks failed to unite their world and keep it strong. Americans have more missionary spirit and a somewhat clearer idea of means and ends, but they have not clearly learned the most apparent lesson of Hellenistic history, which is that order and peace cannot be achieved unless nations surrender their right to determine and defend their self-interests at any costs, in any circumstances. Meanwhile Russia is more clearly analogous to the Macedonia of Philip and Alexander, as a stepchild that is the greatest power in Europe.

In a long view of the future, finally, this analogy suggests still different possibilities. The Greek conquest of the East stimulated a revival among some Oriental peoples, such as the Parthians and the Maccabean Jews. Similarly the Western domination of the East has stimulated a revival in this century, as in Turkey, Arabia, Persia, India, and China. In time, Eastern peoples may again surge back, as the Arabs and Turks succeeded in reconquering the whole dominion of Alexander, and almost succeeded in conquering Europe. But long before these military triumphs the East had won a subtler victory, by religion. In the cosmopolitan Hellenistic world, the naturally easy-going, companionable Olympians soon took Oriental consorts; and these, by temperament and long experience, were better suited to preside over the hard times that followed. The final result of Alexander's conquest was the conquest of the West by the spirituality and the superstition of the mystical, fatalistic East. Hence Toynbee has conjectured that a tide of Oriental religious spirit may again sweep over the West, if the times get bad enough. The growing interest in this 'perennnial philosophy' might be a portent.

Such possibilities, however, offer no clear hope of salvation. The Greeks were not saved by their new gods, or deeply comforted and sustained, if only because they did not really believe in them as the natives did. They could not give themselves up to their Oriental religions unless they also gave up the most distinctive interests and values of their own culture—in other words, unless they ceased to be Greeks. No more, I should assume, could Westerners wholeheartedly embrace a passive, other-worldly spirit, unless their civilization was in ruins.

6. THE LEGACY OF HUMANISM

'You are going to visit men who are supremely men,' Pliny wrote to a friend setting out for Greece. Although the Greeks of Roman times may not have deserved this compliment, it was a handsome acknowledgment of their great legacy to mankind. The supreme goal of their culture had been the making of men—free, conscious, self-reliant, fully developed men. For me, the last word about Greece belongs to the supreme humanism that created its unique glory.

'What is Man, that Thou art mindful of him?' The Greeks gave proud answers to this question, which to the Hebrew Psalmist was merely rhetorical. From the beginning they said in effect that man is the proper study of mankind, if not the measure of all things. Man was the main actor in Homer; the heroes were dearer to him than the gods. Man was the subject of the incomparable sculpture of the Greeks: in their gods they represented the ideal perfection of the human form. For all their living ideals they looked to great men, who spoke for themselves rather than as privy councillors of deity. They had no Moses to bring them God's commandments from Sinai: they got their laws from Solons, men who were patriots, and they got their Bible from Homer, a man who had named the gods and put them in their places. They were always so eager to find a human author for everything they inherited from a shadowy past that we cannot be sure there ever was a Homer, a Hippocrates, or a Lycurgus; but they felt surer of such men than of the gods. When Pericles summed up the ideal faith of Athens in his Funeral Oration, he failed to pay even a perfunctory tribute to the gods. And though Pericles was known to be more skeptical than most, he was appealing to the deepest faith of the Athenians, which was a devotion to Athens itself, the city of free men.

Even the tragic poets, who taught the nemesis of pride, expressed the pride of humanism. The Greeks were the originators of Tragedy because of their very zest for life, which made them feel more poignantly than other peoples 'the pathos of mortality,' the ultimate vanity.

> Nothingness, nothingness,
> Ye Children of Man, and less

I count you, waking or dreaming!
And none among mortals, none,
Seeking to live, hath won
More than to seem, and to cease
Again from his seeming

—so chanted a chorus of Sophocles. Another chorus, however, explains why Sophocles continued to invest this mere seeming with the magnificence of Tragedy:

Numberless are the world's wonders, but none
More wonderful than man . . .
O clear intelligence, force beyond all measure!
O fate of man, working both good and evil!

The life of man was nothing because it was everything. 'When man faces destiny,' André Malraux observes, 'destiny ends and man comes into his own.' Like all Greek art, Tragedy was 'the dance of man casting off at last the yoke of destiny'; what the Athenians admired was 'not man's defeat but the poet's triumph.' And if the poet himself was more aware of the yoke, the wisdom of resignation that he counseled was still not the glad humility that declares, Let Thy will be done. While recognizing the guilt and folly of man, the Greeks had little sense of sin—of inherent unworthiness before their Creator, or of their shortcomings as crimes against their Creator. The mystics aside, they lived neither in fear nor in love of God but went about their own business of making the most of life on earth. Granted a decent piety, their primary duties were to the city-state and to themselves.

This humanism raises a final issue that is often glossed over by conventional admirers of Greece, especially in academic circles. Although 'humanism' is still a fairly honorable word, since it has usually kept dignified company, other words for the Greek spirit are 'naturalistic,' 'secular,' 'worldly' —words that now ring in denunciation of the modern world. The traditional mottos of the Seven Wise Men of Greece (Consider the end, Seize time by the forelock, Nothing is impossible to industry, et cetera) embody a wisdom as secular as Poor Richard's; while the oracles in the national shrines specialized in inside advice about worldly affairs, tips on what the gods might have up their sleeves. Today we are told that such a naturalistic, humanistic faith cannot sustain man, who needs the support of a supernatural power, or else that it has sustained too many men, who are leading our world to disaster. We are told that man cannot be happy and good unless he fears God and confesses his helplessness without God.

And so it may be worth our while to review the familiar story of the religion of Greece.

To the eternal question about the nature of the unseen, unknown powers, the early Greeks answered that the gods were very much like men, superhuman in their powers but quite human in their interests. From this human quality stemmed the obvious limitations of the Olympian gods. They were unsatisfactory for metaphysical purposes, explaining little or nothing about the origin and destiny of the universe. They were as unsatisfactory for moral purposes, even aside from the licentiousness of their private lives; they were arbitrary and capricious in their favors, taking sides in a war fought over a woman, 'laughing pleasantly' at the strife among men or among themselves.[16] They were much too vivid personalities—at once too independent and too deeply attached to their favorite temples—ever to settle down, take on universal duties, administer impersonal laws, and behave like Absolutes. To a purist, indeed, the Olympian religion was not really a religious faith. Homer sometimes smiles at the gods, suggesting the attitude of Voltaire's Spinoza toward God: 'But between you and me, I believe you do not exist.'

By the same token, however, the Olympians were good gods for humanistic purposes. If they were occasionally unpredictable and unaccountable, just as men are, they were never alien or simply fearsome; they could be understood and appeased. If they loved gifts and were touchy about neglect or any open aspersions on their dignity, they were far less jealous than most gods; generally they were reasonable, good-natured, and gracious. They permitted the Greeks to make themselves at home in the world. Above all, they left thought and aspiration free. Wrapped up in their own celestial affairs, they did not demand correct opinions about their nature, confer divine rights on kings, endow a powerful, exclusive church, or encourage holy virtuosos to set themselves apart from ordinary good citizens. They refused to submit to a priesthood or to authorize a Sacred Book. And in their amiability they could be induced to become good Greeks.

---

[16] In fairness to the Olympians, we should remember that they were invaders, who came into Greece with the Northmen and settled among the older gods they found there. The innumerable adulteries of Zeus, for example, were not due to mere wantonness; he had to have affairs with various local goddesses, or become the father of local gods, in order to bring about religious unity and peace. To such honorable purposes he sacrificed his own domestic peace: Hera was especially jealous because she was his second wife, who had once been Queen of Thessaly in her own right. Gilbert Murray reviews this whole story in *Five Stages of Greek Religion.*

One of the great religious reformations in history, which must have been well under way before Homer's time, was this civilizing of the Olympians—the conversion of rude, swashbuckling, thunderbolting mountain-gods into the builders of cities, the patrons of light, order, beauty, love, joy, wisdom, and at length even virtue. Although they remained glorified human beings they were at least glorified, and at best glorious. The best was Apollo, a sun-god of mongrel ancestry who was transformed, in Santayana's view, into 'an ideal standard for action and a perfect object for contemplation.' He is no less admirable when we add that as far as literal truth goes, the new Apollo was as fictitious as the old —that he never really existed, never could exist except in the minds of men. He was more inspiring because he did not inspire dogma. He exemplified the spirit that erected the temple 'To the Unknown God,' which St. Paul found in Athens: a temple implicitly recognizing the symbolical function of religion and the inadequacy of any literal creed.

As Aeschylus, Euripides, Socrates, Plato, and others groped their way toward the idea of One God, universal, nameless, and impersonal, the Olympians were perforce left behind; yet they did not have to be exterminated. They could still be revered as poetic symbols or honorable civic traditions, and indirectly they could even lend aid to these high endeavors. Since they had encouraged a reasonable, tolerant spirit in religious matters, the later Greeks could be serious about their new conceptions of the One God without feeling any obligation to lay down an orthodox creed. To the rhetorical question asked by the Hebrews—'Canst thou by searching find out God?'—they could answer, Yes and no. They said that man should search, and find out the supreme good, but that he could not and need not hope for an intimate acquaintance with God.

Socrates is the best example of this religious spirit. 'To find the Father and Maker of all is hard,' he said, 'and having found him it is impossible to utter him.' He did not pretend to know the divine mind or the divine purposes. Meanwhile he assumed that the proper 'service of God' was a constant search, not a reiteration of faith in God or simple submission to his will. He started mankind on the great quest of wisdom, of justice, of moral order through moral freedom, of a good life that can be justified on rational instead of merely traditional grounds. The habitual irony of his manner sprang from the tension of a life-long quest that realized the full implications of the questing spirit—the implications at once of realism and idealism, humility and pride, skepticism and faith, in the knowledge that wisdom and virtue cannot be won by mere logical rigor or brute moral strength.

In his insistence that a man's first and last concern should be his soul, not wealth or power, Socrates anticipated Christ: 'What shall it profit a man, if he gain the whole world and lose his own soul?' But Socrates did not teach men to save their souls in the Christian sense—save them for God in a life to come. Unable or unwilling to define and explain the soul, uncertain whether there was a life to come, he taught in effect that the soul was the normal consciousness; it was not a supernatural or purely 'spiritual' entity but a natural faculty of a rational animal, the given source of man's distinctive but natural excellence. Hence the highest good that Socrates sought was not supernatural or transcendent—it was a positive human good, good for something in this life, good enough for this life alone. It was a good that all men could achieve by their own efforts, through reason, without benefit of special grace. If the 'inner voice' to which Socrates appealed was ultimately the voice of God, he told men to heed it for their own sake, not for God's sake. In his own 'service of God' he was primarily a servant of mankind.

The martyrdom of Socrates is sufficient proof that irony and skepticism may be consistent with positive faith, and humanism with spirituality. The first great apostle of intellectual and moral freedom, he remains a supreme example of intellectual and moral integrity. He did not become the founder of a higher religion, however. Like most of the poets and philosophers who sounded the deepest religious thought of Greece, Socrates lacked intense religious fervor. He sought wisdom rather than holiness, sanity rather than sanctity. Even in his martyrdom he had none of the fierce exaltation of the prophets of Israel, or of St. Paul. At the end he did not ask in anguish why his God had forsaken him, or in any way invite his disciples to worship him as a martyred Messiah. He could not be resurrected, except by a complete falsification of his message. He offered no guarantee of life eternal.

For most devotees of higher religions, the distinctive religious spirit of Greece is not spiritual enough. Apollo was a god for this world alone; he did not encourage men to stake their hopes on a better world than the actual one. To St. Paul, the temple 'To the Unknown God' was another sign of the foolishness of the Greeks; the Athenian philosophers were merely curious about the One True God who had spoken to Paul from the heavens. As for Socrates, one may say that he was too humble, too sweetly reasonable, to be a religious prophet; or one may say, with Carlyle, that he was too much

made at ease in Zion. At any rate, the Greeks characteristically made it their business to be at ease in Zion, as did both
the Epicureans and the Stoics after Socrates. Hence a Carlyle
might add that in the long run the Greeks did not succeed very
well. Neither the Olympian religion nor the religion of Socrates
proved adequate for bad times, the times that try men's souls.
Neither was a religion for the meek and poor in spirit. So the
Greeks came to seek salvation in mysticism or the mystery-
gods, and at length in the resurrected Christ of St. Paul.

And so we return to the issue of humanism. We may be disposed to draw the obvious moral as we contemplate the ruins
of the Acropolis of Athens, with its temples to dead gods, or
as we see the timeless peasant grazing his goats on the sites
of Mycenae, of Pergamon, of Priene. Vanity of vanities, saith
the Preacher; nothingness, nothingness, ye children of man;
and the deadliest sin is pride. In their proud faith in man, the
Greek states were destroyed, and their peoples vanished from
history; while in their humble trust in God the Israelites survived the destruction of their national state, and as a people
still live. Yet this is not the whole moral that even the pious
draw from the ruins of Greece. These ruins are holy too. As
we contemplate them we are also thrilled by the spirit that
built so superbly. When the Greeks turned to other-worldly
religions they continued to be creative, helping to build the
impressive structure of Christian theology; but we do not
treasure these later works as we do all the splendid creations
of their unregenerate, pagan prime. And their civilization
did not really die. Time, the great enemy they feared, has
brought them a deathless fame, more glorious than even they
dreamed of in their passion for fame, and in a world far
greater than they conceived. Most of their culture still lives, in
us. At the heart of our civilization there is still the naturalistic,
humanistic faith of Greece.

Ordinarily, our civilization is described as fundamentally
Christian. 'Western Christendom' is Toynbee's name for it;
T. S. Eliot declares that 'if Christianity goes, the whole of our
culture goes.' They both believe, however, that Christianity
started going in the late Middle Ages; certainly Aquinas and
Dante are not so close to us in spirit as are Pericles, Euripides, and Socrates; so it would seem clear that our culture
has been molded more by Greek secular ideals.[17] These ideals

[17] It should be added, of course, that Christianity too has been deeply influenced by Greek thought, and is not simply opposed to it. But
if these two main strands in our heritage cannot be separated, they can
and should be distinguished. Christianity includes a Hebraic tradition
that is radically different from the Greek; and the most distinctively
Christian periods or movements in our history, such as the Middle Ages
and the Protestant Reformation, were essentially un-Greek.

were the mainspring of the Renaissance and the Age of the Enlightenment, the rise of science and the rise of democracy. By now the scientific, political, and industrial revolutions have carried us far from Hellas, as from Palestine, into a world at once greater and smaller, where life is more varied and abundant, and more standardized and impoverished. By our faith in the power of reason we have vastly increased our knowledge and understanding, and made much more dangerous the powers of ignorance and irrationality; we have set up the ideal of freedom for all men, and have created machinery of unprecedented efficiency for enslaving the minds and crushing the spirit of men; we have gone much further in the experiment of the open society, and of the totalitarian society. We are therefore more aware of the dangers inherent in the Greek adventure. Nevertheless this is the adventure to which the Western world has been committed, and in the democracies still is.

Today many men are again yearning for more assurance, of more exalted hopes, than Socrates offered. Yet I believe that the natural human goods he stood for still need to be stressed more than the supernatural goods he failed to promise. Toynbee quotes with approval the verdict of Paul Elmer More on classical philosophy, that 'in setting the emphasis so strongly upon knowledge and intelligence, and in leaving so little room for the will and the instinctive emotions,' it failed to touch the great heart of mankind. As a historian, however, Toynbee presumably believes in the value of knowledge and intelligence, and recognizes that the will and instinctive emotions have had ample play throughout history, with dubious consequences. I doubt that mankind has grown too devoted to knowledge and intelligence. The will and instinctive emotions had plenty of room in Hitler's Germany and Mussolini's Italy, and they seem active enough in Russia and America today. If Socrates still fails to touch the great heart of mankind, the reason is that his ideal is too lofty, not that it is too narrow, meager, or cold. Even though his way of life may not accommodate all the religious fervour of the Hebrew prophets, I believe that the world today needs reasonableness even more than it needs fervor.

VI

The Rise of Christianity

1. THE VARIETIES OF CHRISTIAN EXPERIENCE

Although no Christian, I suppose, would deny that Christianity has had a history, few seem really aware of the implications of this truism. Believers naturally tend to assume that their beliefs are the immutable truths revealed or discovered by the founder of their religion. So St. Vincent of Lérins defined Catholicism as 'what all men have believed, everywhere and always'; Protestant sectarians believe that they have returned to the true faith, which was corrupted by Catholicism; liberal Christians assume that all the diverse sects have the same basic faith, which is unfortunately obscured by their wrangling over detail. All overlook the profound changes that have taken place throughout Christian history, and the profound divisions in any given period. As the Epistles of St. Paul reveal, the earliest followers of Jesus disagreed sharply over his teachings; there were some twenty varieties of Christianity by the second century, and at least eighty by the fourth century. The Church Fathers entertained beliefs that are heretical by medieval standards and naïve by modern standards. Today most educated Christians entertain beliefs that would have bewildered or shocked St. Paul, and made them eligible for burning in medieval Rome or in Calvin's Geneva.

The individual believer, accordingly, will continue to find the 'true' meaning of Christianity in his own conception of the highest Christian ideals. To the charge that Christianity has failed he may then answer that it has never been tried. But this could be said as well of all the higher religions and philosophies. Meanwhile we must consider not only the various ideals preached in the name of Christ but the actual behavior of Christian churches and societies, from which a detached observer might not deduce those ideals. The historic meaning of Christianity as an established religion lies not in its origins or its choicest expressions but in its entire history—all the thought, feeling, and conduct that it has inspired, and failed to inspire. And this history, like that of all other human institutions, is wonderfully and woefully mixed. It is shot through with absurd, sublime, and tragic contradictions, of hope and fear, love and hatred, ecstasy and atrocity.

The plainest reason for a survey of this history is that Christianity has been the avowed basis of Western culture, the frame of reference for even its un-Christian and anti-Christian developments. It produced Voltaire, Huxley, and Nietzsche as well as Dante, Milton, and Newton. But a survey is especially pertinent today because of the swelling chorus of voices in the wilderness crying that we can hope to save our civilization only by returning to a faith in God. No one is saying that any old faith will do; so the question is, What faith? What God? No Westerner is arguing for a return to the Orthodox faith of St. Sophia, though this would seem to be as valid a choice as Roman Catholicism and the many varieties of Protestantism. And underlying these sectarian differences are still more fundamental differences in concepts of God and the good life. The Christian tradition includes a greater variety of conflicting traditions than any other high religion.

Specifically, are we to return to a stern, inscrutable God in fear? Or to a loving, lawful God in joy? May we approach him through reason, believing that religious truth may be beyond reason but is not contrary to it? Or must we accept him on faith, and distrust the claims of reason as sinful pride? Is the Kingdom of God within us, in the eternal present, sufficient unto itself? Or must we expect a literal heaven and hell? And if there is a hereafter, may all men achieve salvation simply by being good? Or does salvation require correct opinions about God and the ministry of a church? To a sophisticated generation such questions may seem academic—though in Christian history they have literally been burning issues. Other questions, however, make a vital difference in everyday life. Is the world, as God's creation, a blessing to be used, enjoyed, made the most of? Or a devil's snare to be contended against? Or a vale of tears to be escaped? Should we guard against 'a fugitive and cloistered virtue'? Or should we guard against attachment to the world and temporal interests? Is the body the prison of the soul, the vile flesh the antithesis of spirit? Or are body and soul inseparable, and ideally a harmonious whole? Should we love all men, refrain from all violence, and resist not evil? Or should we hate God's enemies and war on evil? Should we judge, or judge not? Should we concentrate on saving our society, or our souls?

Historic Christianity has given contradictory answers to all these questions. Rationalism and fideism, monism and dualism, optimism and pessimism, worldliness and other-worldliness, mildness and militancy—all have been embraced by the most flexible of religions, while it proclaimed its inflexible devotion to its immutable truths. This diversity is a sign of the vitality of Christianity, which has been able to survive profound changes, adapting itself to good times and bad, accommodating new knowledge and new aspirations. The diversity is also an obvious source of confusion and conflict; it helps to explain why Christianity has never succeeded in stamping a society as indelibly as has Juadism, Mohammedanism, and Confucianism. At any rate, here is the historic meaning, or welter of meanings, that we must consider before we commit ourselves to programs for salvation.

The historians of civilization have made this issue still more pertinent. Spengler pointed out that civilizations in decline have typically been marked by a 'second religiousness'; in disillusionment and despair, they seek to recapture the vital faith of the ancestors, or to manufacture some synthetic substitute. In Spengler's view, accordingly, the symptoms of such religiousness today would signify the beginning of the end—the hopelessness of salvation. Toynbee, once more, gives a different meaning to much the same picture. Although he notes that disintegrating societies are given to 'archaism,' or futile efforts to revive the dead past, he prefers to describe the new religiousness as 'transcendence' or 'transfiguration'; the dying society gives birth to a higher religion, a truer conception of the One True God. In some of his recent essays Toynbee speculates that the great drama of the future may be the counteraction of Islam and the Far East upon Western civilization, which presumably would give rise to a still higher religion, incorporating the best of Christianity and the Oriental religions, and perhaps arriving at some new conceptions. But generally he argues that the Christian God is the One True God. If so, Christianity should be the spiritual heir of all other religions; and one secular Western civilization, which has given it the whole world to spread over, has reason to hope for a reprieve if it returns to its original faith. Once the True God is known to all mankind, his purposes might not demand the continued destruction of civilizations.

To a detached observer, the strongest argument for this possibly arrogant assumption that Christianity is the apex of spiritual progress is an argument that Toynbee does not press. As the last great product of the ancient world, Christianity was a synthesis of Jewish, Oriental, Greek, and Roman thought and feeling; when it converted the lusty Germanic peoples and became the faith of a rising civilization, it ceased to be primarily an end-of-the-world religion; and in recent centuries it has been adapting itself, however tardily and painfully, to the consequences of the political, scientific, and industrial revolutions. Hence it is potentially capable of the further growth and change that would be required of a really universal religion in a going society. In this view, of course, one cannot speak confidently of the nature of the One True God or the religion of the future. But one may at least hope to assess more realistically the possibilities of Christianity as an agent of salvation for our civilization, or as an inheritor of the remnants, the values of the next civilization.

From any point of view, the birth and growth of Christianity is among the most momentous dramas in history, as well as the most fascinating. The immediate question is how and why it triumphed. It had rich soil, made fertile by the decay of the ancient religions of Greece and Rome, and by the uprooting of masses of people; but for the same reason it might have been choked out by the mystery cults that were growing like weeds all over the Roman Empire. The answer is not simple, nor simply edifying.[1] We may concentrate, however, on four major factors (apart from the heritage of Judaism) that distinguished Christianity from other popular mysteries. These are the figure of Jesus, as man and as Christ; the contribution of St. Paul, the greatest of apostles; the development of a theology, which made the new religion philosophically respectable; and the organization of a Church on the Roman imperial model, which made it powerful. We may then consider the fortuitous contribution of the Emperor Constantine, whom the Church had reason to call 'the equal of the Apostles'; his conversion to a despised minority sect enabled it to become the imperial religion. Finally, we may consider the consequences of this triumph:

---

[1] It appears, for example, that many pagans were attracted by the monotheism and stoic ethics of Judaism but repelled by the food laws and especially by the requirement of circumcision, which invited the taunts of their fellows and their womenfolk. Christianity offered comparable attractions without such embarrassments.

what the Church won, and lost, and what the masses brought with them as they were led or driven into it.

Altogether, we may read an epical success story. But even for religious purposes we might do well to read it in the tragic spirit: aware that its happy ending was also an unhappy beginning, and that in affairs of the spirit nothing fails like worldly success.

2. THE HISTORIC JESUS

When Jesus went about his 'Father's business' in the Temple, his parents naturally did not understand him; yet we too are still mystified. The pious, painstaking efforts to recover the historic Jesus, on which scholars have been engaged for more than a century, have revealed how astonishingly little we know for certain about the human life of our Lord. In so far as his gospel seems clear, they have revealed that it was in fundamental respects quite different from the religion that grew up in his name. And they have revealed a prophet who in still other respects is a stranger to us—an unsophisticated villager from an alien world.

Of the meager, conflicting biographical data recorded in the Gospels, the birth of Jesus will do as an example. No one knows, of course, the exact date when he was born. Against the opposition of the East where he had lived, the Western churches elected 25 December because of pagan tradition: it was a festival day that marked the winter solstice (through an astronomical miscalculation) and was therefore holy to the Sun God—especially to Mithra, who was the chief rival to Christ as a Saviour-God. As for the details of the birth, we have our choice of the idyllic story of Luke, with the shepherds and the manger, or the grim story of Matthew, with the slaughter of the innocents and the flight to Egypt. The most significant detail on which these two authors agree is that he was born of a virgin—a detail unmentioned by Mark or John, and foreign to Hebrew tradition.[2] Such scanty

[2] 'Behold a virgin shall conceive and bear a son,' reads the prophecy of Isaiah in the King James Bible. Modern scholars, however, substantiate the protests of the early Jewish opponents of Christianity, that the word translated as 'virgin' meant only a young woman in Hebrew, and that the whole legend of the virgin birth closely resembled the tall stories of the foolish Greeks, who invented such an origin for Plato, Pythagoras, Alexander, and other heroes. (Matthew's story in particular is similar to the legend of Plato, born of a virgin by Apollo.) Some early Christians preferred the theory of Adoptionism implicit in the Gospel according to Mark, who says nothing of the birth and has the Spirit descending upon Jesus after he was baptized by John. In this view, Jesus was born a man but earned divinity by his spiritual achievement, thereby setting a still higher example for other men.

records are not really astonishing. The early Christians were not interested in the human life of Jesus, or the anniversary of his birth. They were interested primarily in his resurrection, on which they staked their whole hope of salvation. 'If Christ be not risen,' insisted St. Paul, 'then is our preaching vain, and your faith is also vain.' Without this belief there would have been no Christianity; and with its rise Jesus disappeared from view, leaving only a few scattered memories that were colored by the faith in the risen Christ.

Even the teachings of Jesus involve considerable uncertainty. The Gospels preserve only fragments of his many discourses—all that is recorded could be said in a few hours—and we cannot be sure that their selection or emphasis is fairly representative; they are interpretations of his message in the light of ideas that grew up after his death. The New Testament was the product of the early churches, not their basis. When Protestantism sought to return to the Bible, it returned to doctrines that were not certainly taught by Jesus himself.

Although some scholars have therefore questioned even the existence of Jesus, this extreme skepticism seems unwarranted. Certain details of the Gospel narratives impress one as unquestionably authentic—for example, the misunderstanding of his family, the denial of Peter, and the flight of the Apostles —because they are scarcely the kind of detail that would be invented to glorify the Christ. The last words of Jesus on the cross, as reported by Mark and Matthew—'My God, my God, why hast thou forsaken me?'—give an especially poignant sense of the human tragedy of Jesus: the physical and spiritual anguish, the final loneliness, the terrible suspicion that his mission has been a failure. (The gentle Luke has the dying Jesus say, 'Father, into thy hands I commend my spirit.' John, who makes Jesus aware of his fate from beginning to end, reports a simple, 'It is finished.') In spite of all their discrepancies, moreover, the gospels of Mark, Matthew, and Luke give so similar an impression of Jesus that they are rightly known as the 'synoptic' Gospels. They picture an inspired missionary who was not profoundly original in his thought but who had a singular sweetness of spirit, a radiant simplicity and breadth of humanity that welcomed the 'publicans and sinners' despised by Pharisees and Greeks alike. They present the basic teaching that has been the main source of Christian idealism, and which remains as noble an inspiration as religion has offered.

This teaching, to repeat, is essentially that of the great prophets of Israel; but it is purer in Jesus. He was still more indifferent to the external forms of religion. He deepened the inwardness of the prophets in his teaching that the Kingdom of God is within men and above all worldly fortunes and misfortunes—a very simple idea that remains the essential spiritual insight. Likewise he was freer from prejudice and more clearly exemplified the ideal of universalism; the neighbor to be loved was not only the good Jew but the sinner and the heathen Samaritan. Nothing in religious history surpasses the sentiment attributed to him at the crucifixion: 'Father, forgive them; for they know not what they do.' Altogether, his deceptively simple gospel of universal brotherhood and love was so revolutionary that it has taken Christians many centuries to realize its implications, and merely to begin to effect them in political and economic life.

Yet the synoptic Gospels also make clear that Jesus did not conceive himself as the revolutionary author of a new world religion, and in a real sense was not the founder of Christianity. According to these Gospels, he made no plain, open claim to divinity. They suggest that he came to regard himself as the Messiah, though he never boasted of the Davidic ancestry that Luke and Matthew are at pains to give him; but even if he had publicly adopted this role, instead of requesting his disciples to keep it a secret, his listeners would not have assumed his divinity—the Messiah of tradition was not the Son of God. In any case, he did not offer salvation through a redeeming Lord. He taught rather that through repentance and righteousness any man could earn the kingdom of heaven, by his own efforts. Then the Church went on to make him the equal of God, and to insist that salvation was possible only through Christ. The central doctrine of Christianity became the doctrine of the Incarnation, which was apparently unknown to Jesus and his first followers.

Similarly the recorded teaching of Jesus was not cultish. He did not baptize, or prescribe baptism as essential; his institution of the Eucharist, as described in the Gospels, suggests a simple memorial with no magical efficacy. Constantly he attacked the formalism of the high priests and the scribes, the blind guides who strained at a gnat and swallowed a camel. 'Be not ye called Rabbi,' he told his disciples, because only One was their Master, and they were all brethren. Then the Church made the sacraments necessary to salvation, after the fashion of other mystery cults (and presently was embarrassed to find that the Devil had instituted the rite of communion in Mithraism, so as to mislead simple Christians). It developed an autocratic priesthood, an elaborate hierarchy of masters; through them alone were the brethren permitted to come to Christ. In time Christianity was torn by fierce wrangling over the letter of the new law—the formalism that Jesus despised. 'In vain do they worship me, teaching for doctrines the commandments of men.'

In general, the Jesus of the synoptic Gospels would have been mystified or appalled by many of the doctrines through which his 'Father's business' came to be interpreted and conducted; so the apparent moral is that we might try to recover the gospel that has been buried under layer upon layer of ritual and dogma. Actually, the moral is not so simple. As we recover the historic Jesus, we find not merely an elevated prophet but an unlettered Galilean who shows little trace of the culture of the ancient world, and who hardly foresaw the peculiar problems of the modern world. We are forced to reinterpret and readapt his teaching, precisely as the early Church was forced to do.

Among other things, Jesus seems to have accepted the popular superstitions of his time and place. Mark has him forever 'casting out devils'—the evil spirits that were supposedly the cause of disease; most of his recorded miracles were of this kind, which was a routine performance for contemporary wonder-workers.[3] Similarly Jesus is credited with the popular apocalyptic visions and with a belief in hell, a 'furnace of fire,' which the Israelites had apparently learned about during their Captivity. Such notions may be spiritualized, as they have been; but in the Gospels they are presented as bald matters of fact. They are hardly consistent with the disinterested love of God and man that Jesus also taught.

Neither can the historic Jesus clarify our conception of God. He had no theology, made no pretense of offering new ideas about God. All his allusions imply a personal God, but he felt no necessity to describe or explain him; for this was the God his lowly listeners already knew. He cannot answer such questions as why a perfect God created so imperfect a world because these questions never occurred to him. The recorded

[3] It is all too easy to ridicule these miracles, on whose authenticity orthodox Christianity has felt obliged to insist. As for evidence, the contemporaries of Jesus had little idea of natural causes and took miracles for granted—there were even manuals on how to revive a corpse. Hence the miracles continued for centuries, to the frequent embarrassment of the Church. Celsus, one of the first known pagan writers who attempted to refute Christianity, could argue that the pagan gods performed bigger and better miracles; and when Christians continued to patronize pagan temples famous for their cures, the gods had to be replaced by the bones of saints. It would also seem unbecoming of a deity to stoop to such arguments, even if they did not involve a kind of rank favoritism, or such plain injustices as that visited on the unfortunate owner of the Gadarene swine. 'You should love your enemies,' Shaw paraphrased the logic attributed to Jesus, 'and to convince you of this I will now proceed to cure this gentleman of cataract.' It is accordingly fairer to Jesus to stress that even the credulous authors of the Gospels indicate his resentment of the incessant demand for 'signs.'

faith of Jesus had indeed a child-like quality. 'Whosoever shall not receive the kingdom of God as a little child, he shall not enter therein'; he thanked God because 'Thou hast hid these things from the wise and prudent, and hast revealed them unto babes.' And his more specific religious ideas are generally more troublesome. If he conceived himself as the Messiah, the conception is ambiguous; it may have been as the Davidic prince of popular conception, or as the Son of Man mentioned in Daniel and Enoch; but neither conception is strictly acceptable or even intelligible to the modern mind.

The indifference of Jesus to 'the wise and prudent' was ultimately an indifference to the whole effort of civilization. He was not, to be sure, an ascetic. He appears to have taken pleasure in nature, wine, and other simple joys; he told his disciples to be not, as the Pharisees, of a sad countenance; he wanted them to 'have life more abundantly.' Nevertheless the perfect world he proclaimed was not so much a completion of human effort in this world as an epilogue, a supernatural kingdom that required the end of the natural world. Hence we have trouble even with the ethical teaching of Jesus, the sublime Sermon on the Mount itself. Almost all Westerners, including agnostics, revere this teaching; almost none, including the most orthodox Christians, really believe its plain injunctions of non-attachment and non-violence. And since Jesus himself sometimes acted in a different spirit, as when he drove the money-changers out of the temple, we might look at the historic setting in which he preached, again remembering that he was preaching to his fellow-Jews, not to all mankind.

Palestine had long been convulsed by fierce struggles against the heathen oppressors of Israel. The preiod of Jesus was one of almost hysterical tension, reflected in the many nervous maladies he cured by casting out demons and in the extensive apocalyptic literature. It has therefore been suggested that in commanding non-resistance to evil Jesus was opposing the Zealots—the party that refused to pay taxes to Caesar, clamored for open rebellion against the Romans, and was especially popular in his own Galilee. Presumably Jesus foresaw the hopelessness of this struggle, which in fact led to the destruction of Jerusalem. If so, his ethical teaching was not revolutionary but conservative and prudent. This might also explain the popular revulsion against Jesus. The people wanted above all to be delivered from the Romans—and he told them to render unto Caesar the things that were Caesar's.

Another, more comprehensive explanation of the Sermon on the Mount is the popular expectation that the Kingdom of God was at hand. Just what Jesus himself meant by the Kingdom is not clear. Some of his reported sayings plainly indicate a spiritual kingdom—one 'not of this earth,' or one 'within you.' Other sayings as plainly indicate an imminent kingdom on this earth, in keeping with the whole prophetic tradition of Israel: 'Verily I say unto you, That there be some of them that stand here which shall not taste of death, till they have seen the kingdom of God come with power.' But there is no question that the early followers of Jesus—including those who preserved, or imagined, the sayings now found in the Gospels—all got the impression that the kingdom was coming any day. As St. Paul announced, 'The time is short.' And given this expectation, the ethical teaching of Jesus is not at all impractical. Laying up treasures on earth, resisting evil, hating enemies, keeping the eye that offends you, taking thought of the morrow—all such activities, which are important enough if society is a going business, become trivial or irrelevant if the morrow is to bring the kingdom of heaven. This would further explain the very fragmentary records of his career: as Guignebert remarks, the disciples would hardly be interested 'in remembering and preserving for the future the details of a teaching which interested them precisely because it limited the future to a few months.' And we might be less troubled by the harsh sayings attributed to Jesus—such otherwise inhuman injunctions as to leave the father and let the dead bury their dead, or even to sever all family ties and hate parents, brethren, wife, and children.

We would then be led to the ironic conclusion that Christian ethics, and the establishment of the Christian Church, resulted from the failure of our Lord's vision; so this possible illumination of his extremism presumably will not be welcomed in orthodox quarters, even though they will continue to discount his principles. For the unorthodox, there are two ways of looking at ideals that are admittedly impossible of realization in a solvent society. Whitehead rejoiced in the 'fortunate ignorance' of the Gospel authors, who could give free rein to their vision of ideal possibilities, without regard for such practical considerations as the preservation of society. In the long run, society may profit more from such visions of the pure ideal, and more nearly realize the ideal. On the other hand, Arthur Murphy maintains that an idealism that is too good for this world is simply not good enough, since it neglects the social conditions under which real goods and real evils are produced. The demand for universal love may be the distinctions essential to the good life, the perhaps higher principle of loving only the lovable and hating the vile; and the condemnation of all use of force, as necessarily evil, obscures the actual necessity of using force to prevent greater evil.

At any rate, it was not the Sermon on the Mount that conquered the world. The ruling ethics of Christianity has been not only more worldly in practice but more militant in principle. If St. Francis of Assisi is the ideal type of Christian, the great Christian leader has more typically been a Bishop Ambrose, a St. Bernard, a Pope Innocent III, a Luther, a St. Ignatius Loyola—a soldier of the Cross. The basically different ethos of Western Christendom is most conspicuous in the American way of life. 'Ye cannot serve God and mammon,' Jesus said flatly; but Americans believe that they can serve both in their land of opportunity, and are very proud of their high standard of living. 'Blessed are the poor in spirit,' the meek, the humble; but the American is supposed first of all to be self-reliant, enterprising, and ambitious. 'Resist not evil,' and turn the other cheek; but the great national heroes were the leaders in the War of Independence, the war to preserve union, and the world wars to make the world safe for democracy. 'Love your enemies'—and who tried to love Hitler?

The American way can be pretty gross and self-righteous. At its best, however, it is the way of resolute, high-minded, heroic endeavor, to oppose tyranny and to extend the blessings of liberty. If the way of Jesus is sublime, it is not necessarily the only good way, or under all circumstances the best way. But the first prerequisite of morality is to be clear-eyed and honest: to know what one does believe, and to assume the responsibilities of that belief. The chief objection to the pure Christian ideal is that in practice it has produced a basic dishonesty, which is the more dangerous because it is usually unconscious.[4]

Also fateful in its consequences for historic Christianity was the indifference of Jesus to anything but the kingdom of God, however he conceived it. He was not a social or political reformer. Although Shaw and many others have tried to make him out as an apostle of socialism, he was as unconcerned about economic opportunity and political freedom as he was about the cultivation of art, philosophy, and science. His failure to protest against slavery is typical of his failure to draw out the social implications of his call for universal brother-

---

[4] President Truman, for example, once told a delegation of churchmen that the foreign policy of the United States is based on the Sermon on the Mount. He was no doubt quite sincere, quite unaware of any inconsistency between this announcement and the contemporary Truman doctrine. And though Americans are notorious for such self-righteousness or innocent hypocrisy, it has always been characteristic of the Christian civilization of the West, and a major offense to the exploited peoples of the East.

hood and his scorn of the wealthy. His followers developed a more positive indifference to these implications. Until the last century, the leaders of Christendom preferred to take seriously the scattered texts in which Jesus offered comfort to the privileged and powerful, notably his injunction to render unto Caesar the things that are Caesar's. The historic Church tolerated slavery and serfdom, supported the divine right of kings to govern wrongly, and generally opposed the popular movements toward equality, fraternity, and liberty. The early champions of democracy were often hostile to orthodox religion for the same reason that the leaders of the Russian and Mexican revolutions were hostile: official Christianity was on the other side.

Such perversions are the inevitable by-products of a revolutionary doctrine that becomes orthodox, and are not to be blamed on Jesus himself. His basic teaching was a gospel of love whose plain meaning has survived all perversion, and whose implications we shall keep returning to as we follow Christian history. We may even see a kind of relativism in his categorical injunctions to judge not and love one's enemies; for as Reinhold Niebuhr points out, these injunctions imply the inevitable fallibility of all human judgment, the finiteness of all social standards of good and evil. Meanwhile the basic paradox remains that the historic Jesus, so far as we can know him, was not directly responsible for either the success or the failure of Christianity. When he was resurrected, he was indeed transfigured by his followers. He became the Christ, a Greek word he was unacquainted with. He was sent abroad to strange peoples, to compete with their mythical savior-gods in a similar mystery of the Mass. He was made to demand rites about which he had cared little, and beliefs about which he had known nothing. He was identified with a *Logos* that he had never heard of, and could not have conceived. As a Saviour, he became the symbol of hopes both grander and meaner than his own.

And he remains a profoundly ambiguous symbol. He became ambiguous in his simplest, most familiar aspect—the grand and awful symbol of Jesus nailed to the Cross, which adorns his churches everywhere. It was this martyrdom—the example more than the teaching—that enabled Christianity to survive persecution, since his disciples were willing or even eager to follow the example of their Lord. Their passion, however, had its naïve aspects. 'Unhappy men,' exclaimed the proconsul Antoninus, 'if you are thus weary of your lives, is it so difficult for you to find ropes and precipices?' More gravely, Marcus Aurelius deplored the 'unseemly joy' with which Christians faced the prospect of release from their earthly duties, and sought an immediate heavenly reward. In time their passion became worse than unseemly. The inspired followers of Christ had been eager to suffer martyrdom; now they were as eager to inflict it. Jesus on the Cross became the symbol of an uncompromising, ruthless idealism that has inspired the most glorious and most terrible deeds in our history. In the name of one who preached peace and the brotherhood of man, Christians have slaughtered millions of their brethren, chiefly their fellow-Christians. 'Any serious attempt to remove the present causes of war,' concludes F. S. C. Northrop, 'must concentrate on the roots of the Christian religion and of Western idealism.'

3. THE MISSION OF ST. PAUL

Among the teachers of the ancient world was one who taught that behind all the gods was a supreme deity, and that the highest goods were love and selflessness. His piety was such that he was reputed to be the son of a god, though he himself made no such claim; he performed miracles, casting out demons and raising a girl from the dead; and when he died, his followers maintained that he appeared to them afterwards, and then went bodily to heaven. The teacher I am referring to was not Jesus, however. He was Apollonius of Tyana, as described by Philostratus. He illustrates the lofty religious ideals against which the followers of Jesus often had to contend. He forces the question of why Christianity triumphed over its rival mystery religions, which are now discredited because they failed, but which also offered high hopes to man and at their best made high demands.[5] One answer to this question is that Jesus alone attracted an extraordinary missionary, unsurpassed in religious history for his devotion, his fervor, and his genius. This was Saul of Tarsus, who became St. Paul.

[5] Mithraism in particular was similar to early Christianity in many ways. Its followers formed secret societies and called themselves Brothers; they admitted the lowly, even to slaves; they performed the rites of baptism and communion; they celebrated their sabbath on Sunday, and an annual festival on 25 December; they had a categorical ethics, stressing continence and abstinence; their dead were resurrected, to go to a heaven above or a hell in the bowels of the earth; their god Mithra had made a sacrifice which saved the human race; and he was a mediator between the supreme God and man. Greek philosophers emphasized all these parallels—to the advantage of Mithraism. Modern scholars are not certain to what extent the two religions borrowed from one another, but it seems probable that their similarities owe largely to their common debt to older religions, especially in Persia.

Paul was the supreme example of a new type of man: the 'fool for Christ's sake,' who had a vivid consciousness of the presence of the Holy Spirit within him, and whose mystical exaltation led him not to a life of contemplation but into the world, into a life of ceaseless activity. While the other Apostles (judging by Acts) preached the ordinary gospel of religious revivalists, exhorting men to repent and be saved on penalty of eternal damnation, St. Paul preached eloquently of the life 'in Christ,' and of how it could make others as it had made him, a 'new creature,' reborn to love, joy, peace, and goodness. A naturally fierce, somber man, he taught this gospel of hope and charity throughout a life filled with peril, privation, and pain. According to legend, he finally suffered martyrdom in Rome, but he constantly suffered from persecution by his fellow-Jews and from controversy with his fellow-Christians. 'I am more' than other ministers, he wrote: 'in labors more abundant, in stripes above measure, in prisons more frequent, in death oft.' Everything he sacrificed gladly to his Lord, the resurrected Christ.

And first of all he sacrificed the historic Jesus. He knew Jesus only by hearsay, and rarely referred to his human life; he never used such terms as the Son of Man. Unlike Jesus in temperament, he at first had a seemingly pathological hatred of Jesus' disciples. Then, while en route to Damascus on a mission of persecution, he had a blinding vision of the resurrected Christ, who called to him from the heavens. This mystical experience, the turning point of his career, is the key to his gospel. The Lord he knew, intimately, overwhelmingly, was a Saviour-God, comparable to the gods of the mystery cults, who had died and been resurrected, and through whom man could achieve immortality. Whereas Jesus had proclaimed a kingdom of God that men could earn simply by repentance and righteousness, Paul taught that salvation was through Christ, and Christ alone. With his deep sense of personal guilt, and of the radical evil of all mankind, he went on to lay the cornerstone of orthodox Christianity in his doctrine of Christ as the Redeemer, who atones for the sins of all men since the Fall of Adam.[6] In complete sincerity, Paul preached a gospel about Jesus that was not taught by the Jesus of the synoptic Gospels. The first great convert of the Nazarene converted his teaching into Christianity, a religion at once higher and harsher.

As a result, the extraordinary missionary achievement of

---

[6] James Parkes aptly summarizes the contrast between Judaism and Christianity in this respect. 'In Judaism God says to man: fulfil my plan for creation; and man replies: I will. In Christianity man returns to God to say: fulfil that part in creation which I cannot because I am foolish and sinful; and God replies: I will.'

Paul has not been greatly admired by Modernists. 'It was Paul,' charged George Bernard Shaw, 'who converted the religion that had raised one man above sin and death into a religion that delivered millions of men so completely into their dominion that their own common nature became a horror to them, and the religious life became a denial of life.' This is hardly fair to the man who wrote so eloquently about the supreme virtue of charity. (And let us remember that charity for Paul did not mean a hand-out, an easy form of good works that permits deductions from spiritual and material income taxes.) Yet Shaw was describing an actual aspect of the tormented life and thought of Paul, and in particular of his enduring influence. Paul has suffered even more from his friends than from his enemies—from the Paulism that has magnified the most dubious elements of his teaching. So in fairness we might stress at once the basic contradictions in the work of the greatest of the Apostles, who in seeking to 'become all things to all men' became both more and less than he knew.

Like Jesus, Paul was a loyal Jew. 'I am verily a man which am a Jew,' he affirmed and 'so worship I the God of my father, believing all things which are written in the law and in the prophets.' Unlike Jesus, however, he was a city man, with a Hellenic as well as Jewish background; although he was scarcely urbane, the air he breathed and the language he spoke were suffused with pagan thought. Hence he made a momentous decision that transformed a Jewish sect into a universal religion. Setting himself against other disciples (apparently including James, the brother of Jesus) Paul was the leader of the faction that decided not only to preach the new gospel to the Gentiles but to exempt them from the ceremonial requirements of Judaism, notably circumcision. In his revulsion against his Pharisaic past, he went on to denounce legalism even more vehemently than Jesus had; so despite his sincere loyalty to the God of his fathers he was largely responsible for the violent break with Judaism. But even so he was not consciously building a religion for the future. Expecting his Lord to return in his own time, and hoping that he would 'come quickly,' he could hardly have foreseen that his hurried letters—now exalted and luminous, now crabbed and obscure—would in time become Scripture.

We should accordingly not expect to find a coherent, systematic theology in Paul. However profound, his thought was essentially an uncritical rationalization of his intense, peculiar experience, reflecting all the vicissitudes of his missionary career, the extremities of both his hopes and his fears; and it naturally yielded some dubious dogma when it was read literally by later Christians. Thus with his doctrine of justification by faith. With Paul there was never a question of faith *versus* good works; once justified, men were more than ever responsible for good works. Too good a Jew to be content with a mere salvation cult, he not only made Christianity a mystery religion but made it more ethical than all other such religions, retaining the moral law of Judaism and much of the spirit of Jesus. Still, faith was foremost—'Without faith, it is impossible to please God'; and though for Paul it meant an intimate, completely responsible conviction, in others it was apt to be mere credulity. As James Shotwell comments, his call to faith was singular in that he gave almost no evidence to support it; he seemed quite indifferent to the historical details of the life of Jesus, on which it presumably rested. His converts, who had not had the benefit of his mystical experience, could be impressed by prophets who were more delirious than inspired. They could accept at once the most grotesque imaginings of the Book of Revelation and the lofty theology of the Gospel of St. John, and even believe that these were the work of the same man.

Again, Paul's central message was a spiritual declaration of independence. All men were one in Christ Jesus: 'There is neither Jew nor Greek, there is neither bond nor free, there is neither male nor female.' But in his devotion to Christ Jesus he attacked both Jew and Greek, and in his indifference to all else he discouraged attack upon the social institutions that actually separated mankind. He provided the text that became perhaps the most influential argument for bondage to absolute monarchs: 'The powers that be are ordained of God. Whosoever therefore resisteth the power, resisteth the ordinance of God; and they that resist shall receive to themselves damnation.' Likewise his experience led him to deny equality and freedom even in the spiritual life: he taught that salvation was by special grace, 'not of ourselves.' Paul felt that his own saving vision of Christ had come only through the grace of God, not through any good works of his own. Then as he preached the message of the Saviour he encountered a strange hostility, which seemed more perverse because it was fiercest in his fellow-Jews, God's chosen people. He concluded that God was hardening their hearts, as in Exodus he had hardened the heart of Pharaoh in order to afflict all Egypt with more plagues. 'Therefore hath he mercy on whom he will have mercy, and whom he will he hardeneth.'

A contemporary apologist, Jacques Maritain, regrets that Paul 'expresses these idea in Semitic style.' They give trouble in any style, however, especially when they are coupled with the ideas of heaven and hell. (St. Augustine also remarked that the unhappy heathens of Tyre and Sidon would have believed in God had they witnessed the wondrous miracles of Christ, but they were damned because 'it was not granted them to believe.') And in any case such ideas were at the very heart of Paul's thought. It is not surprising that the Christ-intoxicated man should stress our absolute dependence on Christ, and utter unworthiness of his grace. Knowing the ultimate in gratitude and hope, he also knew the ultimate in guilt and fear. He was always liable to what Morris Cohen considered the great sin of religion—the disposition to arouse an abject terror and then to deprive man of reasonable hopes, insisting that without religion his condition is hopeless.

This is the major issue raised by the doctrines that Paul bequeathed to Christianity, in particular the cardinal doctrine of the Redemption. The author of the Acts of the Apostles, written to spread the Gospel, knew nothing about the pre-existence of Christ and represented his death as a kind of misfortune that was gloriously redeemed; he seems almost embarrassed by the crucifixion. ('Cursed be everyone that hangeth upon a tree,' it was written in Deuteronomy.) Paul was apparently the first to popularize, if not to conceive, the idea that unlike all other savior-gods Christ had deliberately sacrificed himself in order to redeem mankind. This is the highest hope that religion has ever held out to man. In one aspect it is a magnificent conception—the grandest symbol of the goodness of God, and the humble gratitude of man. In another aspect it may look naïve and presumptuous. Historically, another name for the Redeemer is Scapegoat: the ancient Hebrews had laid their sins on the head of a goat, which was then led off into the wilderness or pushed off a cliff. With Paul, however, there was no question of such an easy evasion of moral responsibilities. The serious objection is again that in offering mankind the wonderful solace of the Redeemer, he also cursed mankind with an absolute need of that solace.

Specifically, he introduced the idea of Original Sin. The prophets of Israel had made little or nothing of the Genesis myth of the Garden of Eden, and Jesus made nothing at all of it; he never mentions the Fall of Adam or the curse of Original Sin.[7] Here Paul may be credited with a stern realism

[7] Given the wide, deep, and lasting influence of this ancient dogma, it might be noted that the plain meaning of the Biblical story of creation does not support it. There is no Satan in Genesis, and little sense of moral outrage. The Lord God's expressed motive in punishing Adam is a jealous fear: 'Behold the man is become as one of us, to know good and evil'; so now, lest he 'take also of the tree of life, and eat, and live for ever,' the Lord God drives him out of Eden. Thus the story contradicts Paul's belief that man was created immortal, and that death resulted from sin. A jealous God never intended his new creatures to become 'as one of us.'

to set against the shallow optimism of the modern world, the too easy comforts of liberal Christianity. His doctrine symbolizes the sense of ancient evil that is at the heart of the tragic as well as the religious view of life, and that today may be redefined in Freudian terms, located in the dark unconscious. Yet the dogma has not made simply for moral realism. When taken literally, the idea that the whole human race should suffer for the fault of a naïve pair in Eden would seem outrageous if it were attributed to anyone short of a deity. Throughout Christian history the conviction that man's birthright is sin has encouraged an unrealistic acceptance of remediable social evils, or even a callousness about human suffering. It helps to explain the easy acceptance of slavery and serfdom, and a record of religious atrocity unmatched by any other high religion.

Paul's legacy to Christianity, at any rate, wrote large this sense of radical evil. For him, God's whole creation badly needed to be redeemed: 'If in this life only we have hope in Christ, we are of all men most miserable.' Hence he contributed a radical dualism of flesh and spirit unwarranted by the teachings of Jesus. Those who live in the Spirit, he wrote, 'have crucified the flesh.' In particular they had to guard against sex. To woman, God's afterthought and the cause of man's fall, Paul assigned a lowly position befitting the indecent manner of her creation; she must wear a hat in church because she was created to serve man and ought to wear upon her head some symbol of her subjection. As for marriage, Paul maintained that it was better to remain a bachelor like himself, or that 'those who have wives should live as though they had none.' He permitted marriage only because he realized that many men had difficulty containing themselves—it was at least preferable to outright fornication. Christian idealism, which later came to pride itself on the highest known ideals of love and marriage, has always been plagued by such worries over their natural basis and function. Paul was the first of a long line of Christian saints, and Protestant reformers, whose spirituality involved a morbid fear or hatred of sex.[8]

---

[8] Jacques Maritain explains that the realism of his teaching is to be found in a 'very high metaphysical meaning,' not in biology or sociology. 'With regard to the service of the Lord and of progress toward perfection, marriage is a difficult state, which bears with it afflictions of the flesh, embarrassments and complications not involved in the state of virginity.' Paul, however, was embarrassed by the complications of virginity. He was saying in effect that wives are useful or tolerable chiefly for relieving their masters of sexual desires, which might otherwise lead men into sin and jeopardize their chances of salvation.

Similarly St. Augustine wrote that we must regret, as the punishment of Adam, the process by which children are begotten; and while the whole Roman world around him was going to pieces, he worried

It was Paul's harsh asceticism, finally, as well as his exalted faith, that made him hostile to Hellenism. 'The Jews require a sign and the Greeks seek after wisdom; but we preach Christ Crucified—unto the Jews a stumbling-block and unto the Greeks foolishness'; and Paul gloried in the thought that God had 'made foolish the wisdom of this world.' (In a similar spirit Mohammed was later to despise the Jews of Medina as 'asses loaded with books.') Here he ushered in the historic conflict between philosophy and religion. The wisdom of this world is always likely to look foolish to the God-intoxicated man, while religious myths may look as foolish to the rationalist. Each may in fact be foolish. The philosopher is prone to overlook the simplicities of human emotion and desire, the salvationist to overlook the elementary claims of reason and knowledge. In the company of the Athenian philosophers to whom he preached, Paul appears at his worst and at his best, in all the narrowness and the strength of his belief, the naïveté and the grandeur of his obsession.

Apparently the Athenians were amused by his idea of the resurrection of the dead. Although Paul did not share the general Christian belief in the 'standing up of the corpses,' thinking that the resurrected would have a finer spiritual body instead of their original flesh, this idea is still foolish enough, by rational standards; no thoughtful, disinterested man would be likely to accept it, unless it had the unquestionable authority of a divine revelation. And Paul had many other naïve ideas. He believed that the Lord himself would soon 'descend from heaven with a shout'; he believed in an Anti-Christ; he believed in a horde of demons that had taken the form of pagan gods. In short, he believed in what an enlightened, civilized man would naturally regard as primitive superstitions —unless, again, he had God's own word for their truth; and Paul's God had spoken only to an uncultured people.

But what did the Athenian philosophers believe? At this time they were schoolmen, reshuffling and rewording the ideas of the masters who had died centuries before. In so far as they were dissatisfied with these academic exercises they were toying with Oriental superstitions, such as Chaldean astrology, that were as gross as Paul's. Generally they were detached from the communal life, with little understanding of their world, and little interest in improving it. Knowing them, Paul

over the problem of whether married folk could go to heaven, and if so where they would rank in the heavenly choir. St. Jerome went further: 'I wholly disapprove of baths for a virgin of full age'; for she should 'blush and feel overcome' at the sight of her nakedness, and should also make haste, by 'a deliberate squalor,' to spoil the good looks that might distract men in pursuit of saintliness.

had reason to tell his followers, 'Ye are all the children of light, and the children of the day.' He was at least preaching a universal message, seeking to be all things to all men. He represented potentially the most creative, liberating force of the age. At the end he was entitled to write, in proud humility, 'I have fought a good fight, I have finished my course, I have kept the faith.' What he kept was not the faith of Jesus himself; it skirted more than one heresy; yet it was a live, glowing faith, which demanded good works and could inspire more than a ritual rebirth.

4. THE DEVELOPMENT OF CHRISTIAN THEOLOGY

The cultivated pagans who first noted the new religion that was seducing the populace considered it a very vulgar affair. Tacitus referred to it as a 'pernicious superstition,' notable for its 'hatred of the human race'; Suetonius also called it a 'mischievous superstition'; and though Pliny, after a conscientious investigation, concluded that its adherents were not monsters, he agreed that it was 'a depraved and extravagant superstition.' As a superstition Christianity was not fatally handicapped: it could hardly have become popular had it not had much in common with the popular mystery religions. Yet it rose above all the competing superstitions. In time it attracted the cultivated pagans, assimilated much of their culture, and became intellectually respectable. Another reason for its triumph is that, with the aid of the foolishness of the Greek it developed an impressive theology.

Theology is so notorious as a dreary, futile word game, an endless shuffling of the counters of all-ness and not-ness, that one may forget its value and its necessity. The other mystery cults flourished like weeds because they involved relatively little conscious labor or systematic cultivation; but for the same reason they could produce only a wilderness. Christian thinkers made an earnest effort to think out their faith, to harmonize it with the claims of reason, to prove that they were indeed St. Paul's 'children of light.' Specifically, they incorporated Hellenic philosophy, the best available thought of their time. They produced an extensive literature that confused but also stimulated and enriched the intellectual life of Christendom. In a crumbling society they built up a tradition that was able to survive the Dark Ages, and to provide the basis for a new civilization.

The key to this remarkable achievement was the struggle

over the relation of reason to faith. Reason was naturally suspect because of its pagan ancestry. 'Away with all projects for a "Stoic," a "Platonic," or a "dialectic" Christianity!' exclaimed Tertullian. 'After Christ Jesus we desire no subtle theories, no acute inquiries after the gospels.' Tertullian summed up his faith in the famous statement 'I believe *because* it is absurd.' Down the centuries to this day Christian thinkers have reverted to this suspicion of reason, scorning it as impotent or denouncing it as dangerous. But other Christians early declared a faith in reason, as they had to if there were to be a Christian theology. Justin Martyr, one of the first Apologists, maintained that 'those who live according to reason are Christians, even though they are accounted atheists'; he included Socrates and other eminent pagans among the saved, in order to show that the Word was really universal. Clement of Alexandria maintained that 'philosophy was a preparation, paving the way towards perfection in Christ.' He and his follower Origen made their greatest contribution by reconciling philosophy and religion, or at least persuading the Greek world that they were not irreconcilable enemies, and by establishing the doctrine that reason is necessary for elucidating the basic truths revealed in Scripture. Ultimately this became the official faith of the Roman Catholic Church.

By this faith Christianity was necessarily transformed. Its followers, however, have generally ignored or denied the plainest implications of its transformation. The heart of the matter is the 'Word' in the Gospel according to St. John, the most original and profound of the Gospels. The Messiah who had become the Christ was here identified with the Greek *Logos*. In the next centuries thinkers worked out the unsuspected implications of this early synthesis of Judaism and Hellenic philosophy. As one thing led to another, they unconsciously moved farther and farther away from the recorded teaching of Jesus, evolving such abstruse doctrines as the Trinity. These developments do not *ipso facto* discredit the Christian claims to divinely revealed truth; one may say that it took the Greek mind to realize this truth, which would naturally be beyond the comprehension of simple fishermen in Galilee. Nevertheless we are manifestly dealing here with human interpretations, not with plain gospel truth. The triumph of rational theology was clouded from the outset by the half-innocent, half-arrogant assumption of its practitioners that they were merely spelling out God's word, not speaking their own word. And so we have to deal with the endless confusion and conflict inspired by a zeal to clarify the true faith and make it truly catholic.

The major trouble with the whole theological enterprise was that the validity of a Christian doctrine could not be determined primarily by reason. The ultimate criterion of the true faith was always the authority of the apostolic tradition. It was a Canon that reason was not permitted to question, but that had not been based on a clear, coherent body of doctrine; that had settled on four different gospels, with little or no knowledge of their origin and history; and that was unified chiefly by a conception of God profoundly at variance with the concepts of Greek philosophy. Reason was further limited by the insistence on faith as the primary requisite for salvation. Justin Martyr's rational, virtuous pagans were banished from the kingdom of God; and with them, before long, went many earnest theologians. Christian thinkers might have welcomed the counsel of the pagan Themistius, who remarked that they should not be distressed by their disagreements: 'God likes this variety of human thought, and is pleased to see his subjects struggle in rivalry to honor his majesty or confess by their differences their difficulty in comprehending it.' The theologians soon agreed, however, that disagreement was unthinkable; they accepted the doctrine laid down by Irenaeus, that God demanded right faith. The dogma that emerged from their furious disagreements, and that continued to change, was held to be divinely revealed truth, which had to be accepted without further question. Variety of opinion or difficulty in comprehending the incomprehensible was branded as heresy, punishable by eternal damnation in hell. Presently heretics were visited with hell on earth.

Although such unreasonableness was due primarily to the jealous exclusiveness of Yahweh, it was aggravated by the very rationality of the Greeks. For one thing, theologians became entangled in purely verbal problems, as ideas originally written in Hebrew or spoken in Aramaic were translated into Greek. Whatever such terms as 'Son of Man,' 'soul,' 'spirit,' and 'kingdom of heaven' meant to the early Jewish-Christians, they were certain to mean something different to Greek philosophers.[9] The typical Greek mode of thought also made for arbitrariness, as the philosophers deduced their absolute truths

---

[9] Needless to add, translation into Latin, and thence into English, has not resolved these difficulties. Thus Christians have long wrangled over the meaning of *is* in 'This is my body.' Did Jesus mean it literally or symbolically? We can never be certain, if only because the Aramaic in which he spoke would not contain the word *is*. Other terms seem more naïve in English than they did in the original. The three 'persons' of the Trinity, for example, suggest a considerably more anthropomorphic concept than the Latin 'personae,' or masks, which in turn is less philosophical than the Greek 'hypostases.'

from unquestioned premises. This made inevitable the head-on collision of science and theology in recent centuries.

Meanwhile the deepest confusions were generated by the loftiest Greek concepts of God, the highly original contributions of thinkers unaware of their originality. Clement and Origen, the first great Christian theologians, read Platonism into Holy Writ. Whitehead thought they improved on Plato by bringing his transcendental Ideas down to earth; they put the *Logos* to work in the actual world. At the same time, Clement introduced the philosophical Absolute: an impersonal God, ineffable, immutable, and impassive in a self-contained perfection. Origen logically added, in agreement with Aristotle, that God's universe is also eternal; its later creation in time would seem whimsical, or imply some previous insufficiency. The Absolute was then identified with Yahweh—a creator in time, a personal and providential ruler, a heavenly busybody incessantly concerned with temporal affairs. This union, which has persisted throughout Christian history, A. O. Lovejoy describes as 'perhaps the most extraordinary triumph of self-contradiction in human thought.'

The contradiction was further complicated by other Platonic ideas. To explain why a self-sufficient God should have created a world, Plato suggested an overflowing goodness—an idea that naturally pleased Christian thinkers. Still, the world that resulted from this overflow of divine love is manifestly full of pain and evil. Hence Christian thinkers have always been attracted by another suggestion of Plato, that the natural world is a pale, inferior imitation of the 'real' world, and is not to be taken too seriously. Still, they had to take it seriously and stress its reality, because Christ himself had lived in it. Some early thinkers, under the influence of Gnostic tendencies, drew a logical conclusion: our bad world should not have been created—it was all Yahweh's fault, which a superior God was trying to redeem. But theologians quickly rejected this heresy. They preferred to maintain that God is self-sufficient, that his absolute perfection required the creation of an imperfect world, that he does not need this world, that he is perpetually concerned about our doings in it, that it resulted from his overflowing goodness and love, that it is a vale of tears and a devil's snare, and that we should love God because by his grace some of us may be saved from the evil of his creation.

In *The Great Chain of Being,* Lovejoy has traced this confusion down through the centuries, with particular attention to the idea of an overflowing Creator who knew that it took many different kinds to make a world, and who wanted a world full of all possible kinds, including all kinds of evil. Early Christians, however, were not so concerned about the Creator. The first great theological battles were fought rather over the nature of Christ, who represented Christianity's chief contribution to the world's religions; and these battles yielded the most distinctive ambiguities of Christian theology.

The Gnostics started the trouble by denying the human nature of Christ, as an inconceivable degradation of deity; his human body must have been mere appearance, since God could not really suffer. This logical doctrine was promptly condemned, for the logical reason that it made nonsense of the resurrection and the whole Gospel story. The serious trouble accordingly came with the Arian controversy. Arius was a simple man who took the common-sense view that Christ, with his human body, was lesser than God—a view quite in accordance with the Gospels. 'I came down from heaven not to do my own will but the will of him that sent me,' Jesus said; everywhere he implies that 'He that sent me is greater than I'; and nowhere does he plainly assert that he is God himself. For such reasons the great majority of churchmen were willing to compromise the issue with a vague formula. Although they did not wholly agree with Arius they wished to keep the peace, and perhaps were fearful of being too bold in these high matters.

But the heroic Athanasius stood forth and refused to hedge. A subtle, acute Greek, he saw that Arianism was fatal to the Paulist doctrine of the Redeemer. Jesus had to be both true man and true God—a man in order really to atone for mankind, a God in order really to redeem mankind. Christianity had to retain both the deity of Christ and the unity of God, for without the one it might lose its salvationism, without the other it would sink into polytheism. At the Council of Nicaea Athanasius won his battle. The majority finally agreed to sign a creed which stated that the Lord Jesus Christ was 'begotten, not made, being of one essence with the Father,' and that all who said that 'there was once when he was not,' or 'before he was begotten he was not,' or 'he was made of things that were not,' or 'is of a different essence'—all these 'doth the Catholic and Apostolic Church anathematize.' This is not a very luminous formula, and it had the further disadvantage that its key phrase—'of one essence with'—nowhere appears in Scripture. Still, it was at least unequivocal, and precluded any compromise with polytheism.

Unfortunately, ecumenical councils were not yet infallible— Athanasius specifically repudiated the claim to infallibility; so the aftermath of Nicaea was violent and indecent. Arianism was not finally condemned until almost a century of ecclesiastical haggle, intrigue, bribery, and brawl, with exchanges of anathema and exile, in which the chief sufferers were the men of highest principle, like Athanasius himself.[10] And the triumph over Arianism led to further controversies that shook all Christendom. Christ was both human and divine—but did he have one nature or two separate natures? The more mystical Christians tended to stress the divine nature at the expense of the human; many were still revolted by the idea that Christ had emerged from a female womb and experienced the embarrassements of the flesh. The more practical, ethical-minded Christians wished at all costs to preserve the reality of his manhood, in order to prevent him from becoming simply a Holy Ghost. There was a pious desire to distinguish the two natures, and as pious a desire to unite them. 'The faith of the Catholics,' wrote Gibbon, 'trembled on the edge of a precipice where it was impossible to recede, dangerous to stand, dreadful to fall; and the manifold inconveniences of their creed were aggravated by the sublime character of their theology.' In this consciousness of awful peril the Monophysites insisted on one incarnate nature of Christ. 'May those who divide Christ be divided with the sword, may they be hewn in pieces, may they be burned alive!' proclaimed one Christian synod at Ephesus. Presently the Monophysites were condemned to eternal burning.

A modern reader is apt to have difficulty in grasping and remembering the fine verbal distinctions of Apollinarius, Nestorious, the Monophysites, and all the other heretics, and still more difficulty in understanding how such terrible passion could be engendered by such super-subtle verbalism. Yet important principles were involved, or at least important differences in ways of feeling. The Nestorians and Monophysites in particular represented a profound revulsion of the Oriental-Hebrew spirit against Hellenic rationalism. Despite their apparent quibbling, they wanted to be done with all metaphysical quibbling, to avoid any kind of monstrous dual personality in Christ, and to return to the original simplicity and

---

[10] Once a Bishop Stephen tried to discredit a Western peacemaker by turning a harlot loose on him in Antioch. As for the solemn councils, Nestorius described the rabble of monks with whose help St. Cyril got him officially condemned at Ephesus, for attacking such ideas as that God had a Mother: 'They acted in everything as if it was a war they were conducting, and the followers of the Egyptian and of Memnon, who were abetting them, went about in the city girt and armed with clubs, men with high necks, performing strange antics with the yells of barbarians, snorting fiercely with horrible and unwonted noises, raging with extravagant arrogance against those whom they knew to be opposed to their doings, carrying bells about the city, and lighting fires in many places and casting into them all kinds of writings.'

purity of Christianity. At any rate, Hellenism triumphed. The Council of Chalcedon finally settled on the formula that is generally accepted by both Protestantism and Catholicism: 'TWO NATURES, WITHOUT CONFUSION, WITHOUT CHANGE, WITHOUT DIVISION, WITHOUT SEPARATION.' Another fierce battle over whether Christ had one or two wills was decided by a similar formula, of two wills harmonized in one person. With this the Holy Ghost was admitted, to form the Trinity. The Church might have settled for two persons instead of three, inasmuch as the Council of Nicaea had paid little attention to the Holy Ghost, but it had already entered the old baptismal formula.

In one sense, all this represented a triumph for reason. Doctrines about Jesus that had little or no foundation in the Gospels were accepted because they were demanded by the logic of the Atonement. The Holy Ghost was also philosophically convenient, enabling constant spiritual relations between God and man. The Trinity as a whole avoided the remoteness of a purely transcendental God while asserting the unity of God that reason requires. (It has been described as the 'perfect society.') And implicit in all these doctrines was a denial of an inscrutable, arbitrary God, beyond human comprehension and human standards of goodness. God had not only revealed himself but himself appeared on earth in human form. He was himself the Word.

In other respects the cause of reason suffered from this triumph. Free philosophical speculation on the nature of God would hardly arrive at the strange doctrines that became orthodox. The Arians, indeed, were trying to make the faith more intelligible; and following their defeat it became steadily more mysterious, until lucidity was almost a proof of heresy. 'The thought that Christianity is the revelation of something incomprehensible,' wrote Harnack, 'became more and more a familiar one to men's minds.' Reason led the wildest of careers in the fourth and fifth centuries, soaring to the dizziest heights of unreason. When Bishop Cyril of Alexandria, for example, expatiated on the union of flesh and divinity in Christ, he leaned heavily on such phrases as 'in a manner indescribable and inconceivable,' or 'by their inexpressible and inexplicable concurrence'; yet he was very positive that he was expressing the absolute truth, and by his passion for anathematizing all who disagreed with him he achieved sainthood. So theologians evolved ever more elaborate conceptions of the inconceivable and dogmatic explanations of the inexplicable, and overrode their opponents in church councils whose decisions, as Archbishop Benson observed, were remarkable in that they were almost uniformly 'uncharitable, unscriptural, uncatholic, and unanimous.'[11]

The long-range consequences of these furious controversies were likewise mixed. Arianism was finally suppressed—as for some years it was upheld—by Roman emperors; so its defeat inaugurated the imperial domination of the Church, from which Eastern Christendom was to suffer thereafter. At that, the issues were not really settled: Western and Eastern Christendom were later alienated by dispute over the *filioque*, the internal relations of the Trinity. In the East, too, Hellenism was finally overthrown by Mohammed, who proclaimed a return to a pure monotheism; in a sense the Monophysites thus enjoyed a posthumous triumph. Even in the West the great masses of Christians remained more or less Arian at heart; they worshiped chiefly the human Son, together with the Mother and the patron saint. Today most Christians are simply ignorant of the whole issue. Not one in a thousand knows or cares about the heresies that once agitated all Christendom, or would be able to make the nice distinctions that once were necessary to escape eternal damnation.

All these basic inconsistencies of early Christianity are summed up, finally, in its greatest thinker, St. Augustine. In him we find the loftiest mystical intuitions, coupled with a theological rigor that tends to reduce them to logical absurdities. We are led to the momentous consequences of the whole enterprise; for his thought shaped Christian history thereafter, providing both the foundation of the Catholic Middle Ages and the chief inspiration of the Protestant Reformers.

As a philosopher steeped in Neo-Platonism, Augustine conceived God as an Absolute whose perfection was so far beyond rational conception that it could be described only in negatives, and might almost be defined as the absolute Not, the quintessence of Not-ness. 'God is not even to be called ineffable,' he said, 'because to say this is to make an assertion about Him.' As a mystic, however, he had had visions of God; he felt impelled to make fervent assertions about His living presence. As a devout follower of the apostolic tradition, he also believed in a personal God who had very positive characteristics, and had revealed Himself to His

---

[11] More rational theologians did not greatly improve matters when they humbly acknowledged that such doctrines as the Trinity were truths known by revelation, not by reason; for the revelation is still unclear. The Gospels, Acts of the Apostles, and Epistles of St. Paul are all ignorant of the Trinity. The text for the doctrine is in the first Epistle of St. John: 'There are three that bear record in heaven, the Father, the Word, and the Holy Ghost: and these three are one.' Scholars regard this text as a later interpolation, however, since it does not appear in the best manuscripts.

chosen people; Augustine was privy to the main plan of this God. As an earnest moralist and a former Manichaean, he tended to a pronounced dualism, in which the power of evil was so strong that it always threatened to limit God's power of good. As an able, energetic churchman, Augustine was concerned with everyday religious needs that could be satisfied by neither his mystical idealism nor his ethical teaching; so he constantly worked to strengthen ecclesiastical institutions in a physical world he deplored. And as a subtle theologian, with a gift for strained exegesis, he combined these disparate elements in a system that remains one of the wonders of human thought for its fervid piety, its logical rigor, its exalted spirituality, and its profound inhumanity.

The saintliness of Augustine derives from his impassioned love of a Neo-Platonic God conceived as the source of all perfection and the only true reality. Nothing apart from God is real or good; what passes for evil is mere absence of good. This absolute divine monopoly implies, however, the absolute dependence of man. Augustine concluded that man cannot have any merit in himself; his salvation must be wholly dependent on the grace of God, which must be a free gift.[12] In choosing to save some men God is rewarding His own good works, not theirs: 'God does not crown your merits as your merits but as His gifts.' At the same time, Augustine had to accommodate the traditional heaven and hell, which imply human responsibility; so he now granted man a positive will to do evil—to oppose the will of his all-powerful God—and made evil a positive reality instead of a mere absence of good. He offered acute observations on the nature of will, as more primary than reason, and on the moral struggle to humble it before the divine will, as he had known this struggle in his own proud, rebellious youth. Yet he could never reconcile this idea of human responsibility with the idea of an Almighty who had foreordained evil. The upshot of his ethical teaching was that man is totally depraved, that he must try to be good, that he can will good only if God chooses to grant him grace, and that he must shoulder the blame for all the evil in God's world.

This whole issue came to a head in the Pelagian controversy. More concerned with the justice than the metaphysical rights of the Almighty, Pelagius rejected the doctrine of original sin and maintained that every man, like Adam, is free to earn heaven or hell. 'Everything good and everything

[12] Augustine did set one limit on God's freedom: the number he is permitted to save is inalterably fixed because it must equal the number of the fallen angels, thereby compensating for their defection. But this proviso only emphasizes Augustine's implicit doctrine of predestination.

evil . . . is *done by us,* not *born with us.'* Augustine succeeded
in having this teaching condemned, if only because it made
baptism unnecessary; although Pelagianism is in effect the
common belief of Christians today, officially it remains a
heresy in both East and West. Nevertheless the Church also
shrank from the logic of Augustine's predestinarianism, which
did not come fully into its own until the advent of Luther and
Calvin; through a series of uneasy compromises it sought a
formula that would at once restrain human pride, promote
human virtue, and keep salvation dependent on the Church.
Augustine himself forgot his logic. As Bishop of Hippo he
worked with heroic energy to save souls, even though God
had supposedly made all his appointments beforehand. Ultimately, he subordinated all his other doctrines to his belief
in the supreme importance of the Church, as the indispensable
mediator between God and man. His most enduring achievement was his contribution to the Roman Church.

With the Roman Empire crumbling, Augustine became
convinced that most Christians would be hopelessly lost without the guidance and discipline of this supra-personal, supra-
national institution, 'the ark of salvation.' He affirmed the necessity of the sacraments, stating that God wills to save man
only through them. He raised the authority of the Church
even above the infallible Bible, for it had formed and interpreted the Canon; although he was unable to locate satisfac-
torily the infallibility of the Church, conceding that bishops
and even councils might err, he prepared the way for the
claims of the medieval papacy. Most important, he contributed
the *City of God.* In this book, written to explain why Rome
had fallen after it had given up its pagan gods for Christianity, Augustine distinguished the Earthly City from the City
of God—the transcendent spiritual reality that was represented
on earth by the Church. The one great work produced by
the fall of Rome, which argued that Rome was not and ought
not to be the Eternal City, it did more than any other single
work to maintain the importance of Rome in centuries to
come.

Briefly, Augustine pictured all history as a constant conflict
between the City of God and the Earthly City, 'built up by
the love of self to the contempt of God'—a conflict that
would not end until the visible Lord in the clouds and the
audible angels with their trumpets announced the resurrection
of the dead and the final judgment. Although this theory was
not original, being implicit in the prophetic books of the
Bible, Augustine made it coherent, comprehensive, and authoritative. His statement of it remained the most influential
philosophy of history in the Western world until the eighteenth

century; and today it has been revived, in modern dress, by Toynbee.

As Augustine left it, the theory was quite arbitrary. It was not based on an empirical study, of course, and adduced no rational causes; such historical evidence as he offered is trivial. The most obvious objection to his argument is that it was based on a vast, provincial ignorance of history. In his outline of the development from the Creation to the Christian world, through a straight line of Hebrew patriarchs and kings, almost all of the history of civilization had to be left out; there was no room for other societies, even if he had known about them, except as they incidentally impinged on Jews and Christians; and the greatest men of antiquity were outcasts, whose achievements had no more meaning in the divine plan than the legends of barbarians. When Orosius, Augustine's disciple, piously filled in the master's outline with his *Historiae adversum paganos,* he filled it simply with gruesome accounts of calamities, in order to prove that mankind had been even worse off before the rise of Christendom and the fall of Rome. His edifying compendium of horrors became the manual of universal history for the Middle Ages.

This obvious objection by no means disposes of the *City of God,* however. Its great importance lies precisely in the fact that Augustine was not really interested in history. It lies even in the ludicrous fact that he seemed more concerned about preserving virgins from marriage than preserving Rome from barbarians. For he was concerned with the abiding interests of the spirit, which were indeed to abide. His work was a triumph of faith, a faith that might not move mountains but could remove the whole Roman Empire; and his faith was justified by the event. Still more, it helped to bring about the event. His own great Church of Africa was to go down before the Arabs, leaving hardly a trace; but the Roman Church was to mother a new civilization. And if this new Earthly City would presumably be of the Devil again, at least Augustine left the future open. He had nothing but scorn for the classical theory of endless cycles. The coming of Christ was a unique event with a unique promise, and signified a kind of spiritual progress; God's hopes for mankind, which had shrunk from Adam to a chosen people to a saving remnant, were now again extended to the whole race. All might aspire to the City of God. Meanwhile a sympathetic reader of Augustine may even gather some wisdom and hope for the conduct of the Earthly City. Christopher Dawson goes so far as to say that he 'first made possible the ideal of a social order resting upon the free personality and a common effort towards moral ends.'

Yet this was not the ideal of Augustine himself. His very purpose in writing the *City of God* was to justify the fall of Rome, and of all Romes. The *polis* itself was the greatest of heresies, in its concern with mere political justice; for him Athens was as shameless as Assyria. Since the Earthly City is always the City of Satan, he called for a constant war on the world and the flesh, and held out no hopes of an ideal social order. He stressed chiefly the vanity of human effort on earth. And so we are forced to consider further the importance of the fact that the most influential philosophy of history in the Western world denied any real importance or value to human history.

Conceivably, theology could have promoted an ideal synthesis of Greek humanism and Christian spirituality. Although Jesus scarcely preached humanism, he was not actively hostile to its ideals; at least the Gospels do not preach the doctrine of the good soul and the evil body. As a Redeemer, too, Jesus had presumably come to redeem life, or even to sanctify it. His God of love logically emphasized the reality and the value of his creation—something Yahweh had always taken for granted. Man might love God more wholeheartedly if he loved God's world and his fellow-creatures—if he loved real things, not merely an imaginary world. And early Christianity sometimes approached this kind of spirituality. The *Shepherd of Hermas*, which was so greatly admired that it was a candidate for inclusion in Scripture, suggests a candor, cheerfulness, a joy in life that was supposedly the privilege of the pagan world: 'Put on therefore gladness that hath always favor before God, and is acceptable unto Him, and delight thyself in it; for every man that is glad doeth the things that are good, and thinketh good thoughts, despising grief.' Especially under the Antonines, Christian communities seemed to be developing a mellow humanistic spirit that was also radiant with the new faith, hope, and charity. 'The church was true for a moment,' wrote Walter Pater, 'truer perhaps than she would ever be again, to that element of profound serenity in the soul of her Founder, which reflected the eternal goodwill of God to man, "in whom," according to the oldest version of the angelic message, "He is well pleased." '

Ideal or no, this was not to be the ruling spirit of Christianity. St. Augustine gave the seal of his authority to the radical dualism of body and soul, and of this world and the other world, which had entered Christian thought with St. Paul. The triumph of this other-worldly spirit was understandable. Early Christians, coming chiefly from the lower classes, had little or no hope of improving their condition in this life; as men without a country, they staked everything on the life to come.

Later Christians were involved in the growing economic and spiritual insecurity of the Roman Empire; the saintliest felt impelled to make a complete break with a world that seemed hopelessly decadent and corrupt. In general, Christianity was indelibly stamped by the defeatism of the age in which it grew up. Its followers rejected the world that Yahweh had considered suitable for all his purposes, including the final establishment of his kingdom. 'This world' became a synonym for misery and evil, a term of reproach; an attachment to it became charged with guilt, as if God had planted some natural delights simply to trap men. Even while insisting on the resurrection of their flesh Christians also insisted that the flesh was vile, so that its most apparent use in the after-life was to enable sinners to suffer more intolerable pain in hell. Charity itself was infected by this other-wordly spirit. Christian love as conceived by Augustine was not primarily love of one's neighbors, in the service of the world, but love of God, as a means to life in another world.

In culture, too, the growth of Christianity meant the decay of Hellenism. Although Augustine was steeped in Greek culture, and like St. Jerome had a guilty reverence for its masterpieces, the effect of his teaching was to destroy it as effectually as the barbarian invaders were destroying it. There was no place in his *City of God* for its great poets, artists, philosophers, scientists, and statesmen. As for natural knowledge, he not only stifled his own interest in it but closed the door to all independent inquiry. He maintained that 'this world must be used, not enjoyed,' and used only for the offchance of admission to the heavenly world; knowledge was useful only when it helped men to understand the Scriptures, which contained all the essential truths about the universe. Hence curiosity became a vice instead of a virtue. The Greek ideal of free, honest, fearless truth-seeking was smothered. All lights went out, except the Faith. When the Emperor Justinian closed the academies of Athens, a century after Augustine, he put the official seal on the Dark Age that had already descended on the West, and that was heralded by the *City of God*.

In time, of course, the Greek heritage was recovered. Likewise the Earthly City came back to life—and a vigorous, abundant life. The other-worldliness often congenial to the East has never gone really far or deep in the West; innumerable Christians have rejoiced in the world and the flesh, on principle as well as in practice. Nevertheless the traditional dualism has had deep and lasting consequences for historic Christianity, aside from the extremes of asceticism and Puritanism. In the Renaissance, the rediscovery of the Greek spirit led to the opposite extremes of sensuality and worldli-

ness. In recent times the reaction against Puritanism has led
to similar excesses. At all times the ancient tradition has made
a frank, wholehearted, unself-conscious enjoyment of natural
goods impossible for many good Christians. It has involved
a vast deal of unconscious hypocrisy, which became more corrosive as Western civilization set about its triumphant exploitation of 'this world.' It is a major source of the notorious
contradictions of the West.

As for St. Augustine himself, his theology has lost much of
its authority. Medieval schoolmen began to question his harsh
logic; St. Thomas Aquinas restored freedom of will and salvation by merit. When the Jansenists in the seventeenth century returned to the teaching of Augustine, they were charged
with heresy. By now his scheme of salvation has been quietly
dropped by Protestantism too. He would be horrified by
the Christian doctrine that is preached in orthodox churches,
including the church whose infallible authority he did so much
to establish.

Yet this is by no means to say that Augustine simply failed.
He remains a religious classic, a rich source of inspiration because of the very inconsistency as well as the profundity of his
thought. Men of all beliefs can find an Augustine to nourish
them—there are more Augustines than Platos. At his most
doctrinaire, his demand for faith was still a demand for understanding. And so with the whole theological enterprise of
the early centuries. The effort to harmonize the faith with the
deepest thought of the ancient world was essential if Christianity was to become a universal religion; and that it failed of
complete success is neither surprising nor distressing. Apart
from the irreconcilable ideas that the theologians sought to
reconcile, and the prehistoric cult that shapes all religions before ideas get to work, rational theology always ends up against
a strictly insolvable problem. God must symbolize an ideal
of perfection, and this ideal must conflict with the fact of a
woefully imperfect world. Thus in *Mysticism in Religion* Dean
Inge argues plausibly that the path upward to God can be
traced, but adds, 'The road down, from the Creator to the
creatures, is no business of ours, and frankly we know nothing
about it.' I fear it is our business, if we are going to reason
at all—Dean Inge himself makes this confession only after a
great deal of speculation. Still, the main business of religion is
to keep clear the possible path upward. The conclusion I
should draw from the adventure of Christian theology is that
in a changing world it is necessarily a continuous venture, and
that the chief menace to it is the claim of final solutions. New
knowledge and new conditions of life call for the creative
spirit of the great theologians who molded orthodoxy. Other-

wise orthodoxy will substantiate the schoolboy's definition of faith, as believing what you know ain't true.

5. THE ORGANIZATION OF THE CHURCH

'The nearer the Church, the farther from God' runs an old proverb. This was evidently the sentiment of Jesus himself, who has scarcely a good word to say for priests. Yet Christianity could not have triumphed without the Church. The strong centralized organization it developed was indeed its chief novelty, more original than its doctrines. The Church gave Christianity an inestimable advantage over all its competitors, and finally enabled it to become the imperial religion. It introduced Roman order and discipline into a fervor that otherwise might have run out into extravagance or the sands of popular superstition. It attained a high degree of wisdom.

Only this was a wordly wisdom—the wisdom of the Earthly City that rightly gave the Church its name. The increasing strength of the Church meant a loss in spirituality, as it must in any faith that is institutionalized. Here is an elementary distinction too often overlooked. The ideals of an inspired prophet are one thing; the doctrines and practices of an established church are another. Whatever its claims to divine origin and guidance, an established church is a human institution, and on its record a fallible one. It must be judged by human standards—'By their fruits ye shall know them.' In the early history of the Church we may find all the seeds of the mixed fruits that have been the historic meaning of Christianity.

Again we should note at once that recorded history does not do justice to the important simplicities. The church documents of the early centuries are filled with accounts of controversy, involving a good deal of unchristian vituperation. They include only a few fragmentary records of the extensive charitable enterprises of the churches, to which much more time and energy must have been devoted. Hence we catch only occasional glimpses of the humble daily activities that largely accounted for the popularity of Christianity: glimpses of the Church as a great philanthropic institution, caring for the poor and relieving the distressed; of the Bishop as a temporal as well as a spiritual leader, a kind of tribune standing between the people and the State; of the Christian community as a genuine community, a brotherhood, a haven of peace in a crumbling world. In *Marius the Epicurean* Walter Pater gives a vivid sense of this 'peace of the church' under the Antonines, with its gentleness, its cheerful service, its generous sympathy with all creatures, its love of beauty—all lit by an enthusiasm for a Christ who was still green in men's memories, and expressed in a worship that was not merely a petition but an act of thanksgiving.

If this is too idyllic a picture, it is at least in keeping with the nature of the early Church, whose organization was not clearly due either to the vision of far-sighted men or to the chicanery of ambitious ones. It was a natural, organic, unconscious growth. The first Christian communities were dependent upon wandering apostles and preachers, such as St. Paul. In the second century they became self-sufficient, under the ministry of a bishop who was elected by the community to serve as pastor, or shepherd. As the communities grew in size the bishop naturally required help and by the third century we hear of an extensive intermediate clergy, ranging from presbyters, deacons, subdeacons, acolytes, exorcists, and readers to doorkeepers. At length this clergy became an ordered hierarchy, whose members were usually required to pass through each of the grades on the way up. Meanwhile the organization between the scattered churches had developed as naturally. The desire for unity of doctrine and practice was especially strong before there was a central authority to impose it. Hence neighboring bishops met to discuss their problems, and from these meetings gradually emerged the institution of the synod or council. With the imperial recognition of the Church, the assemblies became large enough to be called ecumenical, and authoritative enough to formulate the official creeds and the canons of Church law.

This compact organization enabled the Church Militant. Only an army, indeed, could rival the order and discipline of the Christian Church. By the same token, however, the elaborate hierarchy separated the bishop from the community, and became something of a dead weight. Military organization is apt to produce the inflexible, brassy, autocratic type of military mind, which may not be the best for spiritual purposes. (The Shepherd of Hermas thought that 'the angel of righteousness is modest and delicate and meek and quiet.') The important fact, at any rate, is that the Church became aristocratic in structure and autocratic in power, on the Roman imperial model.

Early bishops, including such great ones as Cyprian, Ambrose, and Martin of Tours, had been elected by the people, sometime against the opposition of the clergy or other bishops. But the vested clergy had a clear advantage in such conflicts, and by the end of the fifth century they had largely won the exclusive right to election. The Church became a self-perpetuating government. It was democratic in that it recruited its priests from the ranks of the common people; a poor boy might rise to be a bishop. It was aristocratic in that the people had no voice in the selection of their spiritual rulers or the determination of spiritual law. Its basic principle was made explicit by the Council of Trent: 'To some it belongs to govern and to teach; to others, to be subject and to obey.' It was the governors who separated the sheep from the goats.

Similarly a hierarchy developed among the bishops, with increasing centralization of authority. Although in theory all bishops had an equal vote in the Church councils, in fact those from the more important sees had considerably more power and prestige, which they naturally sought to strengthen. The happiness of the lesser bishops is indicated in a proclamation by the Council of Ephesus:

> Let none of the most reverend bishops annex a province which has not been from the first under the jurisdiction of himself and his predecessors; and so the canons of the fathers shall not be overstepped, nor pride of worldly power creep in under the guise of priesthood, nor we lose little by little, without knowing it, that freedom which our Lord Jesus Christ, the Liberator of all men, purchased for us with his blood.

They did lose that freedom, as the most reverend bishops continued to annex provinces. The great doctrinal controversies of the fourth and fifth centuries were in large measure struggles for domination by the great churches of Alexandria, Antioch, Constantinople, and Rome. Rome had a considerable advantage as the ancient seat of the Empire, besides the tradition that its church had been founded by St. Peter. (Jerusalem, its most logical opponent, had early been destroyed.) At this time Rome and Constantinople triumphed, to battle with each other in the centuries to come.[13]

Meanwhile the historic role of the Church had been clearly

---

[13] The doctrinal basis for the primacy of Rome is a text in Matthew: 'Thou art Peter, and upon this rock I will build my church.' Scholars outside the Catholic Church generally regard this text as a later interpolation, arguing that in Matthew itself Jesus also tells the Apostles 'None among you shall be placed higher than the others,' that nowhere else in the Gospels does he use the expression 'my church,' and that Mark, the supposed companion of Peter, would hardly have omitted a saying so flattering to him. They add that the most explicit source of the Petrine legend was the supposed *Homilies* of Clement, a product of the Gnostic heresy. Nevertheless most of the churches soon began looking up to the Bishop of Rome and asking his opinion on controversial issues. In the fourth century Bishop Damasus definitely formulated the doctrine of the supremacy of the Roman See, and in the next century Leo the Great induced the Emperor Valentinian III officially to decree this supremacy.

defined. 'The bishops throughout the world,' St. Ignatius early declared, 'are the means by which we know Jesus Christ.' By the end of the second century Bishop Irenaeus had asserted the absolute, infallible authority of bishops. He laid the foundations of Catholicism by explicitly making the sacraments, right conduct, and right faith necessary for salvation, thereby fusing the mystical-ethical-legal system that was to be generally accepted. Right conduct was summarized in the Ten Commandments, but the sacraments had to be administered by the Church and the right faith defined by the Church. Although Irenaeus naturally had some trouble in his effort to base these claims on the teaching of the Apostles, feeling obliged to ascribe some anonymous works to them, he did establish his main principle, which made the apostolic tradition the criterion of the right faith, and the bishops the heirs of the Apostles. In particular, he is the first known bishop to insist on their right to condemn and exclude heretics. So when his successors consolidated the position he staked out, a self-governing priesthood had won complete control of the essential means of salvation.

Now, the motive behind this drive to autocratic rule was not mere lust for power. There was a sincere desire to maintain the purity of the true faith, and to protect simple Christians from false beliefs that would jeopardize their salvation. There was even a kind of victory for the populace. Max Weber pointed out that the sacraments are not only a way of sublimating religious ecstasy, and thereby discouraging orgy, but a way of making the sacred values available to all men; otherwise these values might become primarily the property of monks, mystics, and other religious virtuosos, as they did in the Orient. Yet the authority of the Church could be established and maintained only at the cost of considerable impurity in faith and practice. Its triumph created both worldly and spiritual problems.

The principle of continuity asserted by the Church is essentially a magical or supernatural one, since it implies that God not only gave the bishops a divine right to rule but will continue to guide them, and so prevent the radical corruptions that mark all other human institutions. By ordinary standards, however, the history of the Church looks much like the history of an Earthly City. From the beginning there were the usual accompaniments of political strife. St. Gregory of Nazianzus, among others, attacked the endless series of councils with their 'indescribable contentions and strivings for dominion.' The ecclesiastical campaigns tended to grow more violent and unscrupulous as the Church prospered, and election to a greater bishopric meant the inheritance of appreciable wealth and power. (The pagan Ammianus wryly noted that the victory of Damasus over Ursinus, for the honor of appointment as Bishop of Rome, left 137 corpses strewn on the field of battle.) With the triumph of the Church as the imperial religion, which before long made it the largest landowner in the Empire, abuses became more conspicuous. From now on, the Church was to be vulnerable to attack by precisely the most devout, high-minded Christians. The Protestant Reformation was in this aspect only the culmination of centuries of outraged conscience.

Still more troublesome are the spiritual issues. To a philosophical eye, Gibbon remarked , the vices of the clergy are far less dangerous than their virtues. Sincerity, integrity, fidelity, zeal—the best qualities of an ardent bishop may only force the basic issue, which is the claim to absolute spiritual authority. The authority of the Church has unquestionably comforted, sustained, and uplifted innumerable men, from the masses of simple believers to the loftiest spirits. Cardinal Newman, for example, has told movingly how all his religious troubles disappeared when he came to accept the Roman Church as the oracle of God.[14] At the same time, authority is always a potential menace to the inwardness of the true religious spirit, or more specifically to the personal responsibility, freedom, and dignity that many consider the essential teaching of Jesus; they believe that compulsion in matters of the spirit is blasphemous. In the early history of the Church the gains and the losses are illustrated by two heresies—the Montanist and the Donatist.

Montanism was a reaction against the growing worldliness of the Church and an effort to return to the spirit of primitive Christianity. Insisting on an ascetic morality, the Montanists stressed individual purity more than institutionalized faith. They also maintained that men could still be filled with 'the Spirit'; the prophetic or visionary gift had not died with St. Paul and the first Christians but was still alive, and should be welcomed as St. Paul welcomed it (1 Cor. 14:29-33, 39-40).

[14] When he rationalized his saving experience, however, Newman repeated a familiar but curious argument. Because reason is so fallible, he thought it natural that God should 'think fit to introduce a power into the world invested with the prerogative of infallibility in religious matters.' Similarly others have argued that God had to reveal himself through Moses and Jesus, and to perform miracles during the process, because otherwise men would not have known him or believed in the revelation. An omnipotent deity is thus represented as using belated, circuitous, hit-or-miss means of achieving his divine ends, as if he were patching up the flaws in his original handiwork. The Creator who in Genesis said 'Let there be light' now seems to be saying 'Let us try somehow to show some light to some men.' I should say that the psychological argument for the need of an authoritative church is considerably stronger than the logical argument for its divine authority.

They accordingly forced an issue that always vexed Judaism as well as Christianity—how to distinguish true prophets from false ones. Even the enemies of the Montanists were reluctant to condemn them, because of the orthodoxy of their theology and the unquestioned loftiness of their motives—they had won such converts as the great Tertullian. Yet condemned they were. One reason was that they demanded a virtue beyond the powers of most Christians. Another was their obvious liability to superstition and extravagance. (One contemporary reports that 'two females' misled Christians into novelties 'in the form of fasts and feasts, abstinences and diets of radishes.') The main objection, however, was that the Montanists threatened the apostolic norm and the authority of the Church. Men filled with 'the Spirit' can never be trusted. As history was to demonstrate, they are always apt to be unorthodox in belief, and as disrespectful of established legal forms as was Jesus himself. So the Church declared in effect that true prophets are right and false prophets are wrong, and that it alone could distinguish them.

As high-minded and as dangerous were the Donatists. During the persecution under the Emperor Diocletian, numbers of churchmen had renounced the Christian faith in preference to suffering martyrdom; later these backsliders were charitably pardoned and restored to their offices. The Donatists violently refused to accept their ministry, on the grounds that only a pure Christian could administer the sacraments and secure their spiritual efficacy. As far as principle went, they had all the better of the argument. They were demanding that high churchmen in fact be spiritual leaders, superior to their flock; they were trying to preserve the full sacred meaning of the sacraments, which otherwise might become a mere formal transaction, comparable to a wedding performed by a justice of the peace. In general, they wished to preserve the spirit as well as the letter of Church law. Yet the acceptance of Donatism would have been fatal to the Church. Bishops would always be liable to suspicion, or to the charges of fanatics; simple Christians could never be sure of the efficacy of the sacraments, on which they believed their salvation to depend. All Christendom would be perpetually uneasy and insecure. Hence the Donatists were finally condemned, with the help of the Emperor Constantine and St. Augustine, and excluded from the Christian Church.

In other words, the Church followed a policy of expediency and justified it by casuistry. So an established church must do, simply to harmonize its ideals with reality. And these particular compromises may be considered wise and humane. Generally the Church followed a middle path between the worldliness and unworldliness to which Christians were alike prone. When large numbers began to renounce all worldly interests, it stepped in to guide and control their spiritual fervor; it channelized Oriental other-worldliness into a Roman institution of monasticism. At the same time it employed these celibates and ascetics to perform a kind of vicarious holiness for the masses of ordinary Christians, whom it protected from such excessive demands. At best, it accommodated itself to the frailty of man in a spirit of Christian charity. Perhaps the most striking instance is the gradual development of the institution of penance. Early Christians had regarded themselves as a society of saints; they believed that baptism made them free from sin, and that no sins committed thereafter—or at least no more than one or two sins—could be forgiven. With the discovery that Christians nevertheless kept on sinning, they began circumventing the Devil by postponing baptism until late in life, in order to play safe. (Matthew had written that the laborer of the eleventh hour shall be paid as those of the first.) Hence the Church began shifting to the conception of a society of penitents, and developed its great system of penance. For all its liability to abuse, this remains one of the most admirable means of spiritual education, as well as solace, that the religious life of man has evolved.

No less obvious were the losses entailed by these compromises. In condemning the Montanists, and with them all claims to prophetic gifts, the Church discouraged the kind of spiritual fervor that could purify and revitalize it. In condemning the Donatists, it lowered the standards of its clergy and depreciated the spiritual value of its sacraments. And once committed to the principle of expediency, the Church was prone to gross concessions. On the evils of wealth, for example, Jesus was unequivocal: 'Ye cannot serve God and mammon.' The leaders of the Church soon began to equivocate: it was not the possession but the love of wealth, that was evil. By the fifth century a council condemned a doctrine of Pelagius, that the rich can be saved only by renouncing their wealth. This was again charitable as well as sensible—rich men can be good and do good. Nevertheless it was now possible for churchmen to be extremely wealthy, while preaching the ideal blessings of poverty, and to be corrupted by their wealth.

Altogether, the theory of the Church was government of the clergy, by the clergy, and for the people. The power of the clergy was actual, and except for scattered heretics was never seriously attacked until the Protestant Reformation. The interests of the people were a matter of theory, open to considerable question. The natural tendency of the clergy was to discourage open question. So it came to oppose free inquiry, the growth of secular learning, and even the reading of the Bible by laymen. The Church was bound for trouble once the Greek spirit got abroad again and the great popular movements of the Western world got under way.

6. THE CONVERSION OF CONSTANTINE

According to ecclesiastical legend, the Caesar Constantine had a vision of the Cross when he was entering an important battle, and upon winning the battle with this divine aid, he embarked on the career that made him Constantine the Great and a Christian saint. In the famous Edict of Milan (also possibly legendary, since there is no certain evidence of an official edict) he proclaimed the toleration of the 'Christian heresy,' which had just undergone its worst persecution under his predecessor, Diocletian. Later he made this heresy the imperial religion, and on the site of Byzantium built a splendid capital that was to become the 'New Rome.' With imperial aid, a minority sect was at length able to suppress all its powerful rivals, which otherwise might have dwindled but probably would have survived—as old religions have in all other parts of the world. (It is not inconceivable that Mithra would have churches on Broadway today.) The new imperial religion also paid such a price for its victory that historians have described the contribution of Constantine as a 'fatal gift.' In general, the consequences of this gift have been so momentous that historians are still debating his motives.

Some attribute it to cynical expediency. Various pagan thinkers, including the historian Polybius, had made familiar the thesis later taken over by Marxists that religion is a useful opium for the impoverished masses. Other scholars stress the same practical motive but describe it more agreeably as wise statesmanship; they assume that Constantine was acute enough to perceive in organized Christianity the most vital force in his decadent empire, or even far-sighted enough to recognize it as the universal religion, the means to spiritual unity that men had been seeking for centuries. Still other scholars see a genuine conversion in the emperor but differ on whether it was a superstitious respect for a new god who seemed more powerful than the old ones, or a spiritual appreciation of the One True God.

Given this distinguished disagreement, it seems safe to conclude that Constantine's motives were mixed. There is little doubt that he finally became a sincere Christian, thought not a saintly one. (He was almost certainly implicated in the murder of his wife and son.) His coinage, his recorded edicts, and his policies all indicate an increasing devotion to Christianity. They also indicate a natural difficulty in fully comprehending its novel and abstruse doctrines. Constantine tended to confuse the Christian God with his earlier patrons, Hercules and Sol Invictus; he officially recognized the Sabbath as 'the venerable day of the Sun,' and also continued to recognize the god Tyche, or Chance; he could not understand all the fuss over Arianism, requesting the bishops not to permit such trivial differences to disrupt his empire; and when he was baptized on his deathbed he received the sacrament from the Arian Bishop of Nicomedia. Still plainer was his abiding concern for the preservation of the Roman Empire. At least one reason for his conversion was the belief that the Christian God rewarded his devoted followers with success in battle and business. 'It seems,' he proclaimed, 'that when they render the greatest homage to the Divinity, then the greatest benefits befall the commonweal.' To the end Constantine's primary interest was the Earthly City, not the City of God. And so the clearest certainty about his epoch-making policy is that he foresaw neither its immediate nor its long-range consequences. The Church he elected was to survive the Empire he was trying to save. Constantine builded far better than he knew, and far worse.

For his immediate purposes, his pro-Christian policy was a failure: it restored neither material prosperity nor spiritual unity to the Roman Empire. Instead it intensified the disunity, both political and religious, and deepened the split between East and West. Constantine confused, demoralized, or alienated the great pagan majority of the empire, which included the most loyal citizens; while his Christian supporters at once plunged into furious controversy over fine distinctions in dogma. Still more unexpected were the results of his decision to establish a new capital—his most enduring political achievement. Whether Constantinople was born of far-sighted statesmanship, religious exaltation, or the whim of a despot, it grew up to be a mighty stronghold; but what it held was a Greek-Asiatic civilization that Constantine knew or cared little about. As Ferdinand Lot observes, this Latin from the West who was trying to preserve the Roman Empire succeeded only in founding the Byzantine Empire.

To the Church, on the other hand, the miraculous conversion of Constantine quickly brought immense gains in material wealth, social prestige, and political power, with all the privileges that enabled it to play so important a role in history thereafter. Henceforth, except for the brief reign of Julian the Apostate, Christianity was to be opposed only by the most conservative elements—old Roman families, scholars and literary men, and peasant masses. Yet Christian hopes, too, were grievously disappointed. 'The enduring and implacable hatred of nation for nation was now removed,' wrote Eusebius, the contemporary church historian, as he exulted over the miraculous conversion. Actually, the hatred was intensified by the new flames of holy zeal. Constantine's own vision of the Cross in battle became a symbol of militant Christianity, which began by warring upon itself. Without the imperial power it might have torn itself to pieces, but with this power it managed to effect permanent cleavages.

Here again Constantine's transfer of his capital from Rome to Byzantium had immense, unforeseen consequences. The great churches, such as Ephesus, Antioch, Alexandria, and Rome, had owed their rank primarily to the tradition that they were founded by Apostles. Now the Bishop of Constantinople claimed eminence for purely political reasons. When the Council of Constantinople ended the controversy over Arianism, it sowed the seeds of a more dangerous controversy by decreeing that Constantinople ranked second to Rome, and ahead of Alexandria and Antioch, because it was the 'New Rome.' (Although Constantinople dug up an Apostle for the occasion, claiming St. Andrew as its patron, the claim was patently vague and dubious.) The Oriental-mystical party of Christianity thus found a vigorous new champion in its conflict with the Roman ethical-legal party, but this conflict was intensified by the ambitions of the emperors and patriarchs of Constantinople, who could support their contentions only by secular power. Ultimately Western and Eastern Christendom broke apart for good, for reasons both political and theological. Meanwhile Eastern Christendom itself was united at a heavy cost. Resentment of the authority of Constantinople was largely responsible for the secession of the Armenian, Nestorian, and Coptic churches. The Syrian and Egyptian provinces were so weakened by dissension that they quickly succumbed to the Arabs, even welcoming Moslem rule, and were lost to Christendom thereafter.

The 'Peace of Constantine,' in short, was the signal for the wars on heresy; the toleration granted by the Edict of Milan ushered in a long era of intolerance. There was at first little persecution of pagans, except by mobs or bands of monks, if only because there were so many heretics to be taken care of. Under Constantine the pagans retained full civil rights. Still, he had been brought up in the Roman tradition that a State cult was necessary to secure the protection of the gods—and now the Roman god was a jealous god. He felt obliged to take action against heretics out of fear that 'God may be moved not only against the human race but against me myself'; so to preserve unity he called the Council of Nicaea, thus presenting the Church with the double-edged weapon of the ecumenical council. As these councils produced still fiercer dissension, his successors had to go further. Theodosius, the last emperor to rule over a united Roman Empire, closed the pagan temples, made Catholic Christianity the only legal religion of the empire, and denied civil rights to all 'madmen' who refused to accept orthodox doctrine.

Toynbee describes the triumph of Christianity as a triumph of 'the way of gentleness.' Of other religions, such as Mohammedanism, he remarks the 'prohibitive penalty for the moral offence of attempting to impose a religion by political force.' If so, however, Christianity paid this penalty. By gentleness it had converted only a small fraction of the population in the three centuries before Constantine (Norman Baynes estimates 10 per cent); now it imposed itself on the rest by political force. Augustine himself argued for forcible conversion as a labor of love, wrenching his text from a parable of Jesus—'Compel them to come in.' And the Church went still further. The Christian respect for the person had led to wide protest against the execution of the Spaniard Priscillian, the first heretic to be put to death; but in the fifth century Pope Leo the Great endorsed the death penalty for erroneous beliefs, as necessary for the preservation of divine law. The Church adopted his doctrine, which in time led to the Inquisition and the routine of torture. Indeed, it was Christianity that introduced Toynbee's 'moral offense' into history, as a deliberate, consistent policy. Although the world had long known political despotism, it was not accustomed to the idea that conformity in philosophical and religious thought should be enforced, or that the Church should serve as a police-court. Some earlier thinkers might have agreed with Pope Leo that 'Truth, which is simple and one, does not admit of variety'; but almost all would have thought it absurd to impose such truth by legislation, or to punish metaphysical error by death. When Theodosius deprived heretics of civil rights, religious orthodoxy became the price of citizenship for the first time in history.

The strangeness of this policy caught Christians as well as pagans off guard. In the circumstances, to be sure, the alliance of Church and State was natural enough. The Church had got its form and structure from Rome; now it got its power from the same source, and was able to make good its claims as the only true religion. Still, Christians had generally agreed with Tertullian that the idea of a Christian Caesar was a contradiction in terms. While the State became consecrated to the service of God, God had to return the favor and support the State—which by now was pretty brutal and shabby. For a religion that claimed universality it was a dangerous, uneasy alliance, which created a lasting confusion of the things that are Caesar's and the things that are God's.

The immediate problem was to adjust the relative power of the allies. In the East, as we have seen, the Church became subservient to the State. The prestige of Constantine himself gave an aura of sanctity to the throne—at the outset Bishop Eusebius had hailed him as an emissary of God; and though he was reputed to have died in 'stainless white,' he had always worn the purple. In however pious a spirit, he had summoned the Council of Nicaea and commanded the churchmen to settle their differences. The more vigorous of his successors explicitly laid down the law to the Church, which they could control more easily because of its hierarchic organization. In the West, however, the Church asserted its sovereignty. 'The Emperor is within the Church, not over it,' declared Bishop Ambrose; he humbled the mighty Emperor Theodosius himself, once forcing him to do public penance for an act of imperial arrogance. Augustine provided a firm theological basis for the episcopal claims to supremacy. Above all, the Church was aided by the increasing weakness of the Eastern emperors, the steady disintegration of the Earthly City. Hence the dying empire gave birth to the Papacy, which took over the responsibilities of the State when Rome went down.

In this period the Papacy made its greatest contribution to Christendom, by the magnificent resolution with which Gregory the Great in particular resisted the forces of barbarism and preserved some semblance of order. But when Europe emerged from the darkness, the Church again had to wrestle with the problem of adjusting the authority of the two Cities. This became the central political problem of the Middle Ages, with disastrous consequences for the Papacy. And when its bid for supremacy ended in ignominious defeat, the State retained much of the sacredness it had got from its alliance with the Church; it was able to proclaim the divine right of kings. Then the Church itself lent support to its conquerors. Consciously or unconsciously, it allied itself with the ruling aristocracy, to maintain what power it had or to recover as much as it could. In our own time we have been treated to the spectacle of cardinals publicly praying for the success of a Franco.

In the Roman Empire, meanwhile, the masses of Christians had little reason to rejoice in the new political power of their bishops. From the outset the Church had attacked the materialism rather than the tyranny of Rome. In view of its own organization, it could scarcely attack the principle of autocracy. When it became a partner of the State it was naturally disposed to accept the social *status quo*. More precisely, it accepted the change that was taking place, the last stages of the movement toward an out-and-out Oriental despotism; for as Constantine shifted the State to a Christian basis he was also dropping most of the remnants of constitutional government and municipal self-government.[15] The Church came to regard serfdom as the natural social order for man. Extensive philanthropic enterprises, and occasional outbursts of moral indignation, were offset by acquiescence in the basic class structure. Thus Bishop Ambrose, like John Chrysostom in the East, preached so warmly on the terrible contrast between the misery of the poor and the luxury of the rich that he might be suspected of communism; yet he did not propose that either the authorities or the poor should do anything about this injustice. He positively defended the institution of slavery, arguing that slaves had an unusual advantage for the exercise of the Christian virtues of humility, patience, and forgiveness of enemies, and that men cursed with original sin were not fit to govern themselves anyway.

On the whole, the moral and spiritual standards of Christianity were lowered by its triumph. The hordes of pagans who now were led or driven into the Church were rebaptized but hardly regenerated. The Church took over more freely the trappings of paganism, heightening the splendor of its service but affronting the conscience of Christians devoted to the simplicity and purity of their original faith. Many churchmen became reconciled to 'this world,' or even attached to it, just when it was in fact becoming more evil and miserable. The revulsion against this increasing worldliness helps to explain the growth of asceticism in the fourth and fifth centuries, a movement that expressed a kind of spirituality but deprived the Christian world at large of its possible value. Those who fled to cell or cloister contributed little to the spiritual elevation of the Church or the spiritual welfare of the masses.

The last word about Constantine's fatal gift must be spoken by Christianity itself. Meanwhile Toynbee points to one obvious moral, drawn from the failure of Julian the Apostate a generation after Constantine.

---

[15] The reforms he attempted as a Christian emperor were modest efforts to mitigate certain social evils, involving no basic change in imperial society. Typical was his prohibition of divorce except on serious grounds; he specifically excluded such 'frivolous pretexts' as infidelity and drunkenness.

If Hellenism is not yet making the progress which we have
a right to expect (Julian wrote to one of his pagan prelates),
it is we, its devotees, who are to blame. . . Are we refusing to
face the fact that Atheism owes its success above all to its
philanthropy towards strangers and to its provision for funerals
and to its parade of a high puritanical morality? . . . Do not let
us allow hostile competitors to outdo us in our own strong
points while we give way to a slackness and indifference which
are not merely a disgrace to our religion but a downright
betrayal of it.

By Atheism, of course, he meant Christianity. Today Christians in turn are on the defensive, against godless Communists.
The Communists are parading a high puritanical morality,
and are offering the peasant masses of the world an improvement in the worldly lot that has been theirs under Christian
regimes, or regimes supported by the Western democracies.
The excommunication of Communists may be no more effective than Julian's milder restrictions on Atheism unless Christian societies cease disgracing and betraying their religion.

7. Epilogue: Julian the Apostate and Gregory the Great

'Galilean, thou hast conquered!' So legend has Julian the
Apostate exclaiming, at the close of his brief, brilliant, tragic
career. He had failed in his high-minded crusade to establish
a Roman Catholic Pagan Church, and to him the triumph of
Christianity meant that the glories of Greece and Rome were
no more. Today we know better. We can see that Christianity
was the last great creation of the ancient world. For this reason it was able to preserve something of pagan culture, and
finally to revive its glories. But for this reason, too, it was shot
through with pagan thought and feeling. The Galilean was
also conquered by the world he won. And the failure of the
inspired Apostate dramatically illumines this ambiguous
triumph.

Like most cultivated pagans, the Emperor Julian resented
the blasphemous exclusiveness of the Christians, their prof-
anation of ancient shrines, and their seemingly barbarous
fanaticism. Like the Neo-Platonists in particular, he wanted a
more spiritual, mystical religion, objecting to the worship of a
man and to the corruption of the teaching of this man. (As
Porphyry wrote, 'The gods have declared Christ to have been

most pious. . . Whereas the Christians are a polluted set, contaminated and enmeshed in error.') Hence Julian's aim was not merely to restore the Olympians to their thrones. He had a grand, if hazy vision, in which a pantheon of gods under a Sun-God symbolized an ineffable spiritual reality. He sought a synthesis of the fervor of Oriental religions, the dignity of Greek philosophy, the beauty of Greek poetry, the piety of Roman ceremony, and the stoicism of Roman patriotism. Although his dream included considerable superstition too, on the whole it was a magnificent and magnanimous one, the loftiest that the pagan world was then capable of. To the mission of realizing this dream Julian dedicated all the remarkable energy and ability that had distinguished him alike as scholar, soldier, and administrator. He even retained a generous spirit, despite his increasing bitterness—Christians kept complaining because he denied them the glory of martyrdom.[16]

But Athanasius remained calm. 'It will soon pass,' he said; and he was right. Even the spectacular misfortunes of Julian were not simply mischances. When fire or earthquake destroyed the temple he started building for the Jews in Jerusalem, and the pagan temple at Antioch from whose precincts he had removed the unholy bones of a saint, Christians hailed these new miracles; but the apparent accidents now look like the remorseless logic of destiny. Julian's mission was doomed from the outset. The fervor of paganism had gone into the mystery cults, which were groping toward the ideal of universal brotherhood but were still essentially private salvation societies. They could not be organized into the national church that Julian wished to erect; they provided no incentive to self-sacrifice or martyrdom. On the other hand, the rich tradition of Greece that he wished to incorporate in his universal religion survived only in scattered rhetoricians, scholars, and dilettantes, who had piety but little fervor or faith. Altogether, he was attempting an impossible combination. His religion was neither rational enough nor popular enough; it was too good for his world, and not good enough. Julian's beloved gods served him best by fulfilling the gloomy auguries of his soothsayers, when he set out to invade the Persian empire; for his death in battle, at the early age of thirty-two, spared the exalted idealist the almost certain fate of the embittered prophet.

---

[16] Possibly, however, he also had a cynical motive. According to Ammianus, his edict of toleration was inspired by the hope that it would lead Christians to destroy themselves, since he knew by experience 'that there are no wild beasts so hostile to mankind as are the Christians to one another.'

The Christians of his day nevertheless hailed the miracles that foiled the devilish Apostate, believing that his undoing was God's doing; and their belief has persisted. Orthodoxy still proclaims that the greatest miracle—the proof of all the other miracles recorded in Scripture—was the growth and spread of Christianity itself. 'How, without the Hand of God,' asked Cardinal Newman, 'could a new idea, one and the same, enter at once into myriads of men, women, and children of all ranks, especially the lower,' and grow in vigor until it 'broke the obstinacy of the strongest and wisest government which the world has ever seen, and forced its way ... to the fulness of imperial power?' The failure of Julian points to a simple answer. Christianity was not strictly a new idea, or one and the same; the 'good news' announced by the Apostles was very old news, which conformed itself to the different hopes and expectations of their pagan or Jewish listeners. The idea did not enter at once into myriads; the growth and spread of Mohammedanism was far more rapid, or 'miraculous.' The government broken by the idea was no longer strong or wise, but an Oriental despotism serving as a last desperate stopgap. And by this time the Christian Church could hardly have been recognized by the Jesus who supposedly founded it. Like all the higher religions—in particular the revolutionary religions of Buddhism and Mohammedanism—it had grown out of older religions, and in its victory over them had paid the usual price, taking over many of their practices and beliefs. No religion that succeeds can be wholly new. Although it must appear to improve upon the past, it cannot break with the past; it must satisfy hopes and desires conditioned by the past; and as it takes root, it draws still more from the past.

One reason why Julian failed, then, is that Christianity offered a synthesis as familiar as his, and even richer. Its central figure of the Redeemer was at least as old as the Tritos Sôtêr of the early Greeks, and its promise of personal immortality was still older, echoing through the history of timeless Egypt. From Babylonia came the idea of God as the maker of heaven and earth, from Persia the dualism of Satan and God, from Egypt the last judgment, from Syria the resurrection drama of Adonis, from Phrygia the worship of the Great Mother, from Greece and Rome the idea of universal law. From sources too ancient to be identified came its baptism and communion. From the various mysteries came other ritual elements of the mystery of its mass, such as incense, vestments, beads, holy water, genuflection, and chanting. Without this ancient and cosmopolitan heritage, Christianity could scarcely have established its claim to universality.

In addition, Christianity offered Yahweh. In the intense, radiant, and awful presence of this God, the vast imaginings of Julian seemed still more abstract and remote. With him came an interpretation of history, from creation to the final judgment, that ideally reflected the experience of the ordinary man—his awareness of present toil and trouble, his memory of happier days in his youth, his hopes of a peaceful old age. Meanwhile the Church sanctified his life from the cradle to the grave, providing sacraments for all the great occasions, recurrent communion with his Saviour and repeated forgiveness for his sins. It offered him, indeed, somewhat more than Jesus had, and on somewhat different terms. For he had helped to set these terms.

Once more we come to an idea so elementary and obvious that it is generally overlooked in serious discourse. Kirsopp Lake states it simply: 'Catholic Christianity conquered because it was popular, not because it was true.' Its popularity would not make it necessarily untrue, but neither is it a miraculous proof of its truth. The point is merely that the Christianity that has moved the great majority of men, through a gamut of emotions from hope to hysteria, is not the Christianity that is usually discussed in books. Popular religious belief is rather different from religion defined as 'our highest aspiration,' from religion as argued by theologians, even from religion as taught and practiced by the churches. At the same time, it has deeply influenced the doctrine and practice of the churches. On both counts it is an important element of the historic meaning of Christianity, and its historic possibilities. As we seek to realize 'our highest aspiration' we need to consider the realities of popular religion, and the simplicities underlying even sophisticated religion. Here is what T. S. Eliot calls the unconscious, primitive level, on which he finds the basic unity of a religion, and to which, he grants, conscious believers tend to return under stress.

The nature of primitive Christianity is accordingly most apparent today in regions where faith is most nearly universal and unconscious. The great majority of the peasants of southern Europe and Latin America are still *pagani*, whose fatalism, passive brotherliness, and superstition antedate Christianity by thousands of years. (Carlo Levi's *Christ Stopped at Eboli* gives a vivid account of these timeless peasants in Italy.) They know that Providence can't really be trusted. What they worship is not God but the local god or goddess, the patron saint; the saint performs endless miracles in curing ordinary ailments, though he is generally helpless against the evil-eye. What they fear is not Satan but a host of prehistoric demons. They are more akin to Moslem peasants in Anatolia than to fellow-Christians on Fifth Avenue. Yet their worldlier brethren also cling to the ancient belief in magic and miracle. Under stress they pray to supernatural powers to end the drought, to cure the cancer, to deflect the fatal bullet into some other foxhole—to postpone their blessed reunion with their Creator. Lacking the innocence of pure ignorance, they illustrate more plainly the indignities of popular religion. 'Christianity, a religion which is not of this world, suffers humiliation in the world for the sake of the general mass of humanity,' writes Nicolas Berdyaev. 'The whole tragedy of spiritual humanity lies in that fact.'

This universal fate of the higher religions is not, I should say, merely humiliating. At its crudest, the religion of simple men is a pathetic reflection of the hard lot they have generally known, and at that it may express a more genuine piety and humility than the religion of their intellectual betters.[17] Christianity brought higher aspirations to folk culture. It introduced ideals of brotherhood and love, a spirit of gentleness; it gave a new dignity to poverty and manual labor, which could survive exploitation by aristocratic Christians. And the folk in turn contributed to the high tradition. The lowly followers of Christ best exemplified the ideal of brotherhood, the virtues of faith, hope, and charity. Throughout history popular movements have renewed the faith, rescuing Christianity from complacency and corruption.

Other contributions of the folk were indirect or unconscious results of their very limitations. When the worship of images, for example, grew popular under the Christian empire, austere believers protested against it as a reversion to paganism, which it was. The Church supported it on the ground that the image was merely a symbol, which was not itself worshiped. Its logicians added that images make visible the invisible realities just as God himself did in the creation, or in Jesus himself. They chose to ignore the plain fact that many of the faithful did confuse the image with the deity and worshiped the image itself—as among the peas-

---

[17] Readers may recall the little girl, a year or so ago, who appealed for prayers to save her infected arm. Prayers went up from all over the country, but to no avail; the arm had to be amputated. The newspapers reported, however, that she went into the operating room smiling, saying, 'If God wants my arm He can have it.' Here was the quintessential naïveté of popular faith. Why should God want the arm of a little girl? Or who was she to tell Him that He could have it? Yet she was smiling; and who would simply deplore such a faith?

antry they still do. Yet this concession to vulgar belief made possible the later glories of Christian art.

A more curious example is the popular idea of the resurrection of the flesh, which remains in the Creeds that to this day are recited in most Christian churches. 'No doctrine of the Christian faith,' St. Augustine acknowledged, 'is so vehemently and so obstinately opposed.' The most apparent reason why the belief survived opposition was the desire of simple men to enjoy an after-life that was more, not less, than the life they knew on earth. They wanted all this and heaven too. And now intellectuals are dwelling on the admirable humanistic implications of this doctrine. Christopher Dawson points out that it rescues Christianity from the denial of life to which higher religion is always prone; Christian salvation is a complete fulfilment of life, a salvation of the whole man. Similarly Reinhold Niebuhr argues that the resurrection of the flesh is essential to a full justification of human history on earth. When he adds that Christian thought can thereby 'allow an appreciation of the unity of body and soul that idealists and naturalists have sought in vain,' it appears that this doctrine, which seemed foolishness to the Greeks, is the perfect fulfilment of the Greek ideal of harmony.

Or so it might be except for one serious objection, aside from the fact that early Christianity did not realize these admirable implications. The objection is that the doctrine is literally incredible. It is inherently the most improbable, illogical, fantastic view of the after-life that has been offered by the higher religions. Thus neither Dawson nor Niebuhr demonstrates that the doctrine is true—they merely argue that it is very desirable. And so we must consider the vulgar beliefs that made the great liberating force of Christianity a liberation as well from logic, from natural law, and from mature responsibility. A historian of early Christianity should stress that it was free from the grossest superstitions that infected its rivals—for instance the rite of the tauro-bolium, or blood-bath of the bull, that even cultured pagans were pleased to perform. A critical student of high aspirations must also stress all the superstition that did get in, because it is still embedded in orthodox Christianity.

One example is prayer. Prayer may be a communion with God, a withdrawal into an ideal good, an aspiration to grace, a reverent acceptance of destiny. To simple men, however, it is ordinarily a petition for special favors; and orthodox Christianity still teaches that such petitions may literally be granted. This doctrine of the material efficacy of prayer reduces the Creator to a cosmic bellhop, of a not very bright or reliable kind; it declares that the Dahomeans of Africa are right when they explain that the gods are like children, and must be told what to do. It calls for attention because this was the religion of the foxholes—the absence of atheism in foxholes—that seems to gratify many churchmen today. However understandable the prayers of frightened men, they illustrate the humiliating beliefs that pass for high aspirations, and may blind men to their own responsibilities.

More humiliating are the orthodox conceptions of the after-life. Western man, with his gospel of individualism, naturally prefers a personal immortality to the kind of undifferentiated, unparticularized, anonymous oneness with the World-Soul offered by Hinduism and Platonism. John Smith not only wants to live forever—he wants to be forever John Smith, hanging on to everything except his warts; and in a heaven swarming with Smiths he still wants to be set apart, or even catch the eye of the Super-Smith. Still, the Hindu can rightly object that the immortal element in man should transcend the particular self or ego, and that this passion for in-dividual immortality is not only preposterous but shockingly conceited—the plainest example of the overweening pride of Western man. And though it is offset by the doctrine of hell, this may also be regarded as an expression of colossal pride; it only magnifies the injustice it is supposed to com-pensate for, by making evil everlasting, absolute, and irre-mediable. At best, the principle of divine rewards and punishments is not an ethical principle at all. As Kant pointed out, threats by a superior power may extort a prudent obedience but they do not impose a moral obligation; con-duct inspired by hope of reward or fear of punishment is not strictly moral conduct, and does not make the heart better. One may therefore doubt even the practical wisdom of the Church in maintaining hell. Although it has no doubt inspired plenty of fear, the evidence of history bears out the suspicion raised by the endless sermons through the centuries, that the fear never has inspired the masses of men to behave like Christians.[18]

[18] The recent revival of this anachronism in the name of spiritual health (Pope Pius, for example, has called for greater emphasis in Catholic pulpits on the Dangers of Hell) again illustrates the tendency of organized religion to lag behind moral as well as intellectual progress —the inveterate tendency that discredits its claims to spiritual leader-ship. So one might risk the embarrassment of pointing out the elemen-tary objection to the dogma, that an eternity of torture is a shockingly disproportionate punishment for the sins of a lifetime—an infinitesimal moment in eternity—and hardly befitting a God of mercy. Nor can one respect the various efforts of squeamish liberals to hedge on hell, by lowering its temperature to a merely tropical heat, by reducing its pop-ulation to a handful of the very worst men (such as Judas), by anni-

In this respect, at any rate, Julian the Apostate stood for a loftier conception of morality. Like most of the nobler pagans, he believed in virtue for its own sake. As his spiritual father Plotinus had said, 'If a man seeks the good life for anything outside itself, it is not the good life that he is seeking.' The good news announced by the Christian Church, however, was tempered to congregations that contained (as St. Paul said) 'not many wise, not many mighty, not many noble.' It was news of the good life in Christ, for Christ's sake, but it was also a response to ignoble hopes and fears. It is depressing, writes Gilbert Murray, to study 'these obscure congregations, drawn from the proletariat of the Levant, superstitious, charlatan-ridden, and helplessly ignorant, who still believed in Gods begetting children of mortal mothers, who took the "Word," the "Spirit," and the "Divine Wisdom" to be persons called those names, and turned the Immortality of the Soul into "the standing up of the corpses"; and to reflect that it was these who held the main road of advance towards the greatest religion of the Western world.'

Yet they did hold the main road; and the ultimate secret of their success was precisely this combination of low superstition and high aspiration. To the Emperor Julian, the early Christians were very poor in spirit. Repelled by their indifference to aristocratic values, symbolized by their worship of a 'bleeding and dying god,' he could not do justice to the idealism and the heroism that had enabled these obscure Atheists to survive persecution. More to the point, he would have been appalled by Pope Gregory the Great, the inheritor of the remnants of his Roman State (*c.* 540-604). And the career of Gregory—the grand, heroic, benighted saint who came at the nadir of antiquity, represented the very antithesis of Julian's Hellenic ideal, and by sheer force of character unwittingly made possible the eventual recovery of this ideal—affords the final, comprehensive perspective on the main issues of our drama: the whole development of early Christianity, theological, political, and popular; its best and its worst elements, which explain its triumph in defeat and its tragedy in victory; and its potentialities for an age of crisis, or of darkness.

According to the *Catholic Encyclopedia*, Gregory the Great may be regarded as 'the father of medieval Christianity,' who therefore had a momentous influence on the doctrine,

hilating the wicked instead of torturing them, etc. About the best one can say for this doctrine is that its historic acceptance is understandable, since the society in which Christianity grew up was accustomed to autocratic rule and regarded torture as a proper judicial procedure.

organization, and discipline of the Church today. According to Toynbee, he may be regarded as more than any other single man 'the founder of the new civilization of Western Christendom which arose out of the void.' Certainly his achievement was extraordinary—an achievement of character and will more wonderful than the innumerable 'miracles' he was credited with. For he lived in perhaps the darkest age of Rome, an age when it was still a great city with memories of its great tradition, but without the economic, political, or military means to sustain itself. It was cut off from its former empire, surrounded by barbarism, beset by famine and pestilence, and in its impotence afflicted by an appalling pessimism. 'Today there is on every side death, on every side grief, on every side desolation,' wrote Gregory; 'on every side we are being smitten, on every side our cup is being filled with draughts of bitterness.' He himself entered the monastic life, in which he practiced great austerities and from which the Pope summoned him to active duty against his will. He displayed not a trace of worldly ambition or pride. When he was himself elected Pope, tradition has it that he had to be seized and carried to the Basilica of St. Peter.

Despite constant ill health, Gregory worked with tremendous energy and resolution. He carried out extensive ecclesiastical reforms, enforcing a strict discipline in church and monastery, while he himself always exemplified the high ideals defined in his book on the duties of a bishop, which for centuries remained the standard text. He preached innumerable sermons to sustain his own congregation, and sent out missionaries to work among the heathens and the Arians. He recognized and skilfully managed the estates of the Roman Church, comprising some fifteen hundred square miles, and used their income for the benefit of the poor. He held off the Lombards who had overrun northern Italy, negotiating a settlement that maintained the independence of Rome. Above all, he established the primacy of the Apostolic See as the one supreme authority, divinely appointed. Calmly he confirmed or vetoed the decrees of synods, and as calmly upheld the dignity of Rome against the far greater temporal power of Constantinople. Hereafter all Western Christendom looked to Rome for guidance. And all this he achieved without military force and without intrigue, simply by moral authority. The work of Gregory remains the greatest spiritual triumph of the Papacy.

Toynbee therefore acclaims him for having laid the most solid kind of foundation for the civilization to come: he built 'on a religious rock and not on economic sands,' or political bogs. His main concern was indeed a 'supra-mundane order,' not a mere world order. Yet a world order did arise later, and does concern most of us; so we need to examine the religious foundation laid by Gregory. We might expect it to be inadequate for a going concern, since he himself expected the speedy end of the world. He gave the Church an authority that might be abused for mundane purposes, as in time it was. He also bequeathed it the fantastic superstitions and terrors that helped to mold the distinctive piety of the Middle Ages. For his work reflected the barbaric ignorance of his own age.

As the *Catholic Encyclopedia* concedes, the greatness of Gregory did not extend to his powers of thought. He made his important contribution to theology by summing up the teachings of the Fathers before him, notably Augustine. In popularizing these teachings, for his very practical purposes, he sometimes made them more intelligible and humane; but he was generally incapable of grasping the deepest thought of the Fathers, or of perceiving their basic inconsistencies. He took for granted that the Bible and tradition were not only infallible but identical. In particular, he vulgarized church doctrine by raising a great deal of pagan folklore to the dignity of dogma. He was very fond of prodigies and miracles, and obsessed with angels and demons; his works are filled with tales of the grotesque activities of demons. Similarly he believed in prayer as a form of magic. Catholic piety has owed much to his teaching that prayer could enlist the aid of saints and hasten the release of souls from purgatory. Purgatory itself was one of the pre-Christian beliefs he helped to establish as dogma.

More important than any specific doctrines was the informing spirit that Gregory bequeathed to Christianity. Although Augustine often seems credulous, he was at least acquainted with the philosophy and science of the ancient world; he simply chose to ignore it as unimportant. By now, however, such indifference had resulted in the virtual disappearance of classical thought and knowledge. Gregory was simply ignorant. Where Augustine deliberately subordinated all other interests to the hope of supernatural salvation, Gregory was almost unaware that there were other interests; the supernatural was the whole frame of his thought. Hence he welcomed the most preposterous superstitions, while frowning on any lingering traces of other forms of curiosity. Curiosity he considered the root of heresy. Faith alone was acceptable to God, and it must be an unquestioning faith in what the Church taught. If a doctrine was incomprehensible, so much the better: 'Nor is faith

meritorious to which the human reason furnishes proof.'
And faith must be rooted in fear. Gregory's own terrible
struggles between love and fear had taught him that constant anxiety was the best means of escaping hell.

Altogether, the faith that Gregory the Great handed down
to posterity was the common faith of the Dark Ages; and
its essence was despair of life on earth. It is a tribute to
him that this despair did not lead to quietism, as one
might have expected. Nevertheless his legacy was the dark
tradition of fear and hatred of the natural world, with salvation possible only on arbitrary terms dictated by the
Church. Gregory remains a symbol of the attitudes that have
conflicted with the knowledge, aspirations, and ideals of the
Western world in recent centuries. If the atomic age is as
calamitous as his age, it is conceivable that men will return
to his God. Meanwhile we should recognize that this God
is not a God of light and law, and does not welcome the
pursuit of truth and beauty. Faith in him will again mean
that men have lost all faith in themselves, and in the goodness of his creation.

'Amid the ruins of a falling age,' wrote Bishop Cyprian,
'our spirit remains erect'; so he accepted martyrdom, confident of the heavenly life to come. Gregory the Great is a
still grander exemplar of this spirit because he was denied
the dignity or ecstasy of martyrdom, and suffered from
terrible anxieties about the life to come. Yet he illustrates
as well the ultimate reason for the triumph of Christianity in
the ancient world. In Gilbert Murray's famous phrase, it
was 'the failure of nerve'—'a loss of self-confidence, of hope
in this life and of faith in normal human effort; a despair
of patient inquiry, a cry for infallible revelation.' For all
his zeal, the Emperor Julian himself was touched by the
same failure. He once lamented that in all Cappadocia he
could find no true Hellenist, but it is doubtful whether he
could have recognized one. At least there had been one in
Cappadocia not long before his time, in Diogenes of Oeno-
anda—an obscure old Epicurean whose last testament was
a message engraved in marble for all passersby, in order to
'set forth in public the medicine of the healing of mankind.' Diogenes exemplified the noblest spirit of pagan
antiquity—a religious faith in a purely ethical creed, a devotion to goodness for its own sake, without promise of material blessings or heavenly rewards, and without benefit of
mystical ecstasy. Gregory the Great would have been horrified by this pagan, but even Julian would not have
appreciated fully the simple, unpretentious dignity of his fare-

well message: 'Nothing to fear in God: Nothing to feel in Death: Good can be attained: Evil can be endured.' Perhaps the spirit of Diogenes was even more erect than either Julian's or Gregory's.

VII

The Fall of Rome

1. THE ACHIEVEMENT OF ROME

Never before, wrote Polybius, had Fortune 'accomplished such a work, achieved such a triumph,' as the establishment of the Roman Empire. 'What man is so indifferent or so idle that he would not wish to know how and under what form of government almost all the inhabited world came under the single rule of the Romans in less than fifty-three years?' Polybius was a Greek, however. The Romans were less curious, and had less understanding of what they had wrought in these fifty years (220-168 B.C.). They had not consciously set out to rule the world. They had emerged as the greatest power in the Mediterranean by defeating Carthage, in a terrific life-and-death struggle; then one conquest led to another almost in spite of them, and the rolling stone gathered an empire. Some of their senators even tried to circumvent the designs of Fortune, opposing further expansion as a threat to their rule at home. For Rome itself, in fact, the immediate result of the epoch-making triumph was corruption, class war, increasing chaos. Nevertheless the Roman Empire continued to expand, during a century of bloody civil war, until it finally destroyed the Roman Republic.

When the great Augustus restored peace and order, he deliberately called a halt to the career of conquest. Beginning as an unscrupulous, ruthless politician, he ended as the wise, just statesman who established the famous Principate, a monarchy under an elaborate cloak of republican forms—perhaps the most pious hoax in political history. In his old age, deeply troubled by the moral corruption that accompanied the peace and prosperity he had restored to Rome, Augustus thought he had failed. A century later Tacitus was still disposed to agree with him. The greatest of Roman historians had little idea of the momentous history the Empire was making; aware chiefly of its attendant evils, he pined for the grand old days of the Republic. (The Romans in turn apparently had little idea of Tacitus' own greatness, since his friend Pliny is the only known writer to refer to him until three hundred years later, when Marcellinus—a Greek—set about a continuation of the histories.) Yet the creation of Augustus stood up for some centuries. It has been hailed as 'the supreme achievement in the history of statesmanship.' It led the Romans to inscribe the motto *Æternitas* on their coins, and to cling to this illusion while their empire was crumbling, undergoing a still bloodier anarchy than had resulted from its rise. After Rome was sacked by Alaric in the year 410, the poet Rutilius christened it the 'Eternal City'; when Rome finally 'fell,' in the year 476 according to our history texts, contemporaries did not notice its fall—as Ferdinand Lot remarks, it fell without a sound. A few decades later the chronicler Cassidorus saw nothing exceptional in the events of this famous year. And in fact it did not mark the fall of an empire. The Western provinces were taken over by the Germans, who for all practical purposes had long controlled them; but the Eastern Roman Empire went on.

Such, in rough outline, is the story of the Roman Empire, which has haunted Western historians ever since, and whose fall has been considered 'the most important problem of universal history.' Easterners may add ironic postscripts. The rise and fall of Rome did not shake the whole world; it had little effect on the older, wealthier, more populous East. Neither was its endurance so remarkable. Although Westerners are pleased to observe that some great nations have not lasted as long as it took Rome to fall, it can hardly match the East for longevity. Compared to Egypt, which endured for some thousands of years (and remained a major source of the wealth of Rome), it was a flash in the pan. So now our universal historians are tending to reduce it to just another empire. To Spengler it was a mere 'civilization,' the inevitably sordid, futile dying phase of Hellenic culture; he echoes the verdict that the grandeur of Rome was 'a violent and vulgar fraud.' To Toynbee it was a mere 'universal state,' which is the next to the last stage of a disintegrating society; he holds that in this stage the only role for creative personalities is that of savior, and the great Romans were not saviors. They even persecuted the followers of the true Saviour.

Nevertheless the Roman Empire remains one of the greatest historic achievements of man. If the abysmal Dark Ages that followed it are an ironic comment on its presumptions as an Eternal City, they also deepen the tragedy of its fall, which appears as the worst setback in the history of civilization. For East and West alike Rome is far more significant than Egypt, as the grandest symbol of the ideals of universal peace, law, and order that men are again seeking to realize. Created by force and fraud, like all other empires—created almost absent-mindedly, and full of anomalies to the end—it became different from all other empires by aspiring to be a genuine commonwealth. Its greater rulers were concerned with the welfare of their subject peoples, not merely with the power, wealth, and glory of the Romans; after Augustus these peoples were not merely resigned to Roman rule but were grateful for it. It is unique in the extravagant tributes it elicited from its subjects. One example is the oration of Aristeides, a Greek contemporary of Marcus Aurelius:

Before the establishment of your empire the World was in confusion, upside down, adrift and out of control; but as soon as you Romans intervened the turmoils and factions ceased, and life and politics were illumined by the dawn of an era of universal order... You Romans are the only rulers known to History who have reigned over freemen... The lustre of your rule is unsullied by any breath of ungenerous hostility; and the reason is that you yourselves set the example of generosity by sharing all your power and privileges with your subjects ... with the result that in your day a combination has been achieved which previously appeared quite impossible—the combination of consummate power with consummate benevolence... Rome is a citadel which has all the peoples of the Earth for its villagers. And Rome has never failed those who have looked to her.

Rome soon did fail them—wretchedly. Within a generation after Aristeides the empire was convulsed by military anarchy; and the benevolent Marcus Aurelius, the inspiration of the tribute, himself touched off the anarchy by fondly naming his worthless son Commodus as his successor. As with the Greeks, the failure was not a tragic accident—it was a moral and intellectual failure. But it deserves our study because it was a great tragic drama in its own right, not merely an epilogue to the tragedy of Greece. We too owe a tribute to the achievements of the Romans, who were in truth creators and even saviors of a sort.

What they saved first of all was the legacy of Greece. Far less brilliant, original, and versatile than the Greeks, the Romans were content to borrow most of their culture from them. They gave it their own practical bent, however, translating it into terms more suitable for universal use. They were able to transmit it to the barbaric West and thereby to lay the foundations of modern Europe.[1] Thus they systematized education, bequeathing the seven liberal arts to the Middle Ages. They adapted Greek philosophy to daily needs, applying it to government and recasting it into a philosophy of life available to men without high gifts. They developed the type of cultivated gentleman or man of the world—the type of Cicero, Horace, and Pliny the Younger, who were less spontaneous and exciting than the Greeks but more moderate, urbane, and sensible. Even their pompous rhetoricians did a valuable service by consolidating the power and prestige of the word, siring the profession of letters; in time these bores had such progeny as Petrarch, Montaigne, and Voltaire.

The practical sense of the Romans also led to some original contributions, notably their monumental architecture. While the Greeks stuck to their simple post and lintel, the Romans exploited the possibilities of the arch, the dome, and the vault to erect baths, palaces, amphitheatres, and government buildings, which provide a model for public buildings to this day. (Grand Central Station is among their countless offspring.) Still more characteristic were their engineering achievements, such as the famous roads, bridges, and aqueducts. As Frontinus contemplated the fourteen aqueducts, totaling some thirteen thousand miles, that brought Rome as much water as any modern city has, he made a typically Roman remark: 'Who will venture to compare with these mighty conduits the idle Pyramids, or the famous but useless works of the Greeks?' This is the Philistine talking: celebrating size and utility, revealing the deep-seated contempt of the Romans for mere artists, betraying the reason why their art was mostly anonymous, given to shoddy reproductions, and often coarse, gross, even brutal. Yet only a snob, with a vulgar fear of being vulgar, can dismiss the Romans as mere Philistines. In their great building enterprises they often displayed a bold imagination, a vigorous sense of form-and-function, that produced a genuine grandeur. Their architecture was more humanistic than the Greek in that it contributed much more to civic life; nor were they betraying culture when they added the sewer, the bath, and the house with central heating. They built many splendid cities that

---

[1] German historians are fond of talking of the lusty, original genius of the Teutonic peoples and their potentially splendid culture. The fact remains, however, that these peoples did not build a civilization all by themselves. Directly or indirectly, they were educated by the Romans.

were pleasant both to live in and to look at. Their mode of life was at once more comfortable and hygienic than the common life of Europe today, and more gracious than the American.[2]

At least the mighty aqueducts are clearly more admirable than the 'idle Pyramids,' which served no purpose whatever except to gratify the monstrous conceit of the Pharaohs. By contrast with such aspirations to immortality, another secular achievement of the Romans appears still more majestic. This was the Roman law. A code that was at first designed to provide for the commercial needs of foreigners in their cities, in time it generated provisions binding on both foreigners and citizens, and finally, under the influence of Greek philosophical ideas, became the *Jus Gentium*—a universal law such as the Greeks never developed. Much Roman law is still incorporated in Western law, where it may be an anachronism, but its everlasting importance lies in its basic principles. The foundation of Justice, Cicero had declared, was a Law 'implanted in Nature,' discoverable by 'right reason,' and therefore available to all men by virtue of their natural endowment of reason. This 'true law' was universal and inalterable, 'valid for all nations and all times,' above mere custom and opinion; it could not be abolished by any legislation. It implied, as the later jurist Ulpian explicitly declared, that 'all men are equal.' Roman law accordingly protected the individual against the state.[3]

Apart from the shortcomings of Roman legal practice, one may question even the ideal theory of an eternal law independent of man and society, authored by 'Nature.' At least men of reason have not yet been able to reach agreement on the dictates of this absolute, immutable law. Yet they may agree—as the English-speaking peoples in particular have agreed—that the basic law of the land should be above the wishes of any one man or group, and should guarantee rights not subject to majority opinion. Universal principles of equity

[2] The famous American bathroom, incidentally, incorporates only one process of the elaborate Roman bath—a unique institution that is now known as the Turkish bath, because borrowed by the Turks from Byzantium. This civilized institution was completely destroyed by the barbarians of the West, with the aid of Christian ascetics; and when civilization rose anew in the Middle Ages it clung to the squalor of the Orient. As H. J. Randall observes, the ages of faith have been ages of dirt.

[3] On such counts the Roman law was an advance beyond the Code of Hammurabi, the most famous legal achievement of the ancient East. Although this Code included many humane provisions, and in a Prologue announced Hammurabi's divine mission 'to prevent the strong from oppressing the weak,' it contained nothing about the rights of the people against the state.

may be grounded on uniformities in the nature of man and social life, instead of on a deified Nature. They may be just as valid for our time if we grant that they were not valid for the ape-man, and may not be valid for the man of A.D. 1,000,000. The main principles of Roman justice, at any rate, are indispensable for any system of international law, or any hope of a world order. Their law remains their greatest intellectual and moral achievement, their chief contribution to a free society. And it was the foundation of the enduring glory of their empire—an empire that was first won by military conquest but really won by law and peace.

'Rome made a city what was once a world,' Rutilius could sing after it had been sacked. The consciousness of this world mission dawned under Augustus, who inspired Virgil's *Aeneid*—one of the noblest monuments to new ideals in the history of new eras. So grievous were the travails of Aeneas —'so great was the labor of founding the Roman race'—because he was founding a world: the rise of Rome meant 'a new hope for the human race, a hope of peace, of order, of civilization.' In the political terms of Marcus Aurelius, it meant 'a state in which there is the same law for all, a policy of equal rights and freedom of speech, and the idea of a kingly government that most of all respects the freedom of the governed.' Here was the fulfilment of the classical ideal toward which later Greek thinkers had been groping: an Earthly City in which the State is supreme, subordinating the claims of the individual, but subjecting its great power to the claims of natural reason and equity, and devoting itself to the service of man. The *polis* was now *cosmopolis*. 'The whole of this Universe is to be regarded as one single commonwealth of gods and men,' wrote Cicero. 'For me as Antoninus,' added Marcus Aurelius, 'my city and fatherland is Rome, but as man, the world.' His highest obligation, he took for granted, was to the world; and because he took it for granted, and really meant it, he threw in no cant about the white man's burden.

Needless to add, Rome fell short of this ideal; yet it came near enough to haunt the mind of Europe ever since. For it did more than conceive an abstract idealism—such idealism may also be found in Ikhnaton, Ashoka, Akbar, and other great emperors in other societies. Rome alone succeeded in embodying the idea in a heterogeneous empire, maintaining it through different dynasties. It provided such material means to unity as its superb system of roads, which made travel easier, faster, and safer than it was in Europe and the Near East until the last century. It planted cities everywhere, introducing the vigorous civic life of the Hellenistic East to Western Europe. Above all, it brought the *Pax Romana*—the longest period of continuous peace in the annals of imperial history. After Augustus deliberately refrained from further aggression there were occasional campaigns on the borders, but chiefly for defensive purposes. Within the empire there were no serious rebellions except for the uprisings of the intractable Hebrews. For almost two hundred years the Mediterranean world enjoyed a relative peace that it has never known since, least of all in the last hundred years.

According to Toynbee, this period was the 'Indian summer' of the Hellenic society. We can now see that it was the prelude to disaster, and so must presently consider the reasons for the disaster. Yet transitory as it was, the Roman achievement was vastly impressive, and Toynbee oversimplifies both the success and the failure of the empire when he treats it as merely a phase of the 'Hellenic society.' If the Greeks provided the cultural foundations of the Mediterranean world, they failed to organize and unify it, make it a real society. The immediate question is why the Romans succeeded where the brilliant Greeks failed.

As usual, the answer is not simply inspiring. The men who made the empire were not crusaders; and none had the Hebrew faith in a heavenly kingdom on earth, or the modern faith in progress. Nor was religion the inspiration of the Romans. Their ancient religion was wholly practical, a matter of pious prudence rather than deep faith or lofty aspiration. Their countless gods for the occasions of daily life were vague or abstract, 'earth-spirits' who required a scrupulous observance of traditional ceremonies but promised no rewards in a life to come; their priests, in the words of Dean Inge, were 'professors of spiritual jurisprudence,' carefully carrying out the letter of the prescribed contract long after the origin or meaning of the contract had been lost sight of. (G. F. Moore notes that when the antiquarian Varro set out to collect and classify the ancient rituals he found 'gods whose names were perpetuated in the calendar, but whose cult had long since been extinct; priesthoods and sodalities whose functions had been forgotten; rites whose motive and meaning no man knew.') After Augustus, the emperors were added to the old gods, but this new cult induced no more exaltation; although Orientals worshiped the emperors during their lifetime, the practical Romans waited until they had died, and then set them up as deities only if they had earned the honor by good works. When the Romans turned to the mystery religions their more spiritual faith did not carry them to greater heights; the gain in spirituality was a loss in vitality. The faith that made Rome great was essentially secular. The real religion of Rome, as of Periclean Athens, was patriotism.

At the same time, the famed political genius of the Romans calls for serious qualification. Certainly no practical genius was displayed in their institutions. Their Republic was a fantastic system of checks and balances, seemingly designed to prevent any hope of efficiency and continuity. Among its elaborate impracticalities were two consuls, who could veto each other and were changed annually, and ten tribunes, each of whom could veto the consuls and all the rest of the tribunes. While the supreme authority theoretically rested in the popular assembly, the government was in fact run by the aristocratic Senate, which constitutionally had no control over either legislation or executive action, and displayed its astuteness most conspicuously in thwarting or nullifying the will of the voters. When this system broke down, with the rise of the powerful generals and volunteer armies who won the empire that the Senate did not want and could not run, Augustus set up the Principate, which retained all the forms of the Republic and emptied them of political substance. Priding himself upon his constitutionalism, Augustus nevertheless gave supreme power to the Emperor; while supposed to rule in the interests of the State, the Emperor alone decided what those interests were. The popular assembly soon disappeared while the Senate came to act chiefly as an imperial rubber stamp or publicity bureau. And although everything depended on the character and ability of the emperor, there was no one customary or constitutional procedure for choosing him—he might be designated by the ruling emperor, the Senate, or the army.

The apparent political genius of the Romans, in short, was their ability to keep a preposterous system working. They were much like the English in their reverence for forms, their reliance on tradition rather than logic, their habit of muddling through. At best, their practical sense made them more adaptable than the subtler, more ingenious Greeks; sustained by their ancient forms, they could take liberties untroubled by theoretical inconsistencies, or unaware of them. The genius of Augustus in particular lay in his unconscious blend of conservatism and realism. Always maintaining a pious regard for the Senate and the old families, he built his Principate on the enterprising middle class, whose interest in commerce was scorned by the old families. He made it the administrative class, creating the civil service that the aristocratic Republic had failed to set up. The basis of his Principate was not a constitution but a bureaucracy. The guarantor of law and order in his Empire was the institution of red tape, which has also been called the mother of freedom.

Ultimately, I can find no better key to the success of the Romans than the vague, unscientific, old-fashioned concept of 'character.' This does not really explain history, since the origin and persistence of character have in turn to be explained; neither does character guarantee historic success. Nevertheless it is a social reality, and none is more important for our human purposes. Although Livy was unaware of major factors that are now commonplaces of historical knowledge, he was not merely naïve when he made the central theme of his history the faith of the Romans in themselves and their ancient virtues, *gravitas, pietas*, and *simplicitas*. As early as Polybius men were deploring the moral corruption of Rome—the notorious corruption that persisted over six centuries, providing an endless text for Christian preachers and prophets of doom. Yet the famous iron character of the Romans also persisted. They clung to the ideal of discipline they had introduced—an ideal that outside of Sparta was seldom realized by the supposedly measured Greeks. They continued to produce their great types of the soldier, the magistrate, the senator, the proconsul—models of courage, temperance, grave dignity, and high sense of duty. The middle class elevated by Augustus and his successors carried on the tradition of public spirit. The emperors themselves, for all the vicious weaklings and despots among them, maintained a remarkably high average of responsible, patriotic rule. History cannot match the century of Nerva, Trajan, Hadrian, Antoninus Pius, and Marcus Aurelius—a succession of emperors who differed in temperament and policy but alike ruled as devoted servants, not masters of the commonwealth.

As old-fashioned is the most apparent source of this strength of character—the Roman family. Famous for their public spirit, the Romans were nevertheless devoted to domestic life and created the home as we know it (or knew it until this century). Woman had an honored position, as wife and mother; the sense of duty to the parents and the spirits of the ancestors was almost as strong as in China; the household gods—the *Lares* and *Penates*—were the most vital of the deities, long surviving the official religion. Such loyalty to family and home helps to explain why the Romans were more consistently and profoundly patriotic than the early Greeks, whose religion was also patriotism. In their all-engrossing public life, the Greeks were apt to talk too much, get lost in generalities and abstractions, or make a habit of dispute; at least they might have been less volatile and erratic if they had known the privacy, sobriety, and security of the ancestral

Rome. The distinctive virtues of the Romans were also strengthened by their less civilized religion. Unimaginative, unreasoned, and unexalted, it instilled piety and order by endless ritual, solemnizing all phases of public and private life, uniting the family and the nation.

This severe Roman character had severe limitations, which will concern us later. At his best, the good Roman was more admirable than attractive. Strait-laced, distrustful of individuality and genius, suspicious of art and speculative thought, indifferent even to science, incapable of understanding Plato, Archimedes, and Christ alike—'he could only rule the world,' Will Durant concludes. Still, we should first admire his gravity; and if we are sympathetic we may see him unbend. Even the scandal-mongering Suetonius presents some attractive pictures of the Caesars. Thus we see the Emperor Vespasian, the old soldier and commoner, with his habitual expression of one who was straining at stool,' complaining of the wearisome pomp on the day of his triumph, ridiculing the efforts to dress up his lowly ancestors, and on his death-bed remarking, 'Alas, I think I am becoming a god.'

Indeed, the Romans could not have ruled the world so long and so well had they not had a measure of flexibility. In their grave pride, their sureness of themselves, they were capable of a liberality that for practical purposes was more beneficial than the intellectual liberality of Athens. Like the Greeks, they were free from religious bigotry.[4] 'If the gods are insulted,' said the matter-of-fact Emperor Tiberius, 'let them see to it themselves.' The Romans likewise had relatively little racial and cultural prejudice. While looking down on the Greeks as effete, they also paid them many tributes, including the supreme tribute of going to school un-

[4] The notorious persecution of the Christians was not really an exception, for its motives were political rather than religious. In their fear of idolatry, the Christians refused to make the nominal obeisances required by the imperial cult—a patriotic duty comparable to saluting the flag; all who paid such perfunctory respects to the emperor were free to worship their own gods. (At that, the Jews were exempted from these ceremonial requirements, as a peculiar people; the Christians got into trouble only when they separated themselves from the Jews and became still more peculiar.) Until Diocletian, moreover, the persecution sprang largely from popular hostility to a sect known as 'enemies of the human race' because they rejoiced in the prospect of the imminent destruction of Rome, in a universal holocaust. Given all the other popular superstitions about the infernal Christians—such as their reputation for cannibalism, owing to the custom of eating the flesh and blood of the Son of Man—it is surprising that they escaped with so little persecution. The number of victims was greatly exaggerated by later monks, with whom the manufacture of martyrs became a thriving industry. Thus the bones of many ordinary Romans in the catacombs of Rome became the bones of saints.

der them. They regarded their more gifted slaves as potential citizens, permitting them to earn their freedom, and as freedmen to rise to high positions. (Tenney Frank observes that slaves in the Roman Empire had better opportunities than the mass of workers in Europe until recent times.) Hence they enlisted good will by respecting the customs as well as protecting the legal rights of their provincials. They were content with a commonwealth that was indeed a wealth of diverse cultures. In effect, the basic aim of their empire was not uniformity but unity.

This wisdom was discarded after the empire became Christian; the emperors now sought to impose religious uniformity. When medieval Europe tried to recover the Roman universal ideal it made the same mistake; later it was torn by strife because both Catholics and Protestants insisted on the necessity of uniform belief. Today, as men again seek to revive the *Pax Romana* in a world order, they are again wrangling in the conviction that the one world must be all democratic, or all capitalistic, or all communistic. Even high-minded idealists are apt to conceive the ideal as political or religious uniformity; they merely tolerate cultural differences, as an unfortunate necessity. I should say that the Roman ideal of unity amid diversity is not only the most we can hope for—it is the best we could ask for.

2. THE DECLINE AND FALL

It is characteristic of the severe, practical Romans that they distrusted Greek philosophy, that their rulers were brought up on it, and that in Marcus Aurelius they produced the supreme type of philosopher-king that Plato had merely dreamed of. 'If thou findest in human life anything better than justice, truth, temperance, fortitude, and, in a word, anything better than thy own mind's satisfaction in the things which it enables thee to do according to right reason,' Marcus wrote in his *Meditations,* '. . . turn to it with all thy soul.' He found nothing better; so he gave his whole soul to his self-appointed task of ruling in accordance with reason, in obedience to Providence, in the service of his subjects. Right reason led to sad conclusions, however. Although Marcus constantly insisted that all things are ordered by Providence, he found no joy in these things and constantly strove against attachment to the world. He also insisted on the vanity of life, the seeming poverty of the 'all-embracing commonwealth'; then he sacrificed his own life to preserve the vain lives of his subjects. And Providence seemed bent on mocking his selfless devotion. His reign was a succession of disasters, including domestic treason and a terrible plague, and culminating in war and bankruptcy. It marked the end of the *Pax Romana*, 'the felicity of the age' celebrated on his early coins. Providence preferred to seal his benevolent reign with another of his sayings: 'What is the end of it all? Smoke and ashes and a legend—or not even a legend.'

This might serve as the epitaph of the Roman Empire—except that it did leave a legend. Its decline and fall remains the most haunting theme of history. The contradictions in the life and thought of Marcus Aurelius bring up the familiar observation that there can be no adequate philosophy of history until we have an adequate explanation of the tragedy of Rome. Then 'right reason' may seem to lead to another sad conclusion—simply that there can be no adequate philosophy. Historians have offered about fifty different explanations. (Marcus himself has been made the villain of the piece: according to Ferrero, he struck the fatal blow when he forced his vicious son Commodus on the state.) Yet the drama is at least as intelligible as *Hamlet*. Few historians have seen in it an impenetrable mystery; most have made out good reasons for the failure of Rome, all of which are pertinent. Their painstaking, cumulative researches have made it relatively easy for an outsider to discount the simpler theories of the past, or of any one ardent theorist today. Again we can hope to make better sense if we begin by complicating the drama.

Thus the favorite theme of the moral corruption of Rome, the vices of luxury, involves the difficulty that Rome made almost all its great contributions to civilization after it had become corrupted. Its Golden Age, according to Livy, was the period before the last Punic War, the final victory over Carthage; but we should not be studying the history and the culture of Rome if its achievement had ended with this Golden Age—we should have only a legend of military valor and public spirit, to set beside the Spartan legend. Furthermore, we must admit an element of mere accident. J. B. Bury, for one, attributed the fall of Rome primarily to unforeseeable contingencies, such as the coming of the Huns, the untimely death of key men, and the devastating plague that seriously weakened the empire during the reign of Marcus Aurelius. If this theory is too easy and too untidy, denying any real logic to the drama, at least the fall of Rome was not so clearly inevitable as most historians have implied. They keep overlooking the significant fact that the Eastern Roman Empire did not fall, though it suffered from much the same economic, political, moral, and religious diseases as the West. And its vitality points to still another complication. 'Rome' was not the distinct entity assumed by Spengler, Toynbee, or even more cautious theorists. It was the symbol of a mixed people that kept changing, the capital of an empire that included very diverse provinces. The degree of unity achieved by the Roman Empire is so remarkable because of the geographical, racial, and cultural multiformity it embraced.

Hence environmental theories break down. Simkhovitch, for example, argues that a sufficient cause for the fall of Rome was the progressive exhaustion of the soil; but Rostovtzeff points out that while this was to some extent true of Italy and Greece, it was generally not true of Gaul, Spain, North Africa, Egypt, and the Eastern provinces. Similarly with the seductive racial theories. According to Tenney Frank, Rome collapsed because its old stock was exhausted by death in war, emigration to the provinces, suicide or execution during civil wars, et cetera; funeral inscriptions in Rome reveal the great influx of foreigners, suggesting that up to 90 per cent of its residents 'bore the taint of foreign extraction.' Here one might question the excellence of a stock that killed itself off so thoroughly, or that failed to assimilate new peoples as America has done, but blood appears to tell an odd story in any event. Presumably the 'pure' Romans were the patricians and plebeians who succeeded in conquering and uniting most of Italy. The people who went on to conquer Carthage and build up an empire were a mixture of Romans and Italic peoples; under them the provinces were brutally plundered. The people who finally built the stupendous majesty of the Roman peace were extensively 'tainted' by foreign blood; provincials and freedmen were the chief source of energy. (Roman literature in particular would have been a poor thing if it had had to depend on the old stock, for Cicero, Catullus, Virgil, Horace, Ovid, Livy, Tacitus, Pliny, Juvenal, and Martial were all provincials, none of Roman ancestry.) After the century of anarchy following Marcus Aurelius the stock that managed to stave off the collapse of the empire for another century or so was the rude stock of Illyrian peasants, which produced the Emperors Diocletian and Constantine the Great; these sturdy parvenus gave Christians and barbarians time to assimilate enough Greco-Roman culture to preserve it.

This brings up the famous conclusion of Gibbon's *Decline and Fall of the Roman Empire:* 'I have described the triumph of barbarism and religion.' Today historians perceive a profounder irony than could the great master of irony; generally they picture this triumph as a symptom rather than a basic cause of the decline and fall. When the empire was still healthy its disciplined, well-armed legions could handle the barbarians easily enough. At that, there was no sudden, dramatic deluge of barbarians but a series of raids, by armies seldom numbering more than twenty or thirty thousand men, followed by a gradual infiltration, during which the Germans were enrolled in the Roman army and rose to be patricians and army chiefs. Alaric, who gained immortal fame as the first to sack Rome, and who lives in popular legend as the savage leader of a wild horde, was actually a cautious, hesitant politician, possibly even a 'Roman citizen,' who occupied the capital briefly when the authorities failed to pay his political price, and who had no thought of seizing Italy or the throne.[5] Similarly Christianity made little progress until the empire was well along the road to dissolution. If it failed to regenerate the empire, at least it cannot be blamed for the failure of nerve of a people already drugged on magic and mystery religions. In the East Christianity built Constantinople and Hagia Sophia. In the West it cushioned the final shocks by half converting the barbarians, partially curbing their impulse to wanton slaughter and destruction; though it was incapable of civilizing the barbarians or preserving them from the degeneration to which the Romans had succumbed.

There remains, then, a complex of economic, political, and cultural factors in the breakdown of the empire. These cannot be reduced to a single cause. Any one of the 'fatal' maladies of the empire may be found in societies that endured for many centuries, or even in Rome during its vigorous growth. Taken together, they still do not give the strict inevitability that a scientific historian or philosopher might wish for, since the curtain did not go down on By-

---

[5] St. Augustine even hailed Alaric's sack of Rome as a proof of God's infinite mercy, for God might have handed the city over to the much fiercer Radagaisus. 'Yet our wretched pagans,' he complained, 'refuse to give thanks to the immense mercifulness of a God who, when He had determined to chastise with a barbarian irruption a generation that had earned a still heavier chastisement by its vices, still tempered His indignation with an immense compassion—of which He gave proof first in causing Radagaisus miraculously to be defeated.' In fact, the barbarians did promote the cause of Christianity, for among their chief victims was Mithraism, the chief rival of Christianity. As the popular religion of the army, Mithraism had a good chance of becoming the imperial religion; it was favored by Diocletian, shortly before Constantine elected Christianity. But its strongholds were along the frontiers, which bore the brunt of the barbarian inroads. Christianity flourished in the demoralized but relatively secure cities of the interior.

zantium. Yet they all point to failures in intelligence and in character that are basic enough for our purposes.

First the economic factor, which is of particular interest to contemporaries. Although historians differ in their descriptions of Roman economy—especially about the degree to which it approximated 'capitalism'—it is clear that the great builders failed to build a sound material basis for their civilization. While the empire was expanding, its prosperity was fed by plundered wealth and by new markets in the semibarbaric provinces. When the empire ceased to expand, however, economic progress soon ceased. The slow decline that set in was revealed by the increasing fiscal difficulties of the emperors; the desperate measures that Marcus Aurelius had to resort to in order to finance his defensive wars on the border suggest virtual insolvency. Except for the gradual exhaustion of its gold and silver mines, the material resources of the empire were potentially ample enough, but it had grossly mismanaged these resources. The conspicuous proof of its failure was the deterioration even of the economy of Egypt, which for centuries had supported conquerors in luxury, and enabled Romans to live too long in a style to which they were not accustomed.

Economic historians (such as Rostovtzeff and Tenney Frank) point especially to the failure of Roman industry, which for a time gave signs of developing large-scale production. The ruins of Pompeii, for instance, reveal that among the many little shops of petty specialists were big bakeries that made over two thousand loaves a day, and a factory in which Pompeii's famous fish sauces were manufactured for export as well as the local market. Most household goods were apparently bought on the market, and some came from factories elsewhere. Moreover, Pompeii was frankly dedicated to the pursuit of wealth, with the blessing of the gods and the emperors. Its patron goddess, Venus Pompeiana, devoted herself to protecting business, and she had no reason to complain of the emperors, who pursued a laissez-faire policy. Given this free enterprise, as well as the practical spirit of the Romans and the large amounts of capital available in the early empire, one might have expected industry to expand, spawning many Pompeiis. Yet it did not. It was stagnant long before it collapsed during the anarchy of the third century.

One reason was technological backwardness. After the first century there were no important improvements in industrial techniques. 'The invention of a valve in the bellows used in iron furnaces to create a continuous blast,' writes Frank, 'an improvement that any intelligent and interested workman might have conceived, would have revolutionized the iron industry by making smelting and casting possible on a large scale'; but no such simple invention revolutionized this or any other basic industry. Meanwhile production for export was discouraged by the high costs of transportation, which enabled little artisans to produce as cheaply for the local market. Like the resourceful Greeks, the practical-minded Romans failed to make any notable improvements in navigation, on which their empire so largely depended. Transportation by sea remained slow, uncertain, expensive, and in stormy seasons almost impossible. (As Spengler observed, the biggest ships of the classical world were glorified rowboats, which had to keep hugging the shores.) Similarly the Hellenistic Greeks and Romans both failed to develop a source of mechanical power, even though Archimedes had laid the foundations of mechanics, and other technicians knew of the potential power in water, steam, and air pressure.

This lack of inventiveness was again the natural result of a cultural tradition that ignored or scorned the 'base mechanic arts.' Although the Romans were materialistic enough, their ruling class remained disdainful of the economic activities that produced their wealth; to the end their senatorial class was forbidden even to invest in commerce or industry. Rome itself was a parasitic city that produced little or nothing in return for the wealth of the East off which it lived; it promoted chiefly an extensive trade in luxuries, a trade that could not maintain a thriving industry, and that ultimately drained off into the Far East the gold and silver of the West. In the provinces the bourgeoisie had a sharp eye for cash and tangible wealth but not for economic values and possibilities. Aspiring to an aristocratic status, they invested their wealth in property rather than industry or business enterprise. Hence they tended to become a class of rentiers, ceasing to pay their way, spending their unearned wealth for largely unproductive purposes. Even the public spirit that led the bourgeoisie to adorn their cities created a false impression of wealth and prosperity, by a competition in splendor that squandered the limited resources of the empire and concealed its basic incapacity to keep producing wealth.

Roman ignorance of economics was most conspicuous in the great emperors. They showed some concern about the state of agriculture and trade but did nothing to protect or promote industry. Their occasional regulations were inspired by no clear programs; their usual policy of laissez faire amounted to a lack of policy. When they had trouble maintaining the imperial treasury they could think of no better measure than debasing the imperial currency. (The benign

Antoninus Pius, the 'good papa' who was hailed by his subjects as 'the holiest of all times,' was one of the worst sinners in this respect.) Fiscally, the state lived from hand to mouth. There was no annual budget, no national debt to encourage investment, no policy of national loans to spread costs over the years; wars or national emergencies were met by extraordinary levies that further disrupted economic life. After the chaotic third century the only policy the emperors knew was the ancient policy of compulsion. Diocletian and Constantine restored order by their venture in state socialism, setting up price and wage controls, binding peasants, artisans, and officials to their jobs. This was not a daring program of reform but a desperate effort to freeze the *status quo*. In effect it was a reversion to an essentially primitive order, simple and fixed, as the only kind of order that seemed possible in a crumbling society.

The caste system in the last days of Rome merely rigidified a class structure that Rostovtzeff considers the basic weakness of the Roman economy, as of the Hellenistic. It is significant that little is known about the city proletariat and less about the peasantry, whose voice is rarely heard; but the evidence indicates that they did not share in the prosperity of the early empire, and certainly got more than their share of distress in hard times. The immediate source and sign of evil was the institution of slavery. The abundance of slaves led to the growth of the *latifundia*, the great estates that especially in Italy came to dominate agriculture and ruin the free peasantry. Unable to compete with these capitalistic enterprises, the peasants either became *coloni* of the large landowners or drifted to the cities, to aggravate the chronic unemployment there; the workers of the empire had to support a large class of idle poor as well as idle rich. The abundance of slaves likewise kept wages low. Although men of unusual energy and ability could rise in the world, the masses lived in more or less wretched poverty. Economic stagnation was a natural consequence. Absentee landlords were unlikely to promote an efficient, progressive agriculture. Slaves and underpaid workers lacked both the interest and the ability to invent the simple valve that would have revolutionized the iron industry. Entrepreneurs had little incentive to expand once the empire had ceased to expand, since the market was sharply limited by the poverty of the great masses of consumers.

Such inequalities are not clearly fatal, being common to almost all civilized societies, even in their prosperous periods; but they clearly plagued Rome from the outset of its imperial career. While the conquests enriched the patricians and the rising business class, they left the plebeians worse off.[6] Hence the triumphs abroad led to a savage class war at home. When Augustus finally restored peace he introduced no basic social reforms; he merely encouraged the city bourgeoisie, who displaced the old patrician class. The increasing burdens laid on the wealthy as the empire ran into economic distress were ultimately passed on to the poor. A widening gulf separated city and country, upper class and proletariat, with no solid middle class to mediate or cushion the increasing antagonism. That there were no serious insurrections, and but a few local strikes, indicates only the impotence or apathy of the masses, which aggravated the disease. An active class struggle, in accordance with Marxist theory, might have improved conditions. As it was, the alienated proletariat turned to Oriental religions, investing their faith and hope in dying-gods instead of living emperors or revolutionists. The peasant masses were never really assimilated; they supplied soldiers for the imperial armies, but the rest continued to live in their primitive village world, at best resigned and inert. Although Rostovtzeff suggests that the civil wars of the third century after Christ were essentially class wars, in which the peasant armies lashed out blindly and triumphed over the city bourgeoisie, this conjecture also emphasizes the impotence of the masses. No class won these wars, except a small military class; and with the ruin of the bourgeoisie the foundations of prosperity were shattered, leaving the masses worse off than before.

Hence we must drastically qualify the impressive political achievement of Rome, and return to the limitations of its famed political wisdom. The civil wars were sheer folly. Under the Republic they were not fought over programs to improve labor conditions or class relations; the protagonists were ambitious generals, jealous aristocrats, greedy speculators, and unprincipled politicians. The civil wars of the third century were as pointless. They involved no clash of principle between rulers and ruled, no conscious plan to establish a better form of government, no positive program of any kind; they sprang from elemental greed, ambition, envy, and hatred. In the long interim of peace between these two periods the rulers never came to grips with the latent social prob-

---

[6] Their plight was eloquently stated by Tiberius Gracchus: 'The wild animals that range over Italy have a hole, and each of them has its lair and nest, but the men who fight and die for Italy have no part or lot in anything but the air and the sunlight... They are called the lords of the World, and they have not a clod of earth to call their own.' So wrote Jesus: 'Foxes have holes, and birds of the air have nests; but the Son of man hath not where to lay his head.'

lems. The one problem that seriously troubled them was the evil effects of the *latifundia* in Italy, but they never did anything effectual about it. A few emperors, such as Hadrian, made feeble efforts to defend the poor against the rich. The just, wise, saintly Marcus Aurelius made no effort whatever at fundamental social reform.

In this view, the Principate established by Augustus—the great monument of the political genius of Rome—also sealed the failure of the Romans to solve their political problems. At its best, the Principate was indeed a 'Respublica,' or public thing: a highly original form of policy in which the emperor was the First Citizen, ruling by common consent, on the basis of the common law. 'He is the bond that holds the Commonwealth together,' Seneca wrote: 'he is the breath of life that is breathed by subjects, in their thousands, who in themselves would be nothing but a burden and a prey if they were left to their own devices through the removal of a presence which is the soul of the Empire.' But here was the trouble. The whole Roman world did in fact depend upon the soul of one man. It was the emperor, not a constitutional body, that made the fateful decisions. The army belonged to him alone, swearing allegiance to him instead of the state; he alone declared peace and war. 'The gods have given thee supreme power and control over all things, even over thyself.' Pliny told Trajan. And sometimes the gods forgot the last gift of self-control. When Caligula's grandmother tried to advise him he could answer (according to Suetonius), 'Remember that I have the right to do anything to anybody'; in the ferocious exercise of this right he was embarrassed chiefly by the great number of his subjects. 'I wish the Roman people had but a single neck,' he exclaimed. As there was no prescribed way of selecting the Emperor, so there was no legal way of deposing him. When Commodus made a mockery of 'the freedom of the governed' that his philosophical father sought to respect above all, the governed could only hope for his assassination.

The instability to which monarchy is always prone was aggravated by the Roman tradition of republican government. Weak, dissolute, or despotic emperors had to fear not only ambitious generals but public-spirited Romans of the old school, and fear made them recklessly prodigal and atrociously cruel. The very absurdity of their power tended to make them despise their subjects.[7] The many honorable, patriotic

---

[7] Among the most tragic victims of the imperial power was the Emperor Tiberius. Although Suetonius and Tacitus stress the incredible debauchery and cruelty of his old age, they both acknowledge the apparent moderation and justice of his early reign. He refused the title of

emperors suffered as much from the lack of independent political institutions. With the disappearance of the popular assembly and the fatty degeneration of the Senate, the one power that remained was the Army. As early as the first century the Army was making and breaking emperors; in the chaos of the third century it made death in bed a luxury for them. The average caliber even of these short-lived emperors was unusually high, but rude force and fear were now the only means open to them. When Diocletian and Constantine finally gave up the refined pretenses of the Principate, to establish an out-and-out Oriental despotism, they were not acting simply as despots. They were patriots who made the Emperor absolutely supreme because he was indeed 'the soul of the Empire,' the only force that could hold it together.

Meanwhile the municipality—the basis of the empire—had collapsed. At its peak the empire resembled a federation of city-states, governed from Rome by an emperor who allowed them to manage their local affairs. It was not a republican federation, however, since the autonomous cities had no voice in electing the emperor or determining federal policy. Neither did they have a vigorous political life of their own; the Greek tradition of popular government had been decaying before Rome lent its weight to the oligarchic forces, and by the time of Trajan it was virtually dead. Hence the cities grew increasingly dependent on Rome. The letters of Pliny to Trajan reveal how the most routine civic problems were referred to the emperor for decision, and why the ablest emperors took more and more into their own hands; Trajan and Hadrian assumed control of local finances simply in the interests of efficiency. The city fathers, who served without pay, were not disposed to resent any lessening of their administrative responsibilities. During hard times they were discouraged by extraordinary capital levies and compulsory services; public office became an onerous burden. In general, the municipalities were moribund before they received their death-blow in the third century.

'Father of His Country' that the people repeatedly tried to thrust on him; he refused to permit the Senate to take oath to support his acts, warning it against binding itself unreservedly to the support of any man. 'O men, ready for slavery!' he exclaimed. Although he put up with the new cult of emperor-worship, such preposterous honors only exasperated his awareness of his unpopularity, and his fear for his life. So in his old age he turned his back on the empire, retiring to Capri, where he recklessly indulged all the vicious impulses stirred by his loathing of his subjects and of himself. The utter disgust of the wretched old man recalls the question Walter Pater asked of his malignant grandson Caligula: 'And might not this be indeed the true meaning of kingship, if the world would have one man to reign over it?'

Likewise civil liberties declined. 'As to liberty,' wrote Plutarch, 'we have that which the government leaves us; and perhaps it would not be good if we had any more.' Good or no, what the government left depended on the will or whim of the emperor. Although the nobler emperors proclaimed the ideal of freedom of thought and speech, there was no constitutional right to such freedom. The masses of Rome claimed only the right to be fed and amused; they had little interest in anything except their amusements, and later their religious controversies. Writers and thinkers clung to the old republican tradition but could never be sure of their ground. Augustus himself inaugurated censorship in the name of morality, and later tyrants put men to death for the expression of unflattering opinions. Under weak emperors criticism tended to scurrility; under benevolent ones it was drowned in rhetorical gratitude. Tacitus believed that 'genius died by the same blow that ended public liberty.' Longinus complained of the 'utter servility' in which his generation was schooled from childhood: 'We never drink from the fairest and most fertile source of literature, which is freedom, and therefore we show a genius for nothing but flattery.'

There is some question about the major premise of Longinus, since much of the world's great literature has not been written in an atmosphere of freedom. Rome, however, had learned its literature from Greece, had known freedom; and at any rate Roman culture began to decline as early as the first century of the monarchy, after the Golden Age of Augustus. The 'Silver Age' that followed was marked by increasing affectation and strain. Literature reflected the curious staginess of life in the capital of the world, with its constant, self-conscious parade of dignity and grandeur. The austere Tacitus himself indulged in this theatricality, writing history in the manner of Seneca, with his main characters wrapped in the mantle of Tragedy and his great scenes trumpeted by declamation; in his fear of the commonplace in diction, he employed some fifty elegant substitutes for the word 'death.' After this age, early in the second century, there was almost no creativity in any branch of culture except religion. Knowledge became the domain of copyists and compilers. Thought was smothered under oratory and rhetoric; eloquence was never so prized as when it had ceased to serve any real need, merely concealing the fact that great public issues were no longer being debated. Art was so dead that Constantine had to adorn his triumphal arch in Rome with sculpture borrowed from previous arches.

This early degeneration of Roman culture is the clue to the basic defects of the Roman genius. A legend dating from the beginning of their imperial career may serve as the portent and symbol of its tragic end. The legend is that a Roman soldier killed Archimedes while the harmless old man was drawing mathematical figures in the sands of Syracuse.

The practical Romans were unable to appreciate or even understand the work of Archimedes, the greatest technologist of antiquity. They were too practical to be interested in pure mathematics, never going beyond arithmetic and surveying. They were too practical even to cultivate science. Their foremost scientific work was the *Natural History* of Pliny the Elder, a wondrous hodgepodge of fact and fancy that displayed no critical, scientific sense whatever. They made no important contributions to medicine, astronomy, or geography. In general, they had little interest in finding out about the world they called themselves masters of. 'The incuriousness of the Roman rich and the Roman rulers,' wrote H. G. Wells, 'was more massive even than their architecture.'

The murder of Archimedes also illustrates the callousness of the Romans, a fault in character that went deeper than their famous corruption. They were never more brutal than in the period before they were spoiled by their wealth; the empire that was finally dedicated to humanity grew out of frightful crimes against humanity. The elder Cato, the historic champion and exemplar of the old Roman virtues, fought long and fiercely for the utter destruction of Carthage. The noble Brutus practiced usury—the one great national industry that was always thriving—and ruthlessly exploited the provinces under his command. As the Romans grew more philosophical and urbane, they remained oddly insensitive and unimaginative. Cicero wrote eloquently of natural justice and right reason, but he seemed unaware of any inconsistency in his still more eloquent speeches, composed largely of vituperation, which made little or no appeal to reason or pretense of fairness; and though he upheld the ideal of virtue for its own sake, he also wrote, 'What is the use of being kind to a poor man?' [8] Even the loftiest ethical idealism of the Romans discouraged gentleness and pity. 'To feel pain at the misfortunes of others,' wrote Seneca, 'is a weakness unworthy

---

[8] The great man reveals that the grave dignity of the Romans was compatible with a naïve vulgarity when he writes to his historian friends, begging them to celebrate his services 'in warmer terms than you perhaps feel' or 'a little more than truth shall justify,' and to do so at once, so that he may enjoy during his lifetime the honor that posterity owes him. He adds that unless his friends oblige him, he may be forced to write his own panegyric, 'a thing, after all, which has a precedent of many illustrious men.' Pliny the Younger—a more attractive figure—betrays the same embarrassing insensitiveness when he begs Tacitus to find a place for him in his histories.

of the wise man.' From the imperturbability of the Stoic sage it was not a long step down to the callousness of the simple citizen who wrote a letter to his wife expressing the hope that she was well and unworried about their expected child, and advising her 'if it is a boy, let him live; if it is a girl, put it out.' And so the noblest emperors continued to stage the gladiatorial games that have made Roman cruelty a byword. Few Romans complained of these bloody spectacles, and almost none realized the danger of a populace depraved and demoralized by them.

The essential defects of the Roman character appear in Virgil's Aeneas, the paragon of Roman virtue. In spite of his many varied adventures he is a rather tedious hero, middle-aged and stuffy. As he dutifully performs the valorous exploits required of him he recalls the great Roman roads, which marched over hill and dale in a straight line, unwavering and monotonous, because designed primarily for strategic purposes. He is always pious and patriotic, expressing all the sentiments appropriate to his grand mission, but he has little imagination, less warmth and zest, and no humor at all. His high sense of duty is informed by no real love of goodness for its own sake; his deep piety is wanting both in simple humanity and in spirituality. For the sake of Rome he was always prepared to sacrifice his happiness, or the happiness of any other person. He was the hero of a state, whose interests were supreme. He was the symbol of a people who came to conceive the great idea of *humanitas*, but were not humane enough to realize that this idea is a mere abstraction until it is embodied in a social order, imparted to all the human beings in that order.

Character is primarily a matter of sentiment and will, not of intelligence. Still, it may be strengthened and elevated by thought, knowledge, understanding; and the moral limitations of the Romans involved serious intellectual limitations. For one thing, they had a limited understanding of the character they set such store by. Although Tacitus has been praised above all for his masterly delineation of character, he was often unjust because he had no conception of growth or development. Collingwood notes that he regarded character as an unchanging essence, and so explained the crimes of aging emperors as expressions of an evil they had previously dissimulated, not as results of their experience—with him a good man could not become bad. (It should also be noted that his much admired republicanism was quite academic: he was as contemptuous of the masses as hostile to tyrants.) Livy had as little idea of development. The Rome whose early history he glorified had no genesis, no real history; in effect he pictures it as springing into existence overnight, intact, with its character full formed. And this way of thinking reinforced the inveterate traditionalism of the Romans, which was the most obvious source of their strength and the ultimate source of their weakness.

So Rome clung to its ancient political and religious forms long after they had lost their meaning, with a ritualistic reverence that disciplined and dignified its national life and that sapped its resourcefulness. While it cultivated the ideal of universal reason it remained devoted to a non-rational conservatism, which conserved irrational institutions. Its chief innovation, the Principate of Augustus, was a disguised reversion to monarchy, the simplest, most unimaginative form of government. The 'knights' or businessmen, and later the provincials and freedmen, in whom the empire found a new source of energy, were less bound by tradition; but as a ruling class they soon lost their enterprise and grew devoted to the *status quo*. Although historians usually stress that Roman culture was vulgarized by the bourgeoisie, one might say truly that they became too thoroughly imbued with the Roman spirit. Hence the Latinized West succumbed, while the East survived under a Roman name but on an Oriental basis.

Given these static ideals, the Roman Empire was never so vigorous as it seemed. With Augustus it went on the defensive culturally as well as militarily, began living off both its intellectual and its material capital. Even the Golden Age of Roman literature foreshadowed the blight of the imitative, the conventional, the artificial, the commonplace—all the limitations and the excesses of the classical spirit. From first to last the thought of the Romans was guided by authority rather than experience or experiment; they learned everything from the Greeks except the Greek inquiring spirit.[9] For all their remarkable adventures, they were at heart an unadventurous people. They had their one great dream of a *cosmopolis;* thereafter they had little sense of horizons or new possibilities, and discovered or explored no new world of any sort.

[9] A curious example of their timidity was the skepticism of Sextus Empiricus, who demonstrated in the manner of Hume the utter relativity and uncertainty of all human knowledge. We cannot prove our basic assumption of cause and effect, he pointed out, because all we know from experience is a sequence, not a necessary connection. From the changing impressions of things that we get from our limited senses, we cannot be sure of the truth about anything or know which appearance is 'real.' We cannot even make a dogma of our skepticism, for how can we know that we cannot know? But the conclusion of this bold adventure in thought was ultra-conservative: since we cannot be certain of anything, Empiricus tells us that we should accept the conventions of our day and humbly worship the old gods.

Since they assumed that the future was foreordained they were interested chiefly in divining it, not in making it.

And so we might take a last look at Marcus Aurelius, the noblest Roman of them all, suspecting that in his greatness of spirit he may have been greatly mistaken. Certainly he was nothing of a creator, in thought or in action; his very wisdom precluded creative effort. To Plato, even in his defeatist moods, Necessity was an impediment to the human spirit. To Marcus it was a god called Nature, which he worshiped even though it was indifferent to man, and which he called good even though he felt it was evil. His free man was one who asserted no real freedom but was content (like a citizen of the Soviet) to vote Nature's ticket, the only ticket offered him. His conception of life in accordance with Nature required the suppression of natural sentiments and desires, but this may still have been too easy, for the reasons that made Stoicism popular among the upper classes: they could accept Fate more readily than could the millions of poor wretches, and were prepared to sacrifice pity, love, or any other emotion that might endanger their calm. The ideal of universal harmony upheld by Marcus was purely intellectual, quite unrelated to the social realities of his empire. His melancholy and his recurrent doubt suggest that his philosophy was inadequate even for the intellectual needs of his age, but it was clearly inadequate for social needs. In his kindly tolerance he could tolerate great evils, such as the brutal gladiatorial games. In his high-minded contempt of misfortune he was apt to invite misfortune.

3. The Implications for Us

From the melancholy spectacle of the decline and fall of Rome, the skeptical Gibbon was able to derive comfort by reflecting on the manifest superiority of his own enlightened age, and by drawing 'the pleasing conclusion that every age of the world has increased and still increases the real wealth, the happiness, the knowledge, and perhaps the virtue, of the human race.' Today we are no longer so complacent, at least about the increase in happiness and virtue. The fashion now is to dwell on the deadly analogies between the Roman world and our own, in the suspicion that history may repeat itself after all. We have reason to feel that we too may have lost control of our destiny. We know the 'schism in the soul' that Toynbee analyzes in disintegrating societies—the common symptoms of abandon and truancy, drift and promiscuity, vulgarity and barbarism. ('Bongo, bongo,' ran the popular song; then 'Enjoy yourself, it's later than you think.') We are now prone, indeed, to overlook the essential differences between our civilization and the Roman, which have become much more conspicuous since Gibbon wrote. Yet we might well begin with the analogies. We always have to deal with the invariable basic problems of rulers and ruled, haves and have-nots, and to struggle with the invariable enemies, selfishness and greed. More specifically, we have retraced the Roman adventure of brutal conquest and exploitation, followed by ideal aspirations to a universal commonwealth. If the barbarian hordes that finally overran Rome have dwindled to a negligible power, the West has been breeding its own barbarians, of a type still more dangerous. I assume that no thoughtful person believes we shall escape the fate of Rome because the Huns have technically disappeared from history.

Gibbon wrote that the fall of Rome was 'the natural and inevitable effect of immoderate greatness.' Spengler and Toynbee specifically regard empire itself as a historic sign of decadence, instead of the vigorous growth it appears to be. It breeds the disease of gigantism as well as militarism—a swaggering in size and quantity and material power, which corrupts artistic, intellectual, political, and moral standards alike. It gives rise to the great world-city and the city masses. 'There is a new sort of nomad,' wrote Spengler, 'cohering unstably in fluid masses: the parasitical city-dweller, traditionless, utterly matter-of-fact, without religion, clever, unfruitful...' The man on the street is in fact likely to be a shallower and shoddier type than the simple peasant, lacking piety, lacking a genuine folk culture. In ancient Rome he demanded only bread and circuses; he hardly noticed the fall of Rome because the games went on. In America today he glances at the headlines and then turns to the sports page and the comics.

Another consequence of Roman imperialism was the rise of the businessman and the rule of money. Although the growing materialism was cloaked by the traditional contempt of trade, as today it is cloaked by the conventions of Christian service, it corroded the old traditions and cheapened the tone of the national life. The rising bourgeoisie had the limitations typical of their class. At worst, their notion of grandeur was the vulgar ostentation satirized by Juvenal and Petronius; at best, their civic ideals were exemplified by the beloved Antoninus Pius, who was a kind of benign Coolidge. To the administration of the empire they contributed some practical ability but little vision or statesmanship. The plainest analogy is the complacency of the bourgeoisie, rooted in their material well-being, their civic pride, their superficial culture, and their economic ignorance. The voice of Rome under the Antonines, just before the deluge, sounds much like the voice of Victorian England.

It is America, however, that offers the happy hunting ground for the analogist. America too has risen, without conscious plan, to a position of world leadership; and while some of its senators want to pull back and escape the responsibilities of this role, others call for an aggressive leadership that to Europeans looks like Roman imperialism. As the inheritor of a great culture, it stands to Europe much as Rome did to Greece. The Americans too are a practical people who have distinguished themselves by their material contributions, notably their engineering feats; they glory in their roads, bridges, and dams, and in their plumbing. They have the same ambivalent attitude toward Europeans as the Romans had toward the Greeks, now humbly admiring their superior culture, now scorning them as corrupt and effete. They are prone to the same narrow, short view of the useful, the same distrust of theory and 'brain trusts.' Their common sense is as cloudy a sense of the theories they live by.

Hence Americans were as unprepared for the economic and political problems that resulted from their rapid expansion. Both nations entered a feverish get-rich-quick era, marked by prodigies of exploitation and orgies of speculation. On the morning after, both woke up to chronic unemployment, inflation, the cycle of boom and crash, and bitter class war. Rome tried to solve its problems by *ad hoc* 'new deal' measures, which outraged wealthy conservatives but brought only temporary or superficial relief to the poor. (Among the experiments outlined in Haskell's *The New Deal in Ancient Rome* were debt moratoriums, farm-labor acts, resettlement administrations, the ever-normal granary, work relief, and public subsidies or doles.) The outcome was the dictatorship of Augustus, which some Americans saw coming under Franklin D. Roosevelt. Now America faces the further problem that beset the Roman Republic, the necessity of adapting its democratic institutions to its new responsibilities as a world power. Its problem is complicated by reverence for a Constitution designed for a much simpler society, and specifically by the elaborate system of checks and balances that it inherited from Rome. It has a deep-rooted fear of strong government. But the chief bogey of its conservatives remains the kind of prophecy that Macaulay made a century ago. Once there was no longer a frontier to absorb the discontented and unemployed, he wrote, America would be rent by class war and its prosperity destroyed by demagogues bent on despoiling the rich; whereupon either some Caesar or Napoleon would seize the reins of government or the republic would be laid waste by its own barbarians.

So it might be. But now we need to pause in this popular hunt of analogies, and return to the obvious. There is literally a world of difference between America and ancient Rome —politically, economically, socially, culturally. Western civilization as a whole is still more different, sprawling over whole continents, impinging on all other societies, involving the entire world in its destiny; by comparison the mighty Roman Empire was a piddling local affair. Never before has there been a civilization so vast and dynamic, with such immense powers and incalculable possibilities. Never again will there be such a civilization, one might add, given an atomic war; but this possibility only emphasizes the profound differences in our situation. Such differences are not necessarily in our favor and by no means guarantee our success. The point is merely that they must be taken into account before we draw any final lessons from the failure of Rome. They make nonsense of all neat patterns got by analogy, and more especially of the efforts of Spengler and Toynbee to locate the exact position of our civilization on the downcurve of their historic cycles. We cannot even count on the time that Toynbee gives us when he calculates that Western Christendom has experienced only one-and-a-half of the standard three-and-a-half beats he makes out in the rhythm of disintegrating societies.

Briefly, the major differences may be traced to the growth of democracy, science, and technology. These achievements Toynbee dismisses as 'an almost meaningless repetition of something that the Greeks and Romans did before us and did supremely well.' In fact, they are strictly, profoundly unique. Rome experienced nothing like the political, scientific, and industrial revolutions that have created the modern world, and that are still revolutionizing it. Even in its periods of anarchy the Roman world was not a revolutionary world. Even in times of peace the modern world is.

The Industrial Revolution alone has brought the most radical changes in human life since the Urban Revolution with which civilization began. Like all other great societies, Rome ultimately rested on the manual labor of slaves or serfs. However immoderate its greatness, it was spared the problem of managing an immense machine civilization. Likewise its subject peoples were spared the profound disruption that the impact of Western civilization has caused in other societies today; Roman rule brought a change in masters but relatively little economic, cultural, or social change in the

Eastern provinces. By the same token, however, the Roman Empire had nothing like our material resources. Its famed wealth and power were negligible in comparison—the imperial revenues were a mere fraction of the annual income of United States Steel, or the annual budget of the city of New York. Lacking the basic idea of systematically applied knowledge, the Romans had no real command of their physical environment; and as their material resources were depleted by extravagance, plague, war, and exhaustion of mine and soil, they were helpless. They could only turn to magic and prayer. (Thus the medical science developed so brilliantly by the Greeks was swamped by superstitition as the empire was devastated by plagues; it was lost to Europe for a thousand years.) A major symptom of their impotence was a sharp decline in population, which further weakened the empire; whereas another unparalleled consequence of the Industrial Revolution has been an enormous increase in population, which has continued even through the unparalleled slaughter of the world wars.

This immense population is utterly dependent upon science and industry. Its masses, however, are by no means so slavish or inert as the masses of the Roman Empire. Spengler's 'megalopolis' is now productive, not parasitic, and there is no longer a great gulf between it and the country. If the city masses are rootless and formless, they are nevertheless energetic and busy; they earn their bread and enjoy their circuses in their leisure. When they go on relief or demand social security, conservatives are likely to fear for their character, pointing out how the Roman masses were demoralized by hereditary doles and free grain; yet what the modern worker is demanding first of all is the opportunity to work.[10] Hence there is some reason for optimism even in the 'spiritual barrenness' that Toynbee notes in the proletariat today. Since spirituality in his analysis is a portent of worldly doom, our perverse failure to exhibit some of the appropriate symptoms of disintegration (such as a resurgence of asceticism and the sense of sin) leads him to venture the 'cynical conclusion' that our case has not yet reached the advanced stage; but at least he grants that the schism in the soul

---

[10] It is worth recalling that the millions of WPA workers who were pictured leaning on their shovels, reveling in the taxpayers' money, flocked back to the factories as soon as war production offered jobs again. Their character proved to be as sturdy as that of the businessmen who had rushed to Washington for help early in the depression, when relief to workers was still stigmatized as a 'dole'; and businessmen are notable for a peculiarly stalwart character, which enables them to enjoy without loss of self-reliance the benefits of tariffs, franchises, and even outright government subsidies.

of the workers seems to have been repaired. Unlike the Roman masses who took to Oriental gods, they have not lost faith in their society.

One reason for this obstinate faith is that common men now enjoy political rights, or at least the illusion of political power. Nietzsche and Spengler pictured the rise of democracy and socialism as a typical mark of a society in decay, signifying the dominance of the herd-values of the mass-man; but on the face of it this is an astonishing misreading of history. Until recent centuries the masses have had no real political power in any civilization except the Greco-Roman, and there democracy was steadily on the decline after the fall of Athens. The Roman Republic was essentially a timocracy, which in diplomacy and in conquest supported local oligarchies everywhere. The Roman Empire granted a kind of equality before the law, but it granted the masses no rights whatever in the making of the law. As for the socialism of its last phase, with the regimentation that now serves as a horrid example for Chambers of Commerce, this was a far cry from an experiment in the 'welfare state.' It was neither demanded by the common man nor designed for his benefit; it was designed to aid the imperial government, and merely sealed his slavery to the State. In short, never before our own time has virtually the entire population of large nations been a genuine citizenry, with a voice in selecting its rulers and deciding its destiny.

With the rise of democracy has come an unprecedented humanitarianism, in the name of the dignity and worth of the individual. It is often sentimental and unenlightened, seldom a match for prejudice or the profit motive. It makes more hideous such contradictions as the unprecedented horrors of modern war—the barbarism that we cannot afford to regard as a mere 'reversion,' or incidental relic of our primitive ancestry. Still the humanitarianism is a real force, which has brought real changes. The Roman ideal of *humanitas* was an intellectual concept that involved little concern for the individual; under the formal ideals of classicism, the individual was merely an example of some formal 'type.' Good Romans were seldom disturbed by the wretchedness of the masses and saw no particular evil in gladiatorial games, judicial torture, slavery, or war. In the democracies today there are still plenty of social evils, but they are commonly regarded as evils that should be remedied. The barbarism of our times is at least called by that name.

Most important, however, is the active faith on which democracy is based—the faith in reason, freedom, individualism, with its stress on 'opportunity' and the active effort to improve life. The Romans clung to an essentially passive ideal, relying on discipline rather than initiative, encouraging patient endurance rather than wilful endeavor. Their characteristic wisdom was the wisdom of Epictetus: 'Seek not that the things which happen to you should happen as you wish, but wish the things that happen to be as they are, and you will find tranquillity.' This is always a genuine kind of wisdom, and may be the best kind for life in the atomic age; it is no longer necessary to emphasize the dangers of Western wishfulness and wilfulness. Here, at any rate, is the basic difference between the Roman world and ours, the ultimate source of all the specific economic, political, and cultural differences. Rome had no faith in progress, expecting the future to be merely a recurrence; it sought to keep things as they were, and when things went wrong it looked backward, to a Utopian past. We keep looking forward, much less hopefully than we used to, but still with a vivid sense of possibilities, of things that could or should be done. Rome suffered from a lack of energy and enterprise, a stagnation; its decline was a creeping paralysis. We suffer from an excess of energy, or misguided enterprise; and we are likely to end with a bang.

In this perspective, the apparent analogies between the Roman world and our own may take on quite different aspect. Thus the skepticism and irreligion of the educated class, which Spengler and many others view as a symptom of disease, is not the same old story. In Rome such skepticism was apt to be unhealthy because it was primarily negative, reflecting only a loss of faith. Today it is often as unhealthy or even more so, springing from a deeper confusion or a stronger aversion; it is more apt to produce a cynical indifference than a stoical resignation. Yet it commonly springs from a positive faith in reason and science. Many men are critical of the traditional absolutes because of this faith; they insist on the principle of uncertainty implied in the method of science, and in the ideals of freedom and the open society. Modern skepticism has therefore produced much creative criticism, as in Rome it did not. Modern irreligion has generally been an optimistic religion of humanity. Both have been a positive moral force.

For such reasons the ancient faiths may also have a vitality that traditionalism obscures. The genius of Christianity has been more enterprising, resourceful, and versatile than the orthodox make it out to be. It has known a Protestant Reformation—something of which Roman piety was wholly incapable. Today millions of churchgoers recall this piety as they go through their routine rituals, recite ancient Creeds that they do not really believe or even understand; yet many leaders of Christianity are striving to readapt it to the needs of a revolutionary world. Similarly with the arts. Whereas Roman art suffered from a sterile classicism, modern art suffers from a feverish confusion, intensified by the romantic tradition of individualism, self-expression, and free imagination; the obvious trouble with it is not lifeless formality but strain and excess. I should not predict what will come out of all this experimentation. The point is simply that something rich may come out of it—it is a live growth, however deformed.

Again, the social enterprise of modern democracy has always been more extensive and energetic than champions of private enterprise seem to realize. In pointing to the obvious evils of Roman bureaucracy, and the failure of the final experiment in state socialism, they forget that until this experiment the imperial policy was more consistently laissez faire than that of capitalistic America in its nineteenth-century heyday. The Roman government did not restrict free enterprise by patent laws, hamper free trade by tariffs, or interfere in business by giving franchises or subsidies to a favored few. Neither did it enter the postal business or provide socialized education through public schools. Certainly its mismanagement of its economic resources was not due to a rage for 'planning'—it was due rather to a lack of any plan. The Romans were more consistent than conservatives today in their obedience to Nature or Necessity, even though they had not consciously formulated the Laws of Competition and of Supply and Demand. For modern capitalism has never really respected these sacrosanct laws that it has written into its bill of rights. It has always tended to evade them by seeking monopoly; it has always got more or less government protection against them. And if conservatives have stubbornly resisted every measure to extend similar protection to workers and consumers, they have steadily lost ground, and by now take for granted a great deal of social legislation that horrified their fathers. When the national economy is threatened by a rugged individualist like John L. Lewis, who still believes in free private enterprise, they are the first to demand that the government should do something about it. In spite of themselves, they are committed to the Western faith in active intelligence—the faith that man can make his own laws, control his society, and determine his future.

Hence the experience of the Roman Empire is hardly a guide in our experiment of a democratically planned society. It does suggest, however, that the experiment is worth trying. It supports John Stuart Mill's argument that a benevolent autocracy is inferior to self-government, and in the long run even more harmful than a vicious autocracy, because more enervating. Self-government makes for a vigorous, self-reliant people; whereas a people deprived of political life loses energy, becomes mentally passive, at length becomes helpless —as helpless as the Romans proved to be after the reign of Marcus Aurelius.

But Mill also raised the final issue, of the objects of democratic energy and enterprise, the goods sought by free men; and here the testimony of Rome is less clear. In one sense the Roman masses had the last word: their mentality, based on religion, in time dominated their masters. To Toynbee this was a triumph of transcendence, the victory of Christ over Caesar. Worldlier historians have dwelt rather on its immediate meaning, which was the death of a civilization. Rostovtzeff summarizes the whole story of the decline of the Roman Empire as 'the gradual absorption of the educated classes by the masses and the consequent simplification of all the functions of political, social, economic, and intellectual life, which we call the barbarization of the ancient world.' The lesson of Rome, he believes, is that a civilization cannot endure if it rests on a small class, not on the masses; but then he points out that the masses debase a civilization. He concludes with a question: 'Is not every civilization bound to decay as soon as it begins to penetrate the masses?'

It is an open question. The creative achievements of civilization to date have been primarily the work of an elite, and the greatest achievements will always be due immediately to the gifted few. Ideally, democracy would mean not merely a general rise in the culture of the masses but an elite that is freely recruited, that may be enlarged and constantly invigorated by special talents from the ranks. Actually, democracy has indeed enlisted vast reserves of energy and talent, but it has also meant a lowering of standards of excellence, a blurring of the all-important distinction between common and uncommon men. It has produced the half-educated man— a type relatively rare in other societies—who is apt to have less respect for learning and culture than the uneducated man. And with industrialism has come a universal vulgarization. An immense machinery is now geared to the tastes and desires of common men, which are an offense by the standards of all civilizations before ours. It produces the appalling confusion of values reflected in radio programs, on which a breathless announcement of impending world catastrophe is preceded by a jingle in praise of some eyewash and followed by a popular comic.

Let us spell out the worst about this notorious mass-man and his mass-culture. He has a meager idea of the abundant life, confusing quantity with quality, size with greatness, comfort with culture, gadgetry with genius. He has as little appreciation of pure science as of the fine arts, and as little capacity for the discipline that both require; although he may stand in awe of them his real veneration goes to the engineers and inventors, the manufacturers of True Romances and Tin Pan Alley airs. He is frequently illiberal, suspicious of 'radical' ideas, scornful of 'visionary' ideals, hostile to 'aliens'; in America he has developed a remarkable vocabulary of contempt that manages to embrace most of mankind—the nigger, the mick, the chink, the wop, the kike, et cetera. He is the chief foe of the individualism he boasts of, a patron of standard brands in tastes and opinions as in material possessions, with a morbid fear of being thought queer or different from the Joneses; individuality to him is 'personality,' which may be acquired in six easy lessons or his money back, is then turned on to win friends and influence people, and is confirmed by the possession of 'personalized' objects, which are distinguished only by having his initials on them. In short, he appears to be a spoiled child, fundamentally ungrateful to the scientists, political philosophers, social reformers, and religious idealists who have given him his unprecedented opportunities. He is therefore the natural prey of advertisers, politicians, millionaire publishers, and would-be dictators.

Yet he is much more than this, else he would never have got where he has. The 'mass-man' is also a bogey—a monstrous abstraction that conceals the infinite varieties of common men, in interest, ability, character, and aspiration. It conceals all the degrees in culture, the frequent lustiness of the low-brow, the earnestness of the middle-brow. In particular it conceals the idealism that underlies the obvious materialism. This expresses itself in such commonplace sentiments as that every man ought to have a fair chance—a very novel commonplace, in the light of history. In times of crisis it has enabled such loyalty, fortitude, and unpretentious heroism as won the Battle for Britain. At all times it inspires an enthusiasm for vast co-operative enterprises, kindles the energy and imagination that have made the kingdom of common men the most adventurous in history. 'An idealist working on matter' Santayana has called the American; and his fine enthusiasm might be touched to finer issues. Meanwhile it is again an inhuman spirituality that cannot see idealism in the effort to eliminate the poverty and wretchedness once accepted as the will of God, and to enable all men to enjoy the material well-being once enjoyed only by a privileged few—by aristocrats who could afford to exalt non-economic interests and values because they took for granted their wealth and luxury, and seldom had to earn it.

Rostovtzeff's question remains open for the simple reason that common men are having their first real chance in history, and have not had it long. It is hardly surprising if they still fall short of their opportunities and their responsibilities —as throughout history their masters consistently did. In judging this new adventure, accordingly, we must at least face squarely the historic alternatives. Many critics of democratic culture are not candid. They yearn for all the advantages of an aristocratic society without being willing to commit themselves to the moral and intellectual responsibilities of arguing for an aristocratic government, shouldering the human cost. Even T. S. Eliot, who frankly condemns the ideal of equality of opportunity and maintains that a hereditary privileged class is essential to culture, is vague or irresponsible at the critical points of his argument. He arbitrarily dismisses the 'myth' of the mute, inglorious Milton, ignoring the plain reasons for believing that a great deal of potential talent or even genius went to waste among the illiterate masses of the past. He merely asserts that his privileged elite will have special responsibilities, ignoring the historic fact that they usually evaded these responsibilities, and suggesting no safeguards against the historic abuses of privilege. He declares very simply that 'no sane person can be consumed with bitterness at not having had more exalted ancestors,' ignoring the very good reasons for bitterness that millions of poor devils have had. Possibly Eliot's kind of culture does require a hereditary aristocracy; but given the historic record, I should say that a more reasonable ideal is culture and education for all, within their capacities, even if democracy is not the best soil for the very choicest flowers of the human spirit.

As for Rome, at any rate, the masses cannot be held responsible for its fall. If they 'absorbed' the educated classes, the fault lay with these privileged classes, who had failed to educate or uplift them, failed to maintain either the material prosperity or the spiritual health of the nation. Rome illustrates the maxim that societies die at the top. As it rose to greatness it rehearsed the old story of the selfishness and short-sightedness of the elite. The aristocratic families who ran the senatorial machine proved utterly incapable of the statesmanship that the rising empire called for. They turned on their liberal members, such as the Gracchi, with the kind of fury that was inspired by 'that man' Roosevelt; they rejected the compromises that might have preserved the privileges they jealously clung to; and so they perversely brought on the military dictatorship that destroyed their power. The bourgeois class that replaced them was less suicidal, if only because it had less political power, but ultimately it proved as incapable of enlightened leadership. Nor was it enlightened by Roman intellectuals. If the cultivated class was well-intentioned, it proved wanting in creative intelligence and imagination.

For the Romans, we may then speak the last word in charity, and even in awe. They had nothing like our material and intellectual resources; the wonder is not that their empire fell but that it endured so long and so grandly. For us, the last word is a challenge to the educated, privileged classes. The problem today is not merely a matter of improving the minds and tastes of common men. It is also a question of whether the elite can provide better political, intellectual, and spiritual leadership than it has in all previous societies. For if the creative achievements of civilization have been due primarily to the elite, so too have the failures of civilization. 'No civilized minority,' observed Leonard Woolf, 'has yet been found willing to make the necessary sacrifices.'

VIII

The Birth of Western Civilization

1. THE FICTIONS OF THE 'MIDDLE' AGES

The Dark Ages that followed the fall of Rome were in fact long centuries of darkness, during which there was turbulent life but hardly as much light as in the Homeric age. Yet through the night the memory of Rome lived on, to become the inspiration of a grand illusion. From Daniel's prophecy about the Fourth Kingdom, Christians knew that the empire would last until the end of the world. 'When Rome the head of the world shall have fallen,' wrote Lactantius, 'who can doubt that the end is done of human things, aye, of the earth itself?' Since the world had not ended, in spite of their hopes, Christians assumed that Rome had not really fallen. And so when Charlemagne, by a magnificent creative effort, established a new empire in the West, men knew that he had not created anything new—he had merely restored the Roman Empire. His empire was a Frankish kingdom that had no cities, no Senate, no Roman roads or legions or laws, no Roman institutions or long-established institutions of any sort—except the Roman Church; but this was enough to solemnize the fiction. The Church crowned him Emperor in the year 800, and ultimately canonized him.

Charlemagne's empire soon collapsed, for his dynasty ran out in feeble successors who won only their surnames as the Bald, the Stammerer, the Simple, the Fat. The chaos that followed was more appalling than the barbarism that had gone before; attacked at once by Vikings, Magyars, and Saracens, Western Christendom was on the verge of extinction. Nevertheless the ideal memory of Charlemagne's achievement survived. In 962 the German king Otto again restored the Roman Empire, at another solemn coronation in Rome. The dignity of the Emperor was heightened by the assumption that he was head of the world, not merely of the West; the Byzantine emperors preceding Charlemagne were pressed into service to give him an unbroken line of descent from Augustus, while the contemporary Byzantine emperors were dismissed as interlopers or pretenders. In the twelfth century Frederick I further exalted his Roman Empire by calling it 'Holy,' a title that made other European kingdoms jealous but was piously accepted by them. The Middle Ages remained devoted to the wonderful ideal throughout endless civil war, in which the holy emperor struggled to enforce his rights, his reverent subjects struggled to reject his claims, and Italy was the chief sufferer.

The bitterest enemies of the emperor were the popes. They buttressed their pretensions to temporal supremacy by the 'Donation of Constantine' and the 'False Decretals' of Isidore, both crude forgeries that had been produced about the time of Charlemagne, and that no medieval scholar was acute enough or bold enough to expose; this astounding fraud served the purposes of the Church for some five hundred years. Pope Innocent III contributed a fancier fiction in his theory of the 'Translation of the Empire': the Church had taken the empire away from the Greeks to bestow it on Charlemagne and the Germans, and therefore had the right to recall and transfer the gift. When the popes succeeded in breaking the power of the emperors, however, they chose not to transfer the gift. To restore order in Germany, and to protect their imperial revenues, they put a Hapsburg on the throne. So the Holy Roman Empire lived on, surviving long after the Church in turn lost its dominion and became catholic only in name. Although Voltaire pointed out that it was neither holy nor Roman nor an empire, it testified to the vitality of its ancestor by refusing to give up the ghost until 1806, a thousand years after Charlemagne had revived it. Its formal dissolution by Napoleon was a minor diplomatic event—Christians again failed to notice the end of the eternal empire; but then Napoleon too dreamed of becoming the lawful Emperor of the West.

This wondrous fantasy of the Holy Roman Empire is the key to the Middle Ages, and to their enduring legacy. No other age has created such splendid, preposterous fictions; none has been at once so artful and so artless in its make-believe, and so blind to its solid, original achievements. For the fictions were not simple lies. They were spontaneous growths, rooted in an innocent, impassioned piety. They were nourished by a youthful passion for color, drama,

pageantry—for the pomp that to us may look like incidental
show but to medieval men was the very stuff of life. They
were nourished as well by an ideal passion for legality and
consecrated sovereignty, so that even such a gross fraud as
the Donation of Constantine could be perpetrated in good
conscience. They flowered luxuriantly in an imaginative ignorance of the holy past and a lofty indifference to vulgar
fact.[1] All that mattered was the pure, catholic ideal. Requiring a Holy Roman Emperor for their grandiose purposes,
medieval men did not care too much who he was or how
helpless he was; enthralled by magnificent theories, they were
not troubled if no one tried to carry them out. 'At no
time in the world's history,' concluded James Bryce, 'has
theory, professing all the while to control practice, been so
utterly divorced from it.'

The most charming symbol of these incongruities was the
Virgin, in whom Henry Adams saw the main inspiration of
the age. The boundless, indiscriminate graciousness and mercy
that won the heart of the skeptical, snobbish Adams made
even the Devil grow worried over the depopulation of Hell;
in fabliaux he constantly complained to God of her unjust
forgiveness of the rankest sinners. The Virgin was no longer,
however, merely the sorrowing mother. She was Our Lady,
a medieval queen distinguished in portraits by her crown,
throne, and imperious manner. She lorded it over heaven
and earth. ('God is deaf where His Mother is concerned,'
lamented the Devil, 'and leaves her lady and mistress of
Paradise.') The Crusaders made her Queen even of the
Oriental game of chess, replacing a piece called the Minister; they gave her complete freedom while they restricted
the movements of the Knight and the King. She dominated
an age of mighty warriors. Yet the Virgin had little apparent influence on their conduct, which was typically blood-
thirsty. Likewise she failed to raise her own sex from their
status of essential inferiority. The monks who contributed
to the cult of the Virgin (sometimes adoring her in erotic
language) continued to pour contempt on women as the

[1] The historical methods of the period were summarized by Agnellus,
the scholarly ninth-century Bishop of Ravenna who wrote the biographies
of his predecessors. 'Where I have not found any history of any of
these bishops, and have not been able by conversation with aged men,
or inspection of the monuments, or from any other authentic source, to
obtain information concerning them, in such a case, in order that
there might not be a break in the series, I have composed the life myself, with the help of God and the prayers of the brethren.' Countless
saints—including some who had had the wit never to have lived on
this earth—were equipped with appropriate biographies by this method,
though generally without preliminary inquiry into authentic sources.

daughters of Eve. While Albertus Magnus decided that the Virgin possessed a perfect knowledge of the seven liberal arts, educators decided that women should not be taught to read. Legally, woman was not 'a free and lawful person.' Because of her 'frailty' wife-beating was legal.

The Middle Ages have accordingly continued to engender historical fictions, as later generations were charmed by their ideal theory or repelled by their barbarous practice. The very christening of the period was a misnomer: it was not a middle age but a childhood, the dawn of a new civilization. In the late Renaissance and the Age of the Enlightenment men saw only its primitive rudeness. They coined the term *Gothic* to express simply contempt: as the destroyers of Rome, the Goths were the most notorious of barbarians. Voltaire in particular branded the Middle Ages as the main source of all the superstition, prejudice, and tyranny that were impeding human progress. Then the Romantic Movement polished the other side of the coin. Poets discovered the sublime piety that had created Gothic art; novelists (such as Sir Walter Scott) glorified the ideals of chivalry and romantic love. Religious and political conservatives, frightened by the French Revolution, were charmed as well by the medieval principle of hierarchy, the willingness of the many to honor and obey the superior few. This enthusiasm for the Middle Ages ran its course in the last century, but it left a residue. While popular imagination is still captivated by the romance of the days when knighthood was in flower, philosophical and religious thought is still seduced by the dream of the Age of Faith. In current usage, the term *medieval* may be a synonym for benighted and brutal; or it may connote the unity, piety, and grace so woefully lacking in the modern world.

I should not expect to do exact justice to an age in which there is so much to admire and to deplore, but not so much to recover for our living purposes. Its faiths had a child-like simplicity and freshness that we cannot recover by an effort of will, and that are apt to delude us into sentimental, irresponsible wishfulness; its follies and vices were more ancient but also had a quality of innocence that we dare not attribute to our own. Yet this age is important to us because it was *our* childhood. Its incongruities were more fantastic than the incongruities of any other great society—except perhaps our own; and we may assume that the child is father of the man. In any event, the incongruities were basic and went through and through. By stressing them we may at least find that the romance of the medieval world was fresher, lustier, more wonderful, and more illuminating than the romances it wrote or the romances it has inspired.

2. THE BASIC CONTRADICTIONS

The famed unity of the Middle Ages is not a mere fiction. There was a practically universal agreement on the basic ideas by which men professed to live. Catholicism was not only the one Church but the primary inspiration of art, the main source of education, the accepted basis of all philosophy, science, political theory, and economic theory. Medieval men all knew the same absolute truth about the human drama, from the Creation to the Last Judgment. There was also an underlying similarity in social institutions. The world of chivalry was much the same everywhere, and everywhere rested on the hard work of villein or serf; the same literary and art forms were employed all over Europe, or even the same legends of Charlemagne, Alexander, and King Arthur; Latin was the universal language of educated men. There were no strict nationalities, no fixed boundaries, no armed frontiers, no passports. Merchants, students, minstrels, buffoons, pilgrims, pedlars, friars, masons, scribes, pardoners, cheap-Jacks—all wandered freely from place to place, to give the medieval scene everywhere the same gaudy variety.

This is already a profane scene, however. It includes certain unconscious revolutionaries in the merchants, whose worldly business was largely responsible for the very existence of roads, the possibility of safe travel. The rise of Western civilization, as of Greek culture, was inseparably connected with the rise of commerce and industry. Medieval men, like the Greeks, displayed a natural genius for the economic activities they professed to despise. They were much more enterprising and inventive than the Romans, developing trading companies and craft guilds, making notable advances in the techniques of big business. Medieval business also produced its pilgrims, ascetics, and martyrs—such men as Marco Polo and Christopher Columbus, who dared or denied for the sake of gain, and who perhaps did more for the medieval cause of universalism than did the church. Immediately, commerce led to the rise of towns. The towns were congested huddles, dark, unkempt, filthy, and foul-smelling, with a turbulent and often vicious life of their own; but they were the centers of the new art and learning, the seats of the great cathedrals and universities. The towns generated the creative and disruptive forces of the medieval renaissance, as of the later Italian Renaissance.

At that, the merchants were the most sober men in our motley wayfaring company. Although the students, for example, were all connected with the Church, they were notorious as a rowdy lot, given to drinking, gambling, whoring, and brawling. The pilgrims were visiting some shrine known for its wonder-working images or relics, but they were generally out for a gay time as well as a blessing or a cure; pilgrimages became a scandal to the pious spirits of the Middle Ages. The pardoners were engaged in the minor but profitable racket of selling indulgences, and as a sideline were likely to have holy relics for sale.[2] This seamy side of medieval life had its own values, of humor, exuberance, gusto, daring—a love of life and a spirit of freedom that offset the harshness of medieval doctrine. It also vitalized medieval faith—no society of saints could have built so gloriously as did these reckless sinners. In any event, it suggests that we might forget momentarily the doctrines and fictions, and look at the social scene.

It is a much less homogeneous scene than it was in Roman times, when towns looked and lived much alike. Already we find the regional diversity of manner and custom that has so enriched European culture; hence European patriots now look to the Middle Ages for the sources of their rational pride, while fond scholars get as misty about the *Volkgeist* as the *Zeitgeist*. The most distinctive medieval creation, Gothic architecture, points to a further anomaly. This originated in France—not in Italy or Germany, the domain of the Holy Roman Empire. France was the cultural leader, the center of philosophy, the hearth of the Crusades; while Rome, the capital of Christendom, remained its most riotous, dissolute, wretched city. In 1084 Rome had been ferociously sacked by the Normans, suffering much worse from these allies of Pope Gregory VII than it ever had from the Goths or Vandals. When the city recovered it developed neither indus-

---

[2] The cult of relics illustrates the remarkable fertility of medieval imagination. Among the offerings for sale, or on display in the churches, we hear of vials of the Virgin's milk or St. Joseph's breath, hairs from Noah's beard, dung from Job's heap, a bit of the bush in which God spoke to Moses, hay from the stall in Bethlehem, fragments of the loaves and fishes multiplied by Christ, and countless other souvenirs of the Lord—his teeth, sweat, tears, umbilical cord, et cetera. Since no church could be complete without a relic, and many owned hundreds, the total must have run into millions; but the competition led to considerable duplication, and in time to a deal of skepticism. As early as the twelfth century Guibert, Abbot of Nogent, was troubled by the discovery that at least two churches owned the head of John the Baptist. In France alone, five churches claimed possession of the authentic relic of the Lord's circumcision.

try nor art, devoting itself chiefly to wrangling with its most eminent inhabitant, the Pope, of whom it was always proud and suspicious. It built nothing memorable in this great age of architecture. (The artistic glorification of Rome did not begin until the pagan, worldly Renaissance.) It was perhaps the only city in Europe that contributed no recruits for the Crusades. Throughout the Middle Ages there was universal reverence for Rome, and as universal contempt for the Romans. 'What for centuries has been so notorious,' wrote St. Bernard, 'as the shamelessness and arrogance of the Romans?'

The popes themselves inspired similar feelings. Everybody revered the office of the Vicar of Peter, and everybody felt free to despise or hate the Vicar himself. 'To the catholic soul,' remarks Huizinga, 'the unworthiness of the persons never compromises the sacred character of the institution.' Hence the Holy Emperors had no compunctions about warring on the Vicars, and Dante felt positively exalted as he tortured popes in his Inferno. (The greatest of Catholic poets was later put on the Catholic Index of prohibited books.) In general, medieval men were as fond of ridiculing their spiritual shepherds as Americans are of ridiculing their elected representatives in Congress, only their abuse was more heartfelt and indecent. It was even believed that bishops had an especially poor chance of getting into heaven.

The plain reason for this hatred or contempt was the widespread corruption of the clergy, which is an all too familiar theme.[3] Less familiar is the astonishing irreverence that accompanied medieval piety, and gave the clergy as good reason to complain of their flock. The church was a favorite trysting-place of young lovers, and hunting ground of prostitutes. Students had to be discouraged from playing dice on the altars of Notre Dame by threat of excommunication. During church service the congregation sometimes

[3] A rich source of examples is the *Register* in which the thirteenth-century Archbishop Rigaud of Rouen reported his visitations. Of a nunnery, the priory of Villa Arcelli, he gave this account: 'Johanna de Alto Villari kept going out alone with a man named Gayllard, and within a year had a child by him. The subprioress is suspected with Thomas the carter; Idonia, her sister, with Crispinatus; and the Prior of Gisorcium is always coming to the house for Idonia. Philippa of Rouen is suspected with a priest of Suentre, of the diocese of Chartres; Marguarita, the treasuress, with Richard de Genville, a clerk; Agnes de Fontenei, with a priest of Guerrevile, diocese of Chartres... All wear their hair improperly and perfume their veils. Jacqueline came back pregnant from visiting a certain chaplain, who was expelled from his house on account of this. Agnes de Monsec was suspected with the same. Emengarde and Johanna of Alto Villari beat each other. The prioress is drunk almost any night...' This establishment had only thirty-three nuns.

clapped and cheered the sermon, but preachers complain of 'myche jangling and japynge and many other vanytees, settynge nought bi prechinge and techinge of Goddis word.' Obscenities were freely introduced into religious dramas and allegories. Oaths were multiplied in a passion for novelty; blasphemy was never more ingenious and deliberate than in this period, when it meant certain damnation. The Virgin herself was the subject of embryological or even erotic speculating, while her husband St. Joseph became a comic figure, as a kind of holy cuckold.

The clue here is not so much weakness of faith as the strength of the flesh. The gross sensuality that inspired the voluminous bawdy literature of the Middle Ages also appears in the extreme horror of death, a fascinated horror that was intensified by the fears of hell but was centered on the idea of putrefaction, the decay of the despised flesh, the loss of sinful beauty—a theme that obsessed the later medieval artists, and gave their art a grotesque, macabre quality that would have astounded the sensual pagans of antiquity. Again, the fiction of courtly love had an especially luxuriant growth because love was seldom connected with marriage, which was a matter of *convenance,* and because the sexual life of the nobility was exceptionally rude; so the dreams of pure love were matched by extravagant obscenities that suggest a dream of pure lust. But most characteristic was the blend of the ascetic and the erotic, in the Tristrams and Lancelots, and above all in the immensely popular and influential *Romance of the Rose.* This curious compound of the thirteenth century became the medieval encyclopedia of amorous lore. The sweet idealism of Guillaume de Lorris, who started the poem, is complemented by the cynical realism of Jean de Meun, who finished it. The conclusion is the triumph of Love over Chastity—a glorification of seduction that amounts to a defiance of both Christian and chivalrous ideals. The rose itself almost epitomizes the age. It is a frankly sexual symbol in the poem; it also connotes freshness, youth, beauty; and it is a religious symbol, recalling the glorious rose windows of the French cathedrals.

The rose will not quite do, however: we must add gold and blood. Greed was naked and unabashed in the Middle Ages, even though the desire to make a fortune was called avarice instead of normal ambition. It therefore corrupted the clergy and the nobility far more than it did the business class, who did not profess to have such high, unworldly ideals. Although it called out a typically extreme reaction, in the ideal of absolute poverty proclaimed by St. Francis, his new order became wealthy within a generation after his death; and presently the Franciscan friars were notorious for their cupidity and fraud. It appears that greed even came to replace pride as the deadliest of sins, in the estimation of the pious; but this elevation was only an acknowledgment of its actual status, if not a further incentive to the impious.

Bloodshed, on the other hand, was made honorable by the institution of chivalry, which ritualized violence. By origin a Germanic warrior, the medieval knight was given a Roman ancestry; poets discovered that Romulus was the founder of chivalry. The genuine knightly virtues of courage and fidelity were likewise bedecked with Christian and courtly ideals: the knight became Sir Galahad and Sir Lancelot, or a squire of the Virgin, while other poets made the Archangel Michael the father of chivalry. Nevertheless the knight remained at heart a rude warrior, who fought chiefly for the love of fighting, not of God or of ladies, and whose chivalrous code extended only to his peers. The medieval chronicles devoted to his valorous exploits are full of casual examples of his cruelty, lust, and greed, and his habit of pillaging or slaughtering the peasantry. In time he became a professional soldier or a simple mercenary. But from the outset war was commonly fought over trivial causes, involving personal animosities rather than principles. Its absurdity was accentuated by the 'Truce of God,' through which the Church sought to maintain peace at least on holy days and over week ends.

The vain efforts of high-minded churchmen to curb such excesses point to the most violent paradox of medieval life—its phenomenal license. In theory, life was regulated by elaborate forms and codes, hedged in by religious rules that had the most awful sanctions. In fact, life ran wild in uncouth freedom, with a reckless defiance of all the rules upon which salvation depended. Social records indicate that vice and crime were far more prevalent than they are in the skeptical, cynical modern age, which is agitated by mere 'crime waves'; to judge by sermons, they were most prevalent on holy days. Furthermore, much of this lawlessness was condoned. University life is the most striking example because all students were 'clerks,' supposedly in religious orders. As such, they had special privileges and immunities from civil authority; so they carried on with a rowdier exuberance. When they were not brawling among themselves, or threatening vengeance on their Examiners, they were apt to riot and assault the townspeople; not until later centuries did the universities make a serious effort to put a stop to the incessant battles between armed students and burghers. (It is said that more blood has been shed in Oxford than on many famous battlefields.) And though the students entered the universities at a considerably earlier age than modern students, they were subject to nothing like the discipline that cramps the style of our flaming youth. We read of some who were flogged because they had killed fellow students in drunken brawls, but even homicide did not necessarily merit the severe punishment of expulsion from the university.[4]

All these anomalies are summed up in the crowning adventure of the Middle Ages—the Crusades. The crusading hosts were fired by the love of God, of glory, and of booty. They attracted the whole gallery of medieval types, from saintly and heroic knights to seedy adventurers, merchants, and criminals; many were induced to join by special papal dispensations granting forgiveness of their crimes. The First Crusade —the most idealistic, high-spirited, and successful—set off on its two-thousand mile jaunt by massacring Jews, plundering and slaughtering all the way from the Rhine to the Jordan. Its conquest of the Holy City, after heroic endurance of hardship and peril, was celebrated by the massacre of both Moslems and Jews. 'In the temple and porch of Solomon,' wrote the ecstatic cleric Raimundus de Agiles, 'one rode in blood up to the knees and even to the horses' bridles, by the just and marvelous Judgment of God.' Presently the victors became embroiled in jealous strife over the spoils; so by the judgment of God there had to be further Crusades, which were chiefly disasters for Christendom.

There remains the question, then, how and why the Mid-

---

[4] Among the many fantastic anecdotes in Rashdall's *Universities of Europe in the Middle Ages*—the classic on the subject—is one of a constant troublemaker who was excommunicated for an assault on a fellow-scholar, but refused to recognize this cruel and unusual punishment. When forcibly ejected from the Chapel he set his bed on fire and almost burned the college down; he also threw big stones on the roof of the Hall during supper, so that the food was covered with dust. When finally summoned before the Rector, he set up a guard of a dozen armed men to prevent the Rector from attending the assembly. Even then he was not deprived of his privileges until an examination proved that he was of 'rude intellect, not fitted or apt for acquiring proficiency'; whereupon he was threatened with expulsion unless he quitted the college within four days.

The only really strict laws were those laid down by students to professors in the Italian universities, and enforced by the threat of boycott. At Bologna the professors were compelled under oath to obey the Rector elected by the students, forbidden to leave town for even a day without permission, fined if they began or ended their lectures a minute late, fined if they failed to attract an audience of at least five students for an ordinary lecture, and in general subjected to a very rigorous but possibly salutary discipline. By the sixteenth century, however, the tables were turned; university regulation of student life was not only tightened up but enforced. Thereafter students ceased to be gentlemen at large, and gradually turned into the schoolboys of today.

dle Ages grew up in this way. As usual, we cannot give a definitive answer. If a far-sighted historian might have foretold that the union of the Roman Church and the Germanic peoples would produce lusty offspring, the rise of the West was not clearly inevitable. It had to wait centuries for the genius of Charlemagne, and its chances were very dim in the chaos following the collapse of his empire. No determinist—least of all a Marxist—could have foretold the nature of the civilization that grew up thereafter. In retrospect, however, we can at least make out the efficient causes and the conditions of the growth. Given the vital energy that somehow enables some peoples to start rising in the world, we can see the further reasons why they make out as they do. The fantastic incongruities of the Middle Ages are intelligible enough.

To begin with the most obvious reason, our medieval forefathers were very young. They had inherited a venerable tradition of which they stood in awe, but their own soul was barbarian and child-like. They loved gaudy color and spectacle, fighting and adventure, fantasy and romance. They lived in a fairy-tale world, full of marvels. They experienced life vividly and intensely, in blacks and whites and reds. Like children playing house, they made up elaborate rules that they took very solemnly while the game lasted, but forgot when they started romping again. They transformed their great Roman-Christian heritage by their boundless imaginativeness, magnifying its most wonderful and most fearful elements; they also played with it impishly, indulging the grotesque fancy and mischievous humor that adorned their cathedrals with leering gargoyles, scribbling naughty words on the walls; but they were as ingenuous in their piety as their blasphemy. They gave the European landscape its spires, set it ringing with the lovely sound of bells—the bells to scare off the demons that infested their world.

Another manifestation of youthfulness was the remarkable vitality and vigor of the Middle Ages. Even in the worst periods of the Dark Ages, when men ostensibly had no faith in the possibilities of human effort, they continued to make strenuous efforts; they did not draw the logical conclusion of quietism or renunciation. With Charlemagne came a splendid burst of energy, in all fields of endeavor. When the Normans broke in on the remnants of his empire they brought fresh resources of energy. It expressed itself notably in architecture, in the vigorous style of the Romanesque and later the Gothic, and in the scale of building—the hundreds of great churches erected by an age of limited resources. It produced the extraordinary gallery of medieval leaders, the crusaders in thought, spiritual quest, political, military, and commercial adventure—Hildebrand, Peter Abelard, St. Bernard, Richard the Lion-Hearted, Frederick Barbarossa, Innocent III, Roger Bacon, Marco Polo, Dante—who differed widely and often furiously, but were alike in their conspicuous lack of the meekness and mildness preached by the Christ to whom they were all devoted.

Given the relative simplicity of the medieval mind, the most characteristic expression of this energy was boundless passion. Although the ardent schoolboys discovered the uses of logic, and later became famous for the subtlety, exhaustiveness, and aridity of their scholasticism, they apprehended and glorified their heritage primarily through passion. It was elemental passion, a torrent of love and terror, hope and despair. It produced still more violent contrasts because of the elemental greed, lust, and hatred that ran wild in daily life. Typically, men were as facile and prodigal in their feeling as in their building, and as unconcerned about perfect harmony or symmetry. They did not run the gamut of emotions —they swung from one extreme to the other. They surrendered themselves wantonly alike to their ideal aspirations and their brutal impulses, and resented as fiercely any denial of their sublime theories as any interference with their selfish interests. They were not greatly troubled by inconsistency because in their naïveté they were often unaware of it, and in their extravagance they could overcompensate for it. A common medieval type was Philip the Good, famous for the abundance of his bastards and the austerity of his fasts.

Even the extreme formalism to which medieval men were addicted could be a means to license as well as restraint They had ceremonies in which they could renounce vanity, with great pomp. They reveled in such solemn spectacles as the public torture and execution of heretics, in which they could indulge at once their love of drama, their pity, their cruelty, and their piety. (Thus a chronicler reports a 'holocaust very great and pleasing to God,' in which some 180 heretics were burned before a large ecclesiastical gathering.) Their high sense of honor was especially becoming, as a blend of fine conscience and rude egotism that enabled them to set up an ideal of selfless fidelity, seek personal glory, gratify their love of fighting, maintain standards of justice, and wreak a barbarous vengeance on their enemies.

Yet medieval men naturally suffered from their high-strung, overwrought way of life, and from the artificial forms into which they tried to fit their passion. The effort, for example, to unite physical desire, courtly love, and pure spirituality —or rather the tendency to carry both the sensual and the spiritual to the extreme, in separate compartments—created the difficult strained relationship that the modern world inherited.[5] Similarly the very passion for unity, and horror of schism, made for violent disunity. And medieval men could not indefinitely remain unconscious of the profound contradictions in their life. The lusty growth of secular life brought a growing tension between faith and reason, theory and practice. Among simple people, these strains underlying the Age of Faith were nakedly exposed in the frequent outbreaks of mass hysteria, as in the frenzied crowds of flagellante, or the dancing manias that carried off whole communities. Among the cultivated, Dante is the clearest example of the tension.

The *Divine Comedy* is a complete synthesis of medieval thought and feeling, including the theological synthesis of Aquinas, exalting the Roman as well as the Christian heritage, fusing sensual, moral, intellectual, and spiritual values in the elaborate symbolism and allegory beloved by medieval men, and giving fervid expression to their supreme aspirations. It embraces the medieval extremes of the heavenly and the hellish, the ultimate in love and hate, hope and horror. In so doing, however, it also reveals the basic con-

[5] It is this that makes so poignant the famous love letters of Héloïse to Abelard, written after Abelard (typical of medieval brutality) had been castrated by hired thugs, and the lovers (typical of medieval piety) had retired to cloisters. Now Héloïse expresses her remorse over their sinful love, and dedicates herself to God; now she protests that their love was not sinful, and complains of God's cruelty; now she confesses that she is still racked by sinful desire. 'Even in the solemn moments of the mass, when prayer should be the purest...when I should groan for what I have done, I sigh for what I have lost.' Her torment is further aggravated by the ideal unselfishness of her love. In her concern for Abelard's career as a philosopher she quotes from the classics to prove that man cannot be devoted to both a wife and philosophy. She insists that most lamentable and ignominious was the marriage that finally legitimatized their love, because it declared that a man whom God had made for all was now unnaturally bound to one woman, and it denied the free gift of her love to so holy a man. Her chief consolation is a thought displeasing to God: 'God knows that I have always feared to offend thee more than I feared to offend Him, and have desired to please thee rather than Him.'

Also touching are the innocent but passionate yearnings of medieval nuns, who wrote constantly of 'panting with desire' for the God incarnate, and of their intimate ecstasies when the desire was fulfilled. Mary of Ognies spent thirty-five days in a silent trance, broken now and then only by the words 'I desire the body of our Lord Jesus Christ.' The saintly Liutgard of Tongern had more rapturous transports: 'I am my Beloved's,' she exclaimed, 'and His desire is towards me.' Sister Mechthild of Magdeburg had glowing visions of the 'beautiful Youth' Christ, who spoke to her in lovers' language and called her to 'the couch of love.' 'I am a full-grown bride and will have my Bridegroom,' she rhapsodized; and in her supreme ecstasies she became 'Bride of the Trinity.' Writing before the heyday of Freud, the historian Henry Osborn Taylor asked: 'Are these virgins rewarded in the life to come with what they spurned in this?'

traditions. For a supernatural epic it is amazingly full of the business of the world, including much vulgar, mean detail; the sublime message is introduced by fierce invective, which becomes simply nasty when Dante gloats over the infernal torments of his political enemies. For a Christian epic teaching humility and self-surrender it reveals an amazing pride: Dante makes himself the hero, elects himself to the immortal company of Homer, Virgil, and Horace, supposes that three heavenly ladies—Beatrice, St. Lucy, and the Virgin herself—collaborate on the special mission of securing his salvation, and finally dares the ultimate presumption, introducing himself into the presence of God. And with his radiant visions, which symbolize the loftiest ideals of his age, Dante presents a black picture of the age itself, saying in effect that it was spiritually bankrupt.

Altogether, this supreme synthesis was like *The Magic Mountain* of Thomas Mann, a product of actual disunity. What Dante reveals is not a serene faith but an intense yearning, not an achieved harmony but a magnificent effort at harmony. More strictly, the end was not harmony or consistency—it was entirety, infinitude. The final key to the Middle Ages is the Faustian spirit—the insatiable, inextinguishable wilfulness that distinguishes Western civilization from all others.

Hence medieval men built dangerously, with a passion for the vertical and the transcendent, and with little of the reasonableness and orderliness of the Greeks, or the mere massiveness and solidity of the Romans. Their Gothic cathedrals did not rest on the earth with calm dignity, or neatly enclose a dignified volume of space, but soared into the above and beyond, merged with infinite space—a restless, asymmetrical flight of vaults and spires sustained by the thrust of flying buttresses, with containing walls that were structurally unnecessary and served chiefly as great windows on space; and the early builders vied in throwing up even higher towers, to the greater glory of God and the discomfiture of rival towns. Their boundless love for God, whose love was in turn infinite, gave them visions of infinite perfection, and also a terrifying sense of universal, absolute imperfection; knowing the ultimate in ecstasy and despair, they neglected the ordinary possibilities of resignation and consolation, the ordinary effort to promote social welfare; and in their passionate wilfulness, and their surrender to an Almighty Will, they brooded over such insoluble problems as free will, which had troubled neither Greeks nor Hebrews. For earthly love they set up equally exorbitant standards. Their poets introduced a new theme, stressing not so much the fulfilment or frustration of love as desire itself—a passion impossible to satisfy, for which men gave up all. They forever demanded the absolute, in love, truth, power, or joy; so they could never really lose themselves in God or find themselves on earth.

In the Middle Ages this Faustian spirit had to operate in a finite, classical world that had been stigmatized by Christian tradition. It therefore led to the extremes of asceticism and profligacy, the madness in piety and impiety alike. But it finally burst through all the antique fictions. 'We have come to the last age of the world,' wrote Dante, who believed that the world was very old—five thousand years old, indeed; like all medieval men he conceived a static, finished world, without significant growth or change, without hope except for the after-life; and he symbolizes the dynamism of this last age, the tremendous energy, passion, and will that were to make over the entire world.

3. THE MEDIEVAL LEGACY

Offhand, even the enduring achievements of medieval men are melancholy reminders of their lost cause. Their cathedrals give Europe its most hallowed charm and dignity but are ghostly in their silence, forlorn in their isolation from the civil life that once swirled through and about them. (A medieval ghost might be more horrified by the tourists strolling their aisles with guidebooks than he was by the lovers who made them a trysting-ground, or the students who played dice on their altars.) Their great universities—one of the most original of their unconscious creations—remain centers of learning, but of a heretical, worldly kind of learning; their 'cleric' has dwindled into clerk. Their aristocratic ideals of romantic love have become the stock in trade of a vast, vulgar industry, cheap entertainment for the masses they disdained. Offhand, their descendants have made a mockery of all their grandiose aspirations. We might only hope that they sleep well after the fitful fever of their lives; for they grew more despairing as their age waned, and they would hardly be proud of the civilization they sired.

Yet we may be proud of them. We owe our being to their restless striving, their eagerness to experiment and adventure—in particular to the ardor for learning, beauty, and fullness of life that made the twelfth century a profounder, more wonderful renaissance than the official Renaissance. Because we have gone on to build a vastly different world we may forget our kinship, and because we are now prone to their despair we may be seduced by the fond legends of their humble piety; but we owe them something better than sentimental fondness. In a time of confused aims, and much mean endeavor, we may profit by recalling the reality of their idealism, the power of their belief in things unseen. We may escape the easy cynicism that denies such realities, and thereby strengthens the power of unprincipled business and political leaders.

For all its corruptions, Christianity in the Middle Ages was never a mere opium for the masses. It was a truly spiritual force, among the most powerful that have made history. It was the mainspring of the great revival that enabled the barbarians of the West to surge ahead of proud Byzantium. The Gothic cathedrals alone testify to a religious exaltation that has never been surpassed, even in the intensely religious East. Secular life was also enveloped in this exaltation, always colored by it, at times fired by it. The very corruptions intensified the spirituality, for they stirred constant indignation, reawakened conscience, and led men back to purer versions of the Christian ideal. And perhaps the purest was actually realized by St. Francis and his band of brothers, at the turn of the thirteenth century. A century later St. Francis might have been burned at the stake as a heretic, because of his sublime disregard of dogma; but at this moment, which may be considered the apex of the Middle Ages or of Christianity itself, medieval man was able to find the perfect expression for his simple absoluteness, and in the midst of corruption to realize his impossible idealism. The message of St. Francis was pure love and joy—a continuous, radiant spiritual gladness born of a real love for all earthly creatures and things, and an utter indifference to all earthly cares and pains.[6] He forgave God and man for everything, except only the pride of the schoolmen.

St. Francis is not the complete Christian, since he cared nothing for reason, knowledge, and the whole classical heritage. At the same time, he knew nothing of Gregory the Great's terrible fears of the world, the flesh, and the Devil. He could achieve his kind of perfection because by this

---

[6] Once when his clothes were on fire and a comrade ran to put it out he cried, 'Don't, my dearest brother, don't hurt the fire!' Toward the end of his life, when his physician cauterized his face for some neuralgic pain, he ventured to ask for a slight return: 'My brother, fire, noblest and usefulest of creatures, be gentle to me now, because I have loved and will love you with the love of Him who created love.' And at the very end, as Henry Adams observed, he became aware that in his all-embracing love he had overlooked one thing, which was death itself; so on his deathbed he added his gratitude for 'our sister death.'

time medieval men had sufficiently mastered their heritage to take liberties with it. While they retained Gregory's legacy —even elaborating upon it with Germanic and Celtic superstitions, introducing new hordes of gnomes, goblins, witches, and werewolves to a demon-infested world—they also made it over in their own image. To the cult of the Devil they added the complementary cult of the Virgin. To Roman order they brought Germanic ardor and lust for life. They reclaimed patristic Christianity emotionally and imaginatively, through grand symbolism, making poetry of its dogma, realizing in their cathedrals the community of God and man that they so painfully sought to demonstrate in their theology. Their art is the token of their supreme achievement, which was to humanize Christianity. In various ways they approached a religious ideal that could satisfy the whole man, making him at home in both the natural and the social world, fulfilling his needs for truth, beauty, and goodness. If this Christian humanism cannot be called the essence of the medieval spirit, which was always prey to a gross worldliness and a neurasthenic other-worldliness, it was at least a real element of this spirit. For us, I think, it is the most valuable element of the medieval legacy.

An obvious example is the ideal of universality. Although it was a narrower ideal than that of the Roman Stoics, embracing only the true believers, it was less provincial than the patriotic ideal that superseded it. Medieval men tended to regard themselves first of all as Christians; they had their share of local pride and jealousy but relatively little of the violent national prejudice that now splits the West. They were at least free from racial prejudice, persecuting men for their beliefs rather than the color of their skin. The deplorable intolerance they bequeathed was less irrational than modern forms.

No less pertinent is medieval economic theory. As Christians, they naturally considered business a subordinate means to the serious business of the good life, and naturally sought to bring it under the rule of Christian morality. St. Thomas Aquinas, among others, worked out their cardinal principle of the 'just price': instead of charging whatever the market will bear, and thereby taking advantage of the needs of fellow-Christians, producers and merchants should charge just enough to cover the costs of their labor. (As R. H. Tawney points out, 'the last of the Schoolmen was Karl Marx'; for they provided the basis of his labor theory of value.) Later thinkers made the just price more elastic, recognizing the complex variables that affect value, but they still agreed that prices could never be left to the discretion of the seller, since this would simply encourage extortion. They also agreed that speculation, or buying and selling for gain, was an unpardonable sin. They even continued to condemn interest on loans: to extract a guaranteed pound of flesh, without labor of one's own, was contrary to nature, Aristotle, and God. In all this the schoolmen were hopelessly impractical, and seem more so because their theory was so contrary to medieval practice, especially the practice of the papacy. They were naïve enough to believe that business morality might be secured by the mere formulation of sound moral principles. But they were never so naïve as to believe that morality would be promoted, and the good society achieved, by glorifying the profit motive. 'If it is proper to insist on the prevalence of avarice and greed in high places,' Tawney concludes, 'it is not less important to observe that men called these vices by their right names, and had not learned to persuade themselves that greed was enterprise and avarice economy.' [7]

Political theory was less humane. While it proclaimed the high duties of rulers, it provided little freedom for the ruled and little protection against misrule; and St. Thomas himself justified the institution of serfdom on economic grounds. Nevertheless medieval culture contained the seeds of democracy. They flowered briefly in the Italian city-states, fertilizing the soil of the Renaissance; they produced such enduring growths as the common law and parliamentary institutions of England. The Church, moreover, offered a high career that was open to the lowliest men—at least half of the medieval popes were humbly born. And both clerics and nobles kept pronouncing a stereotyped principle of equality: a highly theoretical equality which they made no effort to realize in social life, and which amounted to little more than the melancholy sentiment that all men are equal before death, but which some common men took seriously. Medieval peasants began to claim rights that the peasants of Byzantium hardly conceived. 'At the beginning we were all created equal,' proclaimed John Ball; 'it is the tyranny of perverse men which has caused slavery to arise, in spite of God's law.' Ball was properly hanged, drawn, and quartered, but the authorities could not kill his dream of 'equal liberty, equal greatness, equal power.'

Even the celebrated religious achievements of the Middle

[7] Some respectable types in modern America may find themselves in the lowest circles of Dante's hell. He regarded sins of fraud as worse than sins of violence because they were deliberate and cold-blooded, sins against the mind and soul of man; so he reserved his more horrible punishments for flatterers, seducers, fortune-tellers, hypocrites, evil counselors, et cetera. This company—somewhere below the murderers —would now be swelled by advertisers and publicity men.

Ages have a humanistic significance that conventional piety has obscured. Art was a far more vital force than it is today because it was not fine art. Gothic art was essentially a folk creation, springing from the common people, expressing a common aspiration and joy in creation; it was not monopolized by an elite. (Hence it seemed 'barbarous' to a later age, which set up aristocratic canons of taste and moved art from the workshop to the salon, studio, lecture hall, and finally the museum.) From the outset it broke away from the rigid formalism of Byzantine sacred art, and its progress was toward freedom, exuberance, and naturalism. Sculpture gradually overcame the orthodox suspicion of the evil body; painting took to a realistic treatment of religious subjects. The work of Giotto, the first great painter, expressed a frank pleasure in the flesh and natural world, and amounted to an open repudiation of asceticism and spiritual abstraction. The more exuberant humanism of the Renaissance was a continuation of the medieval trend, not a sudden rebellion.

Similarly with medieval theology. While its immediate aim was to establish orthodoxy, and its most apparent accomplishment was the official theology of the Roman Catholic Church, its inspiration was a faith in human reason, and its most significant accomplishment was its contribution to the whole adventure of thought. In spite of themselves, the schoolmen established the value of doubt and even of heresy.

One reason why the Dark Ages were dark was that there was no thought worthy of the name of heresy.[8] With the first glimmerings of light men began to question Gregory the Great's legacy of blind faith. As early as the tenth century Berengar rebelled against authority in the name of reason. (Disunity, one might say, was the first sign of the famed medieval unity.) Then St. Anselm proclaimed his motto, 'I believe in order to understand,' and made a new effort to understand, producing his noted ontological argument for the existence of God. Peter Abelard was much bolder, maintaining that one can believe only what he understands, and that it is ridiculous to preach to others what one does not understand. With Abelard the renaissance of the twelfth century came into full swing. He discovered that the Church Fathers were not infallible guides, listing in his *Sic et Non* some hundred and fifty propositions on which they flatly contradicted

---

[8] The striking exception is John Scotus Erigena in the ninth century —one of the rare isolated geniuses in the history of culture. While recognizing the authority of the Bible, Erigena held that reason was its source and did not need its support: 'true religion is true philosophy.' His declaration of independence had little influence at the time, however; and when his true philosophy caught the attention of the Church several centuries later, he was condemned as a heretic.

one another. He was nevertheless confident that the true faith was perfectly reasonable, and therefore believed in the positive value of doubt; he thought that even heretics should be reasoned with instead of tortured. Above all, he had a passion for knowledge, insisting that all knowledge was good. He accordingly fell a victim to the pious obscurantism of St. Bernard, the still more impassioned champion of orthodoxy. As a saintly skeptic, Bernard was less horrified by Abelard's specific heresies than by his general assumption that sacred truths should not be accepted unless they are comprehensible; and he got Abelard officially condemned and disgraced. Yet the future belonged to his victim.

Students had flocked to Paris from all over Europe to listen to Abelard. He had much to do with the rise of the University of Paris, which became the great center of theology. Before long the spiritual progeny of Abelard were poring over Aristotle, who had been discovered through the translations of heathen Arabs and Jews. Inflamed by his passion for knowledge, they persisted in studying Aristotle even though ecclesiastical authorities had properly condemned his philosophy as heretical. The triumph of Abelard was sealed when Thomas Aquinas came to the University of Paris. St. Thomas carried to a magnificent conclusion his effort to substitute rational principles for mere appeal to historic authority. Although he acknowledged that certain revealed truths, such as the existence of angels, could not have been discovered by reason, he never wavered in his insistence upon making God as rational as he himself was.

St. Thomas began the hard way, with the dangerous admission that the truth of Christianity or even the existence of God cannot be taken for granted—it seemed self-evident only because of custom. He supplemented the Platonic intuition inherited by Christian theology with the empirical principle of Aristotle. 'The origin of our knowledge is in sense,' he stated, 'even of those things that are above sense.' He therefore opposed the teaching of St. Augustine that knowledge of the natural world is unimportant, or that Scripture tells us all we need to know about it. 'The truth of our faith,' he declared, 'becomes a matter of ridicule among the infidels if any Catholic, not gifted with the necessary scientific learning, presents as a dogma what scientific scrutiny shows to be false.' False ideas about God's handiwork would naturally lead to false conclusions about God himself. Believing that Aristotle's philosophy contained the essential truth about the natural world, St. Thomas made his bold effort to reconcile it with Christianity. He capped his work by an extraordinarily patient, thorough application of the method of Abelard. In his

Summa Theologiae, designed for 'beginners,' he stated honestly some ten thousand 'Objections' to Christian doctrine, and as honestly tried to meet them.

For his own age, in short, Thomas Aquinas was a modernist, or even a radical. Shortly after his death the archbishops of Paris and Canterbury formally condemned his heretical 'materialism'; and it took his Dominican order fifty years of politics to get him canonized. It is this radical spirit that gives enduring significance to his system. The system was indeed a marvelous synthesis of 'science and sanctity,' wrought with remarkable zest, patience, and acumen, unsurpassed in the history of thought for its combination of imaginative breadth, intellectual rigor, and loving care in detail; but its equilibrium was even more delicate and precarious than that of the Gothic cathedrals. Later schoolmen pointed out basic inconsistencies, and with the rise of science the whole foundation of the elaborate structure was undermined. Today the philosophy of Aquinas is a kind of historical curiosity for most of those outside the Catholic Church and the University of Chicago; and most ordinary Catholics, if they tried to read him, would likely find much of his thought unintelligible or irrelevant. Yet there is nothing curious or irrelevant about his essential faith—his grand conviction that the true faith could and should embrace all knowledge, all truth from all sources.

Hence the real curiosity—the tragic irony—is that the revolutionary philosophy of St. Thomas Aquinas has become the very symbol and stronghold of conservatism. When the pioneers of science, still informed by a pious spirit, made revolutionary discoveries about God's handiwork, one might have expected the Church of Aquinas to welcome this natural knowledge, or at least to avoid the ridicule of infidels by revising dogmas that 'scientific scrutiny shows to be false.' Instead, it chose to stand on the dogmas. Though it lost the historic battle that ensued, it continued to betray the spirit of Aquinas by stubbornly resisting the new knowledge. And even more demoralizing than the endless conflict was the deepening confusion. Philosophy, science, and religion, which Aquinas had united, now broke apart and went their separate ways, to produce the hodgepodge of thought and feeling that constitutes the state of mind of most literate Christians today. All in all, the boldness and the integrity of St. Thomas Aquinas provide a melancholy prespective on contemporary Christianity. The orthodox flatly reject the 'higher criticism,' refusing to permit any rational criticism of the Canon that is the basis of their faith. The liberals suffer from the lack of any consistent philosophy, smuggling in traditional beliefs they wish to preserve by talking of symbolism, but evading the intellectual import duties on their symbols. The modern clergyman, lamented the Reverend Kirsopp Lake, is apt to have 'a lower standard of intellectual honesty than would be tolerated in any other profession.'

4. THE FAILURE OF THE MEDIEVAL IDEAL

According to Henry Adams, the Virgin was bankrupt by 1300: the precarious structure of medieval faith had collapsed, and the ideal unity was no more. According to Toynbee, the religious wars of the sixteenth century signaled the breakdown of Western Christendom, though he also stresses the spiritual debacle of the papacy in the thirteenth century. Catholic historians usually minimize this debacle and picture the Reformation as the great tragedy, attributing it to the greed of princes, the pride of heretics, or simple perversity; Hilaire Belloc went so far as to say that 'the breakdown of our civilization in the sixteenth century . . . was an *accident.*' Protestants naturally deny this apparent lapse of Divine Providence, and tend to view the Reformation as a great liberation. My own liberal, humanistic bias would lead me to stress the good that came out of the breakdown of feudalism and absolutism. Yet this good was also implicit in the Middle Ages—the breakdown was not sudden or accidental. The more impartial of modern historians picture Western history from the dawn of the Middle Ages through the Reformation as a drama that had logic and continuity but no definite climax or curtain fall, and that was neither pure tragedy nor simple success story. The issues of this drama are still live, open, and ambiguous.

Now, the chief disruptive force in the medieval world was quite unconscious. Medieval writers commonly divided society into those who work, those who guard, and those who pray, omitting merchants and townsmen; but it was these men without status—an anonymous 'middle' class—who made over the whole society. They developed the money economy that undermined the feudal system, helping the peasants to emerge from serfdom and the kings to dominate the barons. Just why they proved so much more enterprising than their bourgeois forebears in the Greco-Roman world, or in any other civilization, Marxist theory does not explain. At least they did not embark on a conscious class war against those who guarded and those who prayed; generally they were medieval enough to revere the ideal fictions, and bourgeois enough to be content with their material gains. But the fact remains that they were the most vigorous, resourceful class, and therefore rose to power. While the nobility played at tournaments, the bourgeoisie played the leading role in the great historic events that secularized and then revolutionized Western civilization—such key events as the invention of printing, the discovery of America, the Reformation, the rise of science, the growth of republicanism, and the Industrial Revolution.

In general, the rise of a bourgeois, urban civilization—at first commercial, then industrial, and then increasingly nationalistic and imperialistic—is doubtless the major theme of Western history, and the locus of our major problems. We may accordingly note that medieval Catholicism contributed to the continuity of this story. Sombart thought that the great working order of the Benedictines laid the foundations of capitalistic enterprise by dignifying work and instituted the fixed, orderly, punctual life, which now seems very natural even though men naturally rebel against it. Their rule—practiced in forty thousand monasteries—exemplified the bourgeois ideal of being 'as regular as clock-work.' (The mechanical clock itself was a medieval invention.) Later churchmen contributed more directly to the development of finance, since the Church was by far the greatest financial enterprise of the age. Few have heard of Fra Luca Pacioli, the inventor of double-entry bookkeeping; but he has probably had much more influence on human life than has Dante or Michelangelo.

For our philosophical purposes, however, the rise of the bourgeois is not the main issue of the Middle Ages. If economic forces make history, non-economic motives make it significant; and such motives created the unique glory of the medieval renaissance. They made its history a religious drama. The main theme of this drama was the effort to establish a Christian society, united by a catholic faith. The failure of this effort was genuinely tragic, since it was an ideal effort on a grand scale. But out of reverence for human idealism we again need to view the tragedy with some ironic reserve, aware that the grand effort was born in conflict with Eastern Christendom, that it was nourished by ignorance and illusion, that all along it involved radical contradictions, and that it never achieved real harmony or peace.

Since we are cursed by self-consciousness, and are prone to think how happy is a people without a history or a sociology, we might begin by recalling the perils of innocence. 'Every sin arises from a kind of ignorance,' wrote St. Thomas Aquinas. 'A man's will is secure from sinning only when his understanding is secured from ignorance and error.' This alone might serve as the epitaph of the Middle Ages. The ignorance that made possible such gross frauds as the Donation of Constantine and the False Decretals was most conspicuous in the gross superstitions that so often reduced medieval piety to black magic. An ignorance of natural science strengthened the popular fears of devils and witches and the popular hopes of saints and relics, obscuring the natural conditions of good and evil as well as inviting the natural calamities of famine and plague. An ignorance of history blinded men to the political realities masked by their fictions, giving them no perspective on their problems and their possibilities. And all such ignorance was made more dangerous by the absence of a saving skepticism or critical sense. Bold and imaginative, the medieval mind was remarkably hasty in generalization, feeble in judgment, and careless of consequences. It reduced all complexities to simple forms and concrete images, in an habitual indifference to concrete policy or result. So the kings and great warriors set out on Crusades, in high spirits, and without foresight or strategic plan; the sublime St. Louis of France alone led two expeditions that were unparalleled in their folly and futility; and so the Crusades to drive the Turks out of the Holy Land ended with the Turks camped in the heart of Europe.

The schoolmen were essentially as uncritical in their intellectual industry. Amazingly subtle and pertinacious, they never questioned the literal truth of the Scriptures on which their whole industry was based; brilliantly they employed a deductive logic that permitted no fresh discovery and provided no safeguards against fundamental error. Thought was never really free. Hence the brave adventure of medieval theology was doomed to sterility. Its ultimate aim was to demonstrate the truths that were already known, and its progress was the discovery that these truths involved rationally insoluble problems. Once the ardor and daring curiosity of the twelfth century had staled, the schoolmen settled down to endless dispute over the choice of horns in dilemmas.[9] The very triumph of Aquinas was the beginning of the end. As his 'heresy' became dogma, the schoolmen were attacking its inconsistencies, vindicating the warning of St. Bonaventure that Aristotelian philosophy was incompatible with patristic Chris-

---

[9] The famous example is the controversy over realism and nominalism. Nominalism is fatal to orthodoxy; the doctrine that only particulars are real inevitably leads to materialism and skepticism. But the preferred doctrine of realism, or the reality of universals, also leads to impossible conclusions. It threatens the individual immortality that Christians demand, and when pressed it logically ends in pantheism, which the Church abhors.

tianity. William of Occam proclaimed the bankruptcy of the whole enterprise by showing that reason could not prove the truth of the fundamental dogmas of Christianity, and by restoring these dogmas to the realm of pure faith. His Averroist principle of 'double truth,' with separate standards for revealed theology and rational philosophy, was intended to harmonize natural knowledge and Christian faith; but in effect it meant a fatal split, which was widened by the growth of science.

Inasmuch as prominent educators are saying that medieval philosophy is what our universities need, students of the liberal arts might note that it was not very liberal. The schoolmen incidentally certified considerable ugly doctrine, such as the conclusion of St. Thomas that the blessed spirits in heaven are granted a perfect view of the torments of the damned, in order that 'nothing may be wanting to their felicity.' They were always liable to harshness because of their indifference to the concrete and the individual, in the throes of a logic drunk on verbalism and abstraction. More specifically, they tended to scorn the natural world, as intrinsically worthless, and thereby to mechanize or dehumanize nature as effectually as science at its worst; we may say that Christian asceticism prepared the way for atheistic materialism. (One reason for the scandalous vices of medieval students is that they had no authorized, respectable amusements; the universities were disposed to punish sport more than crime.) Even the arts had no place in medieval education—they were included among Aristotle's 'mechanical arts.' Essentially this education was as illiberal as that provided by technological colleges today, and for the same 'practical' reason. Rashdall pointed out that it taught men to think and to work rather than to enjoy, 'while it left uncultivated the imagination, the taste, the sense of beauty—in a word, all the amenities and refinements of the civilized intellect.'

If such illiberality is not fatal in itself, it contributed to the extreme social inequality that obviously worked to disrupt Christian unity. Inequality has a natural charm for pure logicians, as the apparent means to order, structure, system. In our disorderly world today writers are again praising feudalism as 'the Christian social system,' or even the most 'truly democratic,' dwelling on its ideal of a proper reverence for rightful superiors, who in turn would respect their rightful obligations to their dependents. Inequality brings inevitable abuses, however, and in the Middle Ages such abuses were flagrant. If the misery of the serfs has been commonly exaggerated, their life was plainly hard and often wretched; whenever they had a chance they tried to escape from this

Christian social system, showing a preference for the Christian principle of equality. The ruling nobility and clergy always enjoyed exceptional privileges, and by the record often enjoyed them much more than their duties. While the Christian spirit provoked considerable indignation, the uncritical medieval mentality made it generally ineffectual. There was no organized effort at fundamental reform. Resistance to tyranny was justified in theory but given no institutional or constitutional means. The laws on the books, which enabled a thirteenth-century Abbot of Burton to boast that his serfs legally possessed 'nothing but their bellies,' provided cruel punishments for recalcitrant serfs.

Such cruelty may always be attributed to 'the times.' It remains cruelty, however; if 'the times' make men what they are, they are also made by men; and in any event these were religious times, when Christianity was at the peak of its power. They force the question of the quality of medieval religion.

Huizinga and others have noted how Christianity was cheapened simply because it was made an integral part of daily life, introduced into all activities. As the commonplace was made holier, the holy became commonplace. Spirituality was diluted by a ceaseless multiplication of rites and symbols, and adulterated by a vulgar materialism, such as the faith in the wonder-working powers of saints' bones.[10] After the early flush of exaltation, what united medieval Christendom was not so much a glowing faith as an acquiescence in common superstition. And morality in particular suffered from the superabundance of external forms. Although salvation could be earned by good works, it might be secured in spite of bad works through sacraments or the intercession of saints. The humane system of penance, which freed the ordinary mortal from the obligation of suppressing all the desires of his corrupt flesh, was obviously liable to exploitation; and by the late Middle Ages it begot a contractual system of indulgences—a kind of credit system, with bargain rates fixed in advance, that dovetailed into the mercantile scheme of the period. Pope Clement VI made explicit the theory of the 'treasury'—an inexhaustible treasury of merits accumulated by the saints, Mary, and Christ; from this the Church could dispense indulgences in return for worldly treasures, without need of replenishing its spiritual capital or balancing its

[10] Thomas Aquinas was one victim of this faith in corporeal relics, to which he gave qualified approval. When he died in a foreign monastery, the monks decapitated him and boiled his body, so as to preserve its precious store of potential relics. This whole cult became so degraded that the saints quickly folded up under the attacks of Protestant reformers, though witches and demons retained their vitality.

spiritual budget. Especially in Italy, salvation was put on a sound paying basis. A real estate boom in Purgatory was among the boldest, most original of late medieval enterprises.

Although many churchmen were alarmed by these excesses, the authoritative Church tolerated or even encouraged them; so we are brought to its central role in the drama. The Church had claimed and assumed the leadership of the medieval world, providing both the inspiration and the discipline for the experiment of a Christian society. Ultimately the failure of this experiment was due to the failure of this leadership. The Church was simply not up to the earthly role it had assumed. Its claims to the power and perfection of a supernatural society make its history the most striking example of the tragic incongruities that mark all human history, and the most somber witness to the tragic truth that the best may become the worst.[11]

The basic logic of the story is simple enough. In order to represent effectively a 'kingdom not of this world,' the Church became an immense worldly kingdom, with a far more elaborate organization and more extensive properties than any other medieval kingdom. Like all big institutions, it had to devote much of its time and energy to routine matters of organization and finance; most of the ecclesiastical records and correspondence of the period concern the administration of its vast holdings. To justify its wealth it had to compromise with pure Christian ideals, formally condemning as heresy such traditional beliefs as that Christ and the Apostles possessed no property. (One proof it used was Christ's command to Peter—'Put away thy sword'; *thy* indicated that an Apostle owned at lease a sword.) Insensibly,

---

[11] Jacques Maritain has restated the Augustinian distinction between the True Church, which is incorruptible, and the historic Church, which he grants was guilty of 'certain excesses' or 'impurities arising from the spirit of this world.' He insists that the True Church was not involved in these excesses, for it 'has never been bound up with or into any temporal regime whatsoever.' This Platonic conception of the Church is strictly unarguable, since one can neither prove nor disprove the reality of the perfect Idea. One difficulty, however, is that Maritain provides no clear criterion for distinguishing between the two Churches, or recognizing the momentous blunders that in retrospect may be palmed off on the historic Church; whereas the Papacy always speaks as the voice of the True Church, and a Catholic is still liable to excommunication for disobeying its decrees. Meanwhile a student of history is perforce concerned with the historic Church, even though he respects the pure ideal—just as he must consider the actualities of American and Russian history, not merely the pure ideals of democracy and communism. From the record of the medieval Church he might not be able to deduce the existence of the True Church, but assuming its existence he must also assume some connection between the two Churches, suspecting that the pure ideal may sometimes encourage unideal behavior.

the economic activities of the Church led to further compromises with the ideal economic theory of the schoolmen. The popes often had need of money-lenders, whom Innocent IV designated 'the peculiar sons of the Roman Church'; wealthy monasteries took to banking and became capitalists. Corruption naturally set in, in an age of rampant greed, and it naturally centered in Rome, the seat of the big money. The papal court became the symbol of avarice; all over Europe the cry went up that in Rome everything was for sale. By the end of the fourteenth century the sale of ecclesiastical offices was in fact routine. All the scandalous abuses that have been attributed to the worldliness of the Renaissance developed during the Middle Ages.

The tragedy here was not that the Christian spirit was smothered but that it sought refuge outside the Church, or flamed most brightly in opposition to it. Christian zeal led to schism, which in turn led to worse abuses of worldly power. The Church granted considerable latitude to the schoolmen, who were an academic class without popular following, and it was tolerant of popular superstition; but it had always warred on any heresy that threatened its own power. Now it found its great enemy not in unbelievers—there were as yet few of these—but in simple, earnest men, such as the Waldenses and Lollards, who took seriously the simpler ideals of Christ and the Apostles. In fighting to stamp out these heretics it also fought to keep the Bible out of the hands of the people, forbidding its translation into the vernacular. The clergy had some reason to feel outraged because 'the evangelical pearls have been scattered abroad and trampled by the swine'—ignorant people can get strange ideas from the Bible. Still, the Church had made little effort to educate or uplift the swine, and its educational method now was not reasonable persuasion but invective, calumny, and persecution.

Specifically, it developed the most notorious of medieval institutions, the Inquisition. Monsignor Fulton Sheen reminds us of the logic and even the idealism of this institution, which 'burned the thought in order to save society.' One might add that such policies are not necessarily futile: for centuries the Church did succeed in stamping out heresies. (It exterminated the Albigenses so effectually that scholars are still uncertain about the articles of their heresy.) Nevertheless a society that could be saved only by such extreme measures, which other religions have not found necessary, must have lacked a truly catholic faith. The Inquisition is more significant because it was not the invention of a fanatic but a gradual development, responding to a problem of heresy that had become too extensive to be handled by local authorities, and that required a set of officials who could give their whole time to the job. And the apologists for the Inquisition are obviously troubled by the tortures and burnings, which were of the flesh as well as the thought.[12] As obviously, the Church suffered from its police methods. It weakened its claims as a 'perfect society,' antagonizing when not extinguishing the spirit that might have made it more nearly perfect. It violated the great human attributes of Freedom and Dignity, which according to Jacques Maritain were the glory of the Middle Ages. Where it succeeded, as in Spain and in Italy after the Renaissance, it also succeeded in smothering the national genius that had produced their golden ages. The future belonged to the countries where it failed. The apparent lesson of the Inquisition is that insistence on uniformity of belief is fatal to intellectual, moral, and spiritual health.

The lesson is still plainer, finally, in the Church's bid for political supremacy; for here it indisputably suffered a crushing defeat. At the outset the German emperors put the drama on a high plane by their efforts to purify a degenerate papacy. Under the great Hildebrand, who became Gregory VII, the papacy rose to this spiritual challenge. Gregory asserted its dignity by attacking the institution of simony and denying the right of feudal lords to appoint abbots and bishops. In thus starting the fierce struggle over investiture, which disrupted medieval unity in the eleventh century, Gregory was at least fighting for a principle that the Western world has learned to regard as precious—the principle that spiritual interests should be beyond the control of the State. He went considerably farther, however. Whereas the ideal had been a perfect union of Church and State, he was convinced that one or the other must be master, and naturally chose the Church: he asserted that the Pope had the right to depose emperors, and was 'to be judged by no one.' Gregory succeeded in humiliating the Emperor Henry IV, who resisted his claims. But it was a costly victory. He succeeded by political as well as spiritual force, having enlisted the aid of

---

[12] The *Catholic Encyclopedia* explains that 'moderns experience difficulty in understanding this institution' for two major reasons: 'they have ceased to grasp religious belief as something objective, as the gift of God and therefore outside the realm of free private judgment,' and 'they no longer see in the Church a society perfect and sovereign,' whose primary duty is to keep unsullied the authentic gift of God. The author does not argue, however, for the restoration of the institution, much less its methods. Instead he adds the apologetic explanation (rather lame to one acquainted with other religions) that 'a kind of iron law would seem to dispose mankind to religious intolerance.'

rival princes. It was prophetic that he himself died a prisoner and exile; for his career was the prologue to a perfect Greek tragedy.

The drama unfolded with remorseless logic. In making good Gregory's claims to supreme spiritual power, his successors became increasingly ambitious for secular power, and by the thirteenth century were locked in a life-and-death struggle with the emperors. The papacy reached both its spiritual and its temporal zenith under the illustrious Innocent III. 'The Lord entrusted to Peter not only the universal Church,' he proclaimed, 'but the government of the whole world'; he invested the Pope with the new title of Vicar of Christ, instead of merely Vicar of Peter; while sending out the Fourth Crusade that pillaged Constantinople he also called for a crusade against the Holy Roman Emperor; and like a hero in Greek tragedy he vowed the destruction of not only Frederick II but his children. His vow was later fulfilled: the defeat of the emperors was sealed by the murder of Frederick's grandson Conradin, which was approved if not instigated by Pope Clement. The real victors, however, were the French princes whom the popes had called in for aid. At the end of the century the wheel came full circle. 'We declare, we affirm, we define and pronounce that to be subject to the Roman pontiff is altogether necessary to salvation for every human creature,' Boniface VIII declared, affirmed, et cetera in the bull *Unam Sanctam;* and having given complete expression to the theory implicit in Gregory VII, he was seized and manhandled in his own villa by the French king. Following this humiliation came the 'Babylonian captivity,' during which the popes chose to hold court in France instead of Rome, and spent much of their declining spiritual capital in luxurious living. Their eventual return to Rome led to the ultimate degradation of the Great Schism, when the Italians elected one pope and the French another. For forty years the rival popes exchanged anathemas and excommunications, competing in the sale of indulgences and offices to support their wars on each other.[13] The councils of churchmen that finally succeeded in electing a Roman pope acceptable to all represented a movement toward a kind of constitutional, parliamentary church government, which might have restrained the abuses of papal power; but the restored

[13] Among the grotesque scenes of this period is a conference described by Michelet, involving the Emperor Wenceslas, the King of France, and one of the popes. The Emperor was a confirmed drunkard who could do no business except early in the morning; the King was a lunatic who approached sense only late in the afternoon, after he had eaten and drunk; and the Pope was at any time of day the least reasonable, so far as his own interests were concerned.

papacy was obdurate, clung to its autocratic power, continued in its irresponsible ways, and so brought on itself the final disaster of the Reformation.

The Roman Church must be of divine origin, remarked a character in Boccaccio, to be able to stand the kind of government it has had. Whatever God's purposes, it appears that for ordinary human purposes a priestly autocracy is no better than the secular varieties, and that it is apt to be much worse for the highest spiritual purposes. One reason why the Church failed to dominate the State is that it had so little to offer the State. In battling the emperors it fought for its own rights, not the rights of their subjects; still blind to the revolutionary implications of the Sermon on the Mount, it brought to the problem of government virtually no new ideas, social, legal, or political. But the ultimate moral of the medieval drama is a favorite medieval moral—the deadly sin of pride. Pride was the keynote of feudalism and chivalry; pride became most insolent in the medieval papacy. The noble aspiration to perfection was fatally corrupted by the claim that the Church possessed this perfection, and was an infallible judge of all aspiration. Such claims are the ultimate in human self-righteousness, the antithesis of Christian humility and charity. They only accentuate the enormous liability of man to error, and the enormous danger of dogmatic error.

The Western world may find comfort in this tragedy. It owes its distinctive fertility and creativeness to its diversity of creed and custom, and to the division of authority that weakened authoritarianism; in the face of strong independent interests, popes and kings were alike unable to make good their claims to absolute power. Had Europe achieved the relative unity of Rome, or other ancient civilizations, it probably would have become as rigid or stagnant. But Catholics may also find comfort. The True Church, Maritain insists, must never be confused with the actual one. In its overweening pride the medieval Church insisted on identifying them. Today the Church has a better chance of averting a similar tragedy because it has no real chance of making good its claims to universal sovereignty.

5. The Aftermath: Renaissance and Reformation

Life as we know it and feel it, I wrote earlier, began with the Greeks. In our own civilization it began with the Renaissance, when the rediscovery of the Greeks led to the rebirth of hope for a good life on this earth. With the Reformation

the 'protestant' spirit set out on its rebellious career by rejecting the authority of the Roman Church, and presently
the authority of the Reformers too. The seventeenth century,
the great Age of Science, created an extraordinary instrument
for fulfilling the new hopes, and further weakened the ancient
authorities. The eighteenth century, or Age of the Enlightenment, realized the intoxicating implications of this new
power; its faith in reason and in liberty led to the rise of
democracy. The nineteenth century put science to work, revolutionizing industry by a steady succession of technological
triumphs, while democracy spread all over the Western world.
This century was also the watershed of our world. It was
expected to usher in a new era of peace and justice, through
freedom and plenty—an expectation that in a logical world
would be quite reasonable. Instead it ushered in a revolutionary era of vast confusion and profound contradiction, culminating in world wars and counter-revolutions.

This story, or the story of the last century alone, is a
volume in itself, and a different kind of volume from this
one. My purpose is to offer perspectives on our society, not a
continuous, play-by-play account of its development. But this
purpose does call for some survey of the far side of the
watershed, the days of apparent innocence. The new hopes
that were born with the Renaissance are still at the heart of
our living faith, in particular the liberal faith to which this
study is dedicated. It has generally been a tender-minded
faith; today many liberals are still innocent of the elementary facts of democratic life, or else are simply shocked by
them. And so the 'tragic' view is especially apposite at this
point. Given the outcome in our century, we might suspect
that the authors of our faith are as vulnerable to ironic
contemplation as their medieval forebears. As we cherish
their contributions to the life of freedom, we had better attend to the incongruities of their familiar achievements.

Essentially, the distinctive values of the Renaissance were
the Greek values that we have already reviewed. The natural
man had been exuberant enough in the Middle Ages but
had been hidden behind the pious fictions, or portrayed only
as a sinful man. Now the humanists became conscious of his
worth, and gave much freer play to his creative powers. They
idealized both the human body and the human spirit. They
discovered new possibilities of truth, beauty, goodness, and
joy, and the further possibility of harmonizing them. They
discovered the individual, in pride rather than fear, and made
him eager to be himself. And they were the more ardent
because their humanism embraced the good earth and heaven
too. The Church itself promoted the new art and learning.

The popes began to make their worldly capital a splendid artistic image of the City of God, adorning it with the greatest religious painting and sculpture that Christendom has created. It appeared that the West might at last achieve a vital synthesis of Greek excellence and Christian piety.

In fact, however, the men typical of the Renaissance were neither good Greeks nor good Christians. Their 'classical' art was baroque, and became increasingly flamboyant and theatrical. Their learning was pedantic or merely literary; like the schoolmen, they mulled over ancient authorities. Above all, the new humanism was about as remote from social actualities as medieval other-worldliness had been. While the humanists celebrated the wisdom and virtue of the ancients, political and economic life in Italy became more brutal and sordid. While they recommended the golden mean, men remained devoted to medieval license and excess. The Renaissance produced the ideal of the courtier, the perfect gentleman so charmingly described by Castiglione, and it also produced the mercenary and condottiere, who were glorified as 'soldiers of fortune.' It was an age of treachery and devotion, brutality and civility, vice and grace, all fired by a love of gold, of beauty, of pleasure, of fame, and sometimes of God. It might be symbolized by Sigismondo Malatesta, the princely soldier of fortune who became distinguished for his ruthlessness and treachery, who maintained a brilliant court adorned by scholars and poets, and who built the famous church, consecrated to St. Francis and named after himself, where he lies in peace with his mistress, having arranged for the salvation of their souls by the purchase of perpetual masses.[14]

The basic defect of the humanists was their ignorance of their own world, or academic aloofness from it. They displayed little interest in the explorations and inventions that were enlarging and transforming the world. They were as indifferent to science, when not supercilious. They had no clear or firm philosophy—thought did not become systematic again until Descartes. And they had no social or political program. Although the humanists usually served the princes and disdained the common people, their aristocratic bias was

---

[14] Robert Browning—a poet underrated in fashionable critical circles today—wonderfully summarizes the contradictions of the Renaissance in his dramatic monologue 'The Bishop Orders His Tomb at Saint Praxed's Church.' His 'Fra Lippo Lippi,' on the other hand, summarizes the ideal faith of the age:

> This world's no blot for us,
> Nor blank—it means intensely, and means good:
> To find its meaning is my meat and drink.

a matter of temperament or custom rather than principle; they accepted the social order in essentially the spirit of Leonardo da Vinci, who said simply, 'I serve the one who pays me'—and in fact was content to serve a French king who imprisoned for life his generous Italian patron. Fundamentally, they were less honest as well as less acute than Machiavelli, whose forthright acceptance of the realities of power politics has earned him an evil reputation.

In his realism Machiavelli was also aware of the bourgeois spirit that was producing the wealth on which the Renaissance throve. The wise prince, he declared, might judiciously murder some of his subjects, 'but above all things he is to have a care of entrenching upon their estates, for men do sooner forget the death of their father than the loss of their patrimony.' (Thus Franklin D. Roosevelt became the most violently hated man in America.) Machiavelli was less aware, however, of the paradoxes that resulted from the growth of individualism and intellectual freedom. In the medieval order men had known a kind of psychological security; they took for granted all the actual insecurity of life in a vale of tears. With the disintegration of this order the self-conscious individual emerged; no longer bound to a fixed status and purpose in life, he developed a passion for wealth, power, or fame, which led to increasing restlessness, insecurity, and disorder; and presently he became the creator or the victim of new tyrannies.

On the lower levels of society men discovered that their measure of freedom entailed a loss of feudal rights and a slavery to the money market; they were free to sell their services, and free to starve if they found no buyer. The middle class found itself squeezed by its most rugged individualists, who began forming big commercial companies and monopolizing the market. All were subject to the growing power of kings, a secular instead of a theocratic absolutism. The State became the great individualist of the age. The State was an end in itself, wrote Machiavelli, subject to no law except its own interests, and required by these to keep enlarging its power at the expense of other states—it 'must progress or decline.' The growing nationalism made less sense because the new nations were as yet chiefly heterogeneous affairs, arbitrary products of conquest. (They anticipated the irony of the intense nationalism in Yugoslavia today—a nationality that was invented only in this century, and that embraces half a dozen different peoples.) And the most thoughtful men were discovering that the individual free to make his own life may be a lost and lonely man, uncertain of the meaning or purpose of his life. With the new stress on the dignity and worth of man came an increasing skepticism and pessimism about his destiny. With Rabelais came Montaigne. Finally came Hamlet—the epitome of the contradictions of the Renaissance.

Meanwhile the Reformation had brought further complications and contradictions. As 'protestants' against the central authority of the medieval world, the Reformers prepared the way for both religious and political freedom; they established a principle of individualism that was to have an epoch-making career. Their intentions, however, were very different. They were intensely medieval in spirit, obsessed with the medieval problems of sin, grace, and salvation. They were fiercely devoted to the medieval ideal of uniformity of faith and as fiercely intolerant of dissent, permitting less freedom of thought than the Church had. They revived the worst fears of the Middle Ages, of the Devil and Hell and Original Sin, and made man more utterly dependent upon the grace of an arbitrary God by blocking off the familiar avenues to divine grace, banishing the Virgin, the saints, and the father confessor, and abolishing the solemn mystery of the Mass. They left man alone to fight the Devil. They found still more sins for him to combat in the Devil's world, warning him against the possibilities of beauty and joy rediscovered by the Renaissance.

Immediately, then, the Reformation was not so much a shining new hope as a blight upon decent hopes. The incongruities of its inspired unreason and exalted inhumanity are summed up in the teaching of Martin Luther. 'The father of revolutions' would have been unspeakably horrified by the historic consequences of his revolt, and by his own reputation as a great individualist. He was an arch-conservative, seeking to restore a simple purity that had never been. He hated the authority of the Church because he was a more thoroughgoing authoritarian, who hated not only its corruption but its slackness. He worshiped the authority of a Führer God, whose first command was blind faith and obedience; while denying that Christians had to deal with God through the mediation of priests, he also denied them any claims upon God through their own good works. He condemned the whole effort to establish rational relations with God, thundering against 'that silly little fool, that Devil's bride, Dame Reason, God's worst enemy'; and by furious reasoning he defended 95 theses. For earthly purposes he set up the absolute authority of princes, as ordained by God, 'no matter how evil.' A man of the people, leading a popular movement unlike the aristocratic Renaissance, Luther delivered the peasants from the tyranny of the Church into the worse tyranny of the princes. When they rebelled, stirred by the spirit instead of the letter of his preaching, he announced that 'the brute populace must be governed by brute force,' and called upon the princes to make the civil sword 'red and bloody.' ('I, Martin Luther, have slain the peasants who died during this rebellion, for I goaded authority to the slaughter. Their blood be on my head.') As for his own country, in freeing it from the yoke of the papacy Luther achieved a kind of posthumous revenge on Gregory VII for the German emperors; but he completed Gregory's work by preparing the way for the holy wars that ended in the utter devastation of Germany.

The great virtue of the Reformation, according to Reinhold Niebuhr, was its apprehension of the basic sin of pride and self-righteousness, the ultimate tragedy of the spiritual life. It was an inevitable revolt against the pretensions of Rome to perfection on earth; the Reformers faced up to the actual enigma of human history, recognizing that it can be consummated only by the grace of God, in another life. Niebuhr acknowledges that this humility involved a profound obscurantism, a blindness to all the important shades, varieties, and relativities of human goodness and truth. The serious trouble, however, is that the behavior of the reformers and the reformed hardly looked like humility. Their bigotry suggested rather the same deadly sin of pride.[15]

In effect, the Protestant Reformers rehearsed the ultimate tragedy of the spiritual life. Their intolerance became fiercer precisely because it was illogical. They had rejected the one authority that had maintained continuity in Christendom and built up a venerable tradition; so they could salve their consciences for the bold liberties they had taken only by refusing to tolerate any further liberties with the 'true' faith to which they had returned. A compulsive righteousness cor-

---

[15] In his *Escape from Freedom*, Erich Fromm argues plausibly that the root of these excesses was the basic anxiety of the emerging individual, who no longer had a fixed place in the world, and more specifically the impotent fear and rage of the lower middle class, who were victims of the rising capitalism. Luther's doctrine of salvation by faith alone reveals a 'compulsive quest for certainty' rather than a wholesome certainty. No rational answer could satisfy his irrational feeling of helplessness. The natural answer was his ambiguous gospel of faith and fear, hope and humiliation, in which the greatest of these was not charity. (As Calvin later said, to put charity before faith and hope is 'a mere reverie of a distempered imagination.') Lacking genuine self-confidence, Luther stressed the worthlessness of man, making him utterly abject before God, depriving him of the dignity that alone could justify resistance to secular tyranny; but then he offered the ultimate in compensation, teaching that through faith man could enjoy here and now a certainty of eternal salvation—a promise that the medieval Church had never been so arrogant as to offer.

roded their apparent humility from the outset. Having denied that man could earn salvation by his own merit, Luther denied that there could be any goodness outside the Christian faith—the best works of a non-believer 'would really be impious and damnable sins'; and he rejoiced in the 'vast difference between Papists, Turks, Jews, and us who have the word.' Calvin more rigidly separated Christians themselves into the elect and the damned. His followers naturally tended to conclude that they were the elect, preordained to salvation. They acquired an inner conviction of holiness that was much more intense than the hopes inspired by the purchase of indulgences or perpetual Masses, and that encouraged a more callous attitude toward the rest of mankind, who were preordained to damnation.

This kind of opposition was unlikely to soften the temper of the Roman Church. The immediate consequences of the Reformation were the atrocious religious wars—the blackest page in Christian history. For the Roman Church, however, the tragedy went still deeper. Although it carried through its own reformation, purging itself of the grosser forms of corruption, it too reverted to the worst elements of medievalism. It narrowed and stiffened its dogma, grew more intolerant of doubt and dissent. The Council of Trent authorized the dogma that outside the Catholic Church there is no salvation, and at the same time condemned all 'inquisitive curiosity' about its dogmas: 'Faith, therefore, excludes not only all doubt, but even the desire of subjecting its truth to demonstration.' The Index was established to discourage such curiosity, and the list of forbidden books presently became a roster of the masterpieces of Europe. Mild liberals like Erasmus, who might have succeeded in humanizing the Church, were denounced as heretics. Galileo was silenced. The tragedy was that the Church became reactionary just as Europe was entering the age of the 'great renewal'; so it was committed to hostility to the major liberating and creative forces in the Western world. It lost its intellectual and cultural as well as its political and spiritual leadership. Stubbornly it refused to learn or unlearn; and in the last century, when it reached the nadir of its power and prestige, it proclaimed the dogma of Papal Infallibility.

For Protestantism, the aftermath of the Reformation was both triumph and failure, both due to its basic inconsistencies. Authoritarian in spirit, demanding absolute conformity, the Reformers were nevertheless non-conformists who had introduced a principle of spiritual independence and equality. They had started something they could not stop. Furthermore, they had to rest their whole case on the Bible, since they rejected the authority and tradition of the Catholic Church; so they opened the Bible to laymen, with quite natural but unforeseen results. 'After the Bible was translated into English,' complained Hobbes, 'every man, nay, every boy and wench that could read English, thought they spoke with God Almighty.' Protestantism splintered into innumerable sects, united chiefly by their tendency to separatism. By 1650 Thomas Edwards counted 180 sects, all based on the Bible, and almost all dogmatic and intolerant. This career was further checkered by new religious revivals, such as Methodism, which were again reversions to the more primitive elements of Christianity, and which continued to reveal the very imperfect reformation of Christian life. Altogether, the fate of Protestantism would have seemed pure tragedy to Luther and Calvin, its authors. But by the same token it was able to ally itself—in ways conscious and unconscious, direct and devious—with the forces that were making the modern world.

Hence the dogma of Protestantism has never been its forte. The early Protestants were alike in their historical ignorance of the Bible, their belief in its plain, literal truth, and their arbitrary selection and interpretation of this truth. Luther himself had a high-handed way with Holy Writ, dismissing as 'a mere letter of straw' the Epistle of James because it emphasized the necessity of good works. Servetus anticipated the serious dilemma when he pointed out that the Nicene Creed is to be found neither in the Bible nor in the Fathers; so the first reformer really to go back to the Bible was burned by the Calvinists in Geneva. When scholars later followed his lead and undertook a systematic study of the Bible, Protestantism became hopelessly confused and divided over the source of its belief and disbelief. Yet the main cause of this theological dissipation was the most important contribution of Protestantism to religious life. In spite of themselves, Luther and Calvin had asserted in effect that the Christian was a free man, spiritually subject to no human authority, responsible to God alone. Their Church was at heart a democratic community, which was not morally obligated to obey the authority they tried to impose. In time their implicit principle of spiritual freedom made clear the intellectual impossibility of achieving uniformity in belief, and the moral evil of enforcing it. This principle has kept all the varieties of Protestantism essentially non-Catholic. It made for the growth of self-respect and self-reliance, gradually transforming a blind or abject faith in God into an active faith in man. Ultimately it made an incalculable contribution to the cause of democracy.

Another momentous inconsistency was the intense wilfulness of the Protestant spirit, especially Puritanism. This is what distinguished it from the spirit both of Jesus and of the Greeks, and even from the Hebraic spirit it drew upon. While intensifying the basic illogic of Protestant theology, organized wilfulness also enabled its triumph over mere logic. Its God was a superlative Will, unfettered by logic or scruple, who had foreordained the revolt of Satan, the fall of man, the eternal damnation of most of mankind. (As the Scotch minister explained, 'You must understand that the Almighty in His public and judicial capacity is obliged to do many things that in a private and personal capacity He would be ashamed to do.') Nevertheless Protestants insisted on shouldering the full responsibility for his handiwork, dedicating their will to the greater glory of the Supreme Will. Their doctrine of predestination fortified their zeal instead of discouraging it; whether they felt more certain or less certain of salvation, the elect redoubled their effort, waging endless war on Satan, on the human enemies of God, and on the evil that he had sown so prodigally. And as they became more concerned about the business of this world they set up the compulsive gospel of work. 'There is no other period in history,' writes Erich Fromm, 'in which free men have given their energy so completely for the one purpose: work.' Hence Protestantism formed its historic alliance with the rising capitalism, the most energetic, purposeful movement of the age; and in time it became involved in still deeper contradictions.

As a child of the medieval peasant world, Luther had introduced a peasant version of the gospel of work, declaring that humble toil or even housework was 'a service of God far surpassing the holiness and asceticism of all the monks and nuns'; but he had denounced the thriving business class, which was squeezing the poor. It was John Calvin who signed the pact with this class, sanctifying its interests and values. A spokesman for the busy city world, Calvin sought to escape the shocking contradictions between medieval theory and practice in economic life by investing this life with a high seriousness, dedicating it to the service of God. He made the pursuit of wealth and preservation of property a Christian duty, calling for the same arduous discipline as the warfare against the temptations of the flesh. He exalted the acquisitive virtues of enterprise, diligence, sobriety, frugality, thrift. He invented an ideal type hitherto unknown to religion and culture, a type neither humanistic nor ascetic—the God-fearing businessman. And he made it possible for this man to gain the most in both worlds. 'Prudence and Piety were always very good friends,' a Calvinist minister later explained in *The Tradesman's Calling,* and he implied that Profit was their legitimate offspring: a successful tradesman may take it that 'God has blessed his trade.' Altogether, as Tawney has observed, Calvin did for the bourgeoisie in the sixteenth century what Marx did for the proletariat in the nineteenth: he declared their superiority to the existing social order, made them the elect of God (instead of History), and gave them heart and mind to realize their great destiny of inheriting the earth.

Calvin's ideal was an honorable one. The acquisitive virtues that he dignified are real virtues, essential to a vigorous, prosperous civilization; they produce spiritual as well as material goods. All the cant about 'service' today is apt to obscure the important services that businessmen have in fact performed. Certainly the God-fearing businessman was no fiction in early Protestant times. The best of the Puritans did fear God, laboring in his service with tremendous earnestness; they regarded their property as a moral responsibility, not a purely private possession. When their religious fervor began to cool, they still respected their obligations to their community, which perhaps needed their service more than God did. They established a tradition of philanthropy that remained strong if only because it was conventional. (Thus Andrew Carnegie devoted his last years to his immense philanthropic enterprises, proving that he took seriously his naïve 'gospel of wealth'; while the descendants of John D. Rockefeller unto the third generation are still busy giving away his fortune.) Similarly they provided the ascetic quality of business—the curious kind of selflessness that gives so terrific a drive to its supposed self-interest. The good businessman must not retire to enjoy his wealth but must keep producing the goods, die in harness; and he must not simply spend his profits but must invest them to bring further profits, so that the System may prosper. No other society has produced such willing slaves as the free enterprisers.

In general, Calvin's keynote was discipline, not freedom. He would have been scandalized by the doctrines of laissez faire that grew out of his religion of business. He himself drew up elaborate regulations for the business life of Geneva, including price and rent controls. The Puritans were as firm believers in government regulation of business, the 'regimentation' that outrages their descendants. And yet these descendants are not simply wayward or corrupt. Their gospel of economic license is also implicit in the gospel of Calvin.

'We must exhort all Christians to gain all they can and to save all they can,' repeated John Wesley two centuries later:

'that is, in effect, to grow rich.' Wesley was troubled, however, by the fruits of this exhortation: 'But as riches increase, so will pride, anger, and love of the world in all its branches. ... Is there no way to prevent this—this continual decay of pure religion?' The Protestants found no way. Their motto that God helps those that help themselves is readily twisted into the belief that one helps God by helping himself, and it has been observed that presently they began helping themselves to a lot; but at its purest, their ethical and religious program lent itself to such perversion. 'The puritan's economic moralism,' writes Ralph Barton Perry, 'has tended to deflect attention from the purpose of economic life, and to represent it as a drama of retribution, or as a school or discipline, rather than as an attempt through science and cooperation to provide an abundant and equitable satisfaction of human needs.' To them the keynote of this divine drama was Justice, not Mercy or Love; and as success in trade was a proof of God's blessing, so God came to bless all the tricks of the trade. The Protestants began by sensibly accepting the institution of interest, which is a practical necessity of finance; within a century they began accepting extortion, justifying the practice of charging all the market will bear. Property rights became sacred because men of property were godly men. Capitalism as a whole acquired its aura of sanctity because it was God's plan for society. And the wealthy tended to become more materialistic as well as self-righteous because money-making was almost the only worldly activity blessed by their gospel. As the pleasures to be bought with money were evil, they could only go on making more money.

Protestant individualism likewise contributed to the dynamic of this process. The precious ideals of individual responsibility and individual rights are among the most precarious and corruptible of ideals, tending very easily to a neglect of social obligations, ultimately to a profound irresponsibility and unrighteousness. As the individual got in the habit of standing on his own feet he naturally came to think first of his rights to freedom, and to resent any interference with his business. He grew more forgetful of social obligations because of the impersonal, amoral nature of capitalistic enterprise, with its increasing complexity and abstraction; an earnest businessman was unlikely to feel responsible for the social consequences of his private enterprise if only because he was hardly aware of them. The Protestant ethic accordingly moved away from the traditional Christian virtues. While making a notable contribution to the democratic ideal of liberty, it sacrificed both the democratic and Christian ideals of equality and fraternity.

The chief sufferers from this development, naturally, were the poor. In the Middle Ages the poor were objects of charity, however sentimental; poverty itself was sanctified by Christian tradition. In the Puritan scheme of retributive Justice, poverty was a sign of moral failure. The poor became the 'idle poor.' The spiritual fervor that once had focused on the sins of pride and greed now focused on indolence and improvidence. Presently it was discovered that the best way to keep the poor industrious and rescue them from temptation was to pay them low wages, keep them poor. A long line of ministers down to this century preached the necessity of poverty in the divine economy.[16] Protests on behalf of the poor were early denounced as incitements to 'class hatred.' Protestant theology supported a privileged class, with its division of mankind into the elect and the damned, but the pious grew more uncharitable because of their innocence of economics. Like the naïve businessman, they assumed that success or failure was due solely to the individual; they were quite unaware how extensively their society supported and endowed business. With the Industrial Revolution the state became more lavish in its favors to business but continued to deny any responsibility for unemployment, poverty, and distress. Not until the great depression did the American government fully recognize and frankly accept this responsibility.

The final outcome of the religion of business was the sharp separation of major interests that characterizes the modern world. 'There is another combination of vertues strangely mixed in every lively holy Christian,' wrote John Cotton, 'and that is, Diligence in worldly businesses, and yet deadnesse to the world; such a mystery as none can read, but they that know it.' The mixture looked stranger because the diligent businessman, like God himself, felt obliged to do things in his business capacity that he would be ashamed to do in his private, personal capacity; but insensibly the mystery was resolved. The lively Christians came to reserve their deadness to the world for the Sabbath. On weekdays they held to the doctrine that business is business—a separate

[16] An example from the last century was 'A Dissertation on the Poor Laws, by a Wellwisher of Mankind,' by the name of J. Townsend. 'It seems to be a law of nature,' wrote this wellwisher, 'that the poor should be to a certain degree improvident, so that there may always be some to fulfil the most servile, the most sordid, the most ignoble offices in the community. The stock of human happiness is thereby much increased, whilst the most delicate . . . are left at liberty without interruption to pursue those callings which are suited to their various dispositions.' He therefore complained that the Poor Law worked 'to destroy the harmony and beauty, the symmetry and order, of that system which God and nature have established in the world.'

province with its own laws, not to be confused with sentiment. Thus the God-fearing John D. Rockefeller could be utterly ruthless in building his industrial empire, driving to the wall countless little God-fearing Protestants; while Daniel Drew could build a fortune by unscrupulous speculation on the stock market, wiping out the life-savings of countless more little men, and then use his fortune to endow the Drew Theological Seminary. And as the Puritans had separated Church and State with the failure of their experiment in theocracy, so they now tried to keep the State too out of business. Likewise they divorced art and religion, business and culture—the practical and 'the finer things of life.' In general, the Protestant spirit strengthened the tendencies to dissociation in an increasingly heterogeneous society.

All this is not to say that Protestantism is the primary cause of commercialism, or of the sins of capitalism. The business spirit, with its virtues and its vices, is as old as civilization, and was vigorous during the Middle Ages. Protestantism may be considered as much the effect as the cause of the whole development. Yet unless we hold to pure economic determinism and deny religion any independent historic force, we must assume that it was a real influence. It is significant that Protestant countries generally took the lead in the expansion of commerce and industry, as in the rise of republicanism, while Catholic southern Europe remained typically agricultural, monarchical, and feudal. They built up America, sending colonists and traders to the new lands, while the Catholic countries sent soldiers and priests.

Today Protestantism is again changing its course. Although it has been split by the fundamental cleavage between Fundamentalists and Modernists, its churches are attempting to unite. Many of its leaders are active in social reform, making a new effort to Christianize economic and political life. In effect, they are re-exploring the implications of their basic principle of the spiritual dignity, freedom, and responsibility of the individual. The initial revolt against a venerable authority had induced a strong negativistic tendency—an emphasis on freedom *from* rather than freedom *for*. Protestants are now more aware that 'no man is an island,' more concerned with the continent that alone makes it possible for the individual actually to realize his dignity and integrity.

6. THE AGE OF THE ENLIGHTENMENT

While Europe was being convulsed by the religious wars, the most revolutionary development of the period was largely unheeded. The rise of science was the quietest as well as the profoundest revolution in history. Such events as the condemnation of Galileo and the burning of Bruno now seem momentous, but they did not shake the world at the time. While Galileo was silenced, other pioneers carried on his work without serious trouble from the authorities. Bacon trumpeted the cause of 'useful knowledge,' and with Descartes transferred this knowledge to a realm of its own, making it independent of revealed truth; men could study nature in piety because they were studying the Work of God, which was as good as his Word. Descartes outlined a mathematical interpretation of nature. 'Give me extension and motion,' he said, 'and I will construct the universe.' Newton proceeded to do so. The most brilliant achievement of these men was not this feat of construction but the invention of science itself. For the first time, men had discovered a systematic method of discovery—the experimental, mathematical method, which has enabled the extraordinary cumulative progress in useful knowledge. Similarly the most astonishing victory of science was not over religion but over universal tradition, custom, and common sense. We are still living, as Whitehead said, 'upon the accumulated capital of ideas provided ... by the genius of the seventeenth century.'

The immediate dividend was the enthusiasm of the next century, the Age of the Enlightenment. Alexander Pope struck its keynote:

> Nature and Nature's laws lay hid in night:
> God said, Let Newton be! And all was Light.

With this light came a boundless faith in Reason. It suggested some evident corollaries. Reason was the possession of all men, not merely of aristocrats or clerics; thought and speech must be free, since reason had had to overcome stubborn resistance from authority; and as Newton had wonderfully ordered the universe, so men might reconstruct and order their society. Hence the men of the Enlightenment gave the democratic world its basic faiths. As men of reason they were critical, skeptical, distrustful of 'enthusiasm' or extravagance; yet they were given to wild hopes of indefinite progress, or rather of definite progress to universal peace and good will.

Today, accordingly, they are apt to look ludicrous. They would be much more shocked by the state of the modern world than medieval men would be, or than we are. So at this point we who have inherited their faith have the greatest need of the saving grace of irony. The trouble goes much deeper than the familiar ironies of the abuses of science and liberty.

As Whitehead pointed out, the medieval schoolmen had an even purer faith in reason, believing that by deductive reason alone they could know all that was to be known. Science was a reaction against this consistent rationalism: it was 'through and through an anti-intellectualist movement,' which sought to return to brute fact. Its overwhelming success naturally confirmed its bias; so science was saddled with a naïve faith, an unconscious philosophy. 'The scientists had found a metaphysics which suited their purposes,' observed Michael Roberts, 'and therefore proposed that metaphysical speculation be stopped, much as conservatives sometimes plead for the abolition of party politics.' And in some fundamental respects their metaphysics was medieval.

To begin with, science got from the Middle Ages its basic assumption of an orderly universe, a perfectly lawful rational system in which everything could be explained. Like the schoolmen, the scientists regarded this assumption as a fact of nature, not a postulate. 'Nature does nothing in vain,' said Newton. 'Nature is pleased with simplicity, and affects not the pomp of superfluous causes.' The scientists failed to profit, however, from medieval nominalism, with its acute criticism of verbal fictions. Like the orthodox theologians they were realists, regarding 'matter,' 'force,' 'space,' 'cause,' 'natural law,' and all their basic terms as absolute realities, not as convenient concepts. Thus they went on to build up a materialistic, mechanistic scheme that was considered the unvarnished truth about the universe, that denied reality to all immeasurable, intangible, 'subjective' qualities, and that found no room for the values of art, literature, philosophy, and religion. In other words, they were so intoxicated by their discovery of the mathematical method that they forgot the nature and needs of the discoverer. They gave autonomy to a purely quantitative principle that discredited principles of form, quality, purpose, and value. Man himself was an illogical nuisance in the world conquered or constructed by science.

In time, scientists found that they could not fit their own data into their mechanistic scheme. By now they have not merely altered it but recognized that it is strictly a logical scheme—a man-made affair rather than a literal transcript of reality. Human purposes and values are no longer quarantined by scientific laws. To most men, however, 'science' still means the mechanistic philosophy it started out as; this is what they attack or defend. Literary and religious men maintain their values by ignoring or denying the truths of science, making ineffectual claims to some higher or holier kind of truth. Ordinary thought still suffers from the split between science and the humanities, or more profoundly between accepted belief and living consciousness.[17]

Some eighteenth-century philosophers were aware of the potential difficulties. Starting from the scientific premise made explicit by Locke, that all knowledge comes from experience, Berkeley demonstrated that we cannot have knowledge of 'matter,' the corporeal substance that is supposedly the ground or cause of our sensations; all we know is the sensations, which are in our own heads. Then Hume demonstrated that neither can we know 'mind,' the supposedly spiritual substance or thing apart from the stream of sensations. He added that experience does not give us knowledge of 'cause,' a *necessary* connection beyond mere sequence, or give us assurance that the future *must* resemble the past; so in effect he proved that we could not really know anything. (As someone has said of the state of knowledge at this point, 'No matter, never mind.') Hence Kant was impelled to make his remarkably ingenious, elaborate critique of reason in order to account for the plain fact that we do know a great deal; but in so doing he restricted empirical knowledge to mere 'phenomena,' or appearances, and cut it off from the 'real' world, in which he located the moral law. In effect Kant restored the double standard of truth, and divorced morality from experience.

During the Enlightenment, however, few men were really troubled by such puzzles. Most were dazzled by the wonderful achievement of Newton, and from his great authority derived a more naïve faith. Nature and Natural Law were the key-words of the age. From them came Reason, which they identified with Nature; Reason could answer all questions, solve all problems. Since Nature was an open book, philosophers could read in it according to their heart's desire, finding the 'natural rights' of man, finding a 'natural religion' without mystery. God was still in his heaven—he was the Author of Nature. In art as in social life men cultivated ideals of propriety and correctness, in conformity with Natural Law. In their romantic moments they could experience a measured enjoyment from the familiar simplicities of Nature, reflected in their neat formal gardens. Philosophers and

[17] This is a cursory review of the story I have outlined in Chapters 3 and 4 of my *Science and Criticism* (Yale University Press, 1943).

poets alike admired the wonderful fitness of the cosmic order.

The men of the Enlightenment accordingly had deep affinities with the men of the Middle Ages they despised. They had a new gospel of salvation, a vision of a Heavenly City on earth, revealed through Science instead of Scripture. They lived in an immense clockwork universe instead of the medieval bandbox world, but it was still a static, finished universe, completely known to man. In their classicism they too returned to an imaginary past, symbolized by the periwigged Homer of Alexander Pope. Their very scorn of the Middle Ages revealed that they had little more historical sense. For despite their theory of progress they had no real idea of evolution, or even of simple development; they saw only gratuitous error and evil, a 'code of fraud and woe,' in most of the ages during which man was developing. They regarded ancient institutions as deliberate artifices of priests and kings, comparable to inventions of the devil. They recognized several decent periods worthy of the interest of enlightened men—specifically, according to Voltaire, Greece from Pericles to Alexander, Augustan Rome, and the Italian Renaissance. Otherwise they simply resented the past and appeared to consider themselves a miraculous new race, whose pure rationalism had shot up overnight out of the soil of utter ignorance and irrationalism.

The central source of confusion was 'Nature'—a sovereign order under which there had somehow grown up chiefly unnatural institutions. Nature was to go back on the eighteenth-century philosophers: with the continued advance of science the universe became more mysterious, until it now seems to be fundamentally more unintelligible than it has ever seemed in the history of thought. (As one scientist said, it is not only queerer than we suppose but queerer than we *can* suppose.) But Nature was always a vague, ambiguous term, which concealed or evaded the real problems of just what is natural for man. While it remained the god of the rationalists, their opponents could also appeal to it. The approved ideals of propriety and correctness involved so much artificial convention that Rousseau led a 'back to nature' movement; he proclaimed that the natural man was a man of Feeling. Others who looked to 'the state of nature' began to glorify the noble savage, the red man. Later romantics and revolutionists, such as Shelly, Godwin, and Paine, continued to base their faith on Nature and Reason; but meanwhile Edmund Burke had turned the tables on them. He attacked the prejudice of Reason as a violation of Nature. In particular he attacked the revolutionists' favorite doctrine of 'natural rights,' asserting that 'they are so taken up with their theories about the rights of man that they have totally forgotten his nature.'

Burke was at least partly right. When Pope wrote that 'the proper study of mankind is man,' he implied that it was fairly simple study, and the philosophers generally agreed with him. They assumed that human nature, like Newtonian nature, was uniform and invariable. Even Hume, the thoroughgoing skeptic, generalized freely about an immutable human nature, which he identified with the nature of an eighteenth-century Englishman. The philosophers accordingly neglected the force of habit, custom, tradition—the most uniform force beneath all the variables of human society. They neglected the deep non-rational impulses or drives, the sources of irrational behavior. They neglected, in short, the actual and potential evils of human nature. Their conception of man as a rational animal was at once too narrow and too grandiose. They tended to oppose reason to emotion and imagination, identifying mind with pure intellect; at the same time they tended to assume that the power of reason and knowledge automatically made for wisdom, virtue, and happiness. They overlooked such truisms as that a highly intelligent man is not necessarily a good or happy man, and that his knowledge may make him more dangerous or more miserable. Denying the mysteries of being, ignoring the sources of culture, they lost touch with the most elemental kind of natural knowledge.

The crowning faith of the century—the faith in progress—was necessarily vague. Given their static conception of Nature and their contempt for most of the past, the philosophers could hardly represent progress as a definite 'law' of nature and history. They were generally less extravagant than later thinkers, such as Comte, Spencer, and Marx, who formulated such laws. But they did consider progress the natural tendency, at least from their time on; and their too easy assumption of its naturalness was a threat to actual progress. They could not foresee the perils of freedom, the new possibilities of tension and dissension that it would inevitably create. They slighted even the immediate perils. Believing that the tyranny of priests and kings was the only real barrier to the natural unity of mankind, they overlooked the increasing sharpness of racial, national, and class differences. Lacking sympathy for the tragic ardors of the past, they tended not only to a rhetorical enthusiasm for the future but a limited sympathy for the present, especially for the common people who had to bear the brunt of history. We may note a bourgeois quality in some of the philosophers, who in their enthrallment by the cosmic plan could put up with considerable evil, or even take pains to demonstrate its necessity in so admirably rational a plan.[18]

All in all, the men of the Enlightenment lacked the tragic sense of life. Voltaire had reason to attack Pascal as their most dangerous enemy, since Pascal's intense awareness of the paradoxes of man's life led him to a desperate insistence upon religious faith as the only hope; but the rational faith of Voltaire and his fellows was most vulnerable because they slighted these paradoxes. For all their skepticism, wit, and irony, they did not have a really profound sense of irony; they could write great satire and comedy but not great tragedy. And so they left men of good will unprepared for the tragic aftermath of the French Revolution—the historic climax of their efforts, and of the whole century.

The most obvious disaster was the Reign of Terror. Extremists took charge, signaling the failure of reasonableness: the moderate factions were the most numerous but the least effective. As ironical was the restoration of order by Napoleon. Under the cloak of republican forms, and by the will of the people, Napoleon set up a dictatorship comparable to that of the Emperor Augustus; so again it appeared that the people were unfit to govern themselves. But most insidious was the impetus given to nationalism and war. The men who made the Revolution had proclaimed a new religion of humanity, dedicated to the ideals of liberty, equality, and fraternity; they announced that the French people had no designs on Europe, except to help other peoples secure their liberty.

---

[18] The most lunatic extravagances of eighteenth-century optimism are to be found in the religious thinkers. These were inspired as well by the ancient idea of the 'Great Chain of Being,' stemming from Plato, the history of which has been outlined by Lovejoy. In this conception the goodness of God consists of his 'insatiable generativeness.' Thus William King, Archbishop of Dublin: 'God might, indeed, have refrained from creating, and continued alone, self-sufficient and perfect to all eternity; but his infinite Goodness would by no means allow it; this obliged him to produce external things; which things, since they could not possibly be perfect, the Divine Goodness preferred imperfect ones to none at all. Imperfection, then, arose from the infinity of Divine Goodness.' The Archbishop went on to demonstrate that the very perfection of the universe required every possible degree of imperfection, so that there might be no missing link in the Great Chain. Hence another divine rejoiced specifically in the existence of the carnivora, because 'the variety of the creation is thereby very much enlarged and the goodness of its Author is displayed'; and later there was great delight at the discovery of micro-organisms, which revealed that the world was even fuller of a lot of things. Lovejoy notes, however, that the philosophers did not naturally approve of such variety and multiplicity, since they stressed the simplicity and uniformity of Nature; and for simple human reasons a feeling sometimes broke through that the world would be pleasanter if it were not quite so full.

Presently all Europe was embroiled in war, as the defense of France insensibly developed into aggressive wars and then the imperialism of Napoleon; the merely professional armies of the monarchies were no match for the people's armies, inflamed by patriotic and revolutionary zeal. So democracy everywhere was to intensify national pride and key up whole peoples to fight all-out wars, such as absolute monarchs had never dared to impose upon their subjects. And everywhere the popular movements were strengthening the power of a new class—the men of money. The bourgeois had fought the royal power to advance their own interests, not the cause of democracy. John Jay started their credo: 'Those who own the country ought to govern it.'

Yet this was not the credo of the Enlightenment. Its greater writers and thinkers were concerned primarily with humane, civilized values, not with property rights, and spoke least of all of freedom of economic enterprise. Still more plainly, the militarism and imperialism that followed were perversions or betrayals of their ideals. They were shortsighted and sometimes shallow, but they were not unprincipled or mealy-mouthed. Had they lived to see the event, they could have had a clear conscience. We who know the event still owe the last word to their imposing historic achievement.

Briefly, the eighteenth century was in fact an age of enlightenment. It let into Europe a clear, steady daylight, and focused this light on many time-honored prejudices and barbarities, in particular the unreason of political and religious tyranny. It not only diffused knowledge but set up a public standard of truth. Its principles were aboveboard, freely accessible to all men, and not dependent upon an intuitive, mystical, or revealed truth, monopolized by a chosen race, class, or church. 'To indoctrinate the child early with the prevailing world-view of the society and class in which he has been born, to enforce conformity in later life by the thunders of the priest and by the sword of the magistrate'—this, wrote Preserved Smith, 'has been "the wisdom of our ancestors" at every stage in their progress from savagery to civilization.' It remains the wisdom of many spiritual and political leaders today. That it is not—at least in theory—the accepted wisdom of our legislatures, our courts, our schools, and many of our churches is due mainly to the work of the eighteenth century. The men of the Enlightenment established the ideals of tolerance, free thought, and rational consent.

Since this was a purely secular achievement, dedicated to 'the pursuit of happiness,' it has not been universally applauded. 'It would be a gain to this country,' Cardinal New-man declared in the last century, 'were it vastly more supersti-tious, more bigoted, more gloomy, more fierce in its religion than at present it shows itself to be.' In our own unhappy time, Christopher Dawson complains that the eighteenth century 'substituted intellectual abstractions for spiritual reali-ties.' Reinhold Niebuhr stresses the moral evil of its optimism, which he pictures as a 'very clever contrivance of human pride,' essentially dishonest and sinful. Toynbee sees rather a devilish pessimism, explaining its tolerance as a by-product of 'the Mephistophelian maladies of disillusionment, appre-hension and cynicism.' So it goes—and goes, I should say, ever farther from the historic actuality. One is entitled to prefer, with Newman, a fierce, bigoted religion to the liberal faith; but one cannot in justice deny the vitality of this faith or simply discredit its motives. If the men of the Enlightenment grew rhetorical in their odd devotion to Pos-terity, any parent knows that posterity is not a mere intellec-tual abstraction; their secular values were spiritual enough to generate an ardent and effective idealism. If their opti-mistic faith was proud it was not very clever, but it was es-sentially honest and generous. If their tolerance owed much to increasing skepticism and indifference to religion, or dis-illusionment born of the barbarous religious strife, one might say with Preserved Smith that doubt, not faith, has humanized the world; yet to the greater men of the century freedom of thought and conscience was a positive ideal, at once a rea-soned principle and a fighting faith. They introduced the same ideals into political life, about which they were not at all skeptical or indifferent. Their historic importance—their special significance for us today—derives from their rare combination of fervor and reasonableness, in the service of purely humanistic values.

The sublime example is Condorcet. Among the truly glor-ious scenes in man's history—the scenes that make one feel honored to belong to the human race, and not simply un-happy at the thought of dying for it—is that of Condorcet in his wretched garret: a fugitive from the French Revolution he had helped to bring about, living in the shadow of the guillotine, and on borrowed time working on his outline of human progress, to hearten mankind by his vision of its indefinite perfectibility. On a less rarefied level, where visions have to be realized, there are such examples as Voltaire and Thomas Jefferson. A citizen of the world, Voltaire was not by temperament a lover of mankind; yet there has never been a more brilliant, effective fighter in the cause of free-dom, which he conceived as a universal cause. Jefferson was as true to his lifelong motto: 'I have sworn upon the altar of God eternal hostility against every form of tyranny over the mind of man.' As President, harassed by scurrilous abuse at a time of national crisis, he still opposed all effort to coerce or suppress opinion. And perhaps more remarkable was his spirit as a revolutionary—an author of a Declaration of Independence who took for granted the propriety of manifesting 'a decent respect to the opinions of mankind,' and really meant it.

The lip service to these commonplaces obscures their uniqueness. The 'catholic' ideals of the Middle Ages were sectarian, not actually universal or capable of being universalized; and certainly they involved little respect for the opinions of mankind. We have only to recall the preposterous 'universal histories' that until the time of Voltaire had reduced the whole drama of mankind to the events centered about Palestine and Rome. (Thus the eminent Bishop Bossuet had ignored India and China, pictured the Arabs as mere barbarians, and devoted one paragraph to Greek philosophy.) Today nothing is more depressing than the routine insincerity in the manipulation of public opinion, by democratic politicians as well as dictators. Similarly the real religion of Western man has been patriotism, which Voltaire considered an anachronism; in theory as well as practice, the primary loyalty is not to God or man but to the nation. We must therefore repeat that the men of the Enlightenment overrated the power of reason and knowledge, underrated the strength of tribal sentiments and vulgar prejudices. Nevertheless they proposed the kind of world community that is now a practical necessity. They promoted the civilized values of good sense and good will that are indispensable for establishing such a community.

Altogether, the expressed faiths of the Enlightenment are sometimes naïve and never self-evident; yet I hold that they are noble and necessary faiths. They are more necessary because the dignity and the rights of man are not an inalienable birthright, but a hard-earned acquisition. They are essential to any hopes of a better life on earth. And the faith in progress, the *will* to progress, is the most original contribution of the eighteenth century, dignifying men who were generally smaller than their achievement. If the philosophers overlooked possibilities of evil, they recognized real possibilities of betterment. If they overrated the natural goodness of man, they provided a wholesome corrective to the traditional emphasis on his natural depravity. They denied that freedom is simply an invitation to sin, and that obedience or renunciation is good *per se*. They enabled a decent self-respect. The underlying sanity of the age is summed up in the credo of Jefferson:

Although I do not, with some enthusiasts, believe that the human condition will ever advance to such a state of perfection as that there shall no longer be pain or vice in the world, yet I believe it susceptible of much improvement, and most of all, in matters of government and religion; and that the diffusion of knowledge among the people is to be the instrument by which it is to be effected.

Hence we might take another look at the notorious French Revolution. It testified to the power of the ideas and ideals of the Enlightenment, and its testimony was admirable as well as deplorable. Oppressed though they were, French peasants were considerably better off than most other European peasants; the revolution was not a blind uprising or sudden running amuck of a crazed mob, but the work of men who had been brought to see clearly the rottenness and the absurdity of the old regime, and who had a reasoned program for a better political order After the storming of the Bastille, it was an unusually peaceable, orderly revolution. It might have continued so except for the intrigues of émigré nobles and the constant threat of invasion by other European powers, whose aristocracy was frightened by its success. Fear of these dangers was a major cause of the subsequent Reign of Terror. And despite such excesses, and the ironic aftermath, the revolution made solid, enduring gains. The aristocracy and the Church never recovered their feudal privileges; the common people retained substantial political rights and religious freedom. Above all, the French Revolution remained the inspiration of popular causes all over the Western world. When the bourgeois took charge, they could not kill its ideals of liberty, equality, and fraternity.

'Only a world-view which accomplishes all that rationalism did has a right to condemn rationalism,' concludes Albert Schweitzer. The champions of medieval Christianity have no such right. Its supernatural faith inspired a greater art and loftier unearthly ideals, but on earth it tolerated or even encouraged the powers of ignorance, obscurantism, bigotry, and tyranny. The Age of the Enlightenment did more than any other century in Western history to combat these powers, and to give men a better world to live in. Today we may consider ourselves more enlightened—or at least we have the chance of being so. We can better appreciate the values of the Middle Ages, the achievements of the whole past; we are more aware of the problems created by freedom and democracy, and by enlightenment itself; we have learned much more about the non-rational and irrational forces that condition the life of reason and always menace it. We might even learn the wisdom of more modest expectations. Yet rationalism itself has made possible such discount and supplement. The final argument for the faith of the Enlightenment is that it contained the leaven of self-criticism. If the pronouncements of reason are always fallible, they are always corrigible too; and in science it has created the one orthodoxy that welcomes and thrives on constant correction.

IX

'Holy Russia' Byzantine and Marxist

1. THE BYZANTINE TRADITION

'Beyond all doubt,' wrote Dostoyevsky in 1880, 'the destiny of a Russian is pan-European and universal. To become a true Russian is to become the brother of all men... Our future lies in Universality, won not by violence, but by the strength derived from our great ideal—the reuniting of all mankind.' At about the same time Leontyev had a stranger vision: 'Sometimes I dream that a Russian Czar may put himself at the head of the Socialist movement and organize it, as Constantine organized Christianity.' Both Dostoyevsky and Leontyev were political reactionaries, strongly opposed to revolutionary socialism on religious grounds. Both look ludicrous in the light of the historic event: Russia is seeking to unite mankind by violence, flatly rejecting the gospel of Christ on which Dostoyevsky based his whole faith; and Lenin assumed the role of Constantine, while the last czar was shot. Yet both may be called—as Dostoyevsky has been called—prophets of the Russian Revolution. They spoke out of a tradition that contributed immensely to the success of the Revolution, and to its subsequent course. We cannot understand the Soviet today unless we begin by forgetting Karl Marx and examining the history that molded this tradition, which has revolutionized Marxism itself. Or if we wish, we can take our cue from Marx: 'The tradition of all the dead generations weighs like an Alp upon the brain of the living.'

In Russia this incubus has been exceptionally massive. When the empire of the Huns broke down, Slavic peoples spread over the land, which had not yet known a high culture. In the ninth century the Vikings came down from Scandinavia and established themselves at Kiev. Russian history begins with the legend that the Slavic tribes went to the Vikings, saying, 'Come and rule and be princes over us.' As warrior traders, the princes of Kiev sent expeditions to Constantinople, and by the year 1000 were prosperous and civilized enough to contemplate the possibility of a new religion appropriate to their station. After considering various religions, including Judaism, Mohammedanism, and Roman Catholicism, Vladmir I settled on the Orthodox Church, charmed by the splendor of its service; and with no great trouble he imposed this on his subjects. The kingdom of Kiev became a brilliant offshoot of Byzantine culture. In the thirteenth century, however, it was overwhelmed by the Mongols, or Tartars. Except for the Church, Russian civilization was extinguished; while Western Europe was growing up, Russia remained under the dominion of the Tartars. Then refugees in the forests to the north slowly built up power around the town of Moscow, and at the end of the fifteenth century Ivan the Great finally threw off the Tartar yoke. Under his new title of 'Sovereign of all Russia' he began warring on surrounding kingdoms, seeking to unite all Russia. The Church began inventing an illustrious ancestry for him, going back as far as Augustus Caesar. As a Byzantine autocrat, Ivan gave Russia a new yoke.[1]

Ivan had been inspired by his wife, the niece of the last emperor of Byzantium. The fall of Constantinople to the Turks gave him a holy mission. 'Thou alone, in all that is under heaven, art a Christian Czar,' the monk Filofei wrote him. 'And take note, O religious and gracious Czar, that all Christian kingdoms are merged into thine alone, that two Romes have fallen, but the third stands; and there shall be no fourth.' The religious czar graciously did take note: the idea of the Third Rome became the ruling idea of the Muscovite state. Russia became 'Holy Russia,' the guardian of the true faith. Thereafter it would scorn both Catholic and Protestant Europe; it knew that Constantinople had fallen because it had betrayed the true faith, when its last emperors had tried to save their empire by concessions to Rome. Later the Third Rome would give way to the Third International, become 'the Rome of the proletariat' that Sorel hailed; but still the light came from Moscow. All kingdoms shall be merged into the kingdom of Russia.

---

[1] Toynbee dates the 'breakdown' of Russian society in the eleventh century. This would allow it only about two centuries of healthy growth, under foreign rulers at that, and implies that almost its entire history—its most distinctively Russian history—has been only an unhappy, uncreative aftermath. One need not admire this history, however, to suspect that what breaks down here is Toynbee's diagrammatic schema.

More specifically, the official creed became 'Orthodoxy, autocracy, and nationality.' Byzantium gave Russia its writing, its art, its law, but above all its institution of 'Caesaro-papism.' As in Byzantium, this produced some vigorous, patriotic rulers, and on the side some saints; but our immediate concern is its essential logic. The idea of the sacred Autokrator appears in the earliest Russian writings, it was reaffirmed by Ivan the Great, and it was made still more explicit by Ivan the Terrible, who in 1547 became the first reigning czar to be crowned as such. He declared that it was his duty to save souls as well as to govern the state, and that for both purposes he needed absolute power, so as to avoid the weaknesses of Byzantium in its last years. 'The rulers of Russia have not been accountable to any one,' said Ivan the Terrible (who in recent years has been restored his traditional honors as a national hero), 'but have been free to reward or to chastise their subjects.' He in fact did away with the last vestiges of individual rights. In our century the last of the czars repeated the ancient credo: 'Obedience to his authority, not only for wrath but for conscience' sake, is ordained by God Himself.' And the masses of Russian peasants humbly obeyed God's will. Although they often rebelled against nobles and officials, they rarely rebelled against the czar himself. They revered their 'Little Father,' as in recent years they have been taught to revere 'Our Own Dear Father' Stalin.

The Russian peasantry has been widely praised for its broad, fluid humanity, but its most conspicuous virtue was the fortitude that enabled it to endure about as sustained misgovernment as history has known. The czars' exercise of their absolute power was apt to be the more arbitrary and ruthless because they were guided by no political philosophy and restrained by no tradition of chivalry or *noblesse oblige*. Tyranny, terror, and torture have been routine in Russian history. The noblest creation of the czarist regime was a long line of martyrs, who eventually assisted in committing suicide. Its most enduring creation was the glorified State. This it passed on to the Soviet, together with highly centralized authority, a vast bureaucracy, and such institutions as the secret police.

The Orthodox Church was less creative. It was a civilizing influence in the kingdom of Kiev and played a heroic role in the struggle against the Tartars; but its triumph proved fatal. As the guardian of Orthodoxy it narrowed, darkened, and rigidified the ultra-conservative tradition it had inherited from Byzantium. It created no new monastic orders, developed no theology, inspired no crusades, embarked on none of the adventures that invigorated and transformed medieval Christianity. Its bishops later boasted that unlike the Roman Church it had never changed its doctrine, never tampered with the divine truths entrusted to it; and in fact it hadn't. It made a virtue of ignorance and obscurantism. 'Abhorred of God is any one who loves geometry,' said one bishop: 'it is a spiritual sin.' Another cleric wrote, 'A spiritual sin it is to study astronomy and the books of Greece.' About the common garden varieties of sin the Church was less disquieted. Its primary concern was not ethics but ritual.

The one great controversy that did shake the Church was typical. In the seventeenth century the Patriarch Nikon reformed the ritual, correcting mistakes in the sacred texts; the name of Jesus in particular had been misspelled when it was first translated from the Greek. This purification of the texts aroused violent opposition from masses of common people, known as the Old Believers. Passionately they clung to their ancient misspellings and corrupt forms, denouncing the 'foreign' innovations as an outrage upon the Orthodoxy of the Third Rome. With the help of the czar the Church finally suppressed them, hanging some of their leaders; but again it lost by its triumph. Although the Old Believers were more ignorant and superstitious than the official churchmen, they had more moral and spiritual fervor. When they were driven underground they took with them much of the religious spirit of Russia. Out of them grew the millions of dissenting sectarians who in various original ways (including castration) tried to live strictly in accordance with the teachings of Jesus; while the high churchmen returned to their ritual, content that they were spelling his name correctly.

In the same century the Church lost another brief battle. The Patriarch Nikon also attempted to assert its independence from imperial control, using such arguments as the Donation of Constantine. The czar had him condemned and deposed by a church council. Presently the czars began to purify the Church by taking over its immense land holdings, together with some million of its serfs; it became economically as well as politically dependent upon the 'religious and gracious czar.' It had never made a really earnest effort to realize the spiritual freedom and dignity of the individual, teaching chiefly humility and patience. (Its Catechism includes this passage: 'Question. What does religion teach us as to our duties to the Czar? Answer. Worship, fidelity, the payment of taxes, service, love, and prayer—the whole being comprised in the words *worship* and *fidelity*.') Now 'the Orthodox faith which has been confirmed by the universe' became thoroughly identified with the cause of reaction. Upon the outbreak of the Russian Revolution the Church asserted its spiritual leadership by demanding the return of its ancient lands and privileges. Just before the final disasters on the war front, the Archbishop Platon reassured a great State Conference in Moscow with a message that recalls the last days of Constantinople:

I have come here in order from this platform to say to Russia: Do not be troubled, dear one. Have no fear, my own one... If a miracle is necessary for the salvation of Russia, then in answer to the prayers of His church, God will accomplish this miracle.

The immediate contribution of Orthodoxy to the Soviet was its militant godlessness, as a logical reaction against a church that had stood for and with the czar. In time, however, the Soviet found it necessary to make concessions, since the peasantry clung stubbornly to its ancient faith. The Soviet also learned to appreciate the traditional nationalism of the universal Church, which now supports it. And beneath its hostility was a deep kinship, in its own insistence upon unconditional loyalty to the true faith. It too discussed all issues in terms of orthodoxy and heresy; it too hated heretics worse than heathens. As Jacques Maritain has suggested, the Soviet of the future conceivably might denounce atheism as another form of bourgeois decadence.

Altogether, the Byzantine tradition accounted for the notorious backwardness of Russia. In its 'medieval' phase, Russia developed no large-scale commerce and industry comparable to that of medieval Europe, no energetic bourgeois class; while Europe was bursting its medieval shackles, it was shackling itself with the institution of serfdom. It had no Renaissance, no Reformation, no Age of Reason. 'We have lived, as it were, outside of history,' wrote the philosopher Chaadayev in 1829, 'and have remained untouched by the universal education of the human race... Isolated from the world, we have given or taught nothing to the world; we have added no thoughts to the sum of human ideas; we have in no way collaborated in the progress of reason and we have disfigured everything that penetrated to us from this progress.'

Such disfigurement marked the extraordinary achievement of Peter the Great, whose decision to modernize Russia was the turning point of its history. At the beginning of the eighteenth century he drove the Swedes out of the South Baltic after long years of war, and on Swedish soil built his new capital of St. Petersburg, so as to open 'a window on the West.' With inexhaustible energy, zeal, and pertinacity, he set about

Westernizing Russia overnight. He created a modern professional army. To supply it, he founded Russian industry and put the government into business on a vast scale. (The czars also turned over to the Soviet a state economic machine.) He imported many Western experts while sending young Russians abroad to study, as he had gone himself incognito. He built up an administrative system in which rank depended on efficiency rather than birth. He introduced many cultural reforms, correcting and simplifying the alphabet, starting schools for laymen, printing translations of foreign books, bringing out the first manual of etiquette, putting a tax on beards. When the Patriarch denounced the shaving of beards as a heresy, he eventually abolished the Patriarchate and appointed instead a Holy Synod, making the Church completely dependent upon a completely secularized state. He accomplished all this against the opposition of the peasants, the gentry, the Church, and his own son, whom he had killed. The bulk of his reforms nevertheless endured. He succeeded in making Russia an important European power.

Yet it remained a Byzantine state. Peter's reforms were designed chiefly to strengthen the state, not to promote the welfare of the people. Although fond of the peasants, he did nothing for them; rather, he put still heavier burdens on them—in particular the upkeep of a large standing army—and widened the gulf between them and the ruling class. He Westernized Russia by Eastern methods, arbitrarily imposing his reforms from on top, with a ruthless disregard for human costs. Hence he did not really Westernize its heart. By his outrages of this venerable tradition he made Russia more conscious of this tradition, and stirred a more conscious hostility to the alien culture of the West. The Soviet, which has carried on his work of modernization by the same arbitrary methods, with even worse outrages upon Orthodoxy, has also carried through the revolt against the West. It might be considered the triumphant vindication of Holy Russia.

2. THE NINETEENTH-CENTURY INTELLIGENTSIA

Peter the Great was mainly interested in the severely practical knowledge and skill that Russia could acquire from the West. The cultural Enlightenment had to wait a generation for Catherine the Great, a German princess who had no right to the Russian throne, but managed to keep her son off it after she had arranged for the murder of her feeble husband. Vigorous, broad-minded, and highly cultivated herself, Catherine stimulated a free trade in Western culture. A friend of Voltaire, she delighted in the play of ideas and encouraged free thought. She even took up the fashionable new political ideas of the Enlightenment; aspiring to Voltaire's ideal of the benevolent, enlightened monarch, she drew up a political program so liberal that its publication was forbidden in France. Yet her fine principles were not put into effect. Serfdom reached its culmination during her reign, though she herself predicted it would eventually bring on a cataclysm; by now most of the peasants were chained to the soil and their lot grew worse under absentee landlords, as the gentry flocked to the cities to take up the fashionable new culture. Dangerous peasant revolts put an end to all thought of reform. In her last years, frightened by the French Revolution, Catherine ceased to be liberal. Radischev, the first important radical to appear in literature, was thrown into jail for his protest against serfdom.

Catherine the Great set the pattern for Russian intellectual life in the nineteenth century. The Enlightenment was restricted to culture; politics remained absolutist. The measure of freedom that was allowed depended on the whim of the czar. Catherine's son Paul, a pedantic despot on the Prussian model, proscribed the words *society* and *citizen*. His brilliant son Alexander, a sentimental liberal, was exalted by the role of liberator that Europe thrust upon him after his defeat of Napoleon; but then he took to religiosity and ended as a pious reactionary, the most powerful enemy of democratic movements in Europe as in Russia. Thereafter the occasional efforts at reform, such as the emancipation of the serfs by Alexander II, called out conservative reactions and renewed oppression. The State had now replaced the Church as censor, and to an awakened intelligentsia its arbitrary tyranny was more intolerable than the honest, consistent obscurantism of the past.[2]

Early in the century Pushkin deplored 'this lack of public opinion, this aloofness to duty, justice, and truth, this cynical contempt for the mind and human individuality.' In Russia today he might complain of the same contempt. Yet the issue of Russian intellectual life was much more complex, ambiguous, and ironic than a simple liberal would expect. Living in so suffocating an atmosphere, Pushkin became the

---

[2] Under Nicholas I, for example, all works on logic and philosophy were forbidden. A historian was not allowed to say that Roman emperors had been assassinated—they could only 'perish.' Censors deleted such phrases as 'the forces of nature' and 'the majesty of nature,' as possible reflections on the almighty czar. Another writer was asked to explain what he meant by his phrase 'the movement of minds.'

first great Russian writer, and he remains the most popular —many millions of copies of his works have been sold in the Soviet. He fermented the growth of the most original, impressive literature of the nineteenth century, culminating in Dostoyevsky and Tolstoy; all Europe saluted these giants from the East. The ferment produced an astonishing variety of creeds, from the most revolutionary to the most reactionary, but almost all contributed to the attitudes that brought about the Revolution. 'The whole history of the Russian intelligentsia,' asserted Berdyaev, 'was a preparation for communism.'

Their most insidious enemy was not tyranny but isolation and alienation. The two great forces in Russia were the monarchy and the masses, and the intelligentsia were cut off from both. The czar and his court always viewed them with suspicion; the illiterate, tradition-bound peasantry were as suspicious when they were aware of them at all. (When the 'narodniks,' or Populists, tried to go to the peasants, actually living and working with them, the peasants sometimes turned them over to the authorities.) In Dostoyevsky's words, the intelligentsia were 'the great wanderers of the Russian land,' rootless men living on ideas alone. They lived from hand to mouth because they were sustained by no common tradition. 'Their mission as independent thinkers,' Bertram Wolfe comments, 'was to be critics of the world in which they had no place and prophets of a world that had not yet come into being, and might have no place for them either.'

In this unhappy position they might have cultivated a fastidious sense of superiority, such as helps to sustain some Western artists and intellectuals who also feel isolated from a mass civilization; or they might have turned to a gloomy fatalism, which many readers seem to think is the hallmark of Russian literature. But very few Russian writers were precious, and almost none were fatalistic. Rather, their need of justifying their existence only intensified their social consciousness. Since the press was rigorously censored, literature became the chief medium of social and political discussion, and there was little protest that its purity was thereby sullied. 'He who deprives art of its rights to serve social interests debases the reader instead of elevating him,' declared Belinsky, the most influential critic of the century. Most of the greater writers would have seen nothing strange or intolerable in the Soviet demand that art must serve the interests of the State. As a group they had a more acute sense of social responsibility than any other group of comparable greatness in literary history. Even Turgenev, perhaps the finest artist among them, who was by temperament attracted to Flaubert's ideal of pure art, devoted all but one of his novels to the revolutionary movements in Russia.

One effect of this social conscience was the sense of guilt that haunted most Russian writers: guilt because of serfdom and the other evils of Holy Russia, and of the apparent futility or the possible irresponsibility of the writer himself.[3] Suffering, not free, joyous creativity, was the matrix of Russian literature. Another effect was its distinctive realism. A wholly indigenous product, this realism was not a revulsion against romanticism, nor a symptom of the 'modern' spirit, nor a matter of esthetic theory. Its motives were primarily moral. The ideal of Russian writers was prefect truth, not prefect art. Indeed, they tended to a positive distrust of fine art, or even of culture itself. For most of them the Russian people—the peasants—became the great hope; and the peasants needed bread and boots more than fine art; their virtues went deeper than culture. 'Down with culture!' wrote Dostoyevsky: 'the thirst for culture is an aristocratic thirst.' Tolstoy proclaimed his famous doctrine that all art should be comprehensible to the common man, otherwise it is not good art.

Given these common aims, the obvious source of disagreement among the intelligentsia was the question how Russia was to be saved. The central conflict of the century was that between the Westernizers and the Slavophiles—those who looked to the West for salvation, and those who looked to the native tradition.

The Westernizers typically called for a purely secular program. 'All the talk about Russian humility and Orthodoxy is merely helping the reaction,' declared Alexander Herzen. Some where revolutionaries, of the Marxist type. Others were liberals, of the type of Herzen and Turgenev—cultivated, tolerant, humane men, generally devoted to the cause of democracy. And these men, the most genuinely Western in their idealism, were likely to feel the most frustrated and futile. Intellectually, they were men without a country. They had no liberal, humanistic tradition to appeal to, and having no past, they often suspected that they had no future. 'The

[3] Merezhkovsky lamented that Pushkin was the only healthy, whole man among the greater Russian writers, the only one to achieve a harmony of flesh and spirit, life and art. The others were split souls, whose efforts to merge the man and the artist were likely to end in the destruction of both. Merezhkovsky cited Gogol as the first victim of this profound disharmony: Russia's greatest humorist went to pieces as he tried to complete *Dead Souls*, destroyed his manuscript, made a pilgrimage to Jerusalem, and ended in a maudlin religiosity, wondering why God did not destroy such a sinful wretch as he. ('Give me the ladder, the ladder' were his dying words.) Many other writers ended in as sickly a mysticism. And so, finally, did Merezhkovsky himself.

liberal party,' wrote Herzen, toward the end of a life in exile devoted to its cause, 'will be ground out of existence between the two wheels' of right and left. So in fact it was, when the Bolsheviks rose to power. Trotsky had a characteristic name for this type of idealist—'the Hamlet of democratic socialism.' Of Sukhanov, who stood so far to the left that he was close to the Bolsheviks, Trotsky wrote, 'He was and remained, with his Hamlet temperament, the very opposite of a Bolshevik.'

The Slavophiles had the advantage of ancient tradition, and immediately of Western resistance to Russian expansion in Europe; this turned the Russians eastward to Asia and strengthened their conviction that they were a people apart. Some of the Slavophiles were revolutionaries too, because of their devotion to the Russian people. Generally, however, they were political or religious reactionaries. Almost all opposed the rationalism of the West, on the grounds of a mystical faith in the Russian spirit. With the aid of such foreign importations as Rousseau's idea of the natural goodness of primitive man, they made a virtue of the backwardness of Russia. At worst, like Gogol in the last stages of his religious breakdown, they glorified the Church, the Czar, and even serfdom. At best, like Dostoyevsky, they glorified the universalism of the Russian spirit, which could realize the ideal of brotherhood that the West had lost sight of.

Trotsky's name for Slavophilism was 'the messianism of backwardness'; and offhand it was dedicated to a more impossible cause than that of the forward-looking liberals. Its political reactionaries were hopelessly ineffectual—their holy czardom was as rotten-feeble as it was unholy. Its idealists floundered in hopeless confusion and contradiction. Blinking the universal servility to the czar, they were pleased to believe that the Orthodox Church and the Russian people were at heart thoroughly democratic. Exalting Russian universalism, they actually tended to an extravagant nationalism. Dostoyevsky himself was often chauvinistic—in one breath preaching the Sermon on the Mount, in the next calling for a war on Turkey. In general, the Slavophiles could idealize the historic mission of Russia only by resolutely disregarding its historic past. They could not stem, by mere rhetoric, the deepest currents in the modern world. Russia was to turn to Western science, technology, and revolutionary thought.

Yet on the main issue—the unique mission of Russia—the Slavophiles had the better of the historic debate. The Westerners were also patriotic Russians, likely to sound the high notes of national pride. In particular they shared with the Slavophiles a deep aversion to the bourgeois materialism of the West. All classes, Berdyaev declares, agreed in their hearts that bourgeois ideology was sinful; even the nobility did not believe in the sacredness of private property and property rights. The reactionary Leontyev was appalled at the thought that 'the Apostles preached, the martyrs suffered, poets sang, painters painted, and knights glittered in the lists simply in order that the French or German or Russian bourgeois in his horrible or ludicrous clothes might live an individual and collective life complacently on the ruins of all the greatness of the past.' Alexander Herzen, the most famous of the liberals, was often as disgusted by Western complacency. 'Can we be honestly contented,' he wrote Michelet, 'with your threadbare morality, unchristian and inhuman, existing only in rhetorical exercises and speeches for the prosecution?' Elsewhere he wrote, 'I can foresee the inevitable ruin of the old Europe. . . It can be saved neither by martial law nor by a republican form of government, neither by executions nor by charity.' And he saw Russia as the herald of the new age. He believed that Russia could escape the bourgeois capitalistic stage; he celebrated the 'inborn force' that had preserved the Russian people from such evils, noting especially the inherent socialism of the peasants; he saw even the terror in Russia as 'the birth-pangs of the future,' while Europe could look forward only to death agonies. With the coming of these birth pangs the historic debate continued with the Communist party—and the loudest voices still cried out against 'slavish submission to the West.' Today the Iron Curtain protects Russia from the blight of Western ideas.

Such scorn of the decadent, bourgeois West was intensified by the extremism to which the intelligentsia were prone. 'With us,' wrote Chaadayev, 'new ideas sweep away the old because they do not spring out of them.' Lacking a critical-skeptical tradition, very few were capable of anything like the methodical doubt of a Montaigne or Descartes. ('Montaigne is common and vulgar,' said Tolstoy.) Their own tradition disposed them to absolutism, and their isolation from practical, political life strengthened this disposition. They agonized over the ideas that they lived on, and could not put into effect; they dreamed up grandiose projects for the salvation of all mankind; and typically they insisted that their utopian dreams were absolutely necessary and absolutely true. Untroubled by the high mortality rate of revolutionary gospels, they continued to ride every doctrine to its absurd logical extreme. Even in exile they fought furiously with one another over their exclusive doctrinaire programs—as Bolsheviks and Mensheviks battled for weeks on end in international congresses. They were united in their passion for totalitarian solutions, their insistence on going the whole hog, their contempt of the half measure, the happy medium, the middle way—the Western habit of compromise. To them, the utopian dreamer was the liberal, the gradualist, the mere reformer.

The ugly aspects of this all-or-nothing spirit are plain enough. It naturally encouraged a kind of intellectual terrorism, which in turn led to political terrorism. A typical product was the *Revolutionary Catechism* of Nechaev, instructing revolutionaries in the requirements of absolute loyalty to the cause, complete disregard of all personal interest and moral scruple, unflinching readiness to commit or to endure any atrocity—as he himself had murdered a suspected backslider. But the terrible Nechaev also illustrates the religious quality of the most godless extremists, in their uncompromising devotion to a supra-personal ideal. 'We are all nihilists,' wrote Dostoyevsky, the bitter enemy of the avowed nihilists. Nineteenth-century Russia was the chief breeding grounds of militant atheism, nihilism, anarchism—all amounting to an inverted Orthodoxy. The revolutionary anarchism of Bakunin was as idealistic as the Christian anarchism of Tolstoy. None of the mystics had a more exalted Christian spirit than the atheist Belinsky, who cried, 'I do not want happiness even as a gift unless I have peace of mind about my brothers by blood, bone of my bone, and flesh of my flesh.' The intellectuals often began by denying the freedom of the human spirit, denying the values of civilization; but their characteristic aim was to free man, even if it first required the destruction of society.[4]

In short, the nineteenth-century intelligentsia molded the totalitarian mentality of the Soviet today. Some contributed the specific religion of materialism; the rest prepared for the Revolution by their worship of the People, their scorn of bourgeois respectability, their suspicion of a cultured elite, their yearning for the universal solution, their passion for the clean sweep, their scorn of compromise. The Soviet has recognized its debt, honoring the greatest of them, publishing their works in huge editions. (Even Herzen had a big street in Moscow named after him.) If they could return to Russia

---

[4] The extremities and absurdities of their logic were another obvious reason for many split personalities among them. Dostoyevsky's Ivan Karamazov is typical. He argues that if there is no God and no heaven, there can be no basis for morality—'Everything is lawful'; and then he is driven mad by the artificial dilemma he has created. Tolstoy, on the other hand, had no belief in heaven but concluded that men must follow Christ. By temperament a magnificently healthy pagan, he resolved to live as a saint, in strict accordance with the Sermon on the Mount; and so he managed to destroy his own peace and that of his family.

today, most of them would almost certainly be liquidated. Most would nevertheless feel that Soviet Communism was not so wicked and inhuman as Western capitalism.

3. LENIN AND MARXISM

'I will nowhere and at no time appear on the same platform as Herzen,' Marx wrote to Engels in 1855, 'since I am not of the opinion that "old Europe" can be rejuvenated by Russian blood.' He was never fond of the backward Russians, who provided huge armies for the forces of reaction. In time he grew more interested in them, even learning their language in order to keep up with the exciting possibilities of their revolutionary movements; but he remained of two minds about them. Once he wrote that Russia had 'the best opportunity that history has ever offered to a people to escape all the catastrophes of capitalism.' At other times he expressed his animus toward its servile people, and his irritation with the doctrinaire attitudes of its revolutionaries. (More than once he said, 'Je ne suis pas Marxiste.') Engels was still more critical of the Russian revolutionaries. He deplored their intolerance toward the Populists, 'the only people who are doing anything in Russia at this moment.' In 1893 he warned them against their habit of 'interpreting passages from Marx's writings and letters in the most contradictory ways, just as if they were texts from the classics or the New Testament.' He hardly dreamed that in a contemporary young Russian student by the name of Vladimir Ilyich Ulyanov, later to be known as Lenin, Marx was to find his St. Paul.

The analogy is fairly close. After his conversion, Lenin was as completely obsessed with a single cause as the great Apostle had been. 'There is no other man,' wrote Axelrod, one of many comrades he excommunicated, 'who is absorbed by the revolution twenty-four hours a day, who has no other thoughts but the thought of the revolution, and who, even when he sleeps, dreams of nothing but the revolution.' He was as selfless as Paul in his devotion, or even in his egoism; his fierce self-righteousness never sprang from vanity or selfishness, but always from the holy righteousness of his cause. He was as intense and narrow in his thought, scornful of the foolishness of Greeks and liberals. To make converts or to keep control of his party cells he could be all things to all men, but he made no real concessions to any man. Lunacharsky summed up his genius:

He does his work imperiously, not because power is sweet to him, but because he is sure that he is right, and cannot endure to have anybody spoil his work. His love of power grows out of his tremendous sureness and the correctness of his principles, and, if you please, out of an inability (very useful in a political leader) to see from the point of view of his opponent.

And in this tremendous sureness Lenin transformed the gospel of Marx as profoundly as St. Paul transformed the gospel of Jesus. His own writings became Scripture, though they were often as hurried and topical as the Epistles of Paul, and they have also been quoted in the most contradictory ways.

It is therefore well to review some of the basic inconsistencies, or at least ambiguities, in the thought of Marx himself. They stem from his dual role as a scientific analyst and an impassioned evangelist, the one objectively describing the inevitable, lawful, non-moral historical processes, the other bitterly condemning these processes and exhorting men to follow his path to salvation. He was a philosophical materialist whose program was designed to free man once and for all from bondage to the material environment. He made economic determinism his cardinal doctrine, on this basis demonstrating the inevitable triumph of the proletariat and denying the independent power of conscious ideas and ideals; but he also proclaimed that through correct knowledge man could control his destiny, and his own influence on modern history is the most spectacular example of the power of ideas and ideals. He insisted on the relativity of truth in a world of dynamic process, stressing in particular the class bias of all thought; but he also insisted on the absolute, objective truth of his own theory of history, and exempted his chosen class from bias, making the proletariat free from historical error and sin. And while attacking religion, he preached like the fiercest of the prophets the bloody revolution that was to bring the kingdom of heaven on earth.

Lenin swallowed the materialism of Marx whole and raw. In his *Materialism and Empirio-Criticism* he furiously attacked as 'reactionary idealists' other Marxists who were attempting to adapt dialectical materialism to the revolutionary new concepts in physics.[5] Lenin did not really accept, however, the

---

[5] Though his book aroused little interest at the time, it is now the philosophical bible of the Soviet; so one might note that Lenin betrays the thoroughly unscientific spirit of orthodox communism. In refuting his opponents, whose concepts have since become commonplaces of scientific thought, he did not appeal to scientific authority—he clinched

determinism of Marx. He had to take liberties with the 'iron laws' of history, and in effect to stress a principle of freedom, because his life work was to bring about a revolution in Russia, which had not yet reached the capitalistic stage that lawfully had to precede the triumph of the proletariat. His life-long opponents, the Mensheviks, were much more orthodox Marxists; they wanted to obey the laws and first build up a class-conscious proletariat. Similarly Lenin had to rebaptize the peasant class, which Marx considered petty-bourgeois and reactionary; although at first he echoed this view he later announced that the peasants were a revolutionary class, and banned all reference to opposition between them and the workers. Above all, Lenin had to provide the revolution with a political theory. Marx and Engels had thrown out scattered hints for a correct theory, in such phrases as 'the dictatorship of the proletariat,' but they had not made at all clear what this dictatorship was to be like. Marx in particular was handicapped by his doctrine that 'in the last analysis economics determines politics.' Lenin now reversed this doctrine, making politics primary, and later he himself determined the economics of the Soviet.

The problem of power—how to seize it and how to hold it—was the central concern of Lenin's entire career. 'The emancipation of the working class,' Marx and Engels had proclaimed, 'is the work of the working class itself.' Lenin early decided that it would have to be the work of a 'socialist vanguard,' a small, hard, tightly disciplined core; without their iron control the working class would become 'petty and inevitably bourgeois.' At the Unification Congress of 1903, which fought out this issue of centralism, he won the name of Bolsheviki, or 'Majority-ites,' for his faction. In the long series of congresses thereafter the Mensheviks, or 'Minority-ites,' were usually in the majority, but Lenin fought them by shifting power, now to the Central Committee, now to the Central Organ; or if he controlled neither of these he set up a new committee of his own, or called a new con-

all arguments by citations from Marx and Engels, or by what his victim Bogdanov described as 'quotational shock treatment.' 'You cannot eliminate even one basic assumption, one substantial part of this philosophy of Marxism,' Lenin concluded, 'without abandoning objective truth, without falling into the arms of the bourgeois-reactionary falsehood.' Physicists have learned that the advance of objective truth requires a vigilant criticism of *all* basic assumptions. But they are bound to be reactionary by Lenin's standards, if only because they have never used the Marxian dialectic in their pursuit of truth.

His ignorance here, it should be added, owes as well to the whole tradition of the Russian intelligentsia. Concentrating on social and political issues, they never became much interested in the problem of the nature of knowledge.

ference limited to his small faction. He kept splitting the party, expelling those who refused to follow his line, including his oldest and closest comrades. At times he stood virtually alone, attacked by almost all the leading revolutionists of Russia and Europe, who wanted to have only one socialist party because there was only one proletariat; but always Lenin held to his course, and continued to claim the name of Bolshevik for his minority group. Implacable, incorruptible, and immovable, he was the Party.

Throughout this struggle Lenin's strength lay in his flexibility as well as his steadfastness. He had a shrewd realism, a keen sense of changing conditions and the need of adapting principles to them; he took his favorite motto from Napoleon: *On s'engage, et puis—on voit.* While forever excommunicating heretics, he repeatedly denounced the 'formalism' of his fellow Bolsheviks, their pedantic devotion to the letter of the Marxist texts. This formalism has persisted, however. It became more pedantic once the Bolsheviks were strongly entrenched in power. And about this problem of power—the eternal problem of the abuse of power—the master's teaching was equivocal.

There is no questioning the sincerity of Lenin's desire to keep the revolution democratic. When the impetuous young Trotsky once wanted the tiny party to seize power immediately, Lenin wrote, 'Whoever wants to approach socialism by any other path than that of political democracy will inevitably arrive at absurd and reactionary conclusions both economic and political.' He never doubted that his party was acting solely in the interests of the masses, and that it would disappear in the classless society of the future. In *The State and Revolution* he envisaged the happy day when *'all* will take a turn in management, and will soon become accustomed to the idea of no managers at all.' He never for a moment entertained the Fascist principle of government by and for the superior few.

Yet Lenin himself did not approach socialism by the path of political democracy. He denounced as a 'democratic superstition' the Menshevik doctrine of the 'right of the working class to self-determination.' Although he later admitted that he tended to exaggerate in the heat of controversy, his attacks on 'democratism' remain spread on the books; and the driving logic of his whole policy was anti-democratic. The youthful Trotsky turned the tables by attacking Lenin's 'egocentralism,' warning prophetically against its logical outcome: 'The organization of the Party takes the place of the Party itself; the Central Committee takes the place of the organization; and finally the dictator takes the place of the Central Committee.' And Lenin's sainted, humorless incapacity ever to doubt the rightness of his convictions made him a natural enemy of democratic liberties. The first chapter of his early book *What's to Be Done?* was a violent attack on the idea of 'freedom of criticism'; thereafter he never tolerated criticism in matters he regarded as fundamental. He gave ground only as a tactical expedient, never out of respect for the other fellow's opinion or a desire to get along with him. He appeared even more tyrannical than he was because of his ugly manners in controversy—his inveterate habit of questioning not only the logic but the motives of his opponents, and of branding their views as not only false but 'foul.'

Both sides, accordingly, can quote from the scriptures of Lenin; but the undemocratic side has all the better of such argument. Call it his 'splitting mania' or call it prophetic genius, he made the Bolshevik Party, and he made it Russian. He had been brought up in the conspiratorial tradition of Russia, which he once described as 'our Asiatic and barbarous land.' His long life as an exile did not sweeten or mellow his disposition, and even in exile he breathed the atmosphere of absolutism in government and extremism in thought. He was himself entirely free from jealousy, vanity, personal ambition, or the neurotic motives of a Hitler; in one respect he appears even nobler than St. Paul, in that he dedicated his entire life to his cause without benefit or mystical experience or promise of personal salvation; yet he contributed heavily to a regime that many of his old comrades came to regard as a barbarous, Asiatic despotism, and by which they were to be liquidated.

4. The Revolution

When the Revolution finally broke out in Russia, in 1917, it was neither planned nor led by Marxists. No Bolshevik, admitted Trotsky, realized that this was to be the decisive drive. Spontaneous strikes and demonstrations in Petrograd quickly spread; a large czarist garrison, which could easily have suppressed them, as quickly melted away; and within a few days the czarist regime was no more. It had not been overthrown—it had simply collapsed. It bowed out with a spectacular display of inanity. The pious czarina exhorted her dear Nicky to beat down the people as they deserved, expressing the hope that 'that Duma man Kedrinsky' (Kerensky) would be hanged for his horrible speeches; but Nicholas ignored the frantic telegrams of his ministers, once remarking, 'Again that fat-bellied Rodzianko has written me a lot of nonsense, which

I won't even bother to answer.' When he got around to bothering, his ministers had lost all control and his demoralized supporters were reduced to futile gestures. They naturally suffered somewhat from rioting crowds. (As Trotsky noted, 'A revolution is always distinguished by impoliteness, probably because the ruling classes did not take the trouble in good season to teach the people fine manners.') But there was no real class war, and surprisingly little bloodshed; the casualties in Petrograd totaled a thousand or so. The Russian Revolution began as the easiest, most painless cataclysm in all history.

For a month the Bolsheviks were pleased to support the popular coalition government that ruled the country. 'The fundamental problem,' announced *Pravda* (then edited by Joseph Stalin), 'is to establish a democratic republic.' As Trotsky later saw it, 'The most revolutionary party which human history until this time had ever known was nevertheless caught unawares by the events of history'; it followed 'the confused, weak-hearted, cowardly half-road of compromise,' even to the point of tolerating 'doctrinaires' who demanded freedom of the press. But then the German General Staff helped to set them straight. Scheming to weaken Russia and get her out of the war, the far-sighted generals arranged for the famous 'sealed train' that took Lenin through their lines from Switzerland to Russia. Lenin went to work within a few hours after his arrival at the Finland Station, haranguing the errant comrades in a long speech that he summarized the next day in *Theses of April 4*.[6] He demanded that party at once cease all co-operation with the coalition government, or with any other party, and also cease all support of the war. As usual, the majority of the party was opposed to him, but he soon won it over. The Bolsheviks started on the path that led to the October Revolution, when they overthrew the government and seized power.

For Lenin it was a stormy path. He had constantly to fight the overwhelming majority of the socialist leaders, who wanted to unite. They included many Bolsheviks (among them Stalin and a young student named Molotov, whom Lenin once described as an 'incurable dumbbell,' but who from the beginning had the wit to attach himself to Stalin). At least once, when the majority of the Central Committee voted against him, Lenin appealed over their heads to the workers—a violation

---

[6] It should be remembered that all the historic dates of the Revolution are inaccurate. Czarist Russia was backward even in its calendar, which was thirteen days behind the international calendar since adopted by the Soviet. Thus the famous 'February' and 'October' revolutions actually occurred in March and November.

of party discipline that he would never permit in others, and that would be high treason today. A month before the October Revolution, when Lenin summoned the party to insurrection, many leaders still failed to see its 'inexorable' historic necessity; he had to demand the expulsion of Zinoviev and Kamenev, his oldest disciples. On the very eve of the revolution many were still wavering, and some ran out on it.

At first the October Revolution was also amazingly easy and bloodless. In Petrograd the Bolsheviks got complete control within a day or so; the government simply folded up like the czarist government before it, while Kerensky fled. In Moscow the insurrection was bloodier but took little more than a week. The terrible civil wars did not start until some time later. They make plainer, however, that there was nothing inevitable about the triumph of the Bolsheviks. Given the rottenness of the czarist regime, anybody could have predicted the Russian Revolution; but nobody could have predicted with assurance its eventual outcome. The immediate question, then, is why the Bolsheviks did triumph.

According to Trotsky's *History of the Russian Revolution* it was a victory of the masses. He dwells on not only the rapid growth in popularity of the Bolsheviks but the 'spontaneous' dictatorship of the masses. 'Every step forward of the revolution was evoked or compelled by direct intervention of the masses,' who were far to the left of the Bolsheviks. 'Only in October will the party finally fall in step and march out at the head of the masses.' Trotsky falls into apparent inconsistencies, however. While emphasizing the 'immense' popularity of the Bolsheviks he also emphasizes their heroic audacity, periodically describing them as a small or even 'tiny' minority. He is forced to admit certain 'political aberrations' and 'enigmatical contradictions.' The masses continued to give large majorities to the other parties in the democratic dumas—in Moscow the Social Revolutionaries alone got more than 60 per cent of the votes in the June elections; so he explains that the 'mirrors of democracy' failed to reflect 'the real development of the revolution.' For such reasons he indicates that the spontaneity of the masses had to be carefully coached. At first they were taught the slogan 'All power to the soviets,' but when it later appeared that the soviets still tended to compromise and oppose the insurrection, Lenin revised the slogan: 'All power to the *Bolshevik* soviets.' Trotsky confesses that many in the party were shocked by this new policy, failing to understand Lenin's everlasting effort 'to express with the utmost simplicity' the real desires of the people.

Despite this simplicity, it seems clear that the revolution proceeded in accordance with neither Marxist nor democratic principles. The 'soviets' themselves were democratic councils that had not been planned by Marxists but had sprung up spontaneously among workers, soldiers, and peasants; the Bolshevik party then used them for its own purposes, as determined by its leaders. For the Constituent Assembly—a truly national parliament—it found no use. All along the Bolsheviks had attacked the coalition government for postponing the elections for this parliament; when the Assembly at last met, just after the Bolsheviks seized power, they dissolved and abolished it—it too was given to 'political aberrations.' They were opposed by most of the democratically constituted groups, including powerful trade unions. In the critical early days of the revolution they got their most effective popular support from the peasant soldiers, who were not Bolsheviks or even Marxists—they were simple peasants, weary of the war and hungry for land. Still more helpful was a confused, disorganized, demoralized opposition. The Kerensky government, dominated by frightened conservatives, proved utterly incapable of dealing with the mounting crisis due to disasters on the war front, increasing food shortage, and a deteriorating economy. It had no real plan. The Bolsheviks alone seemed to have one. As Miliukov, one of their leading opponents, later wrote, 'They knew where they were going, and they went in the direction which they had chosen once for all, toward a goal which came nearer and nearer with every new, unsuccessful experiment of compromisism.'

Only it was not 'they'—it was primarily Lenin, aided by the fiery Trotsky. As a devout Marxist, Trotsky sought to prove 'the deep natural inevitability of the October revolution,' in which Lenin merely 'helped the masses to recognize and realize their own plan'; but he was always embarrassed by his natural appreciation of Lenin's achievements. Throughout his three-volume history he backs and hauls, swerves and squirms, hedges and counterhedges—only to prove that Lenin made all the fateful decisions, and invariably had to bludgeon the majority of the party leaders into accepting them. 'Lenin became the unqualified leader of the most revolutionary party in the world's history because his thought and will were really equal to the demands of the gigantic revolutionary possibilities of the country and the epoch,' whereas others 'fell short by an inch or two'—and then he repeatedly shows how most of the others fell short by miles. When he reaches the climax of the drama he gives himself away completely. 'The success of the Russian and world revolution,' Lenin told the Central Committee, 'depends upon a two or three days' struggle'—not, it appears, upon the iron laws of history. Trotsky agrees that if the Bolsheviks had not seized power at this time they very probably would never have got it, since the masses would quickly have become disillusioned with them too. And again he shows that the party leaders were hesitant, or even hostile; so again the gigantic historic outcome hinged on the iron determination of Lenin.

In the violent aftermath of the October Revolution Trotsky himself played a brilliant, heroic role, as organizer of the Red armies. The revolution had been based on a serious miscalculation. 'We rest all our hope on the possibility that our revolution will unleash the European revolution,' Trotsky told the Congress of the Soviets. 'If the revolting peoples of Europe do not crush imperialism, then we will be crushed—that is indubitable.' In March 1918, Lenin expressed the same prayerful hope: 'It is absolutely true that without a German revolution we will perish.' Instead of a European revolution the Bolsheviks got counter-revolutionary armies supplied and supported by the Western Allies. A blockade by the British fleet kept out food, clothing, and medical supplies; presently English, French, and American forces invaded the country, to aid the counter-revolutionaries. For two years Russia was convulsed by civil wars. The White Terror was matched by the Red Terror, and both were supplemented by banditry and pogrom; hunger and horror became routine. The Bolshevik government barely managed to survive, and likely would not have survived except for popular resentment of the intrusion of the Allies. It might be said that Germany started the October Revolution by sending in Lenin, and that England France, and America sealed its success.

The Russians were accordingly confirmed in their traditional suspicion or hatred of the West. They were also confirmed in their ancient experience of privation and misery. It is estimated that the civil wars claimed seven million victims. When they finally ended, in the particularly cold, dreadful years of 1920, the following spring brought the worst famine in Russian history, with some thirteen million peasants lacking enough grain even for seed. We must remember that the Soviet was not born in strength, abundance, assurance, or joy. What it first had to share was not wealth but sacrifice. To a long-suffering people, any good that came out of it was all to the good.

5. FROM LENIN TO STALIN

'We shall now proceed to construct the Socialist order,' Lenin had said very simply, when he rose to address the cheering

Congress of Soviets during the October days. Because of mass discontent following the privations of the civil-war period, he reverted to the New Economic Policy, granting free enterprise to peasants, merchants, and small capitalists. The West rejoiced: NEP meant that already he had to confess the bankruptcy of Communism. As usual, however, Lenin was not yielding on fundamentals. He was being characteristically shrewd and flexible, retreating momentarily only to gather forces for a further advance. The Soviet State retained complete control of all major industries and resources. Under Stalin it continued on its socialistic course, collectivizing the farms, instituting the celebrated Five Year Plans. Steadily it built up strength, to the confusion of conservatives in the West. Socialism, they kept insisting, destroyed all initiative and could not possibly work; but it was also making Russia a dangerous power, whose initiative was a major threat to the West.

Meanwhile Marxists themselves were becoming much more confused. They had been conditioned to the idea that socialism called for a world revolution. Then Stalin called for a new policy of national socialism and Russia first, and fought his historic battle with the orthodox revolutionists, led by Trotsky. When he triumphed, the primary objective became to make Russia strong enough to survive even in a capitalistic world. To this end Stalin sought to form a United Front with the democracies, as a protection against Hitler; later he made his pact with Hitler. Meanwhile Trotsky had been exiled, at length to be murdered. Extended purges, climaxed by the Moscow trials, revealed considerable dissension within the party and gave Stalin the appearance of an Asiatic despot. The war revealed that the Soviet was by no means so demoralized as critics had assumed, but its aftermath has further disenchanted many sympathizers. And so the question arises, Does the Soviet represent 'true' communism? Some recall the prediction of Bakunin that Marxism would become a terrible tyranny. Others assert that Stalin has betrayed the principles of Lenin and Marx.

The question cannot be answered positively. Given all the inconsistencies in the Marxist scriptures, the friends and the enemies of Stalin can both find ample quotation to clinch their arguments. A further difficulty is that the Marxist dialectic provides no standards of right and wrong. 'History' alone can decide: future might makes right. Lenin was right only because the October Revolution succeeded; if it had failed the orthodox Mensheviks would have been right—the proletarian revolution could succeed only in advanced capitalistic countries. Yet these very difficulties help to decide the issue. It seems clear enough that whether or not Lenin would have approved of all the developments, Stalin's policies are a quite logical development of his own policies. One may as fairly say of Stalin what Trotsky said of Lenin, that he was 'not an accidental element in the historic development, but a product of the whole past of Russian history.'

Trotsky ridiculed the series of Five Year Plans as 'substituting the multiplication table for a historic perspective.' Others point out that the Soviet today is an artificial creation, not a natural product of economic forces, But so it was as Lenin made it. He started creating a proletariat by industrialization; he planned to socialize the peasants, in order to guard against their petty-bourgeois tendencies; he directed the whole construction of the socialist order. Stalin's further measures appear sound enough in communist principle and have unquestionably advanced Russian agriculture and industry. The most obvious objection is to the immense human cost, notably the deliberate liquidation of the kulaks, or wealthier peasants, in order to collectivize the farms. Even the Webbs, in their sympathetic study of Soviet Communism, admit that hundreds of thousands were destroyed or deported to prison camps. They add, however, that while factions within the party disagreed over matters of practical policy, none argued for mercy for the kulaks. Certainly Lenin was never the type to plead the sanctity of the individual of the right of the minority.

In the split over foreign policy, Trotsky had the better of the textual argument. Like almost all communists Lenin had taken for granted the necessity of a world revolution, often saying that communism could not be achieved in Russia unless it was also achieved in the West. Stalin was plainly dishonest in the pretense that his nationalistic policy was orthodox Bolshevism. But he was at least true to the realistic, flexible spirit of Lenin. At the time there were no prospects whatever of a proletarian revolution in the advanced Western democracies. Trotsky looked like the kind of 'formalist' whom Lenin so often denounced for ignoring concrete realities; during the prolonged controversy he did not debate the practical merits of Stalin's policy but dwelt on its deviation from the expressed views of Lenin and Marx. At any rate, the new policy now appears to have been a shift in tactics rather than a modification of basic philosophy. Sometimes the word from Moscow is that capitalism and communism should be able to live together in the same world; sometimes the word is that they cannot possibly do so. The foreign policy of the Soviet appears to be based on the latter assumption, which is essentially the heresy Trotsky was condemned for. 'History' may prove that both Trotsky and Stalin were right, though Stalin has prepared himself a possible out.

The Webbs were pleased to note that the new policy was adopted only after extensive public debate, illustrating the constant self-criticism in the Soviet. Since they wrote, however, the real issue has become much plainer. Public discussion is restricted to the question whether a given idea or policy is in accordance with the party line—the line itself can never be questioned. There was no public debate at all over such crucial decisions as the pact with Hitler (which a democratic Russia would never have signed) or the foreign policy adopted since the war. For better or worse, the party line is determined by a few men; then any criticism or dissent is treated as high treason. And while the line has followed an amazingly devious course under Stalin, reversing itself several times, he has not been patient or lenient with those who had difficulty in following it. Once in the saddle, he became increasingly suspicious of opposition and increasingly merciless in liquidating it.

Now, the brutalities of 'Stalinism' have perhaps been exaggerated. We must recognize, John Somerville rightly says, that there may be 'essential good faith' at the basis of a system we deplore. In theory, Stalin and his privy councillors are ruling in the true interests of the workers; in fact, they may be perfectly sincere in their devotion to these interests, and wise in their judgment of them. But first we must acknowledge the plainest facts. The Soviet is a totalitarian state run by a dictator. As Bertram Wolfe comments, 'Totalitarianism is not "just another form" of democracy any more than kicking over the checker board is "just another way of playing checkers." ' It may be government for the people; it certainly is not government of and by the people. The fact is that freedom of thought, speech, and conscience is denied on principle, as it was in the medieval Church. It has seemed uglier because the rulers of the Soviet consistently refuse to credit their opponents with 'essential good faith.'

In any case, both the theory and the practice of the Stalin regime come straight from Lenin. Lenin himself planted the seeds of tyranny. He set up the dictatorship, which began silencing the opposition as soon as the Bolsheviks came into power. Bourgeois talk about freedom of the press, he announced, 'halts our headlong course towards Socialism.' Because he knew the 'real' interests of the people he always felt free to override 'formal' majority opinion; as Trotsky noted approvingly, 'The majority is not counted up, but won over.' Trotsky also noted that 'irreconcilable' and 'relentless' were always among his favorite words. Lenin was the more inclined to despise all compromise as cowardice because, though an avowed materialist and rationalist, he could see only heresy and treason in honest differences of opinion. Very possibly he would still have disapproved of the ruthlessness and the extent of the purges under Stalin; he was a more tactful, humane man than Stalin appears to be, and is reputed on good authority to have distrusted him. Nevertheless he sanctified the principles that made the purge the logical way of settling differences of opinion.

Indirectly, Lenin prepared for the Stalin regime by his oversights. Despite his life-long concern with the problem of political power, and his many acute insights, he grossly oversimplified the problem because of his utopian assumption that proletarian dictators would be free from the sins of all previous dictators, and that eventually the state would 'wither away.' Like most Marxist analysts he failed to realize, more specifically, that the Workers' State would naturally generate the involuntary by-products and inner contradictions that plague all other states.

As a victim of it, Trotsky began to realize the natural consequences of a victorious revolution. He became aware of the type of the *epigoni*—the less curious, less imaginative, less masterful inheritors, whose ardor is expressed in revolutionary clichés. He discovered the inherent conservatism and self-interest of a bureaucratic machine. 'The machine,' he now saw, 'can fulfil a revolutionary function only so long as it remains an instrument in the service of the party, so long as it remains subordinate to an idea and is controlled by the mass.' He even admitted that Lenin himself 'was "only" a man of genius, and nothing human was alien to him, therein included the capacity to make mistakes'; so he concluded that the all-too-human party needed 'internal democracy.' Yet Trotsky still failed to realize, or to admit, that he and Lenin had built this party machine, that they had provided no effective means for keeping it subordinate to an idea or—least of all —subject to the control of the mass, that their whole revolutionary policy declared human fallibility and much human sentiment to be alien to the good Bolshevik, and that Lenin in particular had fought internal democracy all his life. In his last years Trotsky did remark that 'it is rather tempting to draw the inference that future Stalinism was already rooted in Bolshevik centralism, or more sweepingly, in the underground hierarchy of professional revolutionaries'; but he resisted this temptation. There is little reason to believe that had he won out he would have been essentially more democratic than Stalin.

Another natural result of revolutionary success was the growth of nationalism and imperialism. The Russian Revolution was to be unlike all others, especially the French; but like the French Revolution under Napoleon it has been followed by a return to historic policies. For this Lenin cannot be held responsible. Though a loyal Russian, he was never a chauvinist. When the First World War broke out, he was one of the few leading socialists to oppose it—even forming his own International and reading out all patriots who favored the war. He consistently denounced the Russian drive to the Dardanelles and Iran. Repeatedly he called for the right of peoples to self-determination; he said nobly, and truly, that no nation that oppresses others can be free itself. Stalin, an Asiatic, has resumed the ancient march of the czars—to the Baltic, to the Mediterranean, to the East. The victorious czars and generals have become national heroes again; Ivan the Terrible was glorified while Trotsky was being branded a fascist traitor. The ideal of self-determination has become the capital crime of 'national separatism.' The Red Army is the nation's pride, and its officers have taken to bemedaled uniforms. Like Napoleon, Stalin has restored the ancient titles, granting himself those of Marshal and Generalissimo. Whereas Lenin rejoiced in the defeat of Russia by Japan as a boon to the cause of the proletariat, Stalin in 1945 rejoiced that this 'dark stain on our country' was at last wiped out. Holy Russia is spotless again.

With this has come the systematic deification of Stalin. The reverence for Lenin is a natural tribute to an extraordinary leader, who accomplished far more than Marxist theory allows for but who never sought personal glory. The reverence for Stalin has been drilled by a high-powered campaign, directed by Stalin himself, which is a disgrace to the revolutionary philosophy and the communistic ideal of both Marx and Lenin. In manufacturing his myth Stalin has been able to draw on the ancient worship of the holy czar, but he has also had to rewrite revolutionary history. Memoirs, official biographies, and official histories published during the early years of the Soviet all make plain that Stalin had always been a minor leader, that (as he himself publicly admitted in 1924) he had been among the 'mistaken' comrades who at first opposed Lenin's views on the revolution, and that he played a minor role in the revolution itself. Now the gospel is that Stalin was always the right-hand man of Lenin and the practical genius of the revolution. The Institute of Party History has forbidden publication of his writings during 1914-17, and suppressed important documents; books published as late as 1934, with official approval, have been burned; anecdotists and historians with inconvenient memories, including old

Georgian comrades, have been purged for maliciously 'falsifying' history.[7] Possibly Stalin fancies himself in the role of Dostoyevsky's Grand Inquisitor, deliberately sacrificing his dignity for the sake of his child-like people, giving them the security they really want instead of the truth and freedom for which they are not yet fit; or possibly he is trying to recapture the lost youth of Russian culture, return to the springtime when heroes become gods. The non-Communist world is apt to distrust a synthetic god in any role.

At least Stalin has clarified a basic issue that was obscured by the genius of Lenin. The Soviet is commonly held up as the plainest example of the sins of rationalism, or especially of a 'scientific philosophy.' Actually, the ideals of the Enlightenment have never had a chance in Russia. Lenin was hostile to the freedom of thought and speech required by the life of reason; under Stalin even science has lost its freedom. Orthodox Marxism is at best a pseudo-scientific philosophy, but in the Soviet it has become a Russian religion.

6. AMERICA AND RUSSIA

The hope of One World has traditionally rested on the faith that with acquaintance comes understanding, and with understanding comes love. It has been too simple a faith. With acquaintance may come distrust or dislike, a livelier awareness that foreign lands are infested with foreigners. With understanding may come fear and hatred; knowing the Russians, one may find less reason to trust or to love them. Still, understanding remains the indispensable first step to agreement. Americans had better try to understand a nation that constitutes the vastest empire in all history. And since they are proud to have conquered a continent, they might have a natural respect for the land of Gogol—'that land that does not care to do things by halves, but has spread a vast plain

---

[7] This whole fantastic story has been thoroughly documented by Bertram Wolfe in *Three Who Made a Revolution*. From Trotsky I cite one example of how bare-faced the fabrication has been. The official edition of Lenin's works published during his lifetime declares that 'Trotsky organized and led the insurrection of October 25th.' In 1918 Stalin agreed; in *Pravda* he wrote, 'All the work of practical organization of the insurrection was conducted under the immediate leadership of the president of the Petrograd Soviet, Comrade Trotsky.' In 1924, however, Stalin wrote, 'We must say that Trotsky played no special role in the October revolution and could not have done so'; and presently he gave orders that all historians must say this, forbidding quotation of his former article.

over half the world, and one may count its milestones until one's eyes are dizzy.'

The two countries in fact have much in common. They are both 'new lands,' lands of many peoples, newly risen to world powers. Both have grown tremendously; even under the czars, the population of Russia increased more than ten-fold after 1700. Siberia in particular has repeated the American experience of the frontier. Explorers, hunters, and trappers were followed by farmers and miners; mass coloniza-tion began about 1860. Instead of driving out the natives, the Russians settled among them and are now trying to assimilate them, but in this way they have made their own melting pot, which is still boiling. And under the Soviet, Russian culture has become more like American culture. The Communists have imported not only the cult of the machine but the gospel of work; if they still dream of ultimately realizing the Marxist ideal of 'to each according to his need,' they are mean-while utterly devoted to the Puritan ideal of 'to each accord-ing to his work.' In this spirit they too have drummed up a passion for production, celebrated their material progress, glo-rified the economic man. At the same time, it is idle to sneer at the Russians as mere materialists. Like Americans they are 'idealists working on matter.' Their revolution has been a spiritual adventure, calling for sacrifices that a real mate-rialist would never make. The fabulous marbled subway of Moscow, built proudly while the workers of Moscow still put up with wretched standards of living, is the cathedral of the Soviet—a monument symbolizing a spiritual fervor compar-able to that which erected Hagia Sophia, and more geniune than that which erected the Cathedral of St. John the Divine in New York.

This spirit is not simply Byzantine or Orthodox. It has been intensified by the Western, 'Faustian' spirit at the heart of the revolutionary Marxist philosophy. Because it is now fashion-able to dwell on the somber Hebraic background of Marx's thought ('The day of the Lord is darkness and not light,' saith the prophet) we may forget that he propounded per-haps the most optimistic version of the modern gospel of progress. No eighteenth-century philosopher dreamed of a more heavenly city than Trotsky envisaged at the conclusion of his *Literature and Revolution:*

Man will become immeasurably stronger, wiser, and subtler; his body will become more harmonized, his movements more rhythmic, his voice more musical. . . The average human type will rise to the heights of an Aristotle, a Goethe, or a Marx. And above this ridge new peaks will rise.

Hence the holy mission of Russia has become much like the American Dream. Russians may feel that theirs is the real land of opportunity, the really new world. They do not have the kind of freedom and opportunity that Americans have, but many apparently feel that they have a more exhilarating kind—the power to make over their world. They have a more ardent purposefulness, a more vivid sense of building something new. 'We will be everything, create everything, open up everything, from the North Pole to the blue sky'—so ran the refrain of a popular song. In other words, they will beat Americans at their own game.

We cannot afford to forget that the October Revolution was fought in the name of a lofty democratic ideal, and stirred a genuine idealism all over the world. The corruption of that ideal, the disenchantment of that idealism, is an old story in history; but it remains high tragedy. It should sober conservatives as well as revolutionaries. In *The God That Failed*—especially in the contribution of Ignacio Silone—they might read, reverently, why men of good will were drawn to the Soviet, as well as why they were ultimately repelled. For the tiresome Soviet clichés about the decadent, corrupt, bourgeois West may dull us to the actual corruption. In the period between the wars the democracies were in fact rotten enough to permit or even to abet the rise of Mussolini, Hitler, and Franco, and at Munich to sign the warrants of their degradation. Say the worst about the fantastic, inhuman dogmas of communism and it only emphasizes the demoralization of the West, that such dogmas should appear reasonable to so many intellectuals, and especially in Europe become the white hope of large masses of workers. We might better begin by admitting the worst about the democracies, and recognizing the best that can be said for communism.

The trouble with America, we often hear, is all the godless skeptics among us (especially among professors). Actually, we can hardly hear such skeptics in the din of the incessant, blatant celebration of the American Way—a tribal chant that frightens our allies more than it seems to have frightened the Russians. The plainest trouble is the shortcomings and the perversions of American democracy, which are glossed over or defended by the most respectable elements in the country. In particular it stems from the rule of money. Although the moneyed men are not naturally more selfish, greedy, or unprincipled than former aristocracies, they glorify a profit system that forces men to be selfish, puts a premium on greed, and encourages socially irresponsible or unprincipled behavior. They confuse democratic idealism by identifying Freedom with economic freedom, whereas laissez faire has meant less actual freedom of life for common men, and has threatened the dignity of man presumed by democracy. They restrict freedom in both theory and practice by proclaiming inviolable laws of competition and supply and demand, and by opposing the democratic effort at a rational control of private enterprise.[8] Their curious theory remains that uncontrolled economic strife will automatically promote the good of all. In fact it has promoted strife—the bitter class-war that has been the chief internal problem of democracy over the last hundred years.

For all classes, however, the central source of corruption is the sacred profit motive. It is a constant menace to justice, fraternity, integrity, sincerity, or simple decency. As the practical man says, 'Business and sentiment don't mix'; so when it comes to a choice, sentiment is dropped. One result is the 'absurd, monstrous contrast' between private life and social relations that led the humane Silone to turn Communist. Another is the debasement of culture by big businesses that exploit the most vulgar, depraved tastes, stimulating or even creating these tastes while pretending merely to satisfy them. (One assumes that the Soviet has plenty of sex, for example, but it has not major industries to manufacture the sexiness that gluts American life.) More insidious is the depreciation of all values that do not 'pay.' Most corrosive is the social acceptance of insincere, dishonest behavior that does pay— the routine hypocrisy in politics, advertising, publicity, commercialized sport, commercialized art, commercialized piety— uniting athletes, beauty queens, crooners, society women, and 'men of distinction' in the aristocracy that endorses eye-wash. It is doubtful whether dishonesty has ever before been so pervasive, systematic, dynamic, and respectable as it is in America today.

For such reasons the Webbs regarded the Soviet as a really new civilization, neither Western nor Byzantine. They drew up an impressive list of its unique achievements. It has abolished the profit motive, condemning as criminally unsocial the kind of speculation and exploitation that the West honors as good business; it has demonstrated the possibility of gigantic, long-range planning for communal production and consumption,

---

[8] The semantic confusion behind their logic is exemplified by a little masterpiece of Edmund Burke's: 'The laws of commerce are the laws of nature, and therefore the laws of God.' In this sonorous dictum Burke managed to confuse at least four different meanings of the word *law*. The laws of commerce are either a body of working rules or rough empirical generalizations, and in either case man-made; the laws of nature are exact statements of invariable relations, independent of man and incapable of violation; the laws of God are commandments, which like the laws set up by man may be broken.

which the West had considered hopelessly impractical, and has thereby eliminated the cycle of boom and bust, the unemployment that has been among the privileges of free workers; it has established a more genuine and universal equality, without race or class distinction, and with obligatory work for all; it has created a new political instrument in the Party, a democratic priesthood whose members are carefully selected, thoroughly trained, and severely disciplined for their 'Vocation of Leadership'; it has introduced a new morality, stressing 'universal individual indebtedness' and self-realization through co-operative endeavor, and setting up a scale of values that applies to all spheres of life; it has frankly and utterly devoted itself to the service of man's life on this earth, introducing the new ideal of freedom *from* religion. Altogether, the Webbs concluded, it has achieved a basic unity that contrasts strikingly with the disharmonies, contradictions, and hypocrisies of Western life. In the democracies, John Somerville adds, individuals may have positive values but the only objective of the society as a whole is the agreement to have no one definite objective. In the Soviet, *'society* has a philosophy, a world view, a set of values'—a very positive idea of the kind of life it wants.

Offhand, totalitarian theory is accordingly as respectable as Roman Catholic theory. The apologists for the Soviet point out that it provides 'real' freedom—not a negative freedom *from* the State but a positive freedom *within* it, with such new rights as the right to work. For the State is not a necessary evil against which the individual must be protected: it is a positive good, a great co-operative enterprise that alone makes possible a fuller life for the individual. Hence it will not permit freedom *against* the State, which would jeopardize the interests of all other individuals. It must guarantee its citizens, as Lenin said, freedom from 'anarchic bourgeois individualism'—from powerful, irresponsible men who want to promote their own selfish interests at the expense of others, and who in the democracies largely own the 'free' press. Its gifted citizens, one might add, will also be free from the romantic fallacies of the West, such as André Gide's dictum that the great artist is necessarily a non-comformist. Its artists and intellectuals will work better because, like the Greeks, they are working with and for the community.

So runs the theory, on paper. The paper is already yellowing with age, however. No talk about 'real' freedom can disguise the real tyranny in the Soviet. As we seek to understand, even as we respect the professed ideals of the Soviet, we must finally dwell on its own sources of corruption. Immediately, the abuses spring from the strange faith that evil methods will automatically produce good, and tyranny will necessarily end in freedom. Ultimately they are implicit in the very ideals that the Soviet has set itself.

The plainest objection to Soviet theory is that the State is not in fact a pure co-operative enterprise, synonymous with Society. It is a government run by a small group, who wield tremendous power. They are supposed in time to surrender this power, but Marx himself insisted that no group in power has ever voluntarily relinquished it. Meanwhile they are more likely to abuse their power because they are not subject to free criticism or public recall. Nor is the Party an adequate safeguard against misrule. It is in a real sense a priesthood, whose periodic internal purges may be viewed as drastic efforts to maintain the highest standards of fidelity to the Vocation, and so prevent the corruption that made the medieval clergy a scandal; but as a priesthood it is liable to 'the chronic disease of orthodoxy' that the Webbs recognized. Its diseases are aggravated by the whole Russian revolutionary tradition, the engrained habits of conspiracy and terrorism. By its addiction to the purge the Party breeds the informer, promotes mutual suspicion and distrust, and puts a premium on cynical expediency and servility. It creates a petty-bourgeois aristocracy of right-thinkers and yes-men, and makes scapegoats of precisely its most thoughtful, independent, courageous members.[9]

Marxist 'realism' is a further menace to the wisdom and virtue of the rulers of the Soviet. In making class struggle the key to all history, and violence the means to the heavenly classless society, Marx nurtured a cult of force that betrayed both his rationalism and his Romantic idealism. In effect he repudiated the faith in reason and reasonableness, denied the dignity and worth of the individual—of man as Man, not merely as Worker. His inhuman logic was epitomized by Trotsky after the Russian Revolution: 'To sanctify the individual we must destroy the social order which crucifies that individual. This task can be fulfilled only by blood and iron.' Evidently Trotsky did not consider that a social order is made up of individuals, and that 'only' blood and iron are as likely

[9] Silone has vividly illustrated the reality of these dangers. As a delegate to the 1927 meeting of the Communist International, he learned that Moscow had ordered the meeting to denounce a document by Trotsky, a copy of which he was unable to procure. The delegates obediently denounced it, even though others admitted to Silone that they had not read it either, and though the document proved to be an attack on Stalin's policy toward Chiang Kai-shek—whom Stalin had publicly praised just a week before Chiang reversed himself and started massacring the Chinese Communists. Silone also reports the uproarious laughter that greeted a simple English delegate who objected to some prescribed tactic because 'it would be a lie.'

to make good Fascists as good Communists; so presently he was himself crucified. And the evil is not simply the violence and injustice—these are common enough in the democracies. The evil is that the men of the Kremlin can be ruthless in good conscience, unscrupulous on principle. In their realism they are corrupting the values—such as sympathy, kindliness, love, and passion for justice—that are indispensable to the realization of the communistic ideal.

Ultimately, the curse of the Soviet is rooted in its famed unity. 'Unity' is always a magic word. Many educators, columnists, and churchmen are now crying that what America needs is a uniform philosophy. They seem to forget that Russia has such a philosophy, just as Somerville seems to forget that medieval society also had a common faith and a definite objective. In this respect there is nothing novel about the civilization of the Soviet. It is profoundly, literally reactionary, reverting to the ancient ideal of absolute conformity; and it is demonstrating again that this ideal cannot be achieved except by repression. To a society that has known freedom or aspires to freedom it means tyranny. For free men will never agree on a uniform philosophy or common objective. They cannot all agree even on the value of their freedom. So Carlyle wrote to Herzen that he much preferred czarism 'to the sheer Anarchy . . . which is got by "Parliamentary Eloquence," Free Press, and counting of heads'; and he praised the Russian people for their pre-eminent talent—'the talent of obeying.' But whatever men value more than freedom they are likely to lose as they lose their freedom—unless their pre-eminent talent is indeed for obedience, as it was not in Carlyle himself.[10]

It is very doubtful that Lenin could have won the October Revolution by democratic means, or at once started constructing a democratic socialistic order. Trotsky observed that Russia was hardly capable of the 'elastic conservatism' that had made England great. To be successful, representative government requires long experience in the arts of compromise and bargain, an engrained willingness to accept popular verdicts that run counter to one's cherished convictions. Still, the soviets provided the nucleus for a democractic government, and many liberals believed that once communist Russia was firmly established it would make steady progress toward the democratic ideals of the classless society. As it kept moving instead toward severer repression, disillusioned liber-

---

[10] He might have considered a very simple observation of Herzen's: 'Until I came to England the appearance of a police officer in a house where I was living always produced an indefinable disagreeable feeling, and I was at once morally on my guard against an enemy. In England a policeman at your door merely adds to your sense of security.'

als have tended to make Stalin the villain of the piece, or to dwell on the ancient evil of egotism; but more fundamental, I should say, is the ancient fallacy of authoritarianism. Simply because we cannot hope to eradicate the ancient evil, we must hope to realize the practical wisdom of democratic controls in political and intellectual life. The 'mere formal freedom' that Marx saw in democracy is in fact the only possible security for any real freedom. 'Liberty,' Silone remarked to a fellow-Communist, 'is the possibility of doubting, the possibility of making a mistake, the possibility of searching and experimenting, the possibility of saying "no" to any authority.' His remark aroused the horrified suspicion that he was a counter-revolutionary; and this sufficiently explains the terrible mistakes it has been possible for good Communists to make.

Since understanding is our theme, we may add that the Soviet not only has made little effort to understand the West but has been committed on principle to an inveterate misunderstanding. Twenty years ago Trotsky predicted that England was headed for 'gigantic revolutionary earthquake shocks' because it had lost its elasticity; its conservatives and even its supposed liberals were now addicted to a 'stark reactionism.' Today Soviet authorities keep insisting that the Western bourgeoisie is becoming ever more reactionary and the Western proletariat ever more wretched; so they attack most fiercely the liberals and the socialists who keep working to disprove their textbook theory. They continue to play the 'pitiful role' so often assailed by Lenin, 'meaninglessly repeating a formula *learned by rote* instead of *studying* the unique living reality.' When the Soviet economist Varga actually studied this reality, announcing that the American economy was thriving and the American proletariat pretty well off, he was officially disgraced.

This 'trained incapacity' to understand the history going on under their eyes is a legacy of Marx himself. He bequeathed a brilliant analysis of pure capitalism; grant his premise of a laissez-faire economy—especially of a free labor market—and his conclusion of the inevitably increasing misery of the proletariat is quite logical. But even as he wrote, this society was changing. The workers heeded his cry to unite; they began to improve their condition by labor unions and collective bargaining. They also exerted enough political pressure to invalidate Marx's thesis that democracy is 'only' a veil for bourgeois dictatorship. Hence increasing social legislation worried as well as gratified the Marxists. Engels lamented that instead of suffering as they should, workers were becoming more and more bourgeois; Lenin and others echoed his horror (in Karl Popper's words) of 'the incredible wickedness of a capitalist system that transforms good proletarians into bad bourgeois.' In general, the trend in the democracies everywhere has been away from laissez faire toward a rationally controlled economy—defying the iron laws of history precisely as the Marxists themselves have done in Russia. The 'free private enterprise' system that Communists say is doomed by its wicked stupidity, and that conservatives say is the only hope of the world, has not existed for a century.

'The fundamental premise of a revolution,' Trotsky wrote, 'is that the existing social structure has become incapable of solving the urgent problems of development of the nation.' The issue, then, is whether the democracies can solve the problems of their development, or specifically of their experiment in a mixed economy, the partial collectivism that has been forced on all of them by industrialism. In terms of ideal values, the issue is whether a society that has to be planned to some extent can be democratically planned and controlled: whether democracy can achieve the degree of socialism required by a complex economy and still retain the essentials of liberty. The most dangerous internal threat to its success has not been communist agitators or arrogant labor leaders but the far more powerful vested interests that denounce as regimentation any effort at social experiment or rational control. They recall the historic selfishness, short-sightedness, and incorrigible stupidity of privileged classes, who when facing disaster have again and again refused to make the concessions that would have enabled them to retain the essentials of their power and prestige. But so far democracy has been able to force such concessions, and to maintain a degree of the economic equality without which political freedom becomes meaningless.

And so we might well conclude, in efforts at understanding, by acknowledging the contributions of Marxism to social intelligence and to the struggle for social justice. André Gide remarked the most difficult complication in judgment of the Soviet today: usually 'truth is spoken with hatred and falsehood with love.' Silone speaks what I judge to be the truth, and speaks in a spirit of love. The 'scientific' theories of socialism are transitory, he declares, but its values are permanent. 'On a group of theories one can found a school; but on a group of values one can found a culture, a civilization, a new way of living among men.' There is perhaps a half-truth in his half-serious remark, that the final battle will be between ex-Communists and Communists.

X

The Timely East

1. THE MEETING OF EAST AND WEST

'Oh, East is East and West is West, and never the twain shall meet,' sang Kipling, the champion of the all-conquering West. Actually, of course, they met and mingled in the ancient world. Persia was an early link, especially for the trade in religious ideas; Satan himself appears to have migrated from India to Persia, and thence to Palestine and Rome. Plato's idealism is akin to Indian transcendentalism, if not indirectly indebted to it, and the Neo-Platonists recognized their kinship, looking to India as the seat of wisdom. Christianity owes much to Eastern religions, in particular its mystical and ascetic tendencies.[1] The continuous intercourse ceased with the fall of Rome, when the West was no longer capable of meeting the civilized East, but as Europe grew up it again drew on the wisdom as well as the wealth of the Orient. The Age of the Enlightenment was dazzled by Confucian China—Voltaire hailed it as the best empire the world had ever seen, with the purest morality. Among the intellectual excitements of the nineteenth century was the rediscovery of Indian thought, which was congenial

---

[1] Scholars have also been struck by the close similarity in some of the parables and legends of Buddha and Jesus, such as the miracles of walking on water and multiplying the loaves and fishes. Although they are unable to trace the possible influence, they have discovered the presence of Buddha among the later Christian saints. In the eighth century John of Damascus wrote a story about one Josaphat, a legendary Christian prince who renounced the world. This became so popular that in the sixteenth century the prince was canonized. It is now clear that St. Josaphat was none other than Bodhisat, or Bodhisatva, and his life that of the Hindu prince who renounced the world to become the Buddha.

especially to German Romantics and American Transcendentalists. Today East and West are met in the United Nations. Their mutual understanding is no longer an academic ideal but a practical necessity.

The need is most pressing for the West, which created it by the blind drive that Kipling celebrated. The East has already received a compulsory education, thanks to which it has roused itself and begun to meet the West on equal terms. Now the West in turn must go to school, to learn the rudiments of the universal history it has been writing and making. As Toynbee emphasizes, its unique achievement in laying the material and intellectual foundations of a world order throws into sharper relief its besetting sin of parochialism. The ugliest instances are its national, racial, and religious prejudices. Underlying these is the general assumption that all history culminates in us; the importance of Eastern civilizations, it appears from incidental chapters in our 'outlines of history,' lies chiefly in their 'contributions' to us. As common is the naïve habit of identifying human nature with Western nature—a habit to which authorities on the eternal verities are especially addicted. The prophets who are crying that 'we' can be saved only by returning to the verities almost always mean, in effect, 'we Westerners.' They seldom take into account those Moslems, those Chinese, those Indians—peoples who also have timeless truths, some of which are considerably older than our own. 'We' may save our individual souls on our own basis, but we cannot expect to understand or save civilization on that basis.

To begin with the elementary, then, we might note that there has never really been a timeless, changeless East—that strictly, indeed, there is no 'East.' There is the continent of Asia, a vast breeding ground of heterogeneous societies. Split it into Near East and Far East and there is still no clear entity; historic China had less in common with India than with Rome. Stick to Asia and we get another elementary lesson in humility. Objectively, its history looks more important than the history of Europe, the peninsula jutting off the Asiatic mainland. (A good primer for Westerners is Nehru's *Glimpse of World History*, written in a British jail: Nehru takes for granted that a world historian will be concerned chiefly with Asia.) It has produced more civilizations, involving a much greater proportion of mankind, over a longer period of time, on a higher level of continuity. As for cultural achievement, we have no universal yardstick; but by one standard on which Western Christendom has prided itself, Asia has been far more creative. It has bred all the higher religions, including Christianity. In Buddhism it produced the first universal religion, and the greatest in number of adherents.

The objective, however, is not merely a decent humility. It is again a clearer understanding of our own world, and a consideration of possible means to a better one. As the Hindu philosopher Radhakrishnan observes, we can never afford to neglect the thought and experience of half of mankind, but today in particular we need to mobilize all the intellectual, moral, spiritual resources at our disposal. Most thoughtful Easterners —including those, like Radhakrishnan and Nehru, who are most appreciative of the scientific and political achievements of the West—still maintain that the East has more to teach than to learn about religion, philosophy, and the art of living. We should at least hope to learn; for we cannot deny the spiritual deficiencies of the West today, by either religious or humanistic standards.

2. THE MYSTICISM OF INDIA

The land designated on the map as India has never been a nation. Large parts of it were occasionally incorporated in transitory empires, but it remained a swarm of diverse peoples, with different languages, who until recently did not aspire to political unity. What has made India a recognizable, discrete civilization is primarily religion. Religion was the basis of its thought, its art, its law, its social structure. Its peoples were generally indifferent to political unity, or even to political independence, because they made religion their major business. The most religious society in history, it is today the only great society in which a spiritual leader such as Gandhi could become a national idol and political leader.

Indian religion is likewise a swarm of diverse sects, embracing countless deities and doctrines. Historically it was split for a thousand years between the rival religions of Brahmanism, Jainism, and Buddhism. But these religions were fundamentally akin, in their indebtedness to the Vedas or ancient scriptures; in time Jainism dwindled and Buddhism disappeared from India proper, partly because the Brahmans had taken over much of their creed; and the innumerable sects that continued to proliferate were united by common doctrines that identify the national religion of Hinduism. Hindus generally agreed that the essence of man is not body or ego but *Atman*, an impersonal soul in the depths of his being. The hordes of deities are subordinated to the great gods Vishnu and Shiva, who in turn are manifestations of *Brahma* —an immanent God or World Soul. The basic doctrine is that man can know God directly, because *Atman* and *Brahma* are one; to seek God is to know oneself. Hindus insist on the primacy of this spiritual consciousness, as the source of all true knowledge. The supreme business of man, accordingly, is to realize his spiritual being, become the supreme being within him. A characteristic means to this self-discovery is the discipline of Yoga (etymologically akin to the Latin *jungo* or join, and to our word (*yoke*), which is a kind of spiritual setting-up exercise designed to free man from his consciousness of self and the sensory world.

Allied with these doctrines are such traditional beliefs as reincarnation and the principle of karma, which declares that the deeds of a lifetime inexorably determine a man's status in his next incarnation. The alliance is not clearly logical, since karma appears to give the impersonal soul a sort of individuality and complicates or obscures its supposed identity with the World Soul. The core of Hinduism, however, is its faith in the Within—the immediate knowledge of an immanent God. This mysticism is the major issue raised by Indian civilization. Radhakrishnan and others believe not only that it is the soundest basis for a universal religion but that it is likely to be the religion of the future. I should say at once that I doubt it will be or could be, if civilization prospers. But at least it illumines religious possibilities, and offers a valuable corrective and complement to Western religions.

To begin with, it is significant that this most spiritual of peoples has got along without beliefs and institutions that many Western thinkers declare are essential to spirituality. Thus Buddha denied the existence of a Creator concerned with man and discouraged the hope of life eternal. He never asserted that he was anything more than a man, never invoked supernatural authority; he merely preached a way of salvation that all men could find by their own efforts, as he had found it, without heavenly aid or further need of his own aid. In time his followers added popular attractions, which the Brahmans also tolerated, but among the educated the religious spirit continued to flourish without the extravagant promises and exorbitant demands by which the West has shored up its spiritual life. The Supreme Being of India is not a personal God and does not offer personal immortality. Neither has it required strict faith and obedience, saddled mankind with original sin, or threatened mankind with eternal torment. It has authorized no church to decree and enforce the true form of worship.

The most apparent virtue of this religious spirit is its genius for fervor without fanaticism. Toynbee laments the 'tragic halt' of Hinduism in permitting the co-existence of the great gods Vishnu and Shiva, instead of exterminating one or the other to make way for a Yahweh; but to Hindus such tolerance is not a mere concession—it is the very essence of religion. 'Truth is one,' it is written in the Vedas, 'the sages speak of it by many names.' Devout Indians have always taken for granted that the Supreme Being cannot be pinned down by human dogmas, and that the innumerable gods and forms of worship represent the naturally limited, historically conditioned efforts of the human mind to conceive the One True God. To them nothing is more irreligious than the self-righteous exclusiveness that claims a monopoly on divine truth and the means to salvation. In an edict of toleration issued five centuries before Constantine, the Emperor Ashoka declared a policy far in advance of Constantine's church: 'He who does reverence to his own sect while disparaging the sects of others wholly because of attachment to his own . . . by such conduct inflicts the severest injury on his own sect.' In this spirit Buddhism became a great missionary religion without exterminating heathens and heretics, or scaring them into the true faith; while Hinduism maintained itself without setting up grand inquisitors or ecclesiastical police. Although Hindus have grown militant in recent times through conflict with Mohammedans and a rising nationalism, the religious ideal of India remains the spirit of Ramakrishna, who in mystical visions was united successively with Krishna, Buddha, and Christ, and could easily have known Allah too.

In effect, Hinduism has regarded religious truth as symbolic, not historical or literal. More specifically, it has asserted a continuous or progressive revelation. While the divine inspiration of the Vedas is one of its unifying tenets, the Vedas did not become a closed canon. The most pious admitted the possibility of new revelations, and through the centuries have produced new scriptures; some sects even consider the Vedas outmoded. No major sect pretends to finality. More than any other religion Hinduism has been even in theory a quest, not a creed. Despite its apparent quietism and its aura of timelessness, it is an 'open' religion, and in this respect better suited to an open society than is most Western religion.

It is also more genuinely universal in spirit. The claims of Hinduism do not rest on the logical validity of a set of propositions about God, or the historical validity of reports about his miraculous activities on earth—dogmas that may be shaken by scientific or historical discoveries, and that are convincing only to men brought up in a particular culture at a particular time. Its claims rest on religious experience, a spiritual consciousness that is the birthright of mankind. It affirms that God is always revealing himself to all men, everywhere.

Similarly it affirms a deeper, closer community than the brotherhood of man under the fatherhood of God. Brothers may separate and quarrel, especially when each is created with a separate, personal soul that he retains through all eternity. The lofty Hindu declares that 'one should love his neighbor as himself because he *is* his neighbor.' All selves are one. Indeed, all are united with all living things, in the divine self that is the soul of the universe.[2]

At the same time, Hindus may claim a profounder realization of the Western gospel of self-reliance. One who knows Brahma is free in mind and spirit, above the selfish hopes and morbid fears that have enslaved Western man. And men can achieve this freedom by their own efforts, without special grace. While both Catholics and Protestants have maintained that there can be no salvation without Christ, the holy men of India have maintained that every man must and can save himself—no god can do it for him, or need die for him. This was the supreme lesson that Buddha taught his beloved disciple Ananda:

And whosoever, Ananda, either now or after I am dead, shall be a lamp unto themselves, and a refuge unto themselves, shall betake themselves to no external refuge, but, holding fast to the Truth as their lamp . . . shall not look for refuge to any one besides themselves—it is they . . . who shall reach the very topmost height! But they must be anxious to learn!

Anxious to learn! The teaching of the Enlightened One was more intellectual, less child-like than that of Jesus; like

[2] This sense of oneness is strengthened by the ancient belief in the transmigration of souls, down to the animal world, which most Westerners dismiss out of hand as a strange superstition; so as another five-finger exercise in cultural tolerance we might consider whether it is not more reasonable than the Christian doctrine of heaven and hell. It implies a kind of conservation of spiritual energy that seems more logical than the endless creation of brand-new souls—supposedly 'immortal' souls that come into existence at a particular moment in time, for no more apparent reason than to swell the eternal congestion. It asserts a principle of unity and continuity that is congenial alike to poets, philosophers, and scientists. It makes more sense of the whole creation, the life of all other animals, which in the Christian view were created only for the sake of man, and must struggle and suffer endlessly through no fault of their own. By any rational ethical standard it is much more just than an eternity of bliss or torment awarded on the basis of a single lifetime. As for the obvious objection, that there is no empirical evidence to support the doctrine, neither is there any such evidence for heaven or hell, or any other theories of a future life. Such intimations of immortality as we may feel are more comprehensible if we assume a pre-existence.

almost all the great religious teachers of India, he regarded knowledge, not faith, as the key to salvation, and ignorance the main source of evil and misery. Another paradox of Indian mysticism is its claim to rationality—to a spirit of truth more akin to Western science than the Western religious spirit has been. Because India has valued truth more highly it has known no serious conflict between faith and reason, religion and science. The Brahmans monopolized knowledge instead of combating it. Except for some periods of foreign rule, religious thought has been remarkably free in India, and remarkably bold and restless, producing a great many schools of philosophy. Almost all have appealed to a spiritual consciousness deeper than reason, but almost none have simply rejected or despised reason. Thus Radhakrishnan says flatly that religion can no longer rest its claims on a dogmatic supernaturalism, because any dogma that is irreconcilable with tested knowledge must be rejected. In a sentence he sums up the dark and deadly pages of Christian history: 'If we believe absurdities, we shall commit atrocities.'

Altogether, the mystical, other-worldly spirit of India may be considered more pragmatic than the religious spirit of the worldly West. It begins and ends in the sense of oneness with a much greater whole that is not an arbitrary assumption but a datum of immediate experience, the ground of art and fellowship as well; by concentrating on this felt harmony —the true religious end—it minimizes the endless dispute over theoretical inferences from undemonstrable premises that has confused, distracted, and exasperated the spiritual life of the West. And these religious differences take on a wider, deeper philosophical import in F. S. C. Northrop's provocative work, *The Meeting of East and West*.

The East, according to Northrop, focuses its attention on the nature of all things as known in immediate experience, emotionally and esthetically. It locates its basic truths in the 'esthetic continuum'—indeterminate, ineffable, and all-embracing—which underlies the relative, transitory objects that may be abstracted from the stream of consciousness.[3] The West perforce begins with this primary experience but focuses its

---

[3] Yoga may be regarded as a technique for experiencing only this continuum, by becoming oblivious of the self and the world of things. Westerners usually assume that the state it aspires to is essentially unconsciousness: if the self and the things are removed, nothing would be left. Indians assert that what is left is the continuum, and that it affords a rich, moving experience, though necessarily indescribable. Similarly the Nirvana to which Buddhists aspire is not mere Nothingness but again the continuum, the basic oneness. It looks like oblivion to the Westerner because he wants individual immortality, or even a resurrection of his flesh.

attention on the particular objects or structures it abstracts, the logical theories it infers; it regards the immediate data as 'mere' phenomena, 'secondary' or spurious. The East is more positivistic, sticking to the concrete facts. It declares that reality is the stuff of consciousness, 'the stuff that dreams and sunsets and the fragrance of flowers are made of.' (Thus it keeps the blue in the sky, where it belongs; while Western thinkers have put the blue in the mind of the observer, and then puzzled over the problem of how it could get there and what the sky is 'really' like.) The certainty and the constancy of Oriental culture derive from its stress on the all-embracing oneness and continuity; its knowledge is not hypothetical or tentative. The radical uncertainty and change in Western culture derive from its stress on abstraction and theory; its eternal truths are secondary inferences that are always open to question and subject to change.

In this view, the East has erred by assuming that the logically inferred and theoretically described are merely subjective, relative, or unreal. Hence it failed to develop science, or to do justice to important aspects of experience that can be positively known. The West has erred by neglecting primary experience, finding 'reality' only in the secondary inference. Northrop concludes that the West should go to the East for religious instruction, as the East has come to it for science. But since both the esthetic and the theoretical components of reality are in fact real, and essential to an adequate understanding of man and the universe, there is no necessary conflict between East and West. Rather, their ways are complementary, and point to an ideal synthesis. Northrop believes that in such a synthesis is the practical answer to the world's problems.

Here, unhappily, a student of history must part company with him, and return to the actual disharmonies. Northrop has plainly oversimplified an 'East' in which he managed to bundle the fundamentally different cultures of India and China. He slights the many anomalies in the culture of India itself. Much of its sacred literature is fearfully pedantic and verbose; the authors of the Upanishads, Brahmana, and later theological writings are often as drunk on abstraction as the medieval schoolmen. Hindu art, which one might expect to be primary or pure, has typically been highly mannered, ornate, crowded, often violent. Classical Sanskrit poetry is distinguished by astounding artifice and delight in cleverness, including such stunts as the 'backwards' poems in which each line can be read either forwards or backwards. Read either way, they are a far cry from the 'esthetic continuum.'

And so we must question the spiritual reality that is immediately known to India. Lovejoy has remarked the different kinds of 'metaphysical pathos,' such as the 'intuitive' conviction of many men that only the everlasting and immutable are worthy of our attachment—even though it is not self-evident that the changeless is excellent, or the one more illustrious than the many. At least this conviction looks like a metaphysical inference; for uniqueness, variety, and change are also given in immediate experience, and would seem to be as 'real' as the continuum. As for the mystical experience, its reality and unquestionable value are still no proof of the reality of God; else there is no hallucination, and all that men see in ecstasy or trance is true. The concept of World Soul that Hindus infer from it is highly theoretical and abstract, but in any event the experience has to be interpreted. Thus Radhakrishnan grants that Hindu mysticism tends to 'exaggerations,' is often 'too emotional,' and 'has its fanatics' —implying a rational criterion of judgment that he does not clearly define, and that evidently is not given by the mystical experience itself. The remarkable fertility that has produced so many schools of thought in India also indicates that the nature of the spiritual reality is not at all clear. And given this restless theoretical enterprise, we are forced to note much the same unresolved dilemmas and logical contradictions that have kept Western theology going. These are summed up in the relation of the World Soul to the sensory world in which men have to live. Hindu thinkers have been inclined to regard the universe as illusion, but then they cannot explain how or why the illusion came to be, and why men can escape an unreal world only by the most arduous effort. Now that they incline rather to regard the universe as real, they cannot explain its manifest evil. Rabindranath Tagore simply asserts that God created the world out of overflowing love and joy; so again we are asked to celebrate the perfection of the Absolute, from which all imperfection flows.

The main question, however, is what kind of civilization was created by the most religious of peoples. If Indian piety is the key to the future, we must consider how it worked out in the past. We cannot judge its claims merely by the ideal theory of its sages and saints, any more than we can judge the claims of Christianity by the life of Christ. We must ask whether it has brought more peace, love, joy, and goodness than have other religions. And we find, as we might expect, the same incongruities, the same absurdities and barbarities accompanying the same high aspirations; only they seem more fantastic in a country that has made religion its main business.

This has not been a wholly spiritual business. The devotion to Brahma is less apparent than the reverence for cows;

the saintly mystics are lost in the crowds of fakirs, temple prostitutes, fortune-tellers, snake-charmers, vendors of spiritual patent medicines. In no other land has superstition been ranker and grosser. Through a multitude of magic rituals the masses of India have sought to propitiate millions of deities and demons. Many have found ecstasy in phallic rites, the mystical union of coition; more have bowed down before the terrible Shiva, the god of destruction, whose ritual demands were often cruel and bloody. If the worship of Shiva may be viewed as a profound realism, a recognition of the evils that the mystics dismissed as illusion, it points to the most obvious source of the religious fervor of India—not the esthetic continuum, but continuous wretchedness. Excepting a few brilliant reigns, the historic lot of its masses has been oppression, pestilence, famine, and grinding poverty. They also became enured to such human evils as child marriage, the burning of widows, and the degradation of millions of Untouchables. Northrop declares that the emphasis on the all-embracing continuum naturally tends to make the East compassionate; but there has been little effective compassion for man or beast. 'No society,' lamented Vivekananda, a disciple of Ramakrishna, 'puts his foot on the neck of the wretched so mercilessly as does India.' Gandhi, who made the same complaint, shocked his pious followers when he killed a dying calf to put an end to its agony.

This is the old story of vulgarization—all popular religions breed their sacred cows.[4] Another familiar theme is a priestly monopoly jealously guarding its privileges. Only the Brahmans could directly attain the Absolute, and they took pains to keep their high secrets to themselves; the lower caste Shudras were forbidden, under penalty of torture, even to listen to the Vedas. Hence the Brahmans appear complacent as well as humane in their hospitality to the swarms of popular deities. As holy virtuosos, who believed in a higher truth for themselves and a lower truth for the common people, they were too willing to tolerate vulgar custom and belief, making little effort to give the masses more elevated conceptions of God.

---

[4] The most striking example is the history of Buddhism. Rebelling aginst the ritualism of the Brahmans, the Enlightened One had scrapped all supernatural accessories. Then his followers transformed him into a savior-god, the author of many miracles; and the religion that spread in his name—the 'higher religion' that sustained Toynbee's dying Eastern societies—took on the full paraphernalia of a popular salvation cult: assistant gods, devils, heavens, hells, purgatories, saints, relics, confessions, incense, holy water, candles, rosaries, et cetera. 'The Buddhist,' observed James Fergusson, 'kept five centuries in advance of the Roman Church in the invention and use of all the ceremonies and forms common to both religions.'

Yet the failure of Hinduism to realize its high spirituality in social life may also be charged to intrinsic defects of this spirituality. The fundamental issue is raised by the familiar objection to the mysticism of India, that it is essentially life-denying and therefore essentially non-ethical—that its main effort is not to improve man's life on earth but to escape life.

As usual, the issue is not clear-cut. Defenders of Hinduism can point to many affirmations of life in its scriptures. The Vedas often express a poetic naturalism like that of the Greeks, or even a pagan ecstasy. ('We drank Soma, we became immortal, we found the gods,' reads one hymn—suggesting that they found the World Soul through alcohol rather than meditation on the continuum.) The later priestly writings made many compromises with the ascetic idea, if only because the Brahmans recognized the necessity of offspring to preserve their caste. The sacred literature of both Hinduism and Buddhism is also rich in ethical commandments that anticipated the Sermon on the Mount. It was India that introduced the great commandment not to kill or harm any living creature. Its positive idealism has been exemplified by a long line of spiritual teachers, from Buddha to Gandhi. The West cannot match the saintly Emperor Ashoka: the one great monarch on record who renounced war after victory, horrified by the misery he had caused, and thereafter devoted himself to setting an example of perfect piety and benevolence. Unlike Marcus Aurelius, he was not resigned but fought against misery, working more actively to promote the well-being of his subjects; unlike St. Louis of France, he renounced the use of any force whatever to promote his devout religious faith. And that he is still revered, in a land notorious for its indifference to history, implies that this is not simply an indifference to life itself.

Yet the dominant theme in Indian religious thought has unmistakably been life-negation. The goal of Buddha was a kingdom of no world; the goal of the Hindu saints and sages has been union with Brahma, through non-attachment to the temporal world; the goal of the anonymous masses has been escape from the endless cycle of rebirth. Neither the World Soul nor the popular deities have given real meaning or value to human history. Mysticism naturally tends to ignore this history, as unimportant or evil. While it always proclaims a metaphysical monism, for living purposes it always implies a sharp dualism between its spiritual reality and the vulgar actuality known to ordinary men. Its highest wisdom, Aldous Huxley is pleased to point out, is a 'holy indifference' to mere worldy causes; as St John of the Cross said, 'Disquietude is always vanity.' And this whole tendency is still apparent in modern Hindus who are attempting to reinterpret their tradition. Radhakrishnan, again, maintains that true Hinduism is an affirmation of life; but he also maintains that true religion is 'essentially other-worldly,' calling first of all for a renunciation of this world, and that Hindus naturally regard themselves 'as strangers and pilgrims on earth,' naturally are content to be 'fit for heaven but of no earthly use.'

Likewise neither the World Soul nor the popular deities of India have identified themselves firmly with a moral law. 'I am indifferent to all born things,' announces the God-head in the Bhagavad-Gita. 'There is none whom I love, none whom I hate.' Since goodness is likeness to God, Indians have naturally sought to attain a comparable indifference. 'The immortal man overcomes both the thoughts "I did evil" and "I did good,"' declare the Upanishads. 'Good and bad, done or not done, cause him no pain.' The Buddhist scriptures often warn against the danger of love, as a form of attachment to the world. The compassionate love preached and exemplified by Buddha himself was not an active love, love for its own sake or for goodness' sake—it was a means to Nirvana. Even the sublime commandment to kill or harm no living creature appears to have been motivated by a desire for purity from the world more than a real love of all creatures. Hence there is no Tragedy in classical Indian drama—the tragic sense of life requires a respect for life. Hence, too, the Bhagavad-Gita justifies war on the grounds that killing is unimportant because death is unimportant. And though this most famous of the Hindu scriptures is unusual in that it approves of a life of action, it stresses the need of relinquishing all desire for the fruits of action. As Albert Schweitzer points out, it prescribes an essentially meaningless kind of activity—an activity that begins by renouncing its natural motives, any usefulness for worldly purposes.

The plain proof that the strongest tendency of Indian thought has been life-denying remains the history of India. Even the modern champions of Hinduism admit that it has been poor in works. Religion cannot be held responsible for the corrupt administrations, the foreign invasions, and all the ills of a teeming, broiling, pestilent land; but it can be charged with the historic indifference to such ills, the failure to combat them. Throughout the long centuries, in a land swarming with priests and holy men, there is hardly a sign of any aspiration to liberty, any concerted effort at social justice, any will to social progress. Indians were not interested in recording their history if only because they had no real interest in improving it. When Northrop explains that Oriental positivism regards all determinate things as relative and transitory, and is therefore suspicious of social reform as a merely determinate effort to eliminate merely transient evils, he is putting the cart before the horse. The obvious reason for the acquiescence of the masses is that they never had reason to hope for anything better than transient reform. The Maharajas and the Brahmans could acquiesce in their own privileges the more easily because of the most disinterested spirituality of India. If the temporal world is illusion there is no important distinction between freedom and slavery, justice and injustice. Holy men who contemplate with equanimity the birth and death of whole universes, in an endless cycle, will not be troubled by the fate of mere societies.

The most practical expression of the Indian spirit was its unique caste system. Although this apparently originated in the effort of Aryan conquerors to maintain their superiority over the much greater native population, in time it was rationalized on a religious basis. We need not dwell on the obvious objections to an institution that arbitrarily determined the status of all men by birth rather than merit or ability, that condemned most men to a lowly status, and that denied the many 'Outcastes,' or Untouchables, any civil or religious rights. We do need to consider its less obvious claims to respect. The institution was moralized by the principle of karma, since the faithful man could hope for a higher status in his next incarnation. The privileged Brahman in turn did not have an easier life at the top but was subject to a severe discipline, on penalty of going down the scale in his next birth; unlike most historic aristocracies, this caste kept producing men of distinguished learning and piety in every generation. All men of caste enjoyed the security of an appointed place and a common tradition. All were protected against the tyranny of economic competition, class conflict, and arbitrary political power. All could seek perfection in their own sphere, aided by the order that was given to every trade and profession by the hundreds of sub-castes, and by the strong sense of continuity in the society as a whole. The caste system held India together for more than two thousand years, through all the vicissitudes of foreign conquest, civil war, and political chaos. How it worked, as late as the nineteenth century, is summed up in the famous observation of Sir Charles Metcalf:

If a country remains for a series of years the scene of continued pillage and massacre, so that the villages cannot be inhabited, the scattered villagers nevertheless return whenever the power of peaceable possession revives. A generation may pass away, but the succeeding generation will return. The sons will take the places of their fathers; the same site for the village, the same position for the houses, the same lands will be reoccupied by the descendants of those who were driven out when the village was depopulated.

In short, this institution represents the most astonishing attempt in history to maintain social stability and arrest change. So here, again, is the issue. In keeping with the metaphysical ideal of a changeless reality, the religious ideal of renunciation, and the ethical ideal of passivity, the ideal of the caste system was an absolutely static order, a completely 'closed society.' It was the closest historic approximation of the Platonic beehive.

Now, the historic achievement of India makes it impossible to say that life-negation is mere futility or failure of nerve. I see no way of demonstrating that the affirmative ideals of the West are absolutely truer or higher.[5] The faith of both East and West has been nourished by illusion; but as the profoundest affirmation has been won from the tragic view of life, so the profoundest negation has sprung from a naturally serene, even cheerful disposition. The sages of India have not been wretched men. Similarly, on the humbler level of everyday life, it is not certain that men are wiser and happier in trying to improve their lot than in trying to accept it, or that freedom at the cost of tension and strife is necessarily better than peace at the cost of surrender. Historically, the dynamic, adventurous societies have generally been more brilliant and heroic, but they have also been relatively short-lived. In the West the active faith in progress is already on trial for its brief life.

Nevertheless I hold that if mankind has any future it belongs to the Western faith. The West itself may go down, or eventually be dominated by the East. A billion peasants are now awaking from their timeless sleep, shaking off their traditional passivity. Even apart from its immense human resources, the awakened East may be considered a better risk for the future, for the reason suggested by Toynbee: it may adapt itself more readily to the demands of a new world

[5] I should add that once I did see a way, in the breezy assurance that Western parochialism makes easy. While defining the 'naturalistic basis of values,' in *Science and Criticism*, I asserted that men 'naturally aspire to abundance of life, fullness of being.' I should still argue that this aspiration is a natural expression of the distinctive potentialities emerging from the biological and social evolution of man. But in India man has as 'naturally' aspired to something very different; his distinctive potentialities plainly include a capacity for renouncing the natural world, defying elementary biology. Most of the moral teachers of mankind, indeed, have counseled the suppression of desire and exalted the passive virtues of humility, patience, obedience, and resignation.

order because it is less liable to the 'nemesis of creativity,' the idolization of outworn institutions and techniques. (Nehru illustrates the more enlightened statesmanship that it is theoretically capable of; he might play the ideal role of mediator between Russia and the Atlantic community.) Yet the significant point remains that the new hopes of the East are sprung from Western ideals, as well as Western science and industry. Its peoples have caught the spirit of independence; from the West they have learned that they were 'underprivileged,' and need not accept their historic lot. All the peoples of the world are now calling for 'human rights'—rights that are variously defined and interpreted but that finally imply Western ideals of self-determination and self-realization.

India is a conspicuous example of this interplay. In recovering its independence it appealed to principles of freedom and justice that it had learned from its British rulers. Gandhi himself was a typically Western reformer, even though he called for a rejection of Western civilization; he attacked the economic causes of wretchedness and denounced such venerable Hindu institutions as child marriage and the Untouchables. The whole caste system is crumbling in the new India, which regards it as an ugly anachronism and an obstacle to national unity. The vanishing Indians today are the Brahmans—the oldest of living aristocracies—while women and workers rise from their traditional status of inferiority. Even the revival of Hinduism owes to Western influence, which has made India much more self-conscious than it was in the past.

As yet, however, East and West are not meeting on the plane of religion, where both Toynbee and Hindu idealists expect to find the most significant outcome. Hinduism has had very little influence on Christianity (or Mohammedanism either) since the ancient world. Such hybrids as the theosophy of Annie Besant and the sophisticated, self-conscious mysticism of Aldous Huxley do not look portentous. Christianity has had as slight an influence on Hinduism, though its missionaries have been at work in India since the sixteenth century. The growth of a more active, worldly spirit has been due to secular rather than religious influences, and is not making converts to Christianity. I can see no prospect of either religion's absorbing the other, short of a forcible conversion that Christianity could not achieve in a healthy world order and that Hinduism could not attempt without betraying its essential genius. If our civilization endures, or if a new civilization rises after universal catastrophe, there remains the possibility of a merger into a universal religion; but then both historic Christianity and historic Hinduism would be profoundly transformed. Christianity would have to forfeit its exclusive, literal theism—the core of its traditional dogma. Hinduism would have to forfeit its traditional passivity and other-worldliness; for if the unworldly inherit dying societies, no civilization has been born by a renunciation of life.

Meanwhile Westerners could learn much from India in composure and peace of mind: an inwardness to offset their incessant busyness and concern with externals; a mildness to soften their aggressiveness, moderate their demands upon one another; a cosmic sense to deepen their sense of solidarity, enlarge their precious selves; a sense of the eternal in the here and now, beyond the march of time, because of which time is not all-important. They might simply become more patient, and feel less lonely and impotent. But their advantage remains that they can learn such lessons, without suppression of their active personality or sacrifice of their will to better life. They can grow, acquire new virtues, more readily than the passive man. Only the active faith can become universal, at least in a going society, in the world known to historians. And if the active personality is always prone to egoism, the pride of life-denial may well be as false. Perhaps the ultimate in vanity is the assertion that disquietude is mere vanity.

3. THE HUMANISM OF CHINA

'Better fifty years of Europe than a cycle of Cathay,' sang another Western poet. Time indeed marched slowly in the long ages of China. A troubled age of 'Warring States' gave birth, in the sixth century B.C., to Confucius and Lao-tse, the heralds of a brilliant creative period in philosophy and literature. Several centuries later China was finally united in a great empire; and with the restoration of order creative thought ceased. For the next two thousand years the Chinese mulled over their Confucian classics. They produced new schools of poetry, painting, and ceramics; they made such 'contributions' as silk, tea, china, paper, printing, gunpowder, and the compass; they tried some political experiments, including price control and the ever-normal granary (an idea Henry Wallace got from them); they had revolutions, saw dynasties rise and fall and invaders come and go; but through all these upheavals their basic social and political institutions and their basic mentality remained unchanged. While Jesus would have felt an utter stranger in every century of Europe, Confucius would have felt quite at home in any century of China until our own.

Better fifty years of Europe, perhaps—but better first to

recognize the phenomenal achievement represented by the cycle of Cathay. China is the oldest of living civilizations, with a cultural tradition going back almost two thousand years before Christ.[6] When Rome was at its peak there was as great an empire in China, which contributed to the fall of the 'Eternal City' by throwing back the Huns, who then turned West. (Later it presented Europe with the Turks.) When Europe was wallowing in the barbarism of the Dark Ages, China was the most civilized land on earth, enjoying one of the most enlightened, polished epochs known to history. When Europe later became aware of China it humbly recognized a superior civilization, and down to the nineteenth century was pleased to learn rather than teach. No society has cultivated more graciously the art of civilized living, or clung more tenaciously to an ideal of culture. The political achievement of the Chinese dwarfs that of Rome, not to mention India. 'Nowhere else,' writes Latourette, 'has any group of mankind succeeded for so long a time . . . in holding together under a single rule so large a section of the earth.'

To Radhakrishnan, as to Toynbee, history shows that 'the world in the end belong to the unworldly.' The immediate significance of the oldest living civilization is that its history shows nothing of the kind. The Chinese never dedicated themselves to the service of God, in love or in fear. They were thoroughly mundane people, whose deep piety was a natural piety, rooted in the worship of ancestors and love of the good earth. They were much like the Romans in their combination of ceremonial piety and practical sense, but they were at once more sensitive and more sensible, or more humane. They kept their eye on the end, the good society, refusing to worship the State, the Law, or any other machinery. Their civilization was humanistic through and through. Its spiritual values were purely human values, unclouded by other-worldliness or notions of pure spirituality. Its highest goods were natural goods,

[6] Toynbee splits it into two distinct civilizations, a 'Sinic' and a later 'Far Eastern,' each with its appropriate time of troubles, breakdown, universal state, etc.; but this again looks like an arbitrary division for appearance sake. Other historians agree with the Chinese themselves on the essential continuity of Cathay, through its many times of trouble. During the interval between Toynbee's two civilizations—several centuries of disorder following the end of the Han dynasty about A.D. 200— China never descended into barbarism. The title of Emperor, the idea of unity, the Confucian tradition, and all the basic institutions came through, to serve the great T'ang dynasty that restored order; whereas Buddhism, the 'higher religion' that entered China during its 'disintegration,' failed to become its universal church or the inspiration of a new order. To this century the Chinese continued to call themselves 'Han Jen,' the men of Han.

good for this life and good enough without the further promise
of an eternal life.

Service of this life was the primary object of China's official
religion, nominally centered upon Heaven. Although the ancient classics indicate a degree of intimacy in the relations between Heaven and man, the deity was never so personal and
purposeful as Yahweh. There were no prophets or seers, no
divinely inspired scriptures, no tables of commandments, no
priests with high privileges, no popular temples. With the rise
of philosophy Heaven became purely impersonal. It was
neither a place nor a being, but was a moral order governing
the universe—in effect the sum of natural laws. As such it was
to be obeyed, not humored, flattered, or propitiated. Worship
was purely ceremonial; the highest religious aim was 'respect for Heaven,' not love of God. Similarly with the large
pantheon of lesser divinities and spirits, made up chiefly of
nature gods, deceased emperors, and distinguished men. 'Respect spiritual beings,' counseled Confucius, 'but keep them
at a distance.' He himself became one of the most eminent
divinities but only as the wisest of men; he was not prayed
to. Men were readily deified because there was no clear bound-
ary between natural and supernatural, no sharp separation of
mankind from Heaven. In their official capacity as 'Son of
Heaven,' emperors were free to promote or demote the lesser
deities, often conferring grandiloquent titles upon their favorites. In this century an imperial decree raised Confucius to the
same rank as Heaven and Earth.

The underlying skepticism suggested by such practices is
confirmed by a Chinese proverb: 'No image-maker worships
the gods—he knows what stuff they are made of.' Even the
common people, who worshiped hordes of deities not included
in the state pantheon, were apt to be disrespectful. 'Work with
the sunrise, Rest with the sunset, Dig the well for my drink,
Plough the land for my food—What do I care for the Power
above?' runs a very ancient ballad; and when the local gods
fell down on their job of preventing drought and famine, their
images might be exposed to the scorching sun, and finally
smashed if they still failed to get the idea. At least the Chinese
felt no need of certitude about the final questions. Their mythology (which characteristically included no flood myth) was
incoherent and inconclusive, and they developed no theology.
Thoroughly pragmatic, they were averse to all metaphysical
speculation about the origin, destiny, or ultimate meaning of
the universe. It was enough for them to have a rough idea of
what man had to do to get along with the gods. They were
typically eclectic, out of a sensible desire to take advantage of
all possible benefits. A Chinese could readily be both a Con-

fucianist and a Buddhist, much as an American can be both an Elk and an Odd Fellow.[7]

Confucianism, however, is the key to Chinese history. A mere man, not a divinity—a man who was not even a prophet or saint—Confucius succeeded in stamping a whole society in his image, leaving a far more distinct and indelible impress than did Christ, or even Mohammed. He simply waived the question of a City of God: 'We don't know yet how to serve men, how can we know about serving the spirits? We don't know yet about life, how can we know about death?' His whole concern was to establish a harmonious Earthly City. The natural basis for this endeavor was *jen:* a sense of sympathy or fellow-feeling, which was not a special gift of divine grace but a basic element of ordinary human nature. (The word in Chinese is made up of two symbols meaning 'man' and 'two.') As means of cultivating sense and sensibility Confucius put great store in poetry, music, and love of learning. His 'superior man' was a cultivated gentleman, reasonable, temperate, tolerant, mellow, humane.

Although the Confucian ideal is much like the Greek ideal of harmony and balance, it differs in some fundamental respects from the Socratic ideal, and from Western humanism. Confucius was no inquirer or seeker of truth. By his own testimony he was 'a transmitter, not a maker, believing in and loving the ancients.' Modern Chinese scholars believe that he took considerable liberties with his beloved ancients, and he certainly selected and adapted, shaping the tradition he transmitted; but his followers took him at his own word. The classics he compiled became the basis of all thought and learning. Likewise his humanism ruled out the ideal of individualism. Living in a period of chaos, he made his main objective not full self-realization but harmonious social relations; the good man was always heedful of his obligations rather than his rights, and the superior man was distinguished by being indistinguishable from other cultivated gentlemen. Hence Confucius emphasized the supreme importance of *li*, or

[7] The chief exception to their usual tolerance was the occasional persecution of Buddhism, but this was due chiefly to political objections: some emperors felt that the Buddhist monasteries were draining off too much wealth and manpower. Similarly with the Jesuit missionaries in the seventeenth century. They were hospitably received by the Chinese and at first made considerable headway—even in imperial circles—because they too were tolerant; in letters home they expressed their admiration of Chinese culture. But then the Pope ordered an immediate halt to the heresy of tolerating heathen customs; and the Chinese Emperor, furious at this insult to venerable traditions, put a stop to the activities of the Jesuits. The Catholic Church accordingly maintained the purity of its faith but lost a real opportunity of converting China.

ritual, ceremony, propriety. *Li* corresponded to the order of the universe, as music did to its harmony; through constant ritual men came to realize their proper place in the natural and social order. As the genius of Confucius lay in his union of conservatism and liberality of spirit, so his unique achievement was to unite a devotion to ancient, even primitive ritual—such as ancestor worship—with a cool rationality and a refined sensitivity, and thereby to give Chinese culture both its remarkable continuity and its exceptional graciousness.

The chief rivals of Confucianism—Taoism and Buddhism—offered more popular attractions, offsetting its tendency to excessive dignity and formality; but ultimately they became supplements rather than rivals, and confirm the practicality and this-worldliness of the Chinese spirit. In its original form, Taoism was akin to Indian mysticism. Lao-tse, its legendary founder, taught that the 'Tao' or true Way was an ineffable oneness with the universe, which might be identified with the World Soul or the 'esthetic continuum.' His aim, however, was a good life on earth through mellowness, not an eternal life through holiness, and it called for no arduous discipline or high aspiration. The Sage was one who had recovered the original simplicity of human nature, shaken off all the artificial concerns of civilization. 'The farther one pursues knowledge, the less one knows. Therefore the Sage knows without running about, Understands without seeing, Accomplishes without doing. . . By doing nothing everything is done.' The ideal of Lao-tse, as of Confucius, was a perfect harmony of body and soul, man and nature, but for him the means was natural rhythm and laissez faire. Fundamentally he was not so much a religious mystic as a primitivist. And as a religion Taoism in time went the way of primitive religions, back to magic. Whereas the early Taoists aimed to simplify life and despised worldly goods, their descendants evolved an elaborate, occult ritual for attaining these goods. Instead of the Tao they sought the elixir of life, which would assure prodigious longevity if not immortality. (At least one Taoist emperor died of an elixir.) Essentially, Taoism seems a vagabond expression of the cheerful, prudential Chinese spirit.

The popularity of Buddhism—the only important cultural importation in China before recent times—is somewhat surprising, since both its ascetic and its metaphyscial tendencies would seem alien to the Chinese. It entered, however, during a particularly troubled period, when the rule of Heaven was hard to discern. Its chief attraction was its promise of salvation, on genial terms that included accommodations for native deities in its spacious pantheon. At any rate, the Chinese made over their new religion to suit their temperament.

Nirvana became a more positive bliss, and was supplemented by personal heavens and purgatories; the way to Buddha-hood was made easier and shorter, through monasteries that were havens of peace rather than schools of discipline; the Buddha of popular worship was typically the fat, laughing Buddha. Although the Buddhist monks contributed about the only religious thinking that was done in China, what persisted was neither a systematic theology nor a life-denying ethic but a worldly church, which at best contributed to a serene, kindly life.[8]

Most characteristic, perhaps, was the Chinese neglect of Motse (or Mo Ti), a great religious teacher during the creative period, who maintained that universal love should be the basis of society. Confucius had warned against the folly of idealists who try to live 'too high, high above the ordinary moral self.' He taught that men should deal with one another as Heaven dealt with them, in a spirit of justice rather than universal love or forgiveness—Heaven and Earth are plainly no overflow of love. He summed up true morality in his 'silver' rule: 'Do not do unto others as you would not have them do unto you.' Mencius, his foremost disciple, accordingly condemned the doctrine of Motse as not only unrealistic but positively fatal to society; true virtue and piety require that one should love some men much more than others, and not love evil men at all. Chuang-tze, the foremost disciple of Lao-tse, also rejected the doctrine as 'too harsh' and 'contrary to the heart of the world.' Hence the works of Motse were virtually forgotten until recent times, when scholars unburied them.

Instead, the Chinese trusted to filial piety. They considered the family the natural school for moral education, and filial piety the best means to all other virtues; good sons and brothers were likely to be good neighbors, good rulers, and good subjects. All obligations were strengthened and elevated by the cult of ancestor worship, which united the living with the dead and with the generations to come. Notions of the

---

[8] In Japan Buddhism was likewise transformed into a cheerful religion, promising bliss without demanding austerities, but it had a stormier career. By the tenth century the monks were a formidable evil because of their immense wealth; they grew lazy, ignorant, debauched, and arrogant, turning their monasteries into fortresses. Reforming sects later rose to power but in turn became corrupt. In the sixteenth century the monks were finally crushed by the shogun Nobunaga, who slaughtered thousands of them. Jesuit missionaries rejoiced in Nobunaga's ruthlessness. 'This man,' they wrote home, 'seems to have been chosen by God to open and prepare the way for our holy faith, without knowing what he was doing.' He did know, however. Before long the Jesuits were expelled from Japan, and a chastened Buddhism remained its faith.

after-life were vague, but in some manner the spirits of the
dead stayed at home, residing in tablets on the ancestral shelf
and listening in on family councils. Deference to them was un-
forced, since the living too were assured of a kind of homely,
intimate after-life, which might be more satisfying than resurrection in some misty, remote heaven. So the spirit of Confucius may rejoice in the knowledge that his grave was still
being tended in the twentieth century by a man claiming lineal descent; while all but one of the dying-gods of the less
ancient Greco-Roman world have long since died for good.

Chinese political institutions were likewise molded by the followers of Confucius, in particular Mencius. The Emperor was
a legacy of ancient tradition, and as a 'Son of Heaven' had
the makings of an Oriental sacred-monarch. Shih Huang-ti,
the powerful emperor who unified China, in fact ruled as a
despot; he anticipated Hitler by his famous decree that all
the Confucian books be burned. He was supported by the
Legalists or Realists—another of the many schools of thought
in the astonishing creative period—who had an essentially
fascist conception of the supreme State, and worried over the
problem of 'how to get the people to die.' But they failed to
solve the problem. The Chinese overthrew Shih's dynasty within a few years after his death, and thereafter rejected fascism
as they rejected the doctrine of universal love. The celestial
emperors were denied any divine right to rule as they pleased.
Although they ruled by a 'mandate from Heaven,' they automatically forfeited this mandate by unjust rule. And the people
were supposed to be the judges. 'Heaven sees as my people see,
Heaven hears as my people hear,' Mencius quoted from the
Confucian *Book of History*. The people had the right of revolution; the Chinese word for revolution means literally 'to
change the mandate.' 'In a nation,' Mencius declared, 'the people are the most important, the state is next, and the ruler is
the least important.'

In spirit, accordingly, the imperial Chinese state was democratic. It was unlike both India and feudal Europe in that it
had no hereditary aristocracy, no hard and fast class distinctions. It was most typically Chinese, however, in its dependence on moral education and moral example instead of
constitutions and institutions. The aim of Confucius was not to
establish good laws but to establish a social order in which
laws and lawsuits would be unnecessary. Where the Christian
West developed another double standard of morality, with
more or less Machiavellian principles for politics, the Chinese
identified politics and ethics and adhered to the Christian principle that reform must begin and end in the hearts of men.
They had no bill of rights and no parliamentary forms for

the same reason that they had no police. The one great institution that they did develop was a unique civil service system, which grew up under the Han emperors and endured until this century. Government officials were selected by rigorous competitive examinations, requiring years of intensive study but open to men of all classes. The Chinese had the singular notion that the chief qualification for public service should be proved merit instead of aristocratic birth, imperial favor, or vulgar popularity. As striking was their conception of merit. The examinations were based on the Confucian classics and designed to test characer and judgment, not technical proficiency; so their public servants were scholars and literati. They were always pleased to call their land 'the land of pen and ink.'

The West borrowed from China the idea of a civil service system. It has borrowed little else, however, from the Confucian tradition. And though this whole tradition is hardly suitable to our society, we might still learn some worldly wisdom from it.

We might regret, specifically, that China did not take up the suggestion of Leibniz and send missionaries to teach Europe natural theology. While Christopher Dawson, for instance, declares that Confucianism is not a religion in our sense, and indeed 'is unintelligible to us by reason of its very rationality,' he grants that it had a stronger hold on Chinese society than any real religion has had elsewhere. Yet he represents the large company of thinkers who harp on the inadequacy of merely rational or secular ideals, insisting that 'man' cannot be happy and good unless he believes he is playing for heavenly stakes or is insured in the heavenly mutual. Similarly Dawson remarks that the Chinese father or ancestor becomes a kind of God-substitute reversing the Freudian idea of God as a Father-substitute; and again he apparently fails to appreciate the deep spiritual satisfaction of such biological immortality, or salvation without a divine savior, which has enabled the Chinese to contemplate death with a proverbial tranquillity that is hardly typical of the Christian West.

Too many thinkers find as unintelligible the simple intellectual honesty of Confucius, who stated that one should claim as knowledge only what he really knows, and admit that he does not know what he doesn't know. The characteristic Western ardor for answering the unanswerable would be more uplifting if it did not entail claims of certitude, and of the necessity of certitude. The Chinese were content to leave the unknowable alone. For the moral questions that must be answered, the *Book of Chungyung,* or the 'Golden Mean,' proposed a reasonable criterion:

Every system of moral laws must be based upon the man's own consciousness, verified by the common experience of mankind, tested by due sanction of historical experience and found without error, applied to the operations and processes of nature in the physical universe and found to be without contradiction, laid before the gods without question or fear, and able to wait a hundred generations and have it confirmed without a doubt by a Sage of posterity.

The Chinese believed there were such universal moral laws, grounded on the nature of man, but their feeling for the universal and the positive made them suspicious of categorical imperatives. 'The superior man,' said Confucius, 'goes through his life without any one preconceived course of action or any taboo. He merely decides for the moment what is the right thing to do.' The plainest requirements for good human relations are sympathy, tact, forbearance, the art of compromise. And in keeping with their distrust of absolute maxims the Chinese were content with relative goods, which they recognized are no less good because they are relative.

In reality, of course, the West has been as devoted to temporal goods; so it might profit still more from the spirituality of the Chinese. Although they suffered enough from greed, for example, they never systematized nor glorified it; they served neither God nor mammon. (The Mongol regime whose wealth and splendor so dazzled Marco Polo is regarded by the Chinese as a vulgar interlude.) Similarly they did not glorify war. As no conqueror was ever considered the equal of Confucius, so both the military and the business classes had far less social prestige than the scholars. Possibly they were naïve in their faith that the pen was mightier than the sword, but the main point here is not their specific scale of values. It is rather that essentially spiritual values were their primary concern. They were more profoundly practical than the West in that they did not mistake means for ends.

Herein lies the curious quality of Chinese naturalism from the Western point of view. They had a wholehearted love of nature, at once spontaneous and engrained, that went deeper than the fashion introduced by our Romantic poets; they respected nature as a moral order, even though it was unusually cruel to them, often visiting them with drought and flood; but they never sought to master it. Despite their practicality they developed no science, remaining as indifferent to physics as to metaphysics. Their aim was to live in perfect harmony with nature. They realized this ideal especially in their art, which has little of the passion and tension of Western art. Their temples and palaces were designed to blend into the landscape, not to dominate it. Their poetry expressed a natural delight in such simplicities as the flight of birds and the blooming of flowers, or a natural sadness upon their passing, but in either event it pictured nature and life as eternal rhythm rather than endless struggle. Their painting, which typically subordinated human figures to landscape, was impressionistic and disregarded perspective or definite point of view, the external object as seen by the individual self; to paint bamboo, they said, one had to 'become bamboo,' paint from within. In general, Chiang Yee declares, the Chinese find incomprehensible the dictum of Leonardo da Vinci that 'art seeks to vie with nature.' Typical of their ideal is the story of Chuang-tze, who dreamed he was a butterfly, and upon awakening was not sure whether he was a man dreaming he was a butterfly or a butterfly dreaming he was a man.

Because they took for granted that man was a part of nature, the Chinese entertained neither the proud Christian belief that man is the reason for the creation of the world nor the strange Christian conclusion that the world is alien to the human spirit. Unlike Kant and other high priests of Western idealism, they did not divorce human values from the natural order. But they also avoided the opposite extremes of philosophical materialism—the absurdly inadequate conceptions of man into which Western thinkers have been deluded by abstract logic, or more particularly by the abstractions of science. Always concerned primarily with values instead of facts, quantities, or mechanisms, the Chinese never lost sight of the nature of man. They escaped the inhuman tendencies of both Western religion and Western science. Without effort they escaped, above all, the sharp dualisms—as of heaven and earth, head and heart, ego and id, ethics and business, art and utility, the individual and society—which symbolize the contradictions of Western civilization.

Ultimately, these contradictions may be traced to the gap between the ideal and the real that has been maintained on principle. Ever since Plato man has been split in two, a spiritual self and a sensual self. The 'fall of man' may be attributed to such idealism—to the angel, not the beast in him. His natural frailty was translated into the curse of original sin, an unnatural sense of unworthiness or guilt. This in turn created the need of faith, of transcendence, of personal immortality, of an all-powerful Father-God to compensate for his weakness, or a Redeemer to compensate for this awful God—of a factitious spiritual security for a factitious unearthly self. For earthly purposes, meanwhile, conscience has had to do the work of natural integrity: a conscience that makes a virtue of inner conflict, intensifies anxiety, deepens instability, and for the sensitive makes wholeheartedness virtually impossible. Such dualism is much too deeply engrained in Western habits of thought and feeling to be argued away, but we might at least recognize that it is a product of Western tradition, or rather of the strongest of Western traditions, and not an essential, permanent condition of human nature. For the Chinese, man has naturally been whole and one.

But now the inevitable question arises. How well did the Confucian theory of social life work out in practice? What kind of history has China enjoyed, or suffered? The answer, as always, is melancholy. The annals of China are much like the annals of all other great societies, shot through with the monotonous themes of corruption, oppression, poverty, strife, and woe.

The Great Wall may do as the symbol. Completed by the mighty Shih Huang-ti, to a length of 1500 miles, it was another wonder of the ancient world, the largest structure ever built by man; it helped to assure the comparative isolation in which China could prosper, and stagnate; and it was another monument to the colossal egoism of despots, built of the sweat and blood and tears of conscript workers. So all the great dynasties of China began brilliantly, became corrupt, and ended in the chaos of civil war. Times of peace and prosperity were exceptions; the rule was misrule. Between the Emperor and the family—the pillars of society—remained a turbulent no-man's land, filled variously by sinister court eunuchs, provincial war lords, and assorted brigands. The scholar-mandarins, who were not subject to public control, were often arrogant when not corrupt; because of the years of study required to pass the civil service examinations, they came chiefly from the leisured landlord class, and as tax-collectors were disposed to shift the burden to the peasants. The serene philosophy, the refined art, the delicate sentiment, the polished manners—all the grace of Chinese civilization rested on the drudgery of more or less impoverished peasants. Heaven did not see or hear the peasants. Always threatened by drought and flood as well as by heavy taxation, they were never secure from hunger and want; countless millions died of starvation. In extent and degree of destitution China has been rivaled only by India.

Hence the people of *jen*, who are famous for their kindliness and courtesy, are also notorious for their casual cruelty, their callous indifference to suffering and death. 'Saving face' was more important than saving life. Hence, too, their extreme superstition. Although some Chinese are pleased to state that they are the first or the only great people to have outgrown religion, or at least to be skeptical about the supernatural, their doubts led to a wild speculation in every conceivable form of magic, suggesting the feverish gambler who tries to play it safe by heeding all possible omens of good and bad luck. However halfhearted, the religion of the common people remained more primitive than that of any other great society, except possibly India. Priests served chiefly as experts in magic. Even the educated indulged such superstitions as *feng shui*, an elaborate hocus-pocus for discovering beneficent sites for graves, buildings, et cetera. Confucian sages managed to rationalize much vulgar practice for attaining goods without real moral or intellectual effort. The scholar-mandarins could discredit any emperor, good or bad, by interpreting a flood, drought, or eclipse as a sign of Heaven's disapproval.

Under Heaven, in short, selfishness and stupidity flourished as they have in all societies, under all gods. Yet this is elementary. Our final concern is not the invariable follies and evils but the more specific, remediable causes; and here the Western humanist may have his say. By his standards, the traditional Chinese way of life also failed to do justice to the whole man, the full possibilities of life in the natural world. The many dreary, woeful pages in Chinese history were due not merely to lack of virtue but to the inherent limitations of the Confucian ideal, the defects of its virtues.

If Confucianism is too rational and utilitarian for the religionist, for the naturalist it is not rational or utilitarian enough. There is no necessary wisdom in an indifference to science and technology. For the Chinese masses the indifference meant a vast deal of needless misery. They remained dependent on a relatively primitive economy; for lack of adequate communication and transport thousands might die of starvation in one province while other provinces had an abundance of food. This explains why an eminently practical, energetic, ingenious people remained addicted to the rankest superstition, and seem at once the most skeptical and the most credulous of peoples. In their ingenuity they discovered the compass—and used it chiefly to discover the most favorable sites for graves (just as they used gunpowder to scare away demons). For the educated, similarly, the indifference to natural knowledge meant a dependence upon a purely verbal knowledge, which limited the self-knowledge they prized. They compiled a vast, dull historical literature that gave them an inadequate understanding of their history. They failed to develop a logic, a means of critical analysis or systematic thought; they had no rational method for verifying or correcting their intuitions. Devoted more than any other people to the belief that the proper study of mankind is man, they failed to create logical or psychological techniques for this study.

In political life the Chinese paid the price of their half-truth that the best rule is no rules, and that the only way to establish the good society is to educate the hearts of men. Whereas the West has depended too much on social machinery, the Chinese suffered from weak laws and political institutions; they had no effective means for making practice conform to theory, or revising theory to fit changing practice. Thus the 'mandate of Heaven' was so vague that emperors could readily identify their own will with the will of Heaven; if the people retained the theoretical right of revolution, civil war was about the only practical means of changing the mandate; and then it was not really changed—a successful revolt brought in only a new ruler, not a new order. Here again the indifference to natural knowledge contributed to slackness and confusion. While all law and right conduct were supposedly 'in accordance with nature,' the Chinese were given to an uncritical, unrealistic view of nature. Assuming that the natural order was a universal harmony, they slighted the natural sources of strife and evil. (Like India, China wrote no Tragedy.) Assuming that it was a moral order, which in the long run always rewarded virtue with success, they put up with a great deal of misrule, resisting efforts at reform as interferences with the natural order. At the heart of Confucianism was a fatalistic passivity that united the mundane Chinese with the other-worldly Hindu, in a common acceptance of wretchedness.

Most obviously, the Chinese paid the costs of their profound conservatism. The ceremonial ideals of piety and propriety that Confucius prescribed for a time of troubles became the rule of life for all times. No other people remained more firmly set in their ancient ways. Despite their famed practical sense they ignored the practical advice of Motse, who denounced their elaborate ceremonies—in particular their very costly funerals—as socially wasteful and harmful. 'The people have three great afflictions,' he cried: 'the hungry go without food, the shivering lack clothes, and the overworked get no rest.' The people chose to endure their great afflictions rather than economize on their rituals or their magic. The educated classes, whose unique prestige was fortified by their mastery of the extremely difficult Chinese script, were the most hidebound. Later Confucianists adopted some elements of Taoism and Buddhism, but they never questioned the essential doctrines of the master; their feats in reformulation, culminating in the work of Chu Hsi in the twelfth century, led only to a straitened orthodoxy. The civil service examinations required an ever more minute knowledge of the classics. The whole bureaucracy, in thought and in government, became increasingly rigid. The celestial empire was rotting away before the West broke in.

All in all, the Confucianist was a more truly 'classical' man than the Greek, or even than the Roman. China best exemplifies the classical virtues of poise, dignity, propriety, serenity. Here Westerners may see most clearly the advantages of a stress on the contemplative instead of the active spirit, duties instead of rights, piety instead of opportunity, peace of mind instead of progress. One who values irony might first consider the paradoxes of Lao-tse. 'To yield is to be preserved whole. To be bent is to become straight. To be hollow is to be filled. . . *To be in want is to possess. To have plenty is to be confused.*' But I have added the italics because this wisdom of Lao-tse may redound to the advantage of the West. Westerners want more of life and may therefore possess more, of the spiritual goods of aspiration itself; their confusion springs not only from material plenty but from the ideal of the life abundant. While Confucius himself was admirably mellow and humane, his 'superior man' was apt to become complacent in a formal perfection—a chill virtue and a sterile wisdom. His ideal found too little room for spontaneous pleasure, active love, natural curiosity, and spirit of adventure. It suppressed healthy, vigorous, creative impulses as well as aggressive ones.

In particular Confucianism tended to stifle individuality. Ideally, the individual fulfilled himself in harmonious human relations, and actually he could find contentment because he was subordinated to his own family rather than the State; unlike the free man in the West, he was not saddled with primary obligations to God, king, country, class, or community chest. Nevertheless he was always subordinated, never encouraged to have a mind or life of his own. Few dared to defy tradition or attempted to stand alone; centuries of revered ancestors worked to smother originality, enforce conformity. The unique achievement of the West, by contrast, was to liberate the individual by proclaiming the value of presonality and giving the support of tradition to his efforts to realize this value, Even the medieval scholars and saints dared much more than the Confucian sages, risking their souls in perilous inquiries and lonely adventures. Renaissance humanists and Protestant reformers strengthened the confidence of the individual in his own powers, and in his free, direct access to the goods of this world or to God. He was then apt to grow overconfident, addicted to the fallacies of absolute individualism or the excesses of rugged individualism. But on the whole he repaid his debt, with handsome interest. Never before, L. L. Whyte remarks, has society owed so much to so many.

The advantage of Western humanism, once more, is that it can more readily accommodate the worldly values of other cultures than they can manage to do without loss of character or face. Like India, at any rate, China has been taking to Western ways. When Europeans broke in during the last century, the Chinese at first regarded them as simply another species of barbarian, a type they had been repelling or absorbing over many centuries. They soon learned that they were dealing with a unique species. The 'Opium Wars,' in which England maintained its lucrative trade by absurdly easy victories, were quickly followed by a long series of humiliations by other powers, including a disastrous war with Japan. The Chinese had to acknowledge the apparent superiority of the hated foreigners. In 1905 the civil service examinations were abolished, and Confucius in effect dethroned. In 1912, after a feeble struggle, the Emperor himself abdicated, granting that the will of Heaven now called for a Republic. Together with science, technology, and industry, the Chinese adopted Western ideas of nationalism and democracy. The 'New Civilization Movement' made a frontal attack on Confucian ideals. Hu Shih declared that there was more spiritual value in the effort to eliminate poverty than in all the famed wisdom of the East.

Conceivably, the Chinese might lead the way to an ideal fusion of Eastern and Western values. No other people appears to have such resources of intelligence, vigor, resiliency, and fortitude. India is handicapped by internal divisions, especially between Moslems and Hindus, as well as by its tradition of unworldliness; Japan is handicapped by limited resources. Given their traditional passion for education, and the practicality and ingenuity that underlay the static forms of their culture, the Chinese are now proving that they are as adaptable as the Japanese. The peasants have been quick to seize on the new hopes of improving their worldly lot; the youth have become more eager, adventurous, and experimental than American youth; women, who had been completely subservient, have risen to complete equality. (Only in China is there a 'Madamissimo' to match the Generalissimo.) At the same time, the Chinese can still respect their ancient tradition, whose intrinsic values have been dignified by their unsurpassed historic achievement. A 'New Life Movement' in the 'thirties sought to preserve the best in Confucianism; Chinese intellectuals have been stressing its values for the West. Conceivably, China might re-establish its ideals of harmony and unity—which the West has dismally failed to achieve—in a more comprehensive humanism, a richer synthesis of material and spiritual well-being based on a more even balance of the active and the contemplative, the logical and the esthetic, the individual and the collective.[9]

The actual outcome to date has been rather different. Western intrusion was a greater shock because of the historic isolation of China; a peaceable, courteous people that for two thousand years had regarded itself as the most civilized on earth had suddenly to endure the ignominy of being treated as 'natives.' The impact of the West was still more shattering because the West itself was undergoing radical change. In a generation China experienced the intellectual, political, and economic revolutions that in Europe had been spread over centuries; and at the same time it had to adjust itself to a world at war, convulsed by new revolutions. Political chaos was intensified by the disintegration of the Confucian tradition, the basis of moral effort and order. The family itself was crumbling. Filial piety was weakened by the new economy as well as the new thought; men left home and land to work in factory and office, where only the most successful could discharge their family obligations by loading the pay roll with relatives.

It is no wonder, then, that the Chinese filled this spiritual void with the cruder interests and ideals of the West. In their practicality they became more materialistic; industry and commerce coarsened their traditionally fine taste in art, dress, and household furnishings. Their spiritual needs were met chiefly by a growing nationalism, instead of the traditional pride in their superior culture. The national leader became a general—a type that hitherto had been placed near the bottom of the social scale, about where an Al Capone stands in America. As Northrop observes, the Chinese

[9] A chastened Japan also has much to contribute in refinement, discipline, sense of obligation, and faith in the power of spirit over matter. (The cruelty of the Japs, it might be remarked, appears to be due to their spirituality rather than to mere callousness; like medieval Christians they are indifferent on principle to the pains of the flesh.) But the ruling ideas of Japanese culture are less universal, or less suitable for export. Where the Chinese based the good life on fellow-feeling and natural piety, the Japs cultivated an artificial kind of propriety, stressing obedience to elaborate codes dependent upon status in an elaborate hierarchy. The principle of hierarchy has been their basic faith. In *The Chrysanthemum and the Sword* Ruth Benedict reports that they were genuinely shocked when the peoples they conquered did not welcome their rule; the national ideal of 'Everything in its place' led them to believe that even a lowly status is far better than no status. In the abstract, of course, this ideal is reasonable enough. The trouble with it is that to other people the place the Japs find for everything seems essentially arbitrary.

learned to fight to the death, like good patriots and Christian idealists. (A few million had been converted to Christianity early in the century, before the violent reaction against foreigners.) As 'a follower of Jesus Christ,' Chiang Kai-shek wrote that the success of the Chinese Revolution depended upon men willing to fight and die for its new principles, and was pleased to find that Christians made the best officers. Now he has found that Communists fight still better. Communism bids fair to restore the unity of China, and to realize the tremendous latent power of the East.

As a 'modern' gospel that is nevertheless anti-Western, Russian Communism has obvious attractions for the Chinese. It is akin to their own tradition in its positivism, its devotion to expediency, its strong social sense, its spiritualized materialism, and its combination of democratic theory and despotic practice. It does not encounter the most familiar motives of opposition, sprung on the one hand from a tradition of freedom and individualism or from strong bourgeois interests, on the other hand from religious feeling, a priesthood, or a hereditary aristocracy. Yet in China, as in Russia, Communism can succeed only by defying Marxist theory, *creating* a proletariat (as its leaders have already invented a 'landless proletariat'); and it may come to defy the Soviet, out of national pride. It will also have to overcome some strong traditions, such as the devotion to the art of compromise, the distrust of absolutes or categorical imperatives, and particularly the ideals of filial piety—the ancestral family will have to move into the background before the State can become supreme. Meanwhile the success of Communism in China appears to be due as much to the failure of the West as to its own positive attractions. An aroused peasantry, no longer willing to put up with the abuses of landlordism, wanted land and the rudiments of social justice; an aroused intelligentsia, weary of social incompetence and corruption, wanted a constructive faith, a program of national regeneration. Communism united them by its promise of a dynamic new order, kindling a faith in the future of China. The West offered abstract ideals of liberty and equality, backed by material aid; but the ideals meant nothing to the landless peasants and were suspect to the intellectuals, because of the Western record of colonial exploitation and racial prejudice, while the lavish material aid was given to the old order, an incompetent regime that was dominated by war lords and landlords, and that made no serious effort at fundamental reform.

And so the West already faces a serious challenge from the resurgent East. Students of China have long been saying that its course would prove decisive for the future not only of Asia but of all mankind. Except for jingoes who had nightmares about the 'yellow peril,' Westerners have regarded such speculation as academic. When most tolerant they were still patronizing. Americans in particular have been complacent about their generosity, lending aid more freely because they took for granted that the grateful, backward Chinese would obey orders. Now they are beginning to realize that four hundred million Chinese may be wrong but must be reckoned with. The American dollar has proved no match for the Russian ideal. The American ideal might do much better if attended by sympathetic understanding. At least it seems clear that the West can no longer dominate the East by material power alone.

XI

Conclusion: The Uses of the Future

1. THE CHALLENGE

The times are not propitious for a resonant Conclusion. 'A frightful queerness has come into life,' wrote H. G. Wells in *Mind at the End of Its Tether*. Perhaps the most frightful thing about life today is that it does not seem queer enough. We have grown used to crisis and horror, as to novelty; we should find queerer a morrow in which there was no threat of further frightfulness. Our fathers now seem queer because they assumed the cause of freedom to have been permanently won. Even after the First World War, when Wells wrote that history from then on was a race between education and catastrophe, most men were confident that education would win. 'We have no millennium to look forward to,' asserted Dean Inge, the 'gloomy dean,' in his *Outspoken Essays;* 'but neither need we fear any protracted or widespread retrogression.' Now Wells, the inveterate optimist who spent a long life in fascinated speculation about the 'Pattern of Things to Come,' has died in the conviction that there is no pattern but clean extinction. 'There is no way out or round or through. . . It is the end.'

This is resonant enough, and might give us the grim satisfaction of facing Doom with open eyes, accepting the full cycle. Yet our life is too queer even for this. We were born to aspire and to hope, and thereby have some grounds for hope. In all sobriety we cannot be sure that it is the end— honesty warns us against the sentimentality of pessimism as of optimism. Given atomic power, we can conceive the possibility of an absolute end, of the race instead of merely a civilization; but we do not really know how great are the

374

destructive possibilities that scientists have developed, or may develop, and we are warned against leaping to melodramatic conclusions. We know that throughout history men have been trumpeting the end of the world. Our very awareness of crisis is a possible advantage, since it might give us an elementary prudence that our ordinary intelligence and virtue would not. (As Burckhardt commented, the Greeks might have done better had they regarded the Peloponnesian War as the great national crisis we now perceive it to be.) Meanwhile we may still view our creations with both pride and alarm. We may stress the gigantic material achievement of a world-wide civilization, and admire the unprecedented effort to establish a world order on principles of equity as the most extraordinary adventure of the human spirit. Or we may stress the unreadiness of man for the extraordinary challenge he has set himself, and fear that the race will die of gigantism or monstrosity, like the dinosaurs before it.

I am not optimistic about our immediate prospects. As I write, we have to live in two worlds, both more or less obsolete. Neither side really believes in the doctrine of co-existence that is the only hope of peace. If there is a world war, only the most naïve patriots can believe that the victor will bring lasting peace and good will to the world; and such patriots are not apt to be good peace-makers. Neither am I optimistic about the saving power of historical knowledge. What history teaches, Hegel remarked, is that men have never learned anything from it; or at least their knowledge has not availed against the ancient enemy. Although the learned have often been blind, simple men have always been aware of this enemy, which is selfishness—the egotism of nations as of individuals. Allied with it are the ageless forces of ignorance and stupidity, greed and envy, fear and hate. Today these forces are as active as ever, and more terribly armed. As the old adage has it, most men want peace but do not know or want the things that make for peace. The odds favor catastrophe again.

Yet as we live we must continue to bet on education, on thought, as our only possible chance. We must bet on it even though as individuals we are apt to feel more helpless than ever before, since the fateful decisions involving life or death for hundreds of millions are still made by a few men, even in the democracies. We must bet because we all nevertheless are involved, and have our own decisions to make. In any event, there is logic as well as art in the convention that calls for a book on history to have a Conclusion, even if history itself doesn't. Although it is not my business to predict or plan the future, a book about the past inevitably contains a reference to the future. Our understanding of recent events comes down to ideas about their probable consequences; our interpretation of the remote past is still colored by ideas about what kind of future is possible, and what kind desirable. The effort to be objective, to ground hope and aspiration on the best available knowledge, is itself a bet on the method of intelligence, or education.

At least the immediate terms of our problem seem clear enough. All would agree, I suppose, that the major practical task of our civilization is to establish some kind of world order strong enough to maintain peace. Our technology has made such an order necessary by giving us terrific power—power that we may regret having, but that we will not and cannot do away with. Technology has also made a world order possible, as it was not in Roman times; ancient empires were always unwieldy because of slow, uncertain communication. The obvious trouble remains that men have not kept pace with their machines. The world has been brought together too suddenly and forcibly to be a good neighborhood; the unaccustomed intimacy has intensified the differences between peoples, multiplied the possibilities of friction. Technology has likewise made possible total, universal war.

Given the long series of empires, history might suggest that a likely outcome is a world order dominated by a single power. Russia appears to have imperial ambitions, while many American internationalists call for a tough kind of 'world leadership' that to the rest of the world looks like domination. Given the invariable fate of empire, however, history suggests no reason for welcoming such an outcome. A Russian world dictatorship might achieve order but only by a tryanny that would crush the spirit of most Western peoples; if it endured it would probably mean a creeping death for most civilized values. (One portent is the degeneration of Soviet painting, literature, and philosophy, which have already lost much of the fresh ardor that once compensated for their addiction to crude stereotypes.) An American world dictatorship might be more generous but would almost certainly be disorderly and short-lived; Americans have little mind or stomach for such responsibilities. Nor can a detached observer be hopeful about the further possibility that the pride of both Russia and America may be humbled by some new power, such as China. Only the arrogant can believe that any one people has enough wit and virtue to rule the world.

I therefore reach the commonplace conclusion that the best hope for the future is some kind of world federation on a democratic basis. The ideal role of America, given the leadership that has been thrust upon it willy-nilly because of its wealth and power, would be to lead the way to such a federation. This is the avowed goal of its statesmen and at least the vague aspiration of most of its citizens. The aspiration is in keeping with the major historic achievement of America as a melting pot, a new land in which many diverse peoples have come to form a community and live in liberty under law. The question remains whether the nation is up to this new role. It has been slow to realize that its vaunted wealth and power are by no means great enough to master a world. Its friends and allies are not too confident of its wisdom and virtue. Nor of their own. Ultimately, the question is whether the ideal values of Western civilization are more vital than they have appeared to be in this century.

Again I cannot be certain of the answer. I still do believe, however, that these values deserve to live, and that the liberal faith offers the only real hope for a decent future. So I propose to recapitulate the main articles of this faith.

2. A Credo

'What kind of people do they think we are?' exclaimed Winston Churchill during the last war. A major cause of Hitler's undoing was that the British proved to be a much sturdier people than he thought. Even so he had reason to think poorly of them, judging by the mediocrity of their leaders before Churchill, and by the gloominess of many of their intellectuals. The behavior of the British points to simplicities that thinkers are prone to forget. Before we get solemn about the ultimate issues we might take a hard look at these simplicities.

Thus it is a commonplace that American soldiers in the last war had a dim idea of what they were fighting for. Presumably they have no clearer idea of why they went to Korea, and certainly they have no passion for dying for any cause. Nevertheless they have fought sturdily, sweating it out, grumbling it through to the end. As ordinary men they have a toughness of spirit that carries them through crises while clear-eyed intellectuals indulge in despair. In one aspect this is insensitiveness or simple coarseness. In another it is simple loyalty to the company—the chance unit of buddies. The 'cause' comes down to such common sentiments as fellow-feeling, pride in workmanship, and self-respect. Our religions, our philosophies, and our histories too seldom take adequate account of these rudiments of human idealism. A philosophy of history might well begin and end with a report I have heard on the French underground that took care of Allied airmen and escaped prisoners in the last war. The report was that the most effective workers in this underground were priests and prostitutes.

In this unphilosophical, unspiritual view we may better understand why democracy has not degenerated into the anarchy and tyranny predicted by its critics, from Plato down —why, on the contrary, it has been able to mobilize its resources for mighty national efforts, and to emerge from two world wars without loss of its basic civil liberties. The very limitations of ordinary men may be sources of strength. The depressing conventionality of Americans, for example, has contributed to their unusual cohesiveness and stability. Their favorite national myth, the success story, has strengthened their faith in themselves and helped to maintain the habits of enterprise and self-reliance. Their spiritual slackness, or incapacity for flaming idealism, is at least in part a saving realism and modesty. The chances for world order and peace are better because they no longer expect wars to end war, and have little sense of manifest destiny, little zeal for making the world safe for democracy at any cost. In a period of deep confusion they can carry on the democratic tradition because they carry much of it unconsciously, in sentiments of equality and fair play learned in kindergarten, habits of tolerance and compromise engrained by everyday give and take. 'A very great deal of the Western way of life,' writes Crane Brinton, 'is thus embedded somewhere in quite ordinary Americans, not in their cerebral cortexes, probably, but in a much safer place which the physiologist hasn't quite located—we used to say, in the heart.'

Yet such realism also forbids us to be complacent about these homely virtues, or about any faith learned by heart. Much paltry sentiment and belief have been learned in the same way.[1] Embedded still deeper are the primitive instincts

[1] An instance is the almost universal assumption of Americans that the profit motive is the only motive that can stimulate men to exert their best efforts. This implies an essentially cynical view of human nature, or at least American nature, and confirms what the Russians say about us; yet it is also an excuse for high moral indignation. One may recall the outraged protests in Congress and editorial offices during the last war, when President Roosevelt proposed that incomes be limited to $25,000 for the duration. The most sober conservatives argued that any such restriction would destroy the incentive of the businessmen on whom we depended for war production. It should be added, however, that like ordinary soldiers and workers—not to mention scientists, ministers, teachers, and other simple folk—many businessmen apparently did a conscientious job without expecting as much as $25,000; so we may believe that they are not necessarily the swine their champions assume they are. Or so we must hope, else we are certainly doomed.

of fear and rage, which now give desperate overtones to the tribal chant of the nation's might and right. Conventional patriotism, oratory, heroics, the fervor of hatred and fear— the conditioned reflexes of national life might still carry us through the present emergency; but they could not make a world order. For the long run we need more sober, lucid, responsible convictions about the kind of people we have been, and will have to be. For wherever the democratic faith is embedded in ordinary Americans, it was not born there and did not settle there by chance. It was engendered by conscious thought; it was propagated by conscious effort. In a revolutionary world it cannot survive indefinitely as mere habit. If we begin and end with the priest and the prostitute, in between we still need more conscious thought and effort.

And so with Western civilization as a whole. The familiar refrains about its 'breakdown' may obscure the extraordinary unflagging creativeness that has made it the richest, most dramatic spectacle in history. It has maintained a high level of creative activity over a longer period of time than have previous societies, which rested on their oars after bursts of great achievement. In particular, as Whitehead observed, thought has been more creative. Whereas in other societies thought served chiefly to explain and conserve, Western man embarked on an endless 'adventure of ideas' and put the ideas to work. He has thrived on the continuous disagreement and disharmony from which he has suffered; his life has always been charged with high tension. Since the dawn of the Middle Ages Europe has known the sense of crisis—the symptoms diagnosed by the specialists in 'breakdowns.' During its most complacent periods, such as the *ancien régime* and the Victorian age, revolutionary forces were agitating the more sensitive spirits and engendering further crises.

Now it may be that the long era of expansion is drawing to a close, and that even if we escape a universal catastrophe the future will be an era of contraction. All history might be charted in terms of such pendulum swings, which are the natural terms of action and reaction. An obvious sign in our time is the growth of totalitarianism—a 'dynamic' reversion to the closed, tribal society. Another sign is the swelling appeal to religion, which might betoken a quest for spiritual freedom but looks more like a yearning for security and rest. At best, such tendencies to contraction represent a healthy desire to order, consolidate, and conserve, to restore community and natural piety, in a healthy recognition of the abuses of freedom and the limitations of reason. Yet we are not likely to enjoy the best, nor are we in a position to make

consolidation the order of the day. Immediately we have
to deal with another revolutionary development, in the unlocking of atomic energy; to conserve anything at all we
shall have to make over our traditional institutions and policies. Given science, we must expect more revolutionary developments, in both our conceptions of the universe and
our operations on it. We cannot count on history to repeat
itself.

Hence I should stress first of all, in very general terms, our
continued need of an adventurous spirit—of still more
creative thought, bold, imaginative, experimental, self-reliant,
critical of all 'infallible' authority. This stress may seem unnecessary in an age notorious for its skepticism and irreverence, and at a moment when revolutionaries are the apparent
menace. Nevertheless these revolutionaries are much less bold
and independent than they appear, what with their childish
faith in guaranteed totalitarian solutions. Our conservatives
are even less enterprising than they appear; the frequent violence of their tactics masks a fearful timidity and unimaginativeness in their basic strategy, when not a downright
panic. And we all have to be wary of another contradiction
in our heritage. While the spirit of adventure has been the
genius of Western thought, at its heart has remained the venerable assumption of a static, finished world, in which truth
is timeless, standards are absolute and fixed, and human nature is always and everywhere the same. Our religion, our
ethics, our poetry, our political and economic theory, our
proverbs and maxims for daily life—our idealism and
our common sense alike are steeped in this assumption, which
is at variance both with our scientific knowledge of human history in an evolving world, and with the conditions of life in a
revolutionary world.

All along I have been identifying the adventurous spirit
with humanism, liberalism, rationalism, the scientific spirit,
the ideals of freedom, individualism, and the 'open society.'
Since these have constituted the distinctive faith of our secular
civilization, I appear to be calling for business as usual, at
the same old stand—the kind of business that has brought on
the present crisis. I should therefore repeat that the adventure in freedom is inevitably precarious. Yet I deny that
this faith is the main source of our folly and evil. In the
world of affairs the obvious menace is the inveterate self-
interest, individual and national, upon which all faiths have
foundered. In the world of thought the chief menaces are
the various forms of authoritarianism and irrationalism. The
worst folly of liberals has been a facile optimism that blinked
both the ancient evils and the new complexities.

Today they are apt to echo the common charge that 'scientific philosophy' is the root of our evils. Science has indisputably inspired much narrow, harsh philosophy, and much pseudo-science; its disciples have often been inhuman. As inhuman, however, is the fashion of branding all the efforts of intelligence as sinful pride, and all the works of science as mere materialism. It appears that to study meteorology and scientific agriculture is to be materialistic, whereas to pray for rain and good crops is to be spiritual. Actually, both procedures have utilitarian motives; the immediate choice is between more or less intelligent, efficacious means of attaining human ends; and as for 'higher' values, pure science is a more disinterested, more genuinely spiritual activity than ordinary prayer or worship. At least science cannot be charged with the nationalism and imperialism that now threaten catastrophe. No war has ever been fought over scientific causes. No nation—least of all Soviet Russia—has proposed its aims or resolved its issues in a scientific spirit. Science has had very little to do, indeed, with the administration of our economic and political life. It remains the author of our major problem, in its gift of tremendous power that has been terribly abused; but for the wise use of this power we need more, not less, of the objective, dispassionate scientific spirit. For our philosophical purposes we need more of its integrity and its basic humility, its respect at once for fact and for mystery.

Many men now take a strange pleasure in emphasizing the limits of scientific knowledge, as if the validity of poetic, metaphysical, or religious claims to higher truth were thereby automatically proved, and ignorance were not merely bliss but wisdom. Many are attacking the claims of reason itself, in the name of faith, intuition, instinct, the heart, the voice of the blood. In the world of affairs such attitudes are translated into the kind of common sense that scorns all 'theory,' ridicules 'brain-trusts,' and identifies learning with absent-mindedness. The way is thus cleared for the positive irrationalism of the dictators, the brutal contempt of mind exhibited in their policy when not their creed. We may then realize that a denial of the claims of reason naturally leads to a denial of the claims of the heart too, and that if its powers are as inadequate as many seem pleased to think, there can be no hope of avoiding catastrophe.

If we must make these imprecise, invidious distinctions, we had better try to keep our heads. Scientific knowledge is no less useful because of ultimate uncertainty; it serves the quite sufficient purpose of enabling us to go about our business in a world whose metaphysical 'reality' we do not absolutely need to know. Reliable knowledge is not enough by itself but nothing can take its place—no arbitrary assertion of higher truths and goods. Whatever higher faculties man may have—of feeling, intuition, or imagination, in vision, trance, or ecstasy—can be trusted only after they have been interpreted and judged by reason. Otherwise anything goes: the visions of Buddha, Christ, Mohammed, Marx, Whitman, Nietzsche, and Hitler are on the same footing; and what goes best is apt to be blind unreason or brute force. No product of social intercourse is more precious than reasonableness, or more essential to attaining and sharing the goods of life; for love itself is a partial sentiment that often goes wrong, leading to division, jealousy, and hatred.

In this spirit reason must then add that love and hatred remain more elemental. Its claims need to be qualified by modest ideas of its functions and its powers; its ideal product is not pure rationality but reasonableness. Traditional rationalism has taken too supercilious an attitude toward the instinctive, spontaneous life, the sentiment and passion that alone can give force to its ideals. In this century many social scientists have displayed an incredibly naïve confidence in the power of intelligence to control the 'behavior patterns' with which they play, talking as if social conflict could be handled in the same way as infectious disease. Liberals generally have set their sights too high, overestimating the rationality and virtue of free men. Yet it is still reason that warns us against such unreasonable expectations. In its most mournful judgments of its frail powers it still proves its necessity, its responsibility, and its power.

To live intelligently, in short, we must recognize that man is not simply a 'rational animal.' To live decently we must also recognize that this definition of him is more adequate than such popular definitions as a beast of prey, an illusioned robot, or an imprisoned soul. He shares his basic drives and reflexes with other animals, and he may or may not have an immortal soul; what most plainly and positively distinguishes him from other animals is the power of conscious thought and responsible behavior. If we respect him at all we must treat him as if he were rational, and enlist his free consent in joint enterprises. The whole argument for liberty and democracy ultimately rests on Pascal's dictum that thought makes the whole dignity of man, and that the endeavor to think well is the basic morality. 'The chief virtue of democracy,' concluded Carl Becker, 'and in the long run the sole reason for cherishing it, is that with all its defects it still provides the most favorable conditions for the maintenance of that dignity and the practice of that morality.'

This is also the reason for cherishing the individual,

as the essential carrier of that dignity and agent of that morality. In his newly won freedom to think and act for himself he has indeed done himself much harm. He has identified his cause with a gospel of economic individualism that meant slavery to a profit system, a loss of dignity for the many and a warped, impoverished humanity even for the successful. He has tended to forget that the sense of community is indispensable even to full self-realization. His excesses have therefore called out an extreme revulsion. Social scientists have referred to the individual as a 'discredited hypothesis,' defining him as a mere cell of the social organism, while dictators have discredited him in fact or put him in cells. Yet there is no doing away with him, or without him. The great creative individual, as John Stuart Mill said, not only personifies but initiates all the wise and noble things that the race has done. In everyday life we are as dependent on free relations with the ordinary decent person. We may best appreciate him in a time of crisis, for he is capable of more wisdom and virtue than collective man ever can be. He is often superior to the best institutions—the greatest States and Churches—which repeatedly fall short of the integrity and the decency we can count on in private life.

The related ideal of equality is more vulnerable. Undeniably it has worked to dignify mediocrity and lower standards of excellence. It has produced the new tyranny of the masses, the chief enemy of true individuality. And always it entails apparent absurdities. 'In the eighteenth century,' wrote Ortega y Gasset, 'certain minority groups discovered that every human being, by the mere fact of birth, and without requiring any special qualification whatsoever, possessed certain fundamental political rights, the so-called rights of the man and the citizen.' Bright sophomores delight in pointing out the self-evident truth that men are *not* created free or equal. We shall always be asked to contemplate the ignoramus and the expert marching to the polls, to cast one vote apiece.

But what are the alternatives? In the past almost all political and religious orders were based on the aristocratic principle of the natural inequalities of man. The ideal argument for this principle is rule by the superior. In practice, however, the ruling classes have seldom been disposed to permit any natural test of their claims to superiority—they simply clung to inherited privileges. We have seen that mediocrity thrives in such societies too; even imbecility has sat on thrones and worn haloes. And the logic of the aristocratic principle is no less vulnerable to analysis. There is no universal standard of superiority, no scale for weighing the diverse claims of strength, skill, valor, intelligence, shrewdness, learning, breeding, virtue, piety, and what have you. For men are not unequal in every respect. Any little man may rightly say that he is a better artisan, a better soldier, a better friend, a better husband and father, or a better Christian than the genius; and he may even be a better citizen than some experts.[2] At the same time, all men are in fact equal in respect of their common structure and their common destiny. The egalitarian principle does more justice to both the diversity and the unity of our common humanity. In these terms the supreme gift of the West to mankind is that it has promoted the sentiment of equality and realized a measure of actual equality, political, economic, and social. It has thereby laid the only possible basis for a world federation.

All these ideals, once more, necessarily lead to disagreement, disquiet, disharmony, disorder, disunity. Still, such costs are not necessarily prohibitive. They seem more alarming because of the conservative disposition to be alarmed by all change, and to spare the past its troubles. Historically, there is no clear correlation between harmony and health, much less growth—no great society has realized the degree of spiritual unity common in primitive societies. Although freedom in thought and political life has always got societies into trouble, none have died of it; dying societies have been marked rather by rigidity, the traditionalism of which Rome in decline is the conspicuous example. The most encouraging sign in the Western world is that it not only recognizes the evils in its way of life but continues to struggle against them. It has not yet lost the pioneering spirit that has made its whole history a migration. There will always be some hope for it so long as it retains its distinctive hope that life on earth can and must be improved.

To this hope—to the whole humanistic endeavor—Christianity, finally, can lend strong support. Although it did not lead the way, it contributed the germinal ideals of spiritual freedom and equality. Today many of its leaders are outgrowing the traditional exclusiveness that has militated against its ideal of universal brotherhood. Some are willing to believe

---

[2] The common man's limitations as a voter may seem less hopeless when he is set beside his betters. His gullibility is hardly more dangerous than the conservatism and self-interest of the wealthy, educated classes, who can usually be counted on to prefer a 'safe' candidate—a mediocrity like Calvin Coolidge. It was primarily the common man who elected the greater presidents, such as Jefferson, Jackson, Lincoln, Wilson, and F. D. Roosevelt—all of whom were violently hated by large segments of the well-to-do.

that religion too is properly an adventure—a progress toward more adequate conceptions of God and the spiritual life, instead of the final truth about them. Meanwhile Christianity remains the most accessible source of saving experience for the West. It can comfort, bind up wounds, and cure as no secular faith can. And simply because it is no longer a flaming, crusading faith it can preach more effectively its gospel of charity and humility, help to keep alive the possibilities of peace. Churchmen of all sects are combating the tendency of political and military leaders to buy slight tactical advantages at great moral cost (as Monte Cassino was blasted, to no gain whatever). The Christian conscience might avert the ultimate horror of a total war to preserve freedom—a war waged in a total disregard of the values that alone make freedom precious, and rehabilitation possible.

Nevertheless I have been arguing that Christianity does not constitute our best hope, at least for our earthly future. An established religion remains by nature a deeply conservative force, not a creative one. The churches have long brought up the intellectual rear of our civilization, and despite their awakened social conscience their claims to spiritual leadership are still weakened by their engrained tendency to resist new knowledge and aspiration. Most are still disposed to a dogmatic supernaturalism that saps the intellectual honesty and courage essential for a responsible idealism.[3] Churchmen persistently narrow our choices by equating 'religious' and 'spiritual,' obscuring all the shriveled, deformed spirituality to be found within the churches and all the healthy idealism to be found outside them. Much of what passes for religious faith today amounts to a side bet, covering a vague belief that 'there must be something' or that man needs to believe (especially when in foxholes); often it verges on sentimentality—the indulgence of feeling without commitments in thought and action. Many churchmen are

---

[3] Thus the greatest of the Christian churches recently affronted the intellectual conscience of many other Christians by proclaiming the new dogma of the Virgin's bodily ascent into heaven, despite the absence of scriptural or historical evidence of such an event. Protestant leaders lamented that the Catholic Church should elect the most crucial moment in Western history to emphasize dogmatic differences, and thereby raise a further barrier to a united Christendom. Although the Pope has made one concession, observing that 'human intelligence sometimes experiences difficulties in forming a judgment about the credibility of the Catholic faith,' he has also warned Catholics against any compromise on their dogmas, insisting that reunion is possible only on the impossible terms set by the Church. Spirituality is further confused when an authoritarian church denounces the tyranny of Communism while it supports Franco as it once supported Mussolini, a dictator whom Pius XI hailed as 'a man sent by Divine Providence.'

trying to reanimate such faith by exploiting the theology of crisis, the ethos of fear—preaching not merely humility but humiliation. Given the historic record, we cannot be simply heartened by the possibility that the future may belong to the churches again.

Humanism, or the religion of humanity, may not do either. Toynbee attacks it as peculiar, perverse, 'even pathological.' It is in fact peculiar enough—it has not had the chance of religion. No doubt it makes too heavy demands on human nature in its present state, especially when it asks men to put humanity above the tribe—something they have never succeeded in doing under the fatherhood of God. Yet I still hold that the Western humanistic faith is not perverse, and not so pathological as historic religion has often been. It has proved itself in many good men, by many good works. It has brought finer possibilities of life to masses of men who in the past could invest their hope only in a hypothetical life to come. The utter defeat of this cause would be the worst tragedy in history. Meanwhile the notorious pride of the modern world is dangerous because it is not a clear, proud faith in the dignity of man or in the uses of mind. The enemy today wears the mask of pride, but its true name is fear.

3. THE PIETY OF HISTORY

Vanity of vanities, said the Preacher, all is vanity; and all history may appear to declare his wisdom and his sorrow. 'Man's historical experience has been one of steady failure.' wrote Berdyaev, 'and there are no grounds for supposing that it will ever be anything else... None of the problems of any given historical epoch whatsoever have been solved, no aims attained, no hopes realized.' There is indeed not the faintest prospect of eliminating the endless travail of life on earth, short of eliminating life itself. Man's historical experience should sober the revolutionaries who know the certain solution to our problems, and sober as well the traditionalists whose solution is a return to the ancient faiths, which have always failed in the past. In this view even the appearance of the Saviour has made no difference, for the history of the Earthly City since Christ has been no better by his standards than the history before him. 'Christianity, too, as a historical *world* religion, is a complete failure,' confesses Karl Löwith.

Berdyaev drew an odd inference, however: 'And this

failure of man means simply that man is destined to realize his potentialities in eternity.' In other words, if at first we don't succeed we're simply bound to win forever. This too is a historic hope, though some find no grounds for supposing that it will be realized either. But at least it suggests some qualification of Berdyaev's account of history. In a modest view, ordinary mortals seldom experience absolute failure; they attain some simple aims, realize some decent hopes. So the failures of the race are offset by a number of enduring achievements; Christianity itself is not a complete failure so long as any men are still comforted or inspired by the message of Jesus. In a profounder view, all is not simple vanity but the complication of good-in-evil and evil-out-of-good: the admirable solutions, which always create further problems; the ideal aims that have been partially attained, thereby stirring new aspirations and producing new shortcomings; the richer possibilities of life that man has discovered, to his greater glory and greater discontent. Furthermore, there *are* new things under the sun. Man's history on earth still looks like an evolution, and in the long view even like a progress. Berdyaev himself has much higher hopes than the cave-man could know, or than Moses knew. Today the historic drama is being acted out with a fuller consciousness, and at best a loftier purposiveness, than ever before; for we can still conceive at least the possibility of a far better world, and have at least the material means of building it.

And so we are led back to the ultimate issue, of the meaning of human history. As far as positive knowledge goes, I declared at the outset, there is no certain meaning. Such knowledge, however, is not the whole story. As we brood over the drama of history, we can hardly help feeling a depth of meaning beyond the reach of mere logic or science. It stirs the 'oceanic sense'—the wondrous capacity of a rickety forked animal to know a cosmos and then to feel his way outside it, beyond time and space, into infinity; and this fact of immediate experience always suggests the possibility that man is attuned to the Absolute, and in his history is fulfilling some superhuman purpose. The world's religions, it must be confessed, have not greatly illumined this purpose. Their conflicting views have been unified chiefly by a common tendency to deplore history and common effort to escape it. In effect they have darkened the mystery of the creation by denying life on earth intrinsic value or significance, confirming the somber witness of Isaiah: 'All nations before Him are as nothing; and they are counted to Him less than nothing, and vanity.' Yet the fact remains that in its vanity mankind has deepened and widened its religious consciousness, and now its historical consciousness. In this knowledge Christian thinkers have been seeking to make history intelligible, or at least to escape the traditional view that its whole meaning lies outside history, in a life to come. The two main possibilities of a modern Christian philosophy of history, as I see it, may be represented by Arnold Toynbee and Reinhold Niebuhr.[4]

Toynbee supplements St. Augustine by a religious version of the theory of progress. Although his picture of history to date resembles Spengler's, with civilizations going through much the same cycles (again with considerable help from the author), he differs from Spengler in denying that this process is predetermined or merely repetitive. 'With God's help,' man may master his own destiny, 'at least to some extent in some respects.' There may be an advance despite the repetitive cycles, just as the wheel moves forward while going round and round, or as the annual procession of the seasons has brought about the evolution of life and man. Specifically, Toynbee suggests that the means of progress may be 'the learning that comes through the suffering caused by the failures of civilizations.' This costly but continuous process has led to ever higher religions, and might culminate in the reign of the 'Church Militant on Earth.' Toynbee is careful to stop short of Utopia: because of the innate sinfulness of man there can never be a real City of God on earth. Still, he believes that the reign of this Church would bring about a 'miraculous improvement,' in both material and spiritual welfare.

For us, it must be said, these high hopes offer a somewhat dubious comfort. While Toynbee suggests possible ways of averting the bloody death of our civilization (and thereby, it would seem, of postponing the birth of a still higher reli-

[4] That there is no one standard Christian interpretation of history was amply demonstrated at a Study Conference on the 'Meaning of History,' held at the Ecumenical Institute in Switzerland in 1949. The assembled professors had assumed a general agreement on fundamentals, but presently they were disputing whether there was such a being as a 'Christian historian,' with a peculiar function or peculiar advantage over ordinary historians. One spokesman warned his colleagues against the danger of *hubris* in such claims, which might lead to a violation of history. Others saw *hubris* in any serious concern about the fate of civilization. Professor Thomas Preiss, who argued most eloquently for the profound unity of the New Testament view of history, stressed the implications of the Last Judgment: history does have a meaning but man cannot know it or judge it. 'The end of the great process of history will be a complete surprise for all,' he concluded, 'even for the elect.' He added that to the man of true faith history is properly a *'mystery'*; it is lack of faith that longs to know the future or raises the question of progress.

gion) ultimately he calls us to prayer. In effect, he echoes the Negro spiritual:

Nobody knows the trouble I've seen—
Glory, Hallelujah!

And after prayer the further trouble remains that his theory is as arbitrary on theological grounds as labored on empirical grounds. The New Testament knows nothing of such progress in history, if only because early Christians expected the world to end shortly. If God has since revealed further truths, it is not clear that Christianity represents the furthest advance. The later religion of Mohammedanism, with its purer monotheism, would seem to be a more logical heir of the divine purpose; only like Christianity it has been less catholic in spirit than the more ancient religions of Buddhism and Hinduism. But most troublesome is the apparent extravagance of the divine plan, with its reckless expenditure of whole civilizations. Toynbee himself is disturbed by 'the historically incontestable fact that illumination and grace have been imparted to men on Earth in successive installments'; he can only express the pious hope that God has provided a salvation of sorts for the countless generations that had to get along with little grace during their pilgrimage on Earth. Even so, an ultimate harmony does not cancel the immense cost in suffering, which seems worse as Toynbee plots in detail the tragedy of civilizations, finding his standard three-and-a-half beats in the rhythm of their prolonged death throes. Hence Berdyaev declared that the theory of progress is the best reason for doubting the existence of Providence.

Nevertheless most Christian thinkers are still imbued with the spirit of progress, and at least are unwilling to believe that the whole adventure in civilization is mere vanity, 'less than nothing.' Others have therefore been seeking a middle course between the impossible claim that the divine plan is clear and the unthinkable conclusion that it is pointless. The most they can say, it seems to me, has been said very well by Reinhold Niebuhr, in such works as *The Nature and Destiny of Man* and *Faith and History*.

The essence of history as Niebuhr sees it is paradox. Man is a thinking animal who is 'both the creature and the creator of history,' knowing both necessity and freedom. In his freedom he can and must aspire to better his history. As an earnest liberal, Niebuhr condemns the passive or merely prayerful idealism of Christian tradition, as well as the obscurantism. But he dwells chiefly on the finiteness and fallibility of man, which the race is always prone to deny because of the ineradicable selfishness and pride at the very core of human personality. He condemns all absolutism, all pretense to finality, admitting the historical relativism that distresses most religious thinkers; every society is necessarily limited in its understanding and biased in its judgment. Likewise he condemns all claims of moral perfection, or the complete rightness of any human cause. Although he concentrates his fire on the modern gospel of progress, with its absurd and sinful faith that man can master his destiny, he recognizes that historic Christianity has been corrupted by the same denial of man's finiteness and fallibility. 'The pride of a bishop, the pretensions of a theologian, the will-to-power of a pious business man, and the spiritual arrogance of the church itself are not mere incidental defects, not merely "venial" sins'—they are the mortal sins of pride and self-righteousness. Hence Niebuhr rejects Toynbee's hope of a Universal Church Militant; for if ever there were such a church, it would be still more fatally corrupted by its assumption of universal authority.

Up to this point, in short, Niebuhr takes the tragic view of history. But now he transcends it. While man is always finite, the most significant thing about him is that he always seeks the infinite. There is a spirit in him that transcends nature, history, reason, self—that belongs to eternity. And because history can never resolve its paradoxes, never redeem itself, Niebuhr finds the clue to its meaning in the Redeemer. Through Jesus on the Cross God takes upon himself the burden of the evil that man cannot remove by his own efforts. Through the Resurrection he promises that history will be consummated on the plane of eternity, where man will realize the success he cannot realize on earth but partially earns by his arduous efforts to do so.

This leap to eternity is an avowed act of faith. Niebuhr admits that his conclusion could not be deduced from the facts of history, and that the divine motive in having a history remains impenetrably obscure. I should therefore conclude that his faith is an honorable one, pointing to a real possibility, but that argument about it is unlikely to be profitable. He himself is not content, however, to rest on mere possibility. He argues that the potential leap to eternity is a practical necessity of the good life. He thereby forces further argument; for if we look before we leap, the old questions recur.

Granted that history can be given an ultimate meaning only by faith, one may still doubt that the life of so finite, fallible a creature *must* have an ultimate meaning, much less so proud a one. (In his finiteness Niebuhr demands a great deal of God, even to the resurrection of mortal personality and the flesh: he demands nothing less than a perfect consummation of history, with complete justice to all aspects of human life on earth.) Granted the appearances of a cosmic order, with its suggestion of a creative intelligence, one may doubt that it is informed with a moral purpose. In the natural world outside of man, with its ceaseless struggle for survival, there is no evidence whatever of 'a power not ourselves making for righteousness'; and in the history of man the principle of righteousness seems to have emerged very gradually from his own painful efforts, uncertain and unblessed. But the major objection is to Niebuhr's highhanded way with honorable alternatives, in his insistence that without his faith men must succumb either to complacency or to despair. It is not 'human nature' but a particular cultural tradition that requires a guarantee of success in eternity. We have seen that whole peoples, such as the Greeks, Romans, and Chinese, managed decently and graciously enough without expecting God to consummate their history. If they were too complacent, they were generally less self-righteous than Christian and Mohammedan peoples, and the Chinese in particular were also less prone to despair. In our own society many men have outgrown the expectation of living happily ever after, yet managed to avoid the excesses of optimism and pessimism. In the future all supernaturalism conceivably might come to seem as archaic as animism now does, though animism was once as universal and 'natural'; for the grounds of belief in the supernatural have been shaken as never before, by scientific-historical knowledge and habits of thought. How the race would then make out is an open question. In our finiteness we have no right to judge the needs of the future solely by the standards of the present.

Yet I should finally dwell on the common ground where naturalist and supernaturalist can meet, once they have both acknowledged the finiteness and fallibility of man. Whatever our faith, we cannot escape mystery. Religious faith itself testifies that the only real certainty is mortality. Although it naturally tends to absolute conviction, it remains a matter of faith because it cannot be absolutely proved; it is a tacit confession that our life is surrounded by darkness, and that men still tend to be afraid of the dark. As for history, its 'meaning' is no less mysterious if we assume a divine author. Either God needs man or he doesn't; the reasons either for his need or for his creation of an unnecessary world are equally obscure. Meanwhile, however, we live on an island of light. As life can be worth living even if we are not going to live forever, so history can be rich in meanings without having a final meaning. In his mortality—because of his mortality—man has realized sovereign values that are no less ideal, and no less real, if they are not eternal. Whatever their faith, men of good will may agree, and in effect mostly do agree, upon the essentials of human idealism, the value of the spirit that seeks truth, goodness, and beauty.

Ultimately, only men can make life worth living. Normally they just find it so, through animal faith or the will to live. All may know the elemental goods, such as physical wellbeing, sport, comradeliness, love, the enjoyment of beauty, the enjoyment of growing, making, or knowing things—goods that are good in themselves, and may be good enough whether or not they make any difference to the universe. 'You can't take them with you'; but once enjoyed, they can't be taken away from you. When men seek some further assurance they may enhance the value of life, through the varieties of religious experience. They may also lose sight of the elemental goods, or even sacrifice them to an uncertain hope of a life to come. More to the point, they are apt to forget that all men know what William James called 'the wider self through which saving experiences come,' or what most men call God. Wherever this experience ends, it begins as a sense of kinship with a larger whole, which we might expect to find in a child of nature grown conscious and social. It may be stirred by music, poetry, or moonlight as well as by religious worship. It may come with simple teamwork. It helps to explain another often forgotten simplicity, that men have always been willing to sacrifice themselves for some larger cause, fighting and dying for their family, tribe, or community, with or without hope of an eternal reward.

And among other things the 'wider self' is a sense of the past. It is a sense of the basic community beneath all the relativities of culture, the basic continuity beneath all the mutabilities of history. For all is not simply whirl or flux. One cannot step into the same river twice, said Heraclitus —or even step into it *once*, some logical purist added; but Heraclitus also said, 'In change is rest.' Apart from the rest of death, change gives us a consciousness of permanence that we could not have in a frozen, static world; we can know change itself only because of the permanencies in the underlying modes and patterns, rhythms and recurrences. So all the adventures of civilization come down to an old story, always strange and always familiar. The study of history may justify itself simply as an act of piety that deepens and widens this esthetic, spiritual, essentially religious sense of continuity and community. I, for one, have never felt more pious than when contemplating the ruins of Athens, or even of little Priene.

Hence I am pleased to believe—out of faith, hope, and charity, as out of respect for truth and for mystery—that history finally solves and settles nothing: that it yields no more certain meaning than Unamuno's call 'to live, seeing that we all have to die; to live, because life is an end in itself.' Such progress as man has made has not been a measurable advance in the pursuit of happiness, toward any demonstrable prospect of a heaven on earth. It has consisted rather in the very faith in progress, the awareness of finer possibilities and further goals, the sense of freedom and the open road—the happiness of pursuit. As Horace Kallen has said, 'The going is the goal.' To keep going we can still hope for the best, and must; but we cannot hope for final solutions, and must not. Because history 'shows' nothing so simple and certain as both progressives and conservatives are wont to make out, it may show something more valuable for our living purposes. It is perhaps the best means to a full consciousness of both necessity and freedom, permanence and change—of the always difficult but honorable terms of mortality, on which man has repeatedly failed, and in failure has created deathless values. In this consciousness we may know more freedom amid our necessities, more rest amid change.

Time, the great destroyer, is also the great preserver. It has preserved much more than we can ever be conscious of —the immense accumulation of products, skills, styles, customs, institutions, and ideas that make the man on the American street indebted to all the peoples of history, including some who never saw a street. But most precious are the works that man has consciously preserved, in defiance of time. For a Jacob Burckhardt, as for many other historians, these constitute the sufficient meaning of history: his deep sense of evil, unrelieved by hopes of progress on earth or in eternity, only heightened his reverence for the permanent values created by man. For men of all faiths, however, these works are the ultimate source of inspiration. Even those who renounce the world commune with the great spirits who discovered the value of renunciation, or with a God who became known only because of the adventure in civilization. So we may round out our story with the words of a royal lady of benighted Byzantium, who worshiped not too humbly in Hagia Sophia, disdainful of the 'simple-minded' Crusaders who had set their hearts on recovering the Holy Land. 'The tale of history forms a very strong bulwark against the stream of time, and checks in some measure its irresistible flow,' wrote Anna Comnena, daughter of the Emperor Alexius, 'so that, of all things done in it, as many as history has taken over it secures and binds together, and does not allow them to slip away into the abyss of oblivion.' As imperial Byzantium was entering its ignominious last phase Anna wrote her *Alexiad*, 'an epic poem in prose'—pure Attic prose; and for her pride she is known chiefly to dusty scholars. Nevertheless she contributed to the cultural renaissance that gave splendor to the dying empire. There was dignity as well as folly in her pride. Even the pathetic, artificial purity of her prose symbolizes the value that Berdyaev himself saw in history, as the 'triumph of memory over the spirit of corruption.'

Today, I suppose, the most apparent use of the 'tragic' view of history is the melancholy one of helping to prepare us for the worst. It gives us vast and eminent company in our misery; for if we feel that our society is damned and doomed, we can add that all the great societies were sufficiently damned and were certainly doomed. We might also remember that written history too seldom shows, that ordinary men have always had to suffer the history their leaders were making. Yet the tragic sense is the profoundest sense of our common humanity, and may therefore be a positive inspiration. If all the great societies have died, none is really dead. Their peoples have vanished, as all men must, but first they enriched the great tradition of high, enduring values. Like Burckhardt we might be heartened as well as sobered by the thought that we shall vanish into the same darkness, and live on in the same tradition. We might be freed from the vanity of grandiose hopes, as of petty concerns. We might learn that 'ripeness is all,' and that it is enough.

Bibliography

The following bibliography is neither comprehensive nor strictly selective. Rather, it constitutes a more detailed acknowledgment of the books I have directly drawn on for this study. In the more specialized sections, however, I have starred the works I found especially useful for my purposes; and these, which for the most part are standard authorities, may serve as a guide for the general reader. Since, for the sake of convenience, I have not included periodical literature, I should add that I have drawn on the rich materials to be found in the *Journal of the History of Ideas*.

General
(Chapters 2, 3, and 11)

Berdyaev, Nicolas: *The Meaning of History,* London, 1936

Brinton, Crane: *Ideas and Men,* New York, 1950

Burckhardt, Jacob: *Force and Freedom,* New York, 1943

Burke, Kenneth: *Attitudes toward History,* New York, 1937

Bury, J. B.: *A History of Freedom of Thought,* New York, 1913
————: *The Idea of Progress,* London, 1921

Campbell, Joseph: *The Hero with a Thousand Faces,* New York, 1949

Childe, Gordon: *What Happened in History,* Harmondsworth (Penguin Books), 1942

Cohen, Morris: *The Meaning of Human History,* LaSalle, 1947

Collingwood, R. G.: *The Idea of History,* Oxford, 1946

Croce, Benedetto: *History, Its Theory and Practice,* New York, 1921

Dawson, Christopher: *Enquiries into Religion and Culture,* New York, 1933

Eliot, T. S.: *Notes Towards the Definition of Culture,* New York, 1949

Fischer, Eric: *The Passing of the European Age,* Cambridge, 1943

Herskovits, Melville J.: *Man and His Works,* New York, 1948

Hildebrand, George H. (ed.): *The Idea of Progress,* Berkeley, 1949

Hook, Sidney: *The Hero in History,* New York, 1943

Kallen, Horace M.: *Patterns of Progress,* New York, 1950

Kroeber, A. L.: *Configurations of Cultural Growth,* Berkeley, 1944

Locke, Alain, and Stern, B. J. (eds): *When Peoples Meet,* New York, 1942

Lovejoy, A. O., and Boas, George: *Primitivism and Related Ideas in Antiquity*, Baltimore, 1935

Löwith, Karl: *Meaning in History*, Chicago, 1949

Mannheim, Karl: *Ideology and Utopia*, New York, 1936

Mumford, Lewis: *Technics and Civilization*, New York, 1934

Neff, Emery: *The Poetry of History*, New York, 1947

Niebuhr, Reinhold: *Faith and History*, New York, 1949

————: *The Nature and Destiny of Man*, 2 vols., New York, 1941, 1943

Northrop, F. S. C. (ed.): *Ideological Differences and World Order*, New Haven, 1949

Ortega y Gasset, José: *The Revolt of the Masses*, New York, 1932

————: *Toward a Philosophy of History*, New York, 1941

Papers of the Ecumenical Institute, No. v: 'On the Meaning of History,' Geneva, 1950

Pareto, Vilfredo: *The Mind and Society*, 4 vols., New York, 1935

Popper, K. R.: *The Open Society and Its Enemies*, 2 vols., London, 1945

Randall, Henry John: *The Creative Centuries*, London, 1944

Robinson, James Harvey: *The Mind in the Making*, New York, 1921

————: *The New History*, New York, 1913

————: *The Ordeal of Civilization*, New York, 1926

————: *Essays in Intellectual History* (dedicated to J. H. Robinson by his former seminar students), New York, 1929

Rowse, A. L.: *The Use of History*, London, 1946

Salvemini, Gaetano: *Historian and Scientist*, Cambridge, 1939

Schweitzer, Albert: *Civilization and Ethics*, London, 1929

Shotwell James T.: *The History of History*, New York, 1939

Social Science Research Council, Bulletin 54: *Theory and Practice in Historical Study*, 1946

Sorokin, Pitirim A.: *The Crisis of Our Age*, New York, 1942

————: *Social and Cultural Dynamics*, 3 vols., New York, 1937

Spengler, Oswald: *The Decline of the West*, 2 vols., New York, 1926

Strayer, J. R. (ed.): *The Interpretation of History*, Princeton, 1943

Teggart, Frederick J.: *Theory and Processes of History*, Berkeley, 1941

Toynbee, Arnold: *Civilization on Trial*, New York, 1948

————: *A Study of History*, 6 vols., London, 1934-9

————, with Pieter Geyl and Pitirim A. Sorokin: *The Pattern of the Past: Can We Determine It?*, Boston, 1949

Turner, Ralph E: *The Great Cultural Traditions*, 2 vols., New York, 1941

Whitehead, Alfred North: *Adventures of Ideas*, New York, 1933

Whyte. L. L.: *The Next Development in Man*, New York (Mentor Books), 1950

Zinsser, Hans: *Rats, Lice and History*, Boston, 1935

(Note: Some of the works listed above—notably those by Spengler, Toynbee, and Turner—were drawn on extensively for the more specialized chapters that follow.)

Greece, Rome, and Byzantium
(Chapters 1, 5, and 7)

Bailey, C. (ed.): *The Legacy of Rome*, Oxford, 1923

* Baynes, Norman H.: *The Byzantine Empire*, London, 1925

Bury, J. B.: *A History of Greece to the Death of Alexander the Great*, New York (Modern Library), 1937

————: *History of the Later Roman Empire, from the Death of Theodosius I to the Death of Justinian*, 2 vols., London, 1923

Cambridge Ancient History, vols. 1, 2, 5, 7, 10, 11, 12, Cambridge, 1911-13, 1925-39

Cornford, Francis M.: *From Religion to Philosophy*, London, 1912

————: *Thucydides Mythistoricus*, London, 1907

Dickinson, G. Lowes: *The Greek View of Life*, New York, 1925

Diehl, Charles: *History of the Byzantine Empire*, Princeton, 1925

* Durant, Will: *Caesar and Christ*, New York, 1944

* ————: *The Life of Greece*, New York, 1939

Ferrero, G., and Barbagallo, C.: *A Short History of Rome*, 2 vols., New York, 1919

Finlay, George: *Greece under the Romans*, London, 1907

————: *History of the Byzantine Empire, from DCCXVI to MLVII*, London, 1906

Frank, Tenney: *An Economic History of Rome*, Baltimore, 1927

* Gibbon, Edward: *The Decline and Fall of the Roman Empire*, 2 vols., New York (Modern Library), 1932

Glotz, G.: *The Aegean Civilization*, New York, 1925

Greene, William Chase: *The Achievement of Greece*, Cambridge, 1923

————: *The Achievement of Rome*, Cambridge, 1933

* Hamilton, Edith: *The Greek Way to Western Civilization*, New York (Mentor Books), 1948

Hansen, Esther V.: *The Attalids of Pergamon*, Ithaca, 1947

Haskell, H. J.: *The New Deal in Old Rome*, New York, 1939

* Herodotus: *The Persian Wars*, New York (Modern Library), 1947

Highet Gilbert: *The Classical Tradition*, New York, 1949

Inge, W. R.: *Society in Rome Under the Caesars*, Indianapolis, 1899

* Jaeger, Werner: *Paideia: The Ideals of Greek Culture*, 3 vols., New York, 1943-5

Livingstone, Sir Richard W.: *Greek Ideals and Modern Life*, Cambridge, 1935

————(ed.); *The Legacy of Greece*, Oxford, 1928

* Lot, Ferdinand: *The End of the Ancient World*, New York, 1931

Marsh, Frank Burr: *Modern Problems in the Ancient World*, Austin, 1943

* Murray, Gilbert: *Five Stages of Greek Religion*, New York, 1925

Oman, C. W. C. *The Story of the Byzantine Empire*, London, 1892

Polybius: *The Histories*, 6 vols. New York (Loeb Classical Library), 1922-7

Rostovtzeff, M. I.: *A History of the Ancient World*, vol. 1, Oxford, 1926

* ———: *The Social and Economic History of the Hellenistic World*, 3 vols., Oxford, 1941

* ———: *The Social and Economic History of the Roman Empire*, Oxford, 1926

Suetonius: *The Lives of the Twelve Caesars*, New York (Modern Library), 1931

Tacitus: *Complete Works*, New York (Modern Library), 1942

* Tarn, W. W.: *Hellenistic Civilisation*, London, 1947

* Thucydides: *The Peloponnesian War*, New York (Modern Library), 1934

Toynbee, Arnold (ed): *Greek Historical Thought*, London, 1924

* Vasiliev, A. A.: *History of the Byzantine Empire*, 2 vols., Madison, 1928-9

Judaism and Christianity
(Chapters 4 and 6)

Albright, W. F.: *The Archaeology of Palestine*, Harmondsworth (Penguin Books), 1949

* Bettenson, Henry (ed.): *Documents of the Christian Church*, New York, 1947

Bevan, E. R., and Singer, Charles (eds.): *The Legacy of Israel*, Oxford, 1927

Burtt, Edwin A.: *Types of Religious Philosophy*, New York, 1939

Cambridge Ancient History, vol. XII

* *Cambridge Medieval History*, vol. I

Cochrane, C. N.: *Christianity and Classical Culture*, Oxford, 1940

Cumont, Franz: *The Mysteries of Mithra*, Chicago, 1910

Dawson, Christopher: 'St. Augustine and His Age,' *Enquiries into Religion and Culture*, New York, 1933

Eyre, Edward (ed.): *European Civilization, Its Origin and Development*, vol. 2: *Rome and Christendom*, London, 1935

Fiske, A. K.: *The Great Epic of Israel*, New York, 1911

Frazer, J. G.: *Folk-lore in the Old Testament*, New York, 1923

Gilson, Étienne: *God and Philosophy*, New Haven, 1941

Glover, T. R.: *The World of the New Testament*, New York, 1931

* Guignebert, C. A. H.: *Jesus,* London, 1935
Harnack, Adolf von: *History of Dogma,* 7 vols., London, 1896-9
Inge, W. R.: *Mysticism in Religion,* Chicago, 1948
Lake, Kirsopp: *Landmarks in the History of Early Christianity,* London, 1920
————: *The Religion of Yesterday and Tomorrow,* New York, 1926
* ————, and Lake, Silva: *An Introduction to the New Testament,* New York, 1937
Lovejoy, A. O.: *The Great Chain of Being,* Cambridge, 1936
Maritain, Jacques: *The Living Thoughts of St. Paul,* New York, 1942
* McGiffert, A. C.: *A History of Christian Thought,* 2 vols., New York, 1932
Moore, G. F.: *History of Religions,* vol. II: *Judaism—Christianity—Mohammedanism,* New York, 1919
Murray, Gilbert: *Stoic, Christian, and Humanist,* London, 1940
Newman, John Henry: *An Essay on the Development of Christian Doctrine* (edited by C. F. Harrold), New York, 1949
* Parkes, James: *Judaism and Christianity,* Chicago, 1948
Pater, Walter: *Marius the Epicurean,* 2 vols., London, 1921
Ransom, John Crowe: *God without Thunder,* New York, 1930
Reinach, Salomon: *Orpheus: A History of Religions,* New York, 1930
Rostovtzeff, M. I.: *Mystic Italy,* New York, 1927
Rudwin, Maximilian: *The Devil in Legend and Literature,* Chicago, 1931
* Santayana, George: *The Life of Reason: Reason in Religion* (*Works,* vol. 4), New York, 1936
Shaw, George Bernard: Preface to 'Androcles and the Lion,' *Nine Plays,* New York, 1935
Simkhovitch, Vladimir G.: *Toward the Understanding of Jesus,* New York, 1921
Wright, G. Ernest: *The Challenge of Israel's Faith,* Chicago, 1944

The Western World

(Chapter 8)

Adams, Henry: *The Education of Henry Adams,* New York, 1918
* ————: *Mont-Saint Michel and Chartres,* New York, 1905
Barnes, Harry Elmer: *An Intellectual and Cultural History of the Western World,* New York, 1937
Barr, Stringfellow: *The Pilgrimage of Western Man,* New York, 1949
* Becker, Carl: *The Heavenly City of the Eighteenth Century Philosophers,* New Haven, 1932
————: *Modern Democracy,* New Haven, 1941
* Bryce, James: *The Holy Roman Empire,* London, 1904

Burckhardt, Jacob: *Civilization of the Renaissance in Italy*, London, 1929

Cheyney, Edward P.: *The Dawn of a New Era* (1250-1450), New York, 1936

Coulton, G. G.: *Medieval Panorama*, New York, 1938

Cram, Ralph Adams: *The Substance of Gothic*, Boston, 1917

Crump, C. G., and Jacob, E. F. (eds.) *The Legacy of the Middle Ages*, Oxford, 1926

* Dawson, Christopher: *The Making of Europe*, 400-1000 A.D., London, 1934

Fromm, Erich: *Escape from Freedom*, New York, 1941

Haskins, C. H.: *Studies in Mediaevel Culture*, Oxford, 1929

* Huizinga, J.: *The Waning of the Middle Ages*, London, 1924

Jusserand, J. J.: *English Wayfaring Life in the Middle Ages*, London, 1891

Kohn, Hans: *The Twentieth Century*, New York, 1949

Lloyd, Roger: *The Golden Middle Age*, London, 1939

MacCulloch, J. A.: *Medieval Faith and Fable*, Boston, 1932

MacIver, R. M.: *The Modern State*, Oxford, 1926

Maritain, Jacques: *True Humanism*, New York, 1938

* McGiffert, A. C.: *A History of Christian Thought*, vol. II: *The West from Tertullian to Erasmus*, New York, 1932

Miller, Perry, and Johnson, T. H.: *The Puritans*, New York, 1938

Olschki, Leonardo: *The Genius of Italy*, New York, 1949

* Perry, Ralph Barton: *Puritanism and Democracy*, New York, 1944

* Randall, J. H. Jr.: *The Making of the Modern Mind* (revised), New York, 1940

Rashdall, Hastings: *Universities of Europe in the Middle Ages*, Oxford, 1895

Roberts, Michael: *The Modern Mind*, London, 1937

* Smith, Preserved: *A History of Modern Culture*, 2 vols., New York, 1930-34

Stephenson, Carl: *Mediaeval Feudalism*, Ithaca, 1942

* Tawney, R. H.: *Religion and the Rise of Capitalism*, New York, 1926

* Taylor, Henry Osborn: *The Medieval Mind*, London, 1911

Weber, Max: *The Protestant Ethic and the Spirit of Capitalism*, New York, 1930

Whitehead, Alfred North: *Science and the Modern World*, New York, 1925

Willey, Basil: *The Eighteenth Century Background*, London, 1940

————: *The Seventeenth Century Background*, London, 1934

Russia

(Chapter 9)

* Berdyaev, Nicolas: *The Origin of Russian Communism*, New York, 1937

Carr, Edward H.: *The Romantic Exiles*, London, 1933

Crankshaw, Edward: *Russia and the Russians*, New York, 1948
Crossman, Richard (ed.): *The God That Failed*, New York, 1949
Lenin (Ulyanov), V. I.: *Materialism and Empirio-Criticism*, Moscow, 1937
* ———: *The State and Revolution*, London, 1933
* Maynard, Sir John: *Russia in Flux*, London, 1941
Pares, Bernard: *A History of Russia*, New York, 1930
Popper, K. R.: *The Open Society and Its Enemies*, vol. 2: *The High Tide of Prophecy: Hegel and Marx*, London, 1945
Slonim, Marc: *The Epic of Russian Literature*, New York, 1950
Somerville, John: *Soviet Philosophy*, New York, 1946
Stalin, Joseph: *Leninism, Selected Writings*, New York, 1942
Stern, Bernhard J., and Smith, Samuel (eds.): *Understanding the Russians*, New York, 1947
Sumner, B. H.: *A Short History of Russia*, New York, 1943
* Trotsky, L.: *The History of the Russian Revolution*, 3 vols., New York, 1932
* Webb, Beatrice and Sidney: *Soviet Communism: A New Civilization* (second edition), London, 1937
* Wolfe, Bertram D.: *Three Who Made a Revolution*, New York, 1942

The East

(Chapter 10)

Benedict, Ruth: *The Chrysanthemum and the Sword*, Boston, 1946
Chi, Tsui: *A Short History of Chinese Civilization*, New York, 1943
Dawson, Christopher: 'The Mystery of China,' *Enquiries into Religion and Culture*, New York, 1933
Durant, Will: *Our Oriental Heritage*, New York, 1935
* Eliot, Sir Charles: *Hinduism and Buddhism*, 3 vols., London, 1921
Garratt, G. T. (ed.): *The Legacy of India*, Oxford, 1937
* Latourette, K. S.: *The Chinese, Their History and Culture*, 2 vols., New York, 1934
Lattimore, Owen and Eleanor: *The Making of Modern China*, New York, 1944
Lin, Yu-t'ang (ed.): *The Wisdom of China and India*, New York, 1942
———: *The Wisdom of Confucius*, New York, 1943
Masson-Ourel, Paul, William-Grabowska, Helena de, and Stern, Philippe: *Ancient India and Indian Civilization*, London, 1934
Moore, G. F.: *History of Religions*, vol. 1, New York, 1913
Nehru, Jawaharlal: *Glimpses of World History*, New York, 1942
* Northrop, F. S. C.: *The Meeting of East and West*, New York, 1946

* Radhakrishnan, S.: *Eastern Religions and Western Thought*, Oxford, 1939

* Schweitzer, Albert: *Indian Thought and Its Development*, New York, 1936

* Suzuki, D. T.: *A Brief History of Early Chinese Philosophy*, London, 1914

T'ang, Leang-li: *The Foundations of Modern China*, London, 1928

Waley, Arthur: *Three Ways of Thought in Ancient China*, London, 1939

Yang, Y. C.: *China's Religious Heritage*, New York, 1943

Yee, Chiang: 'The Philosophical Basis of Chinese Painting,' *Ideological Differences and World Order*, edited by F. S. C. Northrop, New Haven, 1949

Yu-lan, Fung: 'The Philosophy at the Basis of Traditional Chinese Society,' *Ideological Differences and World Order*, op. cit.

Index